IMMIGRATION AND ENTREPRENEURSHIP

IMMIGRATION AND ENTREPRENEURSHIP

Culture, Capital, and Ethnic Networks

Edited by
Ivan Light
Parminder Bhachu

Transaction Publishers
New Brunswick (U.S.A.) and London (U.K.)

Copyright (c) 1993 by Transaction Publishers
New Brunswick, New Jersey 08903

All rights reserved under International and Pan-American Copyright
Conventions. No part of this book may be reproduced or transmitted in any
form or by any means, electronic or mechanical, including photocopy,
recording, or any information storage and retrieval system, without prior
permission in writing from the publisher. All inquiries should be addressed
to Transaction Publishers, Rutgers-The State University, New Brunswick,
New Jersey 08903.

Library of Congress Catalog Number: 92-14137
ISBN: 1-56000-070-8
Printed in the United States of America

Library of Congress Cataloging-in-Publication Data

Immigration and entrepreneurship: culture, capital and ethnic networks /
    edited by Ivan Light, Parminder Bhachu.
        p.   cm.
    Papers presented at a conference held at UCLA on April 26-28, 1990.
    Includes index.
    ISBN 1-56000-070-8 (cloth)
    1. Minority business enterprises--Congresses.
    2. Entrepreneurship--Congresses.   3. Alien labor--Congresses.
    4. Immigrants--Economic conditions--Congresses.   5. Emigration and
    immigration--Economic aspects--Congresses.   6. Emigration and
    immigration--Government policy--Congresses.   I. Light, Ivan Hubert.
    II. Bhachu, Parminder.
    HD2341.I46   1992   92-14137
    331.6'2--dc20   CIP

Contents

Contributors

YURI ARUTYUNYAN is senior researcher at the Institute of Ethnography and Anthropology (formerly Institute of Ethnography) in Moscow. He is viewed as the father of "ethno-sociology" in the Soviet Union. Arutunyan was the leader of a team survey research project that produced two pioneering and important volumes: *Ethno-Sociology: Goals, Methods, and Research Results* (Moscow: Institute of Ethnography of the Soviet Academy of Sciences, 1984); and *Socio-Cultural Face of the Soviet Nation* (Moscow: Institute of Ethnography of the Soviet Academy of Sciences, 1986). Some of this work has been excerpted and published in English in *Soviet Anthropology and Archeology* 27 (1988).

PARMINDER BHACHU, an urban anthropologist, was the postdoctoral fellow of the Institute of Social Science Research and International Studies and Overseas Programs for 1990-91 at the University of California, Los Angeles. She was a research fellow at the Center for Research in Ethnic Relations at the University of Warwick, the director of a major project on "Parental Perspectives on Schooling" at the Thomas Coram Research Unit, Institute of Education, University of London. Bhachu is Luce Professor Cultural Identity at Clark University, Worcester, Massachusetts. She is the author of *Twice Migrants: East African Sikh Settlers in Britain* (Tavistock, 1985), and co-editor with Sallie Westwood of *Enterprising Women: Ethnicity, Economy, and Gender Relations* (Routledge, 1988).

EDNA BONACICH teaches in the departments of sociology and ethnic studies at the University of California, Riverside. Her work has concerned class and race, particularly the superexploitation of people of color. She has published works on the split labor market, middleman minorities, and Asian immigrant labor and business enterprise. She is the co-author of *Immigrant Entrepreneurs* (University of California, 1988) and of *The Economic Basis of Ethnic Solidarity* (University of California, 1980).

MEHDI BOZORGMEHR is a lecturer in sociology at the University of California, Los Angeles. He was the project director of the study of Iranians in Los Angeles, funded by the National Science Foundation from 1986 to 1989. His main research interest concerns ethnic diversity within immigrant and ethnic groups. His area of specialization is Middle Eastern immigration to the United States. He has published several articles and book chapters on these subjects.

WAYNE A. CORNELIUS is the Gildred Professor of U.S.-Mexican Relations and the director of the Center for U.S.-Mexican at the University of California, San Diego. He founded the Center for U.S.-Mexican Studies, at the same institution, in 1979. He holds a Ph.D. in political science from Stanford University and for eight years was on the faculty of Massachusetts Institute of Technology. He has been engaged in field studies of rural-to-urban migration within Mexico and Mexican migration to the United States since 1970. He has published widely on Latin American urbanization, immigration issues, and the Mexican political system. His most recent books are *Mexico's Alternative Political Futures* (edited by Judith Gentleman and Peter Smith, Center for U.S.-Mexican Studies 1989) and *Mexican Migration to the United States: Process, Consequences, and Policy Options* (edited by Jorge Bustamante, Bilateral Commission on the Future of U.S.-Mexican Relations 1990). He is currently writing a book on Mexican migration and U.S. immigration reform, co-authored with Manuel Garcia y Griego, to be published in 1991 by Stanford University.

CLAUDIA DER-MARTIROSIAN is a doctoral student in sociology at the University of California, Los Angeles. Her areas of specialization are ethnic studies and quantitative methods. She was in charge of the Armenian part of the recently conducted survey of Iranians in Los Angeles. Based on this research, she has presented papers and co-authored articles and book chapters.

GEORGE A. DE VOS came to University of California, Berkeley in 1957 and is a professor in the department of anthropology. He received his B.A. in sociology from the University of Chicago in 1946, M.A. in anthropology in 1948, and Ph.D. in Psychology in 1951. His Ph.D. dissertation was a comparison of the personality of immigrants and their children. Since then he has studied the Korean and outcaste minorities in Japan and worked with the University of Paris and the University of Leuvin (Belgium) on labor migrants in Europe. He has studied Japanese motivational patterns and personality and most recently, he has been looking at Korean immigrants to the United States.

STAVROS KARAGEORGIS, a citizen of Greece, attended Wesleyan University in Connecticut. He is currently a graduate student in sociology at the University of California, Los Angeles.

EUN-YOUNG KIM is a Ph.D. candidate in the department of anthropology at the University of California, Berkeley. In her dissertation, "In Search of Self: Korean Ethnicity in Transition in the U.S.," she examines the life experiences of the children of Korean immigrants in the context of minority education. Currently, she is editing a book on Koreans abroad as well as conducting an ethnographic research of undercount in Koreatown, L.A., for the U.S. Census Bureau.

KAREN LEONARD is a professor of anthropology at the University of California, Irvine; her Ph.D. is in history and she specializes in social history and anthropology of India. Her first book, *Social History of an Indian Caste: The Kayasths of Hyderabad*, focused on an urban administrative caste to show considerable flexibility and permeability of subcaste and caste boundaries over two hundred years. She completed a book on the biethnic families formed in the early twentieth century by male immigrants from India's Punjab province and Hispanic women in the American southwest. The title is *Ethnic Choices: California's Punjabi-Mexican-Americans*, and the work investigates the construction of ethnicity in rural California.

IVAN LIGHT is Professor of Sociology at the University of California, Los Angeles and director of the Immigration Research Project, an interdisciplinary effort within the Institute for Social Science Research. In this capacity he planned, organized, and directed the California Immigrants in World Perspective conference. Professor Light is the author of *Ethnic Enterprise in America* (1972), *Cities in World Perspective* (1983), and *Immigrant Entrepreneurs* (1988, with Edna Bonacich).

PYONG GAP MIN, a Korean native, graduated from Seoul National University specializing in history. He earned an M.A. degree in history, and two Ph.D. degrees, one in education, and the other in sociology, all from Georgia State University. Assistant professor of sociology at Queens College of the City University of New York, Min currently teaches classes in marriage and the family, minority groups, and Asian Americans. Ethnic business, Korean immigrants' economic adjustment, and Korean immigrant families have been topics of his research interest over the last seven years. He has published a book on Korean immigrant entrepreneurship in Atlanta, and his second book, evaluating the Korean ethnic market in Los Angeles, is in the process of completion. He has published many articles dealing with Korean and Asian immigrants. This includes "Business Enterprise: Korean Small Business in Atlanta," New York Center for Migration Studies Press.

MIRJANA MOROKVASIC, Ph.D., is a sociologist. She holds her degrees from the Universite Rene Descartes Paris V - Sorbonne and the Ecole

Pratique des Hautes Etudes (now Ecole des Hautes Etudes en Sciences Sociales). She lectured in social psychology and sociology of education at the Universite Lille III from 1970-79 and has since been a research fellow at the Centre National de la Recherche Scientifique Paris. Most of her work has been about international migration. Her recent studies focused on female migration and undocumented labour. Her latest research is a comparative study of entrepreneurial strategies of self-employed immigrant and minority women in five European states. She has authored and edited a number of publications in that field (among others, a special issue of *Current Sociology* [1984], and of *International Migration Review* [1984], and a book on women in migration, *Emigration und Danach* [1987]).

DEMETRIOS G. PAPADEMETRIOU received his Ph.D. in political science at the University of Maryland in 1976. He is the director of Immigration Policy and Research, Bureau of International Labor Affairs, U.S. Department of Labor. Previously, he was Executive Director of Population Associates International, a research and consulting firm specializing in immigration, and a senior consultant on policy and research for the U.S. Catholic Conference. From 1980 to 1983, Dr. Papademetriou was the Executive Editor of the *International Migration Review*. He has taught International Political Economy and Comparative Public Policy at the University of Maryland, Duke University, and the Graduate Faculty of the New School for Social Research. Dr. Papademetriou has published extensively on the immigration and refugee policies of the U.S. and other advanced industrial societies, the impact of legal and illegal immigration on the U.S. labor market, and the relationship between international migration and development. Dr. Papademetriou's most recent works are an edited volume, titled *Migration and Development: The Unsettled Relationship*, to be published by Greenwood Press, and *Reluctant Promised Lands: Immigrant Labor in Advanced Industrial Societies*.

ERAN RAZIN is a lecturer in the department of geography in the Hebrew University of Jerusalem. He received his Ph.D. degree from the Hebrew University in 1986, and the subject of his thesis was: "The Effect of Organizational Structure of Industry on the Development of Peripheral Towns in Israel." In 1986-1987, he was a Post-Doctoral Scholar at the University of California, Los Angeles, studying the role of foreign migrants in urban economies in the United States. He is currently engaged mainly in studies of: (a) location and entrepreneurship among immigrant/ethnic groups in Israel and Canada; (b) evaluation of Israel's spatial industrialization policy; and (c) competition among towns in Israel in a period of local initiative.

GEORGES SABAGH is a sociology professor and director of the Center for Near Eastern Studies at the University of California, Los Angeles. As a social demographer, he has maintained a long-standing interest in migration. While his earlier research concerned internal migration, he has recently focused on international migration. His diverse research in Los Angeles has covered residential mobility, the growth of Mexican-American families, and the social and economic adaptation of Iranians. Additionally, he is initiating a comparative study of Armenian ethnicity in California and in the USSR.

GILDAS SIMON is a professor of geography at the University of Poitiers - France. He is the director of a research team studying international migration (U.R.A. CNRS 1145), and he founded *la Revue Européenne des Migrations Internationales*. The principal research themes he pursues are relations between immigration countries and sending countries, ethnic business, and geographic mobility in the EEC. His recent publications include: "Commercants Maghrebins et Asiatiques en France" (in collaboration with E. Ma Mung, Masson edit., Paris 1990); "Les Effets de la Migration Internationale au Maghreb" (SEDES edit., Paris 1990).

CHANDRA S. TIBREWAL is a Ph.D. candidate in sociology at Jawaharlal Nehru University, Delhi, India. He has worked on voluntary associations and entrepreneurships among Indian business communities.

BRIAN WEARING received his M.A. in modern history and B.Phil. in American history from the Queens' College, Oxford. He is a lecturer in American history at the University of Canterbury, Christchurch, New Zealand. He was a visiting scholar at Inter-American University, San German, Puerto Rico; University of London; University of Texas, Austin; Colegio de Mexico; University of California, San Diego; and A.C.L.S. fellow in Washington, D.C. He has taught survey courses in the history of the United States, Latin America, and ethnicity and immigration. His most recent research and publication has been on U.S. immigration legislation and comparisons with the New Zealand experience.

Acknowledgments

This volume emerged from a conference at the University of California, Los Angeles. Under the dual aegis of UCLA's International Studies and Overseas Programs and Institute of Social Science Research, the newly formed, interdisciplinary Immigration Research Project organized an international conference entitled "California Immigrants in World Perspective," which was held at UCLA in April, 1990. It was the largest immigration conference ever convened on the Pacific Coast. We invited to this conference twelve immigration researchers from the United States and seven from foreign countries. The conferees represented six academic disciplines: anthropology, geography, history, political science, urban planning, and sociology.

Like other books, but more than most, this volume is the product of the work and support of many people other than the authors whose names appear on the articles. These undesignated producers are the people who worked on and funded the conference, on April 26, 27, and 28, 1990. First, we thank those at UCLA who had enough faith in the conference to extend it the essential financial support. The director of International Studies and Overseas Programs, John Hawkins, was certainly the key person in that regard. However, Dean Richard Sisson also came through at a critical moment with enough support to put the project over the top.

Second, the conference depended upon the wise leadership of the Institute for Social Science Research (ISSR) at the University of California, Los Angeles. The ISSR provided the administration and accounting services without which the conference could not have happened. The ISSR's director, Marilynn Brewer, made the courageous decision to offer this support out of her evaluation of the timeliness of the project and its potential for long-range contribution to the welfare of social research at UCLA.

Third, the conference depended upon the labor of several people who did a much better job of organizing, administering, and word processing than anyone could possibly have expected. Of these, Darla Guenzler is the linchpin. At every stage of the conference and editorial preparation of the manuscript, Darla offered generous help, encouragement, long hours, and even her artistic talent. We also thank Tarik Abraha, Hadas Har-Chvi, Kenneth Kan, Georges Sabagh, Artemis Riazi, Maureen Quiros, and the underpaid workhorses at the Social Science Word Processing Facility. Each in his or her own way has contributed immensely to the success of this venture.

Finally, we acknowledge the support of the people of California whom the University of California exists to serve.

It is a measure of the credit owed all these supporters that none gave support contingent upon the kind of results we would provide. Every contributor had complete freedom to publish what he or she thought the truth. Therefore, the editors and authors have full responsibility for any errors of fact, interpretation, or method.

IVAN LIGHT
PARMINDER BHACHU

1

Introduction:
California Immigrants in World Perspective

Ivan Light and Parminder Bhachu

Many nations invite foreigners to work within their borders, but few welcome them. When nations wish to welcome foreigners, they offer them the same political rights that their own citizens already enjoy. Citizenship is the most basic right (Brubaker, 1989). Of the many nations that accept or tolerate foreigners, only five now encourage foreigners to migrate, to settle permanently, and then to obtain citizenship and naturalization.[1] These are Australia, Canada, Israel, New Zealand, and the United States (Salt, 1989: 447-49). Because so few countries welcome foreigners, those that do welcome them receive torrents of immigrants, a pressure that analysts expect to intensify as demographic and social pressures mount in the less developed countries of the world (Montalbano, 1991).

If California were one of the nations that award citizenship to immigrants, it would be the world's second largest center of immigrant reception, behind only the United States itself. By 1990 California had received more immigrants in the preceding twenty years than did Australia, Canada, Israel, or New Zealand. In 1980, California already had more and a higher proportion of immigrants than any other American state (Rumbaut, 1992: Table 5). In the 1980s, a period of revived immigration in the United States,

California also received more immigrants than did any of the other forty-nine American states (Papademetriou et al., 1989: 73; Keane, 1986: 24; Espenshade and Goodis, 1985). By 1990, California had one-quarter of all the foreign born in the United States but only 11 percent of the U.S. population. California's population was 28.9 million of whom 20.8 percent were foreign-born, a percentage unmatched outside Florida.[2]

As a world-class immigrant mecca, California's new stature is novel and unanticipated. When California gained statehood in 1850, California bordered Mexico to the South and faced westward onto the Pacific Ocean just as she does today. However, the number of immigrants who entered from these directions was small. There were several reasons. First, Californians resisted the immigration of Asians, compelling Congress to pass the United States' first exclusionary legislation in 1882. This anti-Chinese law was continued and expanded thereafter. Finally, in 1924 Congress widened Asian exclusion into a national origins quota system which set each nation's annual immigration quota proportional to its share of the 1920 U.S. population. This law remained the basic immigration law of the United States until 1965. Second, nineteenth-century Asian migrants included few women or complete families so that natural increase did not contribute to the long-run growth of Asian population. Third, although Mexicans always crossed American borders in search of work, most came as temporary agricultural laborers, and subsequently repatriated (Massey et al., 1987: chaps. 4, 5). Therefore, the net influx of Mexicans was actually modest in the century that followed California's entry into the United States.[3]

After 1882, California's net population increases from immigration reflected the state's attractiveness to interstate migrants. These migrants were the assimilated children and grandchildren of Europeans whose first settlement areas had been in the Middle West and along the Eastern seaboard (Davis, 1990: 114). This pattern still holds. In 1990, only 36 percent of whites in Southern California had been born in the region. Fifty-one percent were born in the United States outside California, 4 percent in California outside Southern California, and 8 percent abroad. Among Southern California's blacks, only one-quarter were born in the region. Fully 70 percent of whites were interstate migrants (Quintanilla, 1991). California had no European ethnic enclaves that could match New York, Boston, Philadelphia, or Chicago for size or institutional completeness. Nonetheless, the population of California was historically more white than the population of the United States. As late as 1960, the population of the United States was 89.9 percent white. In that year, California's population was 91.9 percent white.

In the last thirty years, the long preponderance of assimilated whites drew to a close in California. In 1990, California's population had declined to 60 percent white whereas that of the United States still remained 84 percent white. The discrepancy became a matter of concern for the national press (Henry, 1990).[4] Now drawing its new population from Asia, Central America, and Mexico, California has introduced new ethnic and racial stocks into its established population. California had in 1990 a higher proportion of Asian and Latino residents than any other state and the second-highest number of blacks and American Indians (Fulwood, 1991). In Southern California, 45 percent of Latinos and 42 percent of Asians were foreign-born in 1991 (Quintanilla, 1991). These Latino and Asian immigrants arrive in California at a moment when the United States, confronting European economic unity, and diminished international economic competitiveness, looks for its economic future to trade with Latin America and Asia more than ever in the past.[5] According to Mike Davis (1987: 67), and other regional optimists, Los Angeles is becoming the "Pacific's economic capital." Naturally, this moment in history provides the United States with new reasons to welcome Latino and Asian immigrants who enable it to communicate better with the societies that sent them. But the burdens of immigrant reception fall heavily upon California, and the Golden State is historically ill-prepared for its new role of entrepot, cultural emporium, and melting pot, however useful that role to the economic future of the United States (Kotkin, 1991).

In general, immigration is most difficult to absorb when immigrants are both numerous and of different ethno-racial stock than the settled population. Both conditions continued to pertain in California, which for this reason, ought to have experienced much immigrant/nonimmigrant conflict in the last two decades. In actuality, however, California has proven surprisingly able to accommodate and integrate the new ethnic stocks into its predominantly white population. Unlike Germany and France, where anti-immigrant riots and political parties have arisen (Tempest, 1991; Miller, 1991; Therborn, 1987), California has seen nothing more organized than ballot efforts to certify English as the state's official language and boycotts of Korean grocery stores in black communities. In a European review of intergroup relations in California, David Manasian (1990) declared Californians "admirably" tolerant. "Few other societies could have absorbed so many different types of people so rapidly without violent conflict. Instead Californians are proud of their cultural diversity."(1990: 58)   This is a common European view, and, in the light of the Los Angeles riot and arson of 1992, it is easy to ridicule. Moreover, this judgment overlooks the intolerance that has historically attended the meeting of peoples in California. California did not have a tradition of tolerance in 1942 when the Japanese Americans were interned, nor did it have one in 1880 when the state was the seat of anti-Chinese agitation (Chan, 1990: 61-67). Where did this intolerance go?

Until the Los Angeles riot and arson of 1992, immigrant/native relations in California had been largely peaceful and devoid of the frank racism that occurs in Europe. Nonetheless, relations were often troubled and tense. A Field Institute (1982) poll found that 62 percent of Californians believed that the volume of immigration into the U.S. should be decreased.[6] Sixty-five percent thought illegal immigration a very serious problem, and 77 percent agreed that government should do more to discourage illegal immigration. The intergroup climate is strained. Journalists declare California's public schools "cauldrons of prejudice" in which racially motivated violence is commonplace, especially between blacks and Hispanics (Woo and Kowsky, 1991). Nationalist blacks boycott the Korean storekeepers who operate in Watts, the black residential capital of Los Angeles. Black/Korean tensions focused around some sensationalized murders. In 1991, the Republican governor blamed undocumented immigrants on welfare for the state's budgetary shortfall (Starkey, 1992). Even so, frank intergroup conflict has been on a more modest scale in California than one might have anticipated given the volume and heterogeneity of immigration in the 1980s (Fong, 1989; Kimble, 1989; Horton, 1989). The oddest complaint comes from Asian Americans some of whom object to the positive "model minority stereotype" that causes "others to resent them," and sometimes reduces their ability to obtain financial support from the welfare state (US Civil Rights Commission, 1992).

Emigration of whites offers a possible explanation of California's surprising absorptive capacity. The Los Angeles metropolitan area had a population of about 8.8 million in 1989, a gain of almost a million persons over 1980. During the 1980s, Los Angeles County added more people than did any other metropolitan area in the United States. Two-thirds of this increase arose from net migration, and one-third from natural increase (Allen, 1990: 2). However, this population growth arose *despite* a net egress of about 403,000 persons in the period 1985-1990 alone. Of these, three-quarters were non-Latino whites who moved to other California counties and other American states.

In 1990, after two decades of white egress (Light, 1988), the non-Hispanic whites were only 42 percent of Los Angeles' population. James Allen (1990: 6) estimates that legal immigrants to Los Angeles County amounted to only 310,000 in the period 1985-1990. This legal influx was not enough to compensate the loss of 403,000 established residents. Allen (1990: 6) concludes that Los Angeles County's net population increase depended upon illegal immigrants. Naturally, the numbers of illegal residents are impossible to establish with precision, but they are certainly numerous. In 1989, Los Angeles County alone accounted for 39 percent of all normalizations of immigrant status made possible under the Immigration Reform and Control Act of 1986.

In the face of an unprecedented influx of documented and undocumented immigrants, known less correctly as illegal aliens, this decade's exodus of non-Hispanic whites supported both quality of life and intergroup accommodation. First, by leaving Los Angeles in the 1980s, seven-hundred-thousand non-Hispanic whites vacated residences and jobs, making vacancies at the top that opened opportunities for immigrants at the bottom (Light, 1981: 58). White egress also made extra space available in the schools, hospitals, parks, beaches, and parking lots of the crowded, polluted region. Second, the enhanced availability of these resources reduced the intensity of inter group conflict, thus contributing to the "tolerance" that *The Economist* identified. However, moving away from an immigrant influx does not represent true tolerance. Since more whites stayed than left, there is this basis for acknowledging the tolerance of the established population, but their tolerance was facilitated by the departure of a significant minority of older homeowners.

Although those who left Los Angeles did not display tolerance toward their immigrant successors, neither did they resist their influx. Unlike Palestinians, Belfast Catholics, Mohawk Indians of Quebec, African Americans of Watts, and others who bear a legacy of hatred toward their dispossessors, Los Angeles' departing whites left their homes and jobs voluntarily and without rancor or hatred. This self-abnegation owed much to the free market for real estate. Real estate prices in California soared in the 1980s for several reasons, some of them unrelated to immigration. Among these reasons were $40 billion of Japanese and Canadian investment in California real estate, the growth of Pacific Rim trading, and accelerated weapons procurement programs put in motion by the Cold Warriors of the Reagan administration (Frantz, 1988; Davis, 1990: 132, 135-38; Bates, 1992). The additional housing demand of the immigrants only added to the conjunctural explosion of demand for California real estate, but did not basically cause it. Nonetheless, as immigrants arrived, home prices, partially in response to their arrival, soared until August, 1989, when they were more than three times the U.S. national average. Using prevailing yardsticks, only 13 percent of Los Angeles County's population could then afford to purchase a home at the median price. Since the majority of non-Hispanic whites were homeowners, these vested incumbents could sell their residences for vast profits and then relocate to other parts of California or the United States. Someone who sold a home in Los Angeles could buy a home as good in Portland, and put $140,000 in the bank. In effect, the soaring real estate market paid homeowners to leave Los Angeles, and so many took this golden handshake that housing shortage was significantly reduced among those who stayed.

Naturally, the egress of homeowners did not improve the quality of life. In response to soaring housing prices, residential over-crowding increased (Martinez, 1992). Traffic congestion increased to catastrophic levels, driving business away from downtown to the consternation of central city real estate interests. Air pollution that had declined in the 1970s began to rise again in response to the many additional, often dilapidated cars and trucks that impoverished immigrants pressed into service. Public primary and secondary education was abandoned to immigrants and nonwhite minorities by Republican legislators more sensitive to the needs of tax-resisting suburban voters than to those of immigrant children. Gang violence and drug traffic reached levels much worse than ever observed before. The percentage of Hispanics in poverty increased from 26 percent in 1979 to 45 percent in 1987 (Sabagh, 1992). To make matters worse, the state suffered a severe drought that strained the ability of the Department of Water and Power to supply water. Even the earthquakes of 1988 contributed to the malaise of the state which discovered, after the fact, that highways and public buildings required expensive retrofitting for earthquake safety. Bad as they were, however, the 1980s would have been even worse had it not been for that 10 percent of the white population who voluntarily vacated residences and jobs, thus freeing resources for successors.

Abrupt increase of population threatens the ability of localities to maintain much less to improve their quality of life (Light, 1983: pt. 4). However, effective, proactive government can buffer the impact of immigration on metropolitan regions by shrewd planning and social programs. Unfortunately, several obstacles frustrated the ability of California cities to field proactive, effective, governmental responses to immigration. First, the well-known fragmentation of local government in California deprived localities of an agency uniquely responsible for metropolitan areas or empowered to act on their behalf (Light, 1988: 88-92). Second, California's minimal government tradition, a legacy of nineteenth-century Liberalism, gave the state's metropolitan regions no tradition of long-range planning upon which to build. Finally, with the populist tax revolt of 1978 (Proposition 13), public authorities experienced further erosion of their already slender tax revenues, thus impeding their ability to respond proactively to the immigrant influx.[7]

Although immigration reduced their quality of life, it did not reduce earnings or job opportunities for native Californians, except, possibly, native-born Hispanics who sustained the most direct effect of wage competition with the low-wage immigrants (Papademetriou et al., 1989: 74, 78; McCarthy and Valdez, 1986).[8] First, the state's defense-based manufacturing sector expanded throughout the 1980s, becoming the state's first-ranked employer.[9] Although economic restructuring added new semiskilled and unskilled jobs for immigrants in the garment industry, the high-technology, high-wage sector held up well in the 1980s. Second, California has long benefitted from unusually high entrepreneurship. This state's persistently high entrepreneurship resulted in a flexible and resilient population of small and medium firms that, as numerous studies have confirmed (Light and Bonacich, 1988: chap. 1), actually provide the bulk of employment. Possibly the entrepreneurial climate facilitated the economic integration of the immigrants who not only took the jobs these small and medium firms provided, but also opened small and medium firms of their own, thus expanding the job base and obviating direct wage competition with native Californians.

The Importance of California's Immigration

Native whites still complain frequently about deteriorating quality of life (Rodriguez, 1990: M8): "They mean there are too many ... immigrants. They tell you they are thinking of moving to Oregon or to Australia." Yet, state authorities project a California population of 35 million in 2000, a gain of 6 million in the decade. Of the next decade's population gain, 42 percent is expected to derive from net migration. Obviously, immigration is by no means over in the Golden State (Muller and Espenshade, 1985) -- nor have the whites stopped leaving.[10] Even so, it is not too early to reflect upon California's experience as a major reception center of international migrants. This concern is local and parochial in one sense. As the Los Angeles fire and arson of May, 1992 have demonstrated beyond cavail, California needs to learn how better to manage its immigration-related responsibilities and challenges, and California will benefit most from the knowledge. But the subject has broader ramifications. First, California now attracts and accommodates a significant proportion of the world's immigrants and refugees. This centrality renders California's experience important to anyone who wishes to understand world immigration trends and topics. Second, California's immigrant-reception experience permits generalizations that simultaneously advance social science knowledge and guide the policies of California and other current and prospective immigrant-reception states.

In order to learn from the California experience, we must distinguish the effects of immigrant culture from those of the reception context. The hazards of this distinction were well illustrated when President Ronald Reagan's secretary of housing and urban development attributed residential overcrowding among California Hispanics to a cultural preference for extended families rather than to low incomes and high rents, the explanation the Hispanics preferred (Kurtz, 1984). Of course, if California were a wholly unique environment, the effects of its reception context would be of no interest outside the state so there would be little point in studying it. This question complicates analysis because, to some extent, like every other place in the world, California is a unique environment. Reviewed above, the conjunctural causes and consequences of high real estate prices are one unique feature of California's recent immigration experience. Nonetheless, we believe that Californians can learn something useful from the immigration experience of other states and countries. Similarly, we maintain that California's unique characteristics do not render the state of no interest to non-Californians. However, comparative methods maximize the interest in and benefit from California's immigration experience for Californians and non-Californians alike. California's uniqueness and sameness can be known only in juxtaposition with other immigrant-reception contexts.

Comparative Migration Studies

Edited volumes normally have multiple objectives. The first objective of this volume is just to assemble and make available information that would illuminate California's recent migration experience which, even before the fire and arson of 1992, we knew to be volatile (Light and Bonacich, 1988: chap. 12; Cheng and Espiritu, 1989). Since Roy Bryce-Laporte's (1980) collection on the new migration to the United States, also produced by Transaction, only one edited book on this subject has appeared even though the volume of immigration research has thundered mightily upward in the intervening decade.[11] Indeed, in an ironic reflection of the immigration process itself, edited books about immigration seem to await socioeconomic maturation of the immigrants, a process that takes decades. Thus, the Statue of Liberty/Ellis Island Foundation has sponsored two recent collections of essays that bear on the immigrant experience of groups that went through Ellis Island in the nineteenth century (Yans-McLaughlin, 1990; Vecoli, 1991). Unsurprisingly, these books are historical in focus because the experience of the European immigrants is now history. Today's new immigration does not pass through Ellis Island, and the immigrants debarking are not yet in a socioeconomic position to sponsor research foundations to tell their story. So it is up to the academics to collect and publish the information about the new migration on their own hook and with whatever slender resources they can mobilize.

A second objective of this volume is to compare immigrant groups and immigration-related issues in California with the same groups and the same issues in other world centers of immigrant reception. In this volume, we match California immigrant groups and immigration-related problems with the same immigrant groups and immigration-related problems elsewhere. This is a classic methodological strategy derived from J. S. Mill (Skocpol and Somers, 1980). By matching a California immigrant group or immigration-related issue with the same group or issue elsewhere, one distinguishes more easily what immigrants brought with them and what is a product of California's reception context (Portes and Rumbaut, 1990). That is, to the extent that immigration-related problems and immigrant behavior are the same in California and elsewhere, we can conclude that the causes of the sameness do not lie in divergent reception contexts. At that point we are confronting the similar effects of similar conditions. Conversely, when we find the same group behaving differently in California than elsewhere, we appropriately conclude that characteristics of the reception contexts caused the difference.

Reviewing numerous immigration collections, recent and not-so-recent, we find no comparable organization in any.[12] Many collections simply assemble available articles that bear upon immigration to or from a particular region.[13] Others impose thematic constraints such as womens' immigration or undocumented immigration to the region.[14] A few compare world regions with respect to an overarching thematic concern, assembling papers that illustrate the thematic concern in the contrasted regions.[15] William Serow (et al., eds., 1990) asked contributors to provide parallel information about immigration to nineteen different nations, assembling the results in a kind of checklist.

Recent collections on the United States invariably have organized their contents topically under thematic headings that reflect the editor's interest. For example, Edna Bonacich and Lucie Cheng (1984, x) organized seventeen independent contributions under three topical headings, alleging that the collection would strengthen the theoretical integration of Asian studies. The contributions consisted of parallel narratives that depicted how five groups of Asian immigrants entered, settled, and worked in the United States. Similarly, Virginia Yans-McLaughlin organized eleven independent contributions under four very broad headings. Within each heading, contributors offered parallel narratives of the immigration experience of different groups who migrated to and within the United States (the Irish come to America, the Italians come to America, the Jews come to America, etc). Endorsing "both the comparative method and a global perspective," Yans-McLaughlin (1990: 5) evidently supposed that parallel narratives were the best way to achieve these objectives.

Although a different groups/same nation approach is a legitimate form of comparison, we do not believe it is the most reliable form of *global* comparison. First, a comparison of different immigrant groups within the same country is not a global comparison at all. Yet, much of what passes for comparative research in this country does not vary the national reception context, implicitly accepting the United States as the horizon of comparison. For example, Virginia Yans-McLaughlin (1990) offered three chapters which described experience of Irish, black, and Hispanic immigrants to and within the United States.[16] Edna Bonacich and Lucie Cheng (1984) offered independent chapters that analyzed the experience of Punjabis, Koreans, Filipinos, Chinese, and Japanese in the United States. Intergroup comparisons within the same nation do not vary the reception context of immigration, thus leaving only the cultural endowment of immigrants to vary. The methodological oversight is particularly striking in Bonacich and Cheng's (1984) collection which sought to extract from their data theoretical insights about how capitalism controls immigration. Second, these different groups/same nation comparisons are not as genuinely global as would have been a comparison of, say, Irish in New York and Irish in London. Reversing the prevailing formula, a same groups/different nations approach focuses upon the differences between the nations, not the groups.

By systematically comparing the same groups and immigration-related problems in California and abroad, we achieve a global comparison that does not implicitly accept the parameters of American law, culture, economy, and society without, however, losing sight of those parameters. The comparative method we have selected emphasizes variation in reception contexts as the cause of differences in immigrant behavior. Since parallel narratives place the opposite emphasis, and these are the only collections now available to deal with immigration to the United States, our structure is a useful corrective. The corrective is needed because the prevailing and naive different groups/same nation comparison obscures the global context of immigration. After all, if one only compares immigrant groups who selected the United States as a destination, one conveys the impression that immigration was an American phenomenon, rather than a global phenomenon. The myth of "American exceptionalism," which Yans-McLaughlin (1990: 5) decries, owes a lot to overuse of editorial perspectives that compare different groups who entered the United States.

Comparative Entrepreneurship

A third objective of this collection is to stress immigrant

entrepreneurship. Entrepreneurship is an important theme of this book for two reasons. First, California has an entrepreneurial economy whose self-employment rate is high. That high rate may have influenced the social as well as the economic integration of immigrants by facilitating the formation of immigrant-owned firms which are also very numerous in the Golden State. Second, and more important, in the theoretical context of the latest immigration literature, entrepreneurship has emerged as a neglected but potent influence upon the economic and social integration of immigrants (Aldrich and Waldinger, 1990). But, the state of the current literature of social science has not caught up with the existing collections that represent it. Acknowledging the ability of immigrants to create wealth, Yans-McLaughlin (1990: 12) even observed that immigrant networks can build businesses as well as find housing. This point is a weighty one indeed. Yet, her collection did not include any investigations of immigrant entrepreneurship. In our keynote presentation, we have built upon the existing, influential literature of immigrant networks, arguing that this literature has overlooked the manner in which migrant networks contribute to immigrant entrepreneurship as well as the manner in which immigrant entrepreneurship influences the volume of immigration. Taking account of that link substantially extends the scope and effectiveness of network theory in immigration studies.

Two researchers have mobilized new evidence that bears upon immigrant entrepreneurship. Eran Razin offers a comparative analysis of immigrant entrepreneurship in Israel, Canada, and California. Utilizing official statistics, Razin's original article is the most technically advanced comparative work in immigrant entrepreneurship that has ever been published. Razin shows also that entrepreneurship is an important part of immigrant economic absorption in all three countries. His international comparison also demonstrates the extent to which California's entrepreneurial economy exaggerates but does not create the entrepreneurship of immigrants. At the same time, his results show that the entrepreneurial performance of immigrant groups depends upon the reception contexts.

Gildas Simon has assembled an original overview of French language literature on immigrant entrepreneurs in France. Although the Anglo-American literature on this subject is already well known in France, the reverse is not true. Americans are unaware how extensive, visible, and influential is the entrepreneurship of immigrants in France. The existing French literature on immigrant entrepreneurs is theoretically informed and much more extensive than Americans realize. Simon's paper will open this research access for anglophone scholars.

The garment industry attracts immigrants in every country. Los Angeles has a gigantic immigrant-staffed garment industry whose gross proceeds now equal or surpass those of the Hollywood film and video industry. But immigrants are making garments in many great cities of the developed world. Edna Bonacich examines the immigrant-staffed garment industry of Los Angeles, and Mirjana Morokvasic examines the same industry in Berlin and Paris. Although these chapters concern immigrants, not entrepreneurs, they continue the theme of entrepreneurship since, as is well understood, the garment manufacturing industry consists of small and medium firms and nearly all the entrepreneurs in this industry are immigrants, too. Both Bonacich and Morokvasic emphasize the dramatic increase in small subcontracting firms which have facilitated the entry of immigrants into the garment industry in Los Angeles, Berlin, and Paris. These firms can respond rapidly to the demand for flexible production according to fluctuations in fashion styles. In comparing garment production in Paris and Berlin, two cities with contrasting opportunity structures for migrants, Morokvasic states that subcontracting doubled in France in the 1980s because it "transfers production risks to contractors." Although Bonacich develops a similar theme of the informalization of garment production in Los Angeles through subcontracting, in which manufacturers are "the kingpins" with mutually dependent relationships with retailers, she focuses on the exploitation by capitalist producers of powerless and frequently illegal Latino immigrants. These illegals are, in turn, oppressed by other immigrants of Asian origin. In contrast, acknowledging the exploitative dimensions of the market in determining production, Morokvasic stresses the skills immigrants themselves bring. These skills "are then shaped by the circumstances of the destination economy which enhances certain types of economic behaviors, whilst jeopardizing others." She emphasizes "the obsolescence of traditional class relationships" noting the limitations of "an analysis that constructs employers as the exploiters and the employees as the exploited, that is, the winners against the losers."

Six chapters offer comparative views of the same immigrant group in different reception contexts: Armenians, Koreans, and Asian Indians. Southern California houses the largest settlement of expatriate Armenians in the United States and one of the largest in the world. Yet, Armenians have received next to no research attention despite their influence and growing numbers. Two papers on Armenians show that the "same" group can be quite different in different settings. Claudia Der-Martirosian and Mehdi Bozorgmehr present survey data derived from a 1988 study of Iranian-born Armenians in Los Angeles County. Iran-born Armenians are frequently entrepreneurs. Their rate of self-employment is three and a half times higher than that of other residents of Los Angeles. However, Iranian Armenians in Los Angeles are rarely artists or scientists. One might suppose that the well-known proclivity of Armenians for commerce is irrepressible. However, Yuri Arutunyan shows that Armenians in Moscow were frequently intellectuals and scientists. The difference between the two groups of Armenians arises from Soviet law as much as from the unique characteristics of the Moscow economy. Soviet internal passport regulations monitored the flow of Armenians to the capital, permitting only those to settle whose occupations were in conformity with manpower needs. Of course, there is no way to prove that Armenians in Moscow were not also active in the black market, but there seems no doubt from Arutunyan's results that Moscow's Armenians were an unusually well educated, high status, and officially integrated population.

Two chapters deal with Koreans, a group very much in evidence in Los Angeles since 1975, and subjected to arson and mob violence during the Los Angeles riot of 1992. But few Americans are aware that Koreans also live in Japan as an immigrant minority. One way to evaluate the effect of California on immigrant Koreans is to compare their situation in Japan. George A. DeVos and Eun-Young Kim use projective tests to measure and describe the contrasting psychocultural adaptation of Koreans in Japan and the United States.

Confronting the same projective stimuli, Japanese Koreans volunteered less achievement imagery than did American Koreans. Interpreting this difference, DeVos and Kim observe that Koreans in Japan have been subjected to forced "Japanization," a process that degraded and negated their cultural and ethnic identity. As a consequence, they suffer generational alienation and have difficulty in sustaining a positive group identity. The group's deprecation even reduces the achievement imagery of individual members.

This depressing situation is in contrast to Korean migration to and settlement in Los Angeles where Pyong Gap Min's research documents their economic success and startlingly high entrepreneurship. True, Korean immigrants in Los Angeles are not a cross-section of Korean society. Rather, they represent a self-selected population of relocated people who "held professional and white-collar occupations prior to immigration." Nonetheless, over half of Korean workers owned at least one business compared to 8 percent of Los Angeles workers. Obviously, Koreans in Los Angeles did not lack achievement aspiration, and one must suppose that the characteristics of California's multicultural reception context are partially responsible. Whatever the problems of immigrants in California, they do not include the denial of entrepreneurial opportunity to those who have the resources to take advantage of them. Moreover, California's multiracial society makes social integration much easier for immigrants than does Japan, an ethnically homogeneous society, proud of its racial purity, and determined to remain that way. Whether Japan succeeds in avoiding immigration, a common fate of rich societies, time will tell. However, it is clear from the highly differential fate of Koreans that Japanese society would have to endure a lot of painful stretching in order to accommodate mass immigration.

Karen B. Leonard and Chandra S. Tibrewal develop similar themes of ethnicity, occupational specialization, and entrepreneurship among Asian Indians in Los Angeles. Asian Indians are little studied in the United States, but, like the much-studied Koreans, Asian Indians are unusually entrepreneurial. Asian Indian firms service coethnics and non-Indians alike. Among the shops that make "appeals beyond the community" are the "notorious motels" owned often by Indian persons surnamed Patel, the trendy and expensive Indian restaurants of San Francisco and Los Angeles, and the salaried and fee-for-service professionals, especially computer consultants and realtors. Leonard and Tibrewal refer to the contextual nature of ethnic identity and explore the extent to "which ethnicity is maintained and reinforced by participation in ethnic business." They conclude that strength of ethnicity is not dependent on ethnically-oriented enterprises but on length of residence in the United States and on security of employment. Hence, they find "higher expressions of ethnicity among the professionally oriented immigrants, rather than, among the newer immigrants who are self-employed." In common with other Asians in the United States, Asian Indians too are characterized by numerous highly educated professional immigrants.

This selective migration is further explored by Bhachu who describes the dynamics of caste and class among a section of the British Asian population, the "twice migrant" East African Sikhs, also of Indian origin, who were highly urbanized prior to migration to metropolitan Britain and also relatively middle class. She uses the term *twice migrants* to characterize groups that have previous historical experience of migration and minority status. The East African Sikhs are settlers, oriented toward permanent residence in their destination economies right from the day of arrival. In comparison to Indian direct migrants, who migrated directly from the Indian subcontinent, "twice migrants" went from India to Africa and thence to Britain, and in the process learned rapidly how to establish the infrastructure of their communities and also how to manage their minority status in overseas settings. In emphasizing the interactive nature of ethnicity and ethnic identities, Bhachu explores the interaction on the British scene of a diverse range of class and caste groups, and the impact of this situation on inter- and intra-group identities. In describing the articulation of caste and class, she finds that the "caste status of East Africans was emphasized in the U.K., not because of their own consciousness of it but as a result of their interaction with direct migrants who are more conscious of their caste and village ties, being more familiar about functioning caste hierarchies." Also, East African Asians entered as middle class public sector workers in contrast to the direct migrants who were predominantly working class. These differences are publicly and institutionally expressed, and "the expression of their differences is not only produced by their different caste positions but also by their different class positions in Britain."

We wanted to offer some comparative material about immigration laws and the legislative process as well as about social and economic conditions among immigrants (Kubat, 1979). Immigration laws shape the volume as well as the character of migrations. Current high levels of immigration in California are the product of new immigration laws crafted in Washington, a city whose politicians and administrators cannot see beyond the Beltway, much less the Rocky Mountains. Although California does not make immigration laws, it does participate in the political process from which revised immigration laws continue to emerge, heavy with implications for the welfare of the state. Then Director of the U.S. Department of Labor's International Labor Office, and a Washington insider, Demetrios Papademetriou explains the terms of the debate that shaped 1990's revisions in the 1965 Immigration and Nationalities Act, still the basic immigration law of the United States. His discussion provides the finest-grained account of political processes that churn out immigration laws. Brian Wearing brings out points of similarity and dissimilarity between American law and that of New Zealand which is, like the United States, one of the five countries of the earth that offers citizenship to immigrants. Now, as in the past, the legislative similarities are startling but explicable when one recalls that fashion rules in immigration laws nearly as much as in haute couture.

The last chapter in this volume offers an overview of California's Mexican migrants, the largest single group of migrants in the Golden State. No discussion of immigration in California can ignore Mexicans who are not only much the largest group, but who have contributed the place names of the whole state as well as the numerous restaurants that purvey their national cuisine to grateful customers. Director of the USA/Mexico Research Center in San Diego, Wayne Cornelius demonstrates that the profile of Mexican migration to California has changed radically since the 1960s and even since the 1970s. Whereas the earlier period was characterized by the stereotype of young adult male migrants who came to California for seasonal agricultural work, leaving their immediate relatives behind in villages of origin to which they returned annually, the 1980s saw the development of a rapidly settled, heterogenous and balanced Mexican population of complete families. Cornelius offers four main reasons for this dramatic shift. First, "the changes in the California economy" affected "the nature and magnitude of the demand for Mexican immigrant labor." Second, the protracted economic crisis in Mexico affected the motives of emigrants. Third, the Immigration Reform and Control Act of 1986 impacted Mexican migrants more than those of any other national origin. Finally, the "earlier waves of immigrants to California" resulted in the formation of "transnational migrant networks" that reached maturation during this period. On a pessimistic note, Cornelius predicts that this changing "social composition and spatial concentration of the Mexican immigrant population provide a stern test of California's capacity to develop as a multicultural society in the 1990's and beyond." Early signs are not encouraging. Intolerance toward Latino immigrants is rising in heavily impacted areas of the state. Even though California is not prepared to accept a settled Latino immigrant population in its midst, "public debate in California will gradually shift to how to deal more effectively with Mexican immigrants as a settler population and to the problems of 'assimilating' the second and third generations." Indeed, this challenge of "integrating" and "assimilating" future generations emanating from current immigrants, already constitutes a central topic of economic and political debate in a rapidly changing world.

Notes

1. See the accounts in Serow et al., eds. 1990. For a visual display of world migration, see Kidron and Segal, 1987: map 32.
2. These trends are projected to continue for another decade. See *American Demographics* 8 (1986/87): 66.
3. Ironically, California joined the United States in 1850 after decades of Yankee and European migration into a Mexican state had finally tipped the demographic and economic balance in favor of the ci-devant immigrant "minority," thus encouraging the migrants to petition the United States for statehood.
4. These ethnic statistics influenced the 1990 revision of the immigration

statute that greatly improves opportunities for European immigrants. "Look West, Young European," *The Economist*, 8 December, 1990, 24.

5. As these words are written, President Bush is touring Latin America where, in the opinion of journalists, he is making known that the United States has new interest in economic cooperation with the other American nations to the south. At the same time, European farmers in Brussels are protesting the "threat" of American agricultural exports.

6. *Time* magazine's poll found that 56 percent of Americans thought that immigration was too high. Yet, two-thirds thought immigrants would ultimately make productive citizens. See Otto Friedrich, "The Changing Face of America," *Time*, 8 July, 1985, 18-24.

7. Usually attributed to an abrupt and inexplicable upsurge of ideological conservatism, the California tax revolt actually owed more to the upsurge of house prices that began in 1974. Under the old law, county assessors levied property taxes on the basis of assessed current valuation of a home. When home prices rose, the owners confronted bigger tax bills. When home prices tripled as they did between 1974 and 1978, the owners confronted tripled tax bills on salaries that had not tripled. Confronting what they took to be outrageously enhanced government spending, harried home owners voted overwhelmingly for a tax-control proposal that disconnected their property tax from the market value of their home. Basically, homes were assessed at 1 percent of the original purchase price, and subsequent assessment increases beyond this level were limited to 2 percent per year, much below the actual appreciation of the property. The popular measure permitted homeowners to capture the unearned value added to their residence's sale price as a result of immigration and foreign investment. However, it stripped local governments of any share of this gain, thus inhibiting their ability to protect the quality of life in a context of immigrant influx.

8. Muller and Epenshade (1985: 110) found that the wages of "low-skilled manufacturing jobs in Los Angeles" increased less than did comparable jobs outside the regions. The authors found "little doubt" that the "relative wage decline" resulted from an influx of Mexicans and Central Americans.

9. *Los Angeles Times* 27 January, 1992.

10. *Los Angeles Times* 27 January, 1992.

11. This book is Fawcett and Carino (1987), but it treats only Asians, ignoring Lain Americans, Central Americans, and Middle Easterners.

12. See Vecoli, ed., 1991; Serow et al., eds., 1990; Bean et al., eds., 1990; Yans-McLaughlin, ed. 1990; Buechler and Buechler, eds., 1987; Simon and Brettell, eds., 1986; Bonacich and Cheng, eds., 1984; Kubat, ed.,

1984; Mortimer and Bryce-Laporte, eds., 1981; Bryce-Laporte, ed., 1980; Kritz et al., eds., 1983; McNeill and Adams, eds., 1978; Holmes, ed., 1978; Scott, ed., 1968.

13. See Holmes, ed., 1978; Kubat, ed., 1984.

14. See Bean et al., eds., 1990; Fawcett and Cariono, 1987; Buechler and Buechler, eds., 1987; Bonacich and Cheng, eds. 1984; Mortimer and Bryce-Laporte, eds., 1984.

15. See Simon and Brettell, eds., 1986; Scott, 1968.

16. These are chapters 4, 5, and 6. The same objection can be raised to chapters 2 and 7-11. In this comparative and global book, only two of the excellently crafted chapters deal with immigration outside the United States.

References

Aldrich, Howard E., and Roger Waldinger. 1990. "Ethnicity and Entrepreneurship." *Annual Review of Sociology* 16: 111-35.

Allen, James. 1990. "Migration Into and Out of Los Angeles County in the 1980s." *Perspective* 7: 2-6, 16.

Bates, James. 1992. "Japan's New Investment in US Real Estate Down 61%" *Los Angeles Times* 2 February: A1.

Bean, Frank D., et al., eds. 1990. *Undocumented Migration to the United States*. Santa Monica, CA: RAND Corporation.

Bonacich, Edna, and Lucie Cheng, eds. 1984. *Labor Migration Under Capitalism*. Berkeley and Los Angeles: University of California Press.

Brubaker, Rogers. 1989. "The French Revolution and the Invention of Citizenship." *French Politics and Society* 7: 30-49.

Bryce-Laporte, Roy. 1980. *Sourcebook on the New Immigration*. New Brunswick, NJ: Transaction.

Buechler, Hans, and Judith-Maria Buechler, eds. 1987. *Migrants in Europe: The Role of Family, Labor, and Politics*. New York: Greenwood.

Chan, Sucheng. 1990. "European and Asian Immigration into the United States in Comparative Perspective, 1820s to 1920s." In *Immigration Reconsidered*, edited by Virginia Yans-McLaughlin. New York: Oxford University Press.

Cheng, Lucie, and Yen Espiritu. 1989. "Korean Businesses in Black and Hispanic Neighborhoods." *Sociological Perspectives* 32: 521-34.

Davis, Mike. 1987. "The Internationalization of Downtown Los Angeles." *New Left Review* 164: 61-86.

Davis, Mike. 1990. *City of Quartz*. London: Verso.

Espenshade, Thomas J., and Tracy Ann Goodis. 1985. *Recent Immigrants to Los Angeles: Characteristics and Labor Market Impact*. Washington:

Urban Institute.

Fawcett, James, and Benjamin Carino. 1987. *Pacific Bridges: The New Immigrants from Asia and the Pacific Islands*. New York: Center for Migration Studies.

Field Institute. 1982. "California Opinion Index: Immigration." San Francisco: Field Institute.

Fong, Timothy P. 1989. "The Unique Convergence: Monterey Park." *California Sociologist* 12: 171-194.

Frantz, Douglas. 1988. "Japanese Pour $8.96 Billion into US Real Estate." *Los Angeles Times* 10 October: pt. IV.

Fulwood, Sam. 1991. "California Is Most Racially Diverse State." *Los Angeles Times*, 13 June: A3.

Henry, William A. 1990. "Beyond the Melting Pot." *Time*, 9 April: 28ff.

Holmes, Colin, ed. 1978. *Immigrants and Minorities in British Society*. London: George Allen & Unwin.

Horton, John. 1989. "The Politics of Ethnic Change: Grass-Roots Responses to Economic and Demographic Restructuring in Monterey Park, California." *Urban Geography* 10: 578-92.

Keane, John G. 1986. "Population: Sources and Trends." *Migration World* 14: 22-26.

Kidron, Michael, and Ronald Segal. 1987. *The New State of the World Atlas*. New York: Touchstone.

Kimble, Bobbie, 1989. "Impact of Soviet Armenian Immigration on Los Angeles County." Los Angeles: County of Los Angeles, Commission on Human Relations.

Kotkin, Joel. 1991. "If Moldova Can Go Its Separate Way, Why Not the Golden State?" *Los Angeles Times*, 13 October: M6.

Kritz, Mary M., et al., eds. 1983. *Global Trends in Migration*. Staten Island: Center for Migration Studies.

Kubat, Daniel, ed. 1979. *The Politics of Migration Policies*. New York: Center for Migration Studies.

Kurtz, Howard. 1984. "Official Says Latinos Prefer Overcrowding." *Los Angeles Times*, 12 May: sec. I, p. 15.

Light, Ivan. 1981. "Ethnic Succession." In *Ethnic Change*, edited by Charles Keyes. Seattle: University of Washington.

Light, Ivan. 1983. *Cities in World Perspective*. New York: Macmillan.

Light, Ivan. 1988. "Los Angeles." In *The Metropolis Era*. Vol. 2, edited by Mattei Dogan and John D. Kasarda. Beverly Hills: Sage.

Light, Ivan, and Edna Bonacich. 1988. *Immigrant Entrepreneurs: Koreans in Los Angeles, 1975-1982*. Berkeley and Los Angeles: University of California Press.

McCarthy, Kevin F., and R. Burciaga Valdez. 1986. *Current and Future*

Effects of Mexican Immigration in California. Santa Monica: RAND Corporation.

McNeill, William H., and Ruth S. Adams, eds. 1978. *Human Migration.* Bloomington: Indiana University Press.

Manasian, David. 1990. "A Survey of California." *The Economist,* 13 October: 3-22.

Martinez, Gebe. 1992. "Putting the Squeeze on Crowding." *Los Angeles Times,* 2 January: sec. I, p. 1.

Massey, Douglas, Rafael Alarcon, Jorge Durand, and Humberto Gonzalez. 1987. *Return to Aztlan.* Berkeley and Los Angeles: University of California.

Miller, Judith. 1991. "Strangers at the Gate." *New York Times Magazine,* 15 September: sec. 6, p. 33ff.

Montalbano, William D. 1991. "A Global Pursuit of Happiness." *Los Angeles Times,* 1 October: H1.

Mortimer, Dolores, and Roy S. Bryce-Laporte, eds. 1981. *Female Immigrants to the United States: Caribbean, Latin American, and African Experiences.* Washington, DC: Smithsonian Institution.

Muller, Thomas, and Thomas J. Espenshade. 1985. *The Fourth Wave: California's Newest Immigrants.* Washington, DC: The Urban Institute.

Papademetriou, Demetrios G., et al. 1989. *The Effects of Immigration on the U. S. Economy and Labor Market.* Washington, DC: U.S. Department of Labor, Bureau of International Labor Affairs.

Portes, Alejandro, and Ruben G. Rumbaut. 1990. *Immigrant America: A Portrait.* Berkeley and Los Angeles: University of California Press.

Quintanilla, Michael. 1991. "No Place Like Home." *Los Angeles Times,* 27 October: E1.

Rodriguez, Richard. 1990. "The Dragon in the Dream Factory - the Native Born." *Los Angeles Times,* 30 December: M1, M8.

Rumbaut, Ruben. 1992. "Passages to America: Perspectives on the New Immigration." Paper presented at the Third Annual Sociological Symposium, California State University, San Diego, 27 March.

Sabagh, Georges. 1992. "Los Angeles, a World of New Immigrants: An Image of Things to Come?" In *Migration Policies in Europe and the United States,* edited by Giacomo Luciani. Dordrech, Netherlands: Kluwer Academic Publisher (forthcoming).

Salt, John. 1989. "A Comparative Overview of International Trends and Types, 1950-80." *International Migration Review* 23: 431-56.

Schmidt, William E. 1990. "For Immigrants Tough Customers." *New York Times,* 25 November: E5.

Scott, Franklin., ed. 1968. *World Migration in Modern Times.* Englewood Cliffs, NJ: Prentice-Hall.

Serow, William, et al., eds. 1990. *Handbook on International Migration.* New York: Greenwood.

Simon, Rita, and Caroline Brettell, eds. 1986. *International Migration: The Female Experience.* Totowa, NJ: Rowman and Allanheld.

Skocpol, Theda, and Margaret Somers. 1980. "The Uses of Comparative History in Macrosocial Inquiry." *Comparative Studies in Society and History* 22: 174-97.

Starkey, Danielle. 1992. "Pete to Immigrants: Don't Huddle Here." *California Journal* 23: 127-130.

Tempest, Rone. 1991. "France is the Immigration Litmus Test." *Los Angeles Times*, 1 October: H1.

Therborn, Göran. 1987. "Migration and Western Europe." *Science* 237: 1183-88.

U. S. Civil Rights Commission. 1992. "Civil Rights Issues Facing Asian Americans in the 1990s." Press release dated 28 February.

Vecoli, Rudolph, ed. 1991. *A Century of European Migrations, 1830 to 1930.* Champaign-Urbana: University of Illinois.

Woo, Elaine, and Kim Kowsky. 1991. "Schools' Racial Mix Boils Over." *Los Angeles Times*, 14 June: A1.

Yans-McLaughlin, Virginia, ed. 1990. *Immigration Reconsidered.* New York: Oxford University Press.

2

Migration Networks and Immigrant Entrepreneurship

Ivan Light, Parminder Bhachu, and Stavros Karageorgis

In the last decade, immigration research has refocused on the issue of migrant networks in both contemporary and historical migrations (Bozorgmehr, 1990; Portes and Borocz, 1989; Fawcett, 1989; Boyd, 1989; Morawska, 1989: 260; Wilpert and Gitmez, 1987). Massey (1988: 396) defines migration networks as "sets of interpersonal ties that link migrants, former migrants, and nonmigrants in origin and destination areas through the bonds of kinship, friendship, and shared community origin." A long-standing concern (Tilly, 1978; Light, 1972), migration networks became of renewed interest when researchers sought to connect macro and micro determinants of immigration. *Micro* determinants govern the migration choices of individuals. Micro theorists conceptualize the decision makers as solitary and independent (Sell, 1983; De Jong and Fawcett, 1981; Lee, 1966). Often placed in a world systems context, *macro* influences are regional and international in scope. Thus conceived, macro influences affect whole groups directly, exerting their effect without the mediation of social networks (Burawoy, 1976; Portes and Walton, 1981; Gardner, 1981; Williamson, 1988; Sassen-Koob, 1989). In contrast to these approaches, migration network theorists conceive of migration as embedded in social networks that span continents and decades, and which arise, grow, and ultimately decline. A network approach fits individual decision makers within groups, and it interposes groups between macroscopic social and economic conditions and actual migrations.

True, at any stage of a migration, some migrants arrange their relocation on their own and without any help from social networks. These are unassisted migrants, and migration network theory cannot fully explain their locational choices. However, decades of research have shown that the decision to migrate or to stay, the selection of destination, and the adjustment process at the destination are massively influenced by ethnic, kinship, workmate, neighbor, and friendship networks in which people participate (Hugo, 1981: 208; Morawska, 1990; Grieco, 1987). Rarely do migrants make no use of networks in any of these three moments. Linking populations in origin and destination areas, networks create self-sustaining migration flows that are at least partially independent of the conditions that caused them to develop in the first place (Boyd, 1989: 641). Although based on already familiar ideas, Massey's formula of "cumulatively caused" migration drew together and focused current thinking about migration. According to Massey (et al., 1987; 1988), migrations forge networks which then feed the very migrations that produced them. Therefore, whatever macrosocietal political/economic conditions may initially have caused migration, the originating pushes and pulls, the expanding migratory process becomes "progressively independent" of the original causal conditions. In effect, migrations in process self-levitate above the conditions that caused them to begin, leading thereafter an independent existence.

Networks promote the independence of migratory flows for two reasons. First, once network connections reach some threshold level, they amount to an autonomous social structure that supports immigration. This support arises from the reduced social, economic, and emotional costs of immigration that networks permit. That is, network-supported migrants have help in arranging transportation, in finding housing and jobs at their destination, and in effecting a satisfactory personal and emotional adjustment to what is often a difficult situation of cultural marginality and material deprivation (Goodman, 1981: 137-48; Hugo, 1981: 200-4; Findley 1977: 78). These benefits make migration easier, thus encouraging people to migrate who would otherwise have remained at home. Unless migrants are uprooted refugees, who lack any choice about departure, only immigration affording them any hope of survival (Bozorgmehr and Sabagh, 1990; Pedraza-Bailey, 1985), potential migrants always have the option of staying home. Given that choice, the reduced cost of migration enhances the number who can and will choose to leave, thus increasing the volume of migration from a labor-exporting locality.

Second, Massey has made the same case for networks under the assumptions of a risk-diversification model. According to this model, families allocate members for labor within the constraint of their own needs and aspirations in a cost-efficient and risk-minimizing way. Many Third World households are economically precarious. Such households jeopardize their well-being, even survival if they select nonmigration. Moreover, modernization and development create social and economic dislocations that intensify the unstable and unpredictable economic environment created by the usual risks of drought, crop failure, and natural disasters, for rural as well as urban areas. In the absence of other ways to insure against such risks, diversification of family members' location minimizes overall family income risk (Massey, 1988: 398).

Migration is a risk-diversification strategy. International migration diversifies risk because international borders create discontinuities that promote independence of earnings at home and abroad. Good times abroad can help households survive bad ones at home. Even in the absence of earning differentials, international migration offers an effective risk-diversification strategy, especially when migrant networks already exist. Migration networks reduce the economic risks of immigration, thus rendering the strategy more attractive from a risk-diversification perspective. Expanding networks "put a destination job within easy reach of most community members" (Massey, 1988: 398) and make migration a virtually riskless and costless labor investment in the household's survival portfolio (DaVanzo, 1981: 113; Massey, 1988: 398).

Both internal and international migration restructure both sending and receiving economies, thus affecting subsequent migration flows in the very process of migration (Brown and Sanders, 1981; Hugo, 1981; Massey et al., 1987; Massey and Espana, 1987; Massey, 1988; Sassen-Koob, 1980; 1984; 1988). In this context, scholars have analyzed the role of remittances and return migration in restructuring the sending economy (e.g. Massey et al., 1987; Massey, 1988: 396-401) and the role that migrant networks play in facilitating and encouraging the creation and expansion of employment opportunities for prospective migrants in the host society (Brown and Sanders, 1981: 161-62). More specifically, it has been argued that migrant networks are most significant in the setup and development of migrant ethnic enterprises and enclaves (Boyd, 1989) and in the concentration of migrants from particular ethnic groups and localities in particular occupational and ecological niches in destination societies (Hugo, 1981).

Critique of Network Theory

Although a serious improvement over the individualistic and economistic approaches that preceded it, including world systems theory, migration network theory suffers some self-imposed limitations. Most notably, it concentrates upon facilitation and efficiency, slighting structural changes caused by immigration networks in the destination economy. That is, in existing network theory, networks make it easier for immigrants to find housing, jobs, protection, and companionship (Lin and Dumin, 1986). This facilitation is their *raison d'être*. As they grow, networks also increase their efficiency. Efficient networks expose every job and apartment that exist in some immigrant-receiving locality or region, thus maximally facilitating the introduction of new immigrant newcomers into them. Without increasing the supply of jobs or housing, networks only facilitate participants' access to that existing supply.

Economic saturation poses the obvious limit to existing network theory. As Gregory (1989: 17) has noted, the supply of job opportunities exercises a "restraint on the volume of migration." *Economic saturation* arises when localities and regions have no work or housing to offer new immigrants. Under saturated conditions, a newcomer can only obtain a job or housing when an incumbent vacates it just as one can only find a parking space in a saturated parking lot when someone leaves it. Even hyper-efficient networks cannot find jobs, housing, or parking spaces where none exist. Admittedly, saturation of jobs and housing is neither inevitable nor common. Nonetheless, particularly when migratory influx is rapid, and outstrips economic growth, localities may encounter a short and declining supply of jobs and housing as a consequence. If previous migrants have saturated the job and housing supply, then hyper-efficient networks alone will not find jobs or housing for newcomers. At the point of real economic saturation, a saturation crisis exists. In a saturation crisis, a migration network cannot locate the jobs or housing that provide its *raison d'être*. Unemployment increases, immigrants return to their homelands, and renewed migration has to wait upon the release or creation of new migrant-supporting niches in the destination economy. The existing migration network goes into latency, and begins to deteriorate. This unravelling of migrant networks or, at least, their protracted dormancy, tends to undo the cumulative causation of migration, thus returning the labor-exporting and labor-importing regions into their premigration independence.

Of course, migrant networks can locate new destinations too, a process that yields some ability to explain unassisted migration on the basis of social networks. Confronting saturation or, at least, diminished opportunities in established destinations, a migration network diverts flow to new localities. This reallocation also affects the flow of immigrant entrepreneurs (Goldberg, 1985). Some or all migrants who would have gone to the established destination now flow into the new, unsaturated ones, thereby increasing the demographic pressure upon the local economy. Assuming that the enhanced influx continues, these new destinations will reach saturation sooner than they otherwise would have, thus plunging the migration network into another crisis. If the migration network is to continue after it encounters economic saturation in a destination region, absent other existing regions into which to spill, the migration network has to shift destinations, attaching itself to a new, non-saturated region[1]. How this redirection can happen is unclear as, by definition, networks require linkages between people already in a place and those not yet there. Although the initial movement of pioneers into a new locality is not a network process, its timing is. Network theorists have not shown how networks find, designate, and target new migrant-supporting localities when existing destinations have been saturated.

The Supply of Opportunities

The diversion of networks from saturated regions is not, however, our subject. Even though undertheorized, network diversion still only refers to finding existing jobs and housing rather than to creating them. Instead, we examine the migration network's largely ignored role in increasing earning and housing opportunities in a labor-receiving locality or region. Networks accomplish this objective by improving the efficiency of searches, by increasing the actual supply of opportunities, or both. Improving search efficiency enables migrants to find jobs and housing faster, more reliably, and with less effort. Improving searches either brings immigrants into vacancies in the job and housing markets or it transfers opportunities from natives to immigrants. That is, if the networks direct immigrants to vacant housing or jobs, they improve the immigrants' search without direct economic effect upon non-immigrants. However, if networks help immigrants to obtain jobs that natives were also trying to locate and would have accepted, then the migration networks helped to exclude natives from vacant jobs and housing in their own economy (Waldinger, 1992). Such exclusion makes the networks a competitive ethnic resource of the immigrant population (Grieco, 1987: 41).

But networks also increase the aggregate supply of local opportunities, a function much less studied than the others. In adding new opportunities, the migrant network modifies the economy in the destination region or locality, thus postponing or possibly even avoiding economic saturation. The same migrant networks that relocate co-ethnics from one nation to another have or can assume a role in developing and increasing the migrants' earning and housing opportunities in the destination economy. Three methods encourage this result. First, reliable networks encourage non-immigrant entrepreneurs to shift capital into the immigrant-receiving locality from other locations in the destination economy. This shift enhances the supply of jobs available to immigrants. An example are the numerous immigrant-staffed factories that now exist on both the Mexican and the American side of the U.S./Mexico border (Davila and Saenz, 1990). These factories have grown up with immigration; they did not precede it.

Second, immigrant entrepreneurs buy existing firms from indigenous owners, staffing them with co-ethnic immigrant workers who may replace incumbents. Similarly, immigrant entrepreneurs can buy existing housing from native owners, transferring the units to occupancy by immigrant co-ethnics or by themselves. In both cases, immigrant entrepreneurs expand the supply of jobs and housing available to co-ethnic immigrants, thus forestalling saturation and permitting more immigrants to enter the destination economy. Admittedly, the transfer occurs at the expense of displaced, non-coethnic tenants and employees. Entrepreneur capture of existing jobs and housing transfers the rights to immigrant co-ethnics without expanding the absolute supply of either jobs or housing.

Third, immigrant entrepreneurs create new firms or expand existing ones in the locations of destination, creating new jobs and housing for co-ethnics without reducing the supply available to non-coethnics (Wong, 1987). Immigrant entrepreneurship creates and opens new immigrant-owned firms and immigrant-owned housing in destination economies. New, immigrant-owned firms create employment for their owners and for co-ethnic employees without displacing indigenous workers. Immigrant-owned housing, including apartment housing, creates residences for co-ethnics without displacing vested tenants. Although it makes a difference whether immigrant entrepreneurs transfer rights to existing jobs and housing, or create new jobs and housing, the *immigrant economy* consists of self-employed immigrants and their co-ethnic employees.[2] The immigrant or ethnic economy supplements the earnings opportunities available to co-ethnics in the general labor market. Similarly, when immigrant entrepreneurs build new housing or rehabilitate and expand existing housing, they increase the supply of housing available to co-ethnics without reducing the supply available to natives (Werbner, 1990b: 28-36).

If we represent the general labor market as G, the immigrant economy as I, and economic carrying capacity as S, then the earnings and housing opportunities[3] available to immigrants are:

$$S = f(G + I) \quad (1)$$

Unless I is zero, $G + I$ must always exceed G. G is the unsupplemented job supply available to immigrants in the general labor market. In the limiting case G is 100 percent of jobs, but, in reality, G is usually a fraction of the employed labor force. G threatens economic saturation in that, when its limit is attained, the general labor market can support no more immigrants. $G + I$ is the general labor market plus the immigrant economy. Since $G + I$ normally exceeds G, saturation of a locality's or region's economy requires saturation of both G and I. If G is saturated, but I is not, or vice versa, then the local economy is not saturated. Under that circumstance, we normally expect growth in the unsaturated component until that component too attains saturation. Conversely, if an immigrant population depends upon some balance of G and I to support it, but political or economic changes reduce the capacity of one or the other component to carry its normal load, enhancement of the other component represents a possible alternative to return migration. In exactly this sense, Simon explains in Chapter 6 the growth of immigrant self-employment in Europe following hard upon the decline of wage earning jobs for immigrants: I expanded when G contracted.

A treatment of immigrant networks that ignores I, concentrating upon G alone, underestimates the immigrant carrying capacity of destination economies. Existing network theory generally makes this error, and Massey's synthesis reflects it as well. First, one finds no reference to the immigrant economy in Massey et al.'s (1987) index, nor any appreciation of its implications for job creation in his text. Massey (1988: 398) writes that migrant networks "put a destination job within easy reach of most community members," but he neglects the enhanced access to business ownership which this same migration network affords. True, like other macro theorists, Massey acknowledges the role of non-immigrant entrepreneurs. Migrations cause economic expansion in the target economy because non-immigrant entrepreneurs move capital from high-wage areas to low-wage areas. Massey argues that this capital flow reinforces wage pressures of labor migration, downward in high wage-areas and upward in low-wage areas. He also observes that econometric analyses using simultaneous equations models to specify and estimate the nonrecursive relationship between migration and employment have shown that on balance migration creates employment more than employment creates migration.

Massey argues that employment growth stimulates migration, which stimulates employment growth, which stimulates further migration. Therefore, Massey discerns a process of cumulative causation at work. Massey (1990: 15) claims that "a variety of factors underlies the reciprocal causal relationship" but describes only the one which he deems the most important. This underpinning is, he professes, the selectivity of international migration. Migration selects "the younger, better-educated, and more highly productive workers - those with the greatest endowment of human capital." He argues that this selectivity leads to higher economic growth and labor demand in receiving areas but decreases growth and demand in sending areas, leading to additional migration, and thus creating circular and cumulative causation.

TABLE 2.1.
Cuban and Haitian Refugee Employment in Miami, 1980: In Percentages

	Cuban Mariel Refugees	Haitian Refugees
Immigrant Economy		
Self-Employed	15.2	0.5
Working in Coethnic Firms	30.9	0.2
General Labor Market		
Unemployed	26.8	58.5
Employees	27.1	40.8
Total in Percentages	100.0	100.0

Source: Alex Stepick, "Miami's Two Informal Sectors," In The Informal Economy, ed. Alejandro Portes et al. Baltimore: Johns Hopkins University. Reproduced by permission.

In this discussion, Massey acknowledges only the response of the host economy to immigrant labor. The more efficient the immigrant networks, the more efficiently host capital responds because migrant networks reduce employers' costs of labor recruitment. This response does, indeed, augment the job supply in the general labor market, thus delaying economic saturation, and promoting cumulatively caused migration just as Massey claims. But Massey's recital overlooks the immigrant economy. In effect, Massey operates from a model in which $G = S$, and G expands in response to labor influx. Even if G's expansion proceeds infinitely, as Massey implies, Massey's treatment of the general labor market overlooks the immigrant economy. The larger the immigrant economy, the larger this flaw.

Haitians and Cubans in Miami

To illustrate this claim, Table 2.1 shows the sectoral representation in 1980 of Cuban Mariel refugees and Haitian refugees in Miami. Derived from the work of Alex Stepick, (1989), this table is based ultimately upon official statistics. The three sectors are: unemployment, the immigrant economy, and the general labor market of Miami. Cuban Mariel refugees are working-class Cubans, expelled from their homeland, who arrived in a massive exodus in 1979. A significant proportion of these Cuban refugees were black. Haitians are impoverished blacks who claimed political refugee status in the U.S. but whom the U.S. government defined as economic refugees.

The sectoral representation of Haitians and Cubans was drastically different. Haitian refugees had 58.5 percent unemployed, 0.7 percent working in the immigrant economy, and 40.8 percent employed for wages or salaries in the general economy. In contrast, Cuban Mariel refugees had 26.8 percent unemployed, 46.1 percent employed in the immigrant economy, and 27.1 percent employed in the general economy. In effect, the Haitian economy lacked an immigrant economy and so approximated the one-sector economy Massey's network theory assumes across the board. Haitian employment in the general economy was 13.7 percent higher than Cuban employment in that sector. But Haitian unemployment was 31.7 percent higher than

Cuban unemployment. This discrepancy implies that 18 percent of Cubans who were employed in the Cuban immigrant economy would, in fact, have been unemployed had no immigrant economy had existed to employ them. Discharged from the immigrant sector, the remaining 13.7 percent of Cubans would have found wage-earning jobs in the general economy.

If immigrant opportunities are defined strictly in terms of the general labor market, overlooking the immigrant economy, the oversight would seemingly matter little for Haitians. However, as Stepick (1989: 116-25) shows the impression is misleading. Haitians in Miami operated a very extensive informal economy that these official statistics did not and could not measure. Although operated for cash only and without the knowledge of tax collectors, the Haitians' informal economy amounted to "informal self-employment" (Stepick, 1989: 122). Haitian entrepreneurs created jobs for themselves and for a few other Haitians. Their informal firms were chiefly in dressmaking, tailoring, food preparation, childcare, transport, construction, automobile repair, and electronic repair (Stepick, 1989: 122). In point of fact, then, a significant immigrant economy existed among the Miami Haitians as well as among the more affluent Cubans, but this Haitian economy was too marginal to measure. Hard to measure does not mean nonexistent.

Thanks to the official statistics, this point is easier to make for the Cubans among whom the immigrant economy was sufficiently large to permit its measurement. To overlook the Cuban immigrant economy would be to fall into two serious errors. First, this oversight would exclude 45.4 percent of Cuban workers from observation. Examining only 54.6 percent of workers, we would fancy that we examined all. Second, such treatment would overlook the choice context in which Cuban workers operated. In the general labor market, workers chose between a wage job and unemployment. These make two choices only. In fact, Cuban immigrants had three choices: a wage job in the general economy, unemployment, or the immigrant economy.

This third option creates a new choice context. As Fernandez-Kelly and Garcia (1989: 248) have put it, the existence of an immigrant economy "shields" immigrant workers "from the mainstream labor market." This sectoral shield permits immigrant workers to exert some upward pressure upon the general labor market that, if it wants their services, must make offers that are not only superior to unemployment, but are also superior to what they could otherwise obtain in the immigrant economy, whether as employees or as self-employed. The mere fact that a substantial percentage of immigrant workers select the immigrant economy reduces the supply of immigrant labor in the general wage economy, thus exerting upward pressure on wage rates and working conditions for those in the general labor market.

In the case of immigrant women, frequent employees in the immigrant economy, the scholarly controversy about relative wages in the immigrant economy and general labor market (Phizacklea, 1988: 21; Zhou and Logan, 1989) overlooks "ideological and subjective" influences upon women's work decisions (Schmink, 1984: 93).[4] Flexible hours, part-time work, and liberal child care policy are important non-wage attractions that cause immigrant women to prefer the immigrant economy to the general labor market (Dallalfar, 1989: 161-84). Precisely insofar as women workers have the option of an immigrant economy, the general labor market experiences pressure to modify its unyielding job requirements in order to lure women employees away from the immigrant economy where, if sometimes underpaid, they are flexibly accommodated (Portes and Jensen, 1989: 941; Zhou and Logan, 1989). Moreover, many immigrant women can only work when child care policies are liberal and hours flexible. Otherwise they must be full time home-makers and baby-sitters. For such women, the general labor market offers no satisfactory alternative to unemployment. Neither is acceptable. Only the immigrant economy permits them to work at all. In this sense, the immigrant economy's flexibility increases the percentage of immigrant women who can *work for wages at all*, thus bolstering the gross income of their households and of the immigrant community (Ong, 1987).

Networks and Entrepreneurship

Contemporary network theory overlooks the role of immigrant networks in creating the immigrant economy. This oversight is remarkable in view of the stress network theorists properly lay upon the migrant network's cost-reducing and risk-diversifying properties in the mainstream economy. In overlooking the economic effects of immigrant networks in the destination economy, Massey and others overlooked a network function of great importance and one, moreover, that complements and expands network theory (Birley, 1985; Zimmer and Aldrich, 1987; Johannisson, 1988). These objections to Massey's rendition of network theory are friendly because they expand network theory's scope and utility. Whatever other functions they also serve, migrant networks are entrepreneurial resources that *expand the economic opportunities* immigrants confront in destination economies.

When migrant networks support coethnic entrepreneurship, thus creating an immigrant economy, they modify the existing economy in the destination locality (Gibson, 1990). This modification permits that destination economy to increase its saturation threshold, thus permitting more immigrants to find work in the target economy than would have been possible had the general labor market been the only dispenser of employment. Naturally, the modification of the destination localities begins after the migration network has begun to land workers there. The length of this lag is variable and probably depends upon political restraints on immigrant enterprise. These political restraints have been much more prominent in European countries than in North America (Ward, 1987; Blaschke et al., 1990). Nonetheless, the network's favorable modification of the target economy creates a "pull" influence that supports and seconds the "cumulatively caused" migration of network theory. Therefore, migration networks are actually more effective than theory acknowledges because the networks not only lower the costs of migration, they also augment economic opportunities in destination economies.

The migration network enhances immigrant entrepreneurship in three principal ways. First, the network feeds low cost coethnic labor to immigrant entrepreneurs just as it does to non-immigrant entrepreneurs (Cardenas et al., 1986: 159, 169). Immigrant entrepreneurs routinely employ coethnics at rates vastly above chance levels (Engstrom and McCready, 1990: 36). Pyong Gap Min (1989: 66) reported that 30 percent of employed Koreans found jobs in firms owned by fellow Koreans even though Koreans were only one percent of the Los Angeles County population. More tellingly, Hansen and Cardenas (1988: 233) compared the employment rolls of Mexican immigrant employers, native-born Mexican employers, and non-Mexican employers in Mexican neighborhoods of California and Texas. They found that Mexican immigrant employers were "most likely to hire undocumented Mexican workers," and were also most likely to express very favorable evaluations of the quality of these workers, not just their cheapness. Next in line came the native-born Mexican employers. Last were the non-Mexican employers who employed the least undocumented labor and, when asked about it, stressed its cheapness, not its quality. This result shows that the migration network fed foreign-born Mexican workers to coethnic employers who knew how to get more work out of them and had more favorable opinions of them.

Information is a second support resource (Bailey and Waldinger, 1991). Migration networks feed economic information to immigrant entrepreneurs and aspiring entrepreneurs (Wells, 1991). This information concerns the best industries to enter, pricing, technology, business methods, and the like. Werbner (1990b: 12) talks of a "shared pool of technical knowledge and experience" generally available to immigrant Pakistanis in Manchester. Economic information follows the migration network for natural reasons. The migration network is a frequently used channel of communication along which all kinds of messages easily and inexpensively flow. Business information is just another message. The migration network's messages are credible because of the relationships of mutual trust that link members. This credibility is especially important in business. In many cases, the migration network appeals to participants' ethnic chauvinism. Chauvinism encourages participants to hoard useful information while concealing it from outsiders. Under these conditions, the network becomes the channel by which knowledgeable immigrants hoard and conceal information to the benefit and advantage of their ethnic group.

Migration networks also provide access to various kinds of mutual aid and assistance other than and in addition to information. Credit is an obvious and central example (Werbner, 1990a: 70, 133, 200;

Light et al., 1990). Many immigrant entrepreneurs acquire their initial training in business in the course of an apprenticeship passed in the business of a coethnic. Once established in business, they can call upon primary social relationships, embedded in the migration network, for help in business. This help includes purchasing at advantageous prices, dealing with public bureaucracies and courts, customer and supplier relations, financial and production management, labor relations, industrial engineering, quality control, marketing, and the introduction of new products or techniques (Light and Bonacich, 1988: chaps. 7-10; Light, 1985). In some cases, immigration networks provide access to rotating credit associations and through them to business capital (Light et al., 1990; Engstrom and McCready, 1990: 23-24; Werbner, 1990a: 133, 200, 315). In all these cases, the existing literature documents the utility of the entrepreneur's network connections when confronting standard and inescapable business problems.

Cultural and Religious Influences

Although the network literature has paid scant heed to religious and cultural influences, implicitly treating one network as identical to another, networks are in fact the product of ideologies and beliefs. They are cultural; therefore, they are unique. Often there are culturally-shaped beliefs about migration's desirability as a result of which some networks promote migration more than do others. This difference applies as much to the production of resources as to their management and investment in both migrants' country of origin and of settlement. Immigrant cultures also differ in respect to home orientation. Especially in early stages of settlement, direct migrants and twice migrants differ in respect to home orientation (Bhachu, 1985). Twice migrants intend to stay in their destination economy right from the moment of entry. They also prefer to invest in that destination economy and to acquire the skills and expertise necessary to operate effectively in its markets. Twice and thrice migrants have a much more rapid entrepreneurial impact on their destination economies than do direct migrants, who also utilize migration networks. This generalization applies both to their rapid development of commercial enterprises and a capital base in destination economies. This contrast is apparent in Britain between the highly organized Ismailis (Morris, 1968), and some of the other Gujarati groups, who have rapidly reproduced their entrepreneurial and trading expertise established in India and Africa since the nineteenth century (Gundara, 1990), in comparison, to the directly migrant and predominantly working-class Indians and Bangladeshis. The latter, have not been as efficient in establishing their networks nor in utilizing them for business development.

Inter-group variation in the entrepreneurial efficacy of networks commonly reflects their traditional positions in the occupational hierarchies of their homeland prior to migration. For example, for many South Asian migrants, caste position influences entrepreneurship. Migrants from "commercial cultures" (Gundara, 1990: 7), like the Parsis, the Banyas, the money lending Bhatias, the Memons, the Bohras, the Khojas -- all Gujarati groups -- long dominated trade and commerce in West India and later in East Africa as well. These are precisely the most entrepreneurial of the "South Asians" in Britain and the United States where they reproduced their business expertise overseas much more rapidly than the nonmercantile caste groups could learn them in the first place. Prior to their second emigration, the twice migrants already formed the most efficient entrepreneurial networks and were the pioneering groups who established and monopolized a range of commercial niches in East Africa. They incorporated their kinsmen and caste mates into their businesses, and passed on their entrepreneurial expertise, permitting them to expand and dominate particular sectors of commerce and trade. In the last two decades, East African Asians have brought their developed commercial culture to Britain, Canada, and the United States.[5]

These powerful mercantile traditions are perpetuated almost regardless of the economic situations in which the immigrants are situated. Mercantile castes avoid wage employment unless it be for the purpose of learning skills that can be subsequently utilized for entrepreneurship. Hence, the cultural ethos of mercantile castes legitimizes and encourages entrepreneurial effort and success in concordance with caste ideals, a religious justification that people from noncommercial and nonmercantile castes do not enjoy. If a commercial caste background is combined with the expertise acquired in the course of previous migration, the entrepreneurial impact in transforming destination economies becomes yet more powerful. In fact, among mercantile castes of South Asian origin, profit remains now as it has long been in the past the *raison d'être* for migration. Hence, the migration networks of commercial castes are qualitatively entrepreneurial right from their point of entry into the destination economies. In contrast, other migrant groups, of non-commercial caste background develop entrepreneurship more slowly or not at all in their destination economy.

For example, the majority of Sikh migrants all over the world belong to agricultural and related craft castes. That is, their traditional occupations were farming and artisan, not commerce. As a result, they have been slow at establishing enterprises (if at all), because their caste status is not, and was not, defined by commercial concerns. This remark does not imply that there are no mercantile Punjabi Sikh castes, and no successful Sikh business owners. Some do exist. Nonetheless, the various South Asian caste and cultures still evince uneven interest in entrepreneurship and, unsurprisingly, have enjoyed uneven entrepreneurial success. Naturally, economic and political conditions sometimes shift caste orientations over a protracted period of time. In estimating cultural impacts upon entrepreneurship, one cannot ignore cultural change. In the ramshackle economic circumstances of Thatcherite Britain, Sikhs and some other nonmercantile South Asians, who were until recently in public or private employment sectors, and who even disesteemed commerce, have turned to self-employment to escape job ceilings and racial discrimination in the general labor market. Further encouraging this trend were state policies intended to stimulate private enterprise. As a result, "a culture of entrepreneurship" (Werbner, 1984), has rapidly grown up even among "traditionally non-mercantile" South Asians.

In addition to their influence upon the occupational choice of the migrants, religious ideas also influence propensity to migrate at all. Because unequally entrepreneurial in orientation, caste groups respond unequally to migratory opportunities (Kessinger, 1976). Punjabi migrants are mainly from the Eastern Doaba (McLeod,

1989; Ballard and Ballard, 1977; Ballard, 1989; Barrier and Dusen-bury, 1989) whereas, the entrepreneurial Gujarati migrants are pre-dominantly from Kutch and Kathiawar (Metcalfe, 1986). The fiercely competitive Sikhs (Pettigrew, 1972) have migrated overseas in larger numbers than Hindus of a similar caste level (Saberwal, 1976: 99). One reason for the historically lower levels of Hindu migration is the Hindu religion, which declared ocean voyages a profanation (Mazumdar, 1984: 318, Metcalfe, 1986: 371). Even until the first decades of this century, severe religious penalties awaited Hindus who had crossed an ocean. Upon repatriation, ocean-crossers had to undergo complex cleansing rituals before reintegration into their castes. None of these religious restrictions applied to the Sikhs, whose values encouraged travel and gain. Here, Sikh religious ideas facilitated overseas migration and thus resulted in far-flung immigra-tion networks whereas Hindu ideas inhibited and stigmatized migration.

Conclusion

A big improvement over existing push and pull theories of migra-tion, including world systems theory, immigration network theory still needs to recognize that immigrant networks create employment and housing; they do not just improve the efficiency of searches. Therefore, the migration network can expand the resources in the destination economy, postponing or avoiding altogether the satura-tion crisis that would end or redirect the migration network. Addi-tionally, immigrant networks are qualitatively different from one another, a point overlooked by existing network theory. From the point of view of entrepreneurship, some networks are more produc-tive than others. Independent of class resources, qualitative dimen-sions of the immigrant network sometimes affect the network's capacity to reconstruct the economic environment in destination localities, and thus affect the capacity of the network to produce the economic conditions for its own magnification and persistence.

Taking account of the entrepreneurial functions of networks, we are in a position to explain the migration network's otherwise puzzling self-levitation over the normal material constraints that govern migration decision-making. Massey's formula of "cumulative causation" properly calls attention to the network's self-perpetuating functions without, however, explaining the network's capacity to create the economic growth on which it depends. Once fully underway, networks generate economic growth that promotes their survival. True, migration networks never attain immortality. Ultimately, they collapse and disintegrate. Still, the networks often outlive the economic conditions that gave rise to them. One reason is the overlooked capacity of immigrant entrepreneurs to create the very economic opportunities that migration networks require for survival.

Notes

1. Thus, if no more jobs or housing exist in Belgium, the network can continue to exist only if it locates vacant jobs or housing in the neighboring Netherlands, elsewhere in Europe, or somewhere else in the world.
2. The immigrant economy also includes employment and self-employment in illegal enterprise as does the mainstream economy. We distinguish illegal enterprise from predatory crime which we exclude from this analysis even though it represents, strictly speaking, an earning opportunity. On this subject, see: Light 1974 and 1977.
3. Earnings opportunities exclude transfer payments such as public welfare, private charity, or remittances to the immigrants from abroad. On welfare and immigration, see Peterson and Rom, 1989. Housing opportunities arise when immigrant entrepreneurs acquire real property, creating new residence opportunities for co-ethnics.
4. The literature reads as if all immigrant women became employees. Most do; women are less likely to become self-employed than men. Nonetheless, some immigrant women become entrepreneurs. A complete account of the gender-specific effect of the immigrant economy would need to bring in women entrepreneurs too. See Goffee and Scase, 1983.
5. Werbner (1984) reports a similar process, in describing a "culture of entrepreneurship" that grew up among Manchester Pakistanis in Britain. This culture afforded participants numerous advantages of motivation, skill, expertise, credit, mutual aid. It emerged from what Werbner labelled as migrant "entrepreneurial chains" (Werbner, 1987: 214), in which the earlier business starters supported later ones with advice, patronage, loans and encouragement (1984: 186).

References

Bailey, Thomas and Roger Waldinger. 1991. "Primary, Secondary, and Enclave Labor Markets: A Training Systems Approach". *American Sociological Review* 56: 432-445.

Ballard, R. 1989. "Differentiation and Disjunction amongst the Sikhs in Britain." In *The Sikh Diaspora*, edited by N. J. Barier and V. A. Dusenbery. Columbia, MO: South Asia Publications.

Ballard, R., and C. Ballard. 1977. "The Sikhs: The Development of South Asian Settlements in Britain." In *In Between Two Cultures: Migrants and Minorities in Britain*, edited by J. L. Watson. Oxford, England: Basil Blackwell.

Bhachu, Parminder. 1985. *Twice Migrants: East African Sikh Settlers in Britain*. London and New York: Tavistock Publishers.

Birley, Sue. 1985. "The Role of Networks in the Entrepreneurial Process." *Journal of Business Venturing* 1: 107-17.

Blaschke, Jochen, et al. 1990. "European Trends in Ethnic Business." In *Ethnic Entrepreneurs*, edited by Roger Waldinger et al. Newbury Park, CA: Sage.

Boyd, Monica. 1989. "Family and Personal Networks in International Migration: Recent Developments and New Agendas." *International Migration Review* 23: 638-70.

Bozorgmehr, Mehdi. 1990. "Internal Ethnicity: Armenian, Bahai, Jewish, and Muslim Iranians in Los Angeles." Ph.D. diss., University of California, Los Angeles.

Bozorgmehr, Mehdi, and Georges Sabagh. 1990. "A Comparison of Exiles and Immigrants: Iranians in Los Angeles." In *Iranian Exiles and Refugees*, edited by Asghar Fathi. Costa Mesa, CA: Mazda Publishers.

Brown, Lawrence A., and Rickie L. Sanders. 1981. "Toward a Development Paradigm of Migration with Particular Reference to Third World Settings. " In *Migration Decision-Making*, edited by Gordon F. De Jong and Robert W. Gardner. New York: Pergamon.

Burawoy, Michael. 1976. "The Functions and Reproduction of Immigrant Labor: Comparative Materials from South Africa and the United States." *American Journal of Sociology* 81: 1050-87.

Cardenas, Gilberto, et al. 1986. "Mexican Immigrants and the Chicano Ethnic Enterprise: Reconceptualizing an Old Problem." In *Mexican Immigrants and Mexican Americans*, edited by Harvey L. Browning and Rodolfo de la Garza. Austin: Center for Mexican American Studies of the University of Texas.

Dallalfar, Arlene. 1989. "Iranian Immigrant Women in Los Angeles: the Reconstruction of Work, Ethnicity, and Community." Ph. D. diss.

UCLA.

DaVanzo, Julie. 1981. "Microeconomic Approaches to Studying Migration Decisions." In *Migration Decision-Making*, edited by Gordon F. De Jong, and Robert W. Gardner. New York: Pergamon.

Davila, Alberto, and Rogelio Saenz. 1990. "The Effect of Maquiladora Employment on the Monthly Flow of Mexican Undocumented Immigration to the U.S., 1978-1982." *International Migration Review* 24: 96-107.

De Jong, Gordon F., and James T. Fawcett. 1981. "Motivations for Migration: An Assessment and a Value-Expectancy Research model." In *Migration Decision-Making*, edited by Gordon F. De Jong and Robert W. Gardner. New York: Academic.

Dusenbury, A. Verne. 1989. "A Century of Sikhs beyond Punjab." In *The Sikh Diaspora: Migration and Experience Beyond the Punjab*, edited by N.J. Barrier and V.A. Dusenbury. Columbia, MO: South Asia Publications.

Engstrom, David W., and William McCready. 1990. "Asian Immigrant Entrepreneurs in Chicago." Chicago: Center for Urban Research and Policy Studies of the University of Chicago.

Fawcett, James. T. 1989. "Networks, Linkages, and Migration Systems." *International Migration Review* 23: 671-80.

Fernandez-Kelly, et al. 1989. "Informalization at the Core: Hispanic Women, Homework, and the Advanced Capitalist State." In *The Informal Economy*, edited by Alejandro Portes et al. Baltimore: Johns Hopkins University Press.

Findley, Sally E. 1977. *Planning for Internal Migration*. Washington, DC: U.S. Department of Commerce, Bureau of the Census, International Statistical Programs Center.

Gardner, Robert W. 1981. "Macrolevel Influences on the Migration Decision Process." In *Migration Decision-Making*, edited by Gordon F. De Jong and Robert W. Gardner. New York: Pergamon.

Gibson, Robert W. 1990. "Networks of Chinese Rim Pacific." *Los Angeles Times*, 22 July: sec. 1, p. 1.

Goffee, Robert, and Richard Scase. 1983. "Business Ownership and Women's Subordination: A Preliminary Study of Female Proprietors." *The Sociological Review* 31: 625-48.

Goldberg, Michael A. 1985. *The Chinese Connection*. Vancouver: University of British Columbia.

Goodman, John L. 1981. "Information, Uncertainty, and the Microeconomic Model of Migration Decision Making." In *Migration Decision-Making*, edited by Gordon F. De Jong, and Robert W. Gardner. New York: Pergamon.

Gregory, Peter. 1989. "The Determinants of International Migration and Policy Options for Influencing the Size of Population Flows." *Working Papers of the Commission for the Study of International Migration and Cooperative Economic Development*, no. 2.

Grieco, Margaret. 1987. "Family Networks and the Closure of Employment." In *The Manufacture of Disadvantage*, edited by Gloria Lee and Ray Loveridge. Milton Keynes, England: Open University.

Gundara, Jagdish S. 1990. "British Extraterritorial Jurisdiction, Imperial Enterprise and Indians in Nineteenth Century Zanzibar". Paper presented at the *Indian Diaspora Conference*, at the University of Toronto.

Hansen, Niles H., and Gilberto C. Cardenas. 1988. "Immigrant and Native Ethnic Enterprises in Mexican American Neighborhoods: Differing Perceptions of Mexican American Workers." *International Migration Review* 22: 226-42.

Hugo, Graeme J. 1981. "Village-Community Ties, Village Norms and Ethnic and Social Networks: A Review of Evidence from the Third World." In *Migration Decision-Making*, edited by Gordon F. De Jong and Robert W. Gardner. New York: Pergamon.

Johannisson, Bengt. 1988. "Regional Variations in Emerging Entrepreneurial Networks." Paper presented at the 28th Congress of the Regional Science Association, 23 August, Stockholm.

Kessinger, Tom G. 1976. *Vilyatpur 1848-1968: Social and Economic Change in a North Indian Village*. Berkeley, Los Angeles, and London: University of California Press.

Lee, Everett S. 1966. "A Theory of Migration." *Demography* 3: 47-57.

Lin, Nan, and Mary Dumin. 1986. "Access to Occupations Through Social Ties." *Social Networks* 8: 365-385.

Light, Ivan. 1972. *Ethnic Enterprise in America*. Berkeley and Los Angeles: University of California Press.

Light, Ivan. 1974. "From Vice District to Tourist Attraction: The Moral Career of American Chinatowns, 1880-1940." *Pacific Historical Review* 43: 367-94.

Light, Ivan. 1977. "The Ethnic Vice District, 1880-1944." *American Sociological Review* 42: 464-79.

Light, Ivan. 1985. "Ethnicity and Business Enterprise." In *Making It in America*, edited by M. Mark Stolarik. Lewisburg, PA: Bucknell University.

Light, Ivan, and Edna Bonacich. 1988. *Immigrant Entrepreneurs*. Berkeley and Los Angeles: University of California Press.

Light, Ivan, et al. 1990. "Korean Rotating Credit Associations in Los Angeles." *Amerasia* 16: 35-54.

McLeod, W. Hew. 1989. "The First Forty Years of Sikh Migration:

Problems and some Possible Solutions." In *The Sikh Diaspora: Migration and Experience Beyond the Punjab*, edited by N.J. Barrier and V.A. Dusenbury. Columbia, MO: South Asia Publications.

Massey, Douglas, et al. 1987. *Return to Aztlan*. Berkeley and Los Angeles: University of California Press.

Massey, Douglas S. and Felipe Garcia Espana. 1987. "The Social Process of International Migration." *Science* 237: 733-738.

Massey, Douglas S. 1988. "Economic Development and International Migration in Comparative Perspective." *Population and Development Review* 14: 383-413.

Massey, Douglas S. 1990. "Social Structure, Household Strategies, and the Cumulative Causation of Migration." *Population Index* 56: 3-26.

Mazumdar, Sucheta. 1984. "Colonial Impact and Punjabi Emigration to the United States." In *Labour Immigration Under Capitalism*, edited by L. Cheng and E. Bonacich. Berkeley, Los Angeles, and London: University of California Press.

Metcalfe, Thomas R. 1986. "Indian Migration to South Africa." In *Studies in Migration: Internal and International Migration in India*, edited by M.S.A. Rao. Delhi, India: Manohar Publications.

Min, Pyong Gap. 1989. "Some Positive Functions of Ethnic Business for an Immigrant Community: Koreans in Los Angeles." Final Report Submitted to National Science Foundation. Unpublished document.

Morawska, Ewa. 1989. "Labor Migrations of Poles in the Atlantic Economy, 1880-1914." *Comparative Studies in Society and History* 31: 237-72.

Morawska, Ewa. 1990. "The Sociology and Historiography of Immigration." In *Immigration Reconsidered*, edited by Virginia Yans-McLaughlin. New York: Oxford University Press.

Morris. H. S. 1968. "Ethnic Groups". In *International Encyclopedia of the Social Sciences* 5: 167-72.

Ong, Paul. 1987. "'Immigrant Wives' Labor Force Participation." *Industrial Relations* 26: 296-303.

Pedraza-Bailey, Sylvia. 1985. *Political and Economic Migrants in America*. Austin, TX: University of Texas Press.

Peterson, Paul E., and Mark Rom. 1989. "American Federalism, Welfare Policy, and Residential Choices." *American Political Science Review* 83: 711-28.

Pettigrew, Joyce. 1972. "Some Notes on the Social System of the Sikh Jats." *New Community* 1, 5: 354-63.

Phizacklea, Annie. 1988. "Entrepreneurship, Ethnicity, and Gender." In *Enterprising Women*, edited by Sallie Westwood and Parminder Bhachu. London and New York: Routledge.

Portes, Alejandro, and Jozsef Borocz. 1989. "Contemporary Immigration: Theoretical Perspectives on its Determinants and Mode of Incorporation." *International Migration Review* 23: 606-30.

Portes, Alejandro and John Walton. 1981. *Labor, Class, and the International System*. New York: Academic Press.

Portes, Alejandro and Leif Jensen. 1989. "The Enclave and the Entrants: Patterns of Ethnic Enterprise in Miami Before and After Mariel." *American Sociological Review* 54: 929-49.

Saberwal, Satish. 1976. *Mobile Men: Limits to Social Change in Urban Punjab*. New Delhi, India: Indian Institute of Advanced Study with Vikas Publishing House Pvt. Ltd.

Sassen-Koob, Saskia. 1980. "Immigrant and Minority Workers in the Organization of the Labor Process." *Journal of Ethnic Studies* 8 (Spring).

Sassen-Koob, Saskia. 1984. "Growth and Informalization at the Core: The Case of New York City." In *The Urban Informal Sector: Recent Trends in Research and Theory*. Proceedings of the Seminar on the Informal Sector in Center and Periphery. Baltimore: The Johns Hopkins University.

Sassen-Koob, Saskia. 1988. *The Mobility of Labor and Capital*. Cambridge, England: Cambridge University Press.

Sassen-Koob, Saskia. 1989. "New York City's Informal Economy." In *The Informal Economy*, edited by Alejandro Portes et al. Baltimore: Johns Hopkins University Press.

Schmink, Marianne. 1984. "Household Economic Strategies: Review and Research Agenda." *Latin American Research Review* 19: 87-102.

Sell, Ralph. 1983. "Analyzing Migration Decisions: the First Step -- Whose Decisions?" *Demography* 20: 299-311.

Stepick, Alex. 1989. "Miami's Two Informal Sectors." In *The Informal Economy*, edited by Alejandro Portes et al. Baltimore: Johns Hopkins University Press.

Tilly, Charles. 1978. "Migration in Modern European History." In *Human Migration*, edited by William H. McNeill and Ruth S. Adams. Bloomington: Indiana University Press.

Waldinger, Roger. 1988. "The Social Networks of Ethnic Entrepreneurs." Paper presented at the 1988 Meeting of the National Economic Association, 30 December, in New York City.

Waldinger, Roger. 1992. "Taking Care of the Guests: The Impact of Immigrants on Services - An Industry Case Study." *International Journal of Urban and Regional Research* 16: 97-113.

Ward, Robin. 1987. "Resistance, Accommodation, and Advantage: Strategic Development in Ethnic Business." In *The Manufacture of Disadvantage*, edited by Gloria Lee and Ray Loveridge. Milton Keynes, England:

Open University.

Wells, Mirriam. 1991. "Ethnic Groups and Knowledge System in Agriculture." *Economic Development and Cultural Change* 39: 739-71.

Werbner, Pnina. 1984. "Business on Trust: Pakistani Entrepreneurship in the Manchester Garment Trade." In *Ethnic Communities in Business: Strategies for Economic Survival*, edited by Robin Ward and Richard Jenkins. Cambridge, England: Cambridge University Press.

Werbner, Pnina. 1987. "Enclave Economies and Family Firms: Pakistani Traders in a British City." In *Migrant Workers and the Social Order*, edited by Jeremy Eades. London and New York: Tavistock Publications.

Werbner, Pnina. 1990a. *The Migration Process: Capital, Gifts and Offerings Among British Pakistanis*. Oxford, England: Berg Publishers.

Werbner, Pnina. 1990b. "Secret Ephemera: Immigrant Enclaves and the Nature of Knowledge in the Manchester Fashion Industry." *Migration* 8: 6-36.

Williamson, Jeffrey G. 1988. "Migrant Selectivity, Urbanization, and Industrial Revolutions." *Population and Development Review* 14: 287-314.

Wilpert, Czarina, and Ali Gitmez. 1987. "La Microsociet 'e des Turcs a Berlin" *Revue Europeenne des Migrations Internationales* 3: 175-196.

Wong, Bernard. 1987. "The Role of Ethnicity in Enclave Enterprises: a Study of the Chinese Garment Factories in New York City." *Human Organization* 46: 120-30.

Zhou, Min and John R. Logan. 1989. "Return on Human Capital in Ethnic Enclaves: New York City's Chinatown." *American Sociological Review* 54: 809-20.

Zimmer, Catharine, and Howard Aldrich. 1987. "Resource Mobilization Through Ethnic Networks: Kinship and Friendship Ties of Shopkeepers in England." *Sociological Perspectives* 30: 422-45.

3

Asian and Latino Immigrants in the Los Angeles Garment Industry: An Exploration of the Relationship between Capitalism and Racial Oppression

Edna Bonacich

Capitalism is a system based on competition in the market between private owners of productive property, whose purpose is the maximization of their profits. Because private owners, a small minority of the population, control the economy, major social decisions are made without the democratic participation of those affected by them. Indeed, the social welfare is typically ignored in favor of the "bottom line" of private companies.

There is a widespread belief in the United States, fostered by the Reagan and Bush administrations, that capitalism is "colorblind." Race is supposedly irrelevant to the market, which is only concerned with accomplishment. In the absence of discriminatory legislation, abolished by the U.S. government in the 1960s, the operations of the competitive market ought gradually to lead to racial equalization.

In fact, conditions for people of color have deteriorated substantially since Reagan took office in 1980, despite increased reliance on the market. True, a few individuals have managed to move into the middle class. But for millions of people of color, poverty and despair have intensified.

This reality is clearly evident in Los Angeles (Ong, 1989). The city is becoming increasingly polarized between affluent, generally white, owners, professionals, and managers, who have enough disposable income to satisfy every consumerist desire, and bitterly poor, mainly African American and Latino, workers and unemployed. Housing is one area where the division is starkly demonstrated. Some people are leveling the tops of mountains to build mansions vying with the Hearst Castle for size and luxury. Meanwhile, an estimated seventy thousand Angelenos are homeless, and many thousands of working poor have to pay over 50 percent of their meager earnings to rent crammed and squalid slum apartments.

The purpose of this chapter is to examine how capitalism produces and reproduces racial oppression, by examining the dynamics of one industry in one location: the garment industry in Los Angeles. The L.A. garment industry uses immigrants from Latin America and Asia as workers and contractors. I plan to show how both groups are oppressed by the system, although differentially, by laying out the entire structure of relations in the industry, and the role of immigrants in it. In the course of describing the industry, I hope to demonstrate its excessive corruption at all levels, a corruption endemic to capitalism. A system characterized by such social decay is totally unequipped to solve such fundamental social problems as massive impoverishment and racial oppression.

Method of Study

An eclectic methodology was used to conduct the research for this paper. The available literature, including unpublished works, was searched out and read, along with official statistics and the trade journals. Several garment factories were visited, and state registration data on garment factory ownership was obtained and analyzed.[1]

The most time-consuming and informative method used was interviewing people knowledgeable about the industry. Altogether about forty people were interviewed, mainly during the summer of 1989. They represented all levels of the industry, from bankers to workers, with retailers, importers, manufacturers, contractors, state agents, union officials, newspaper reporters, students of the industry, and officers of various organizations in between.

The process of finding more knowledgeable people and pursuing leads is almost endless and could have gone on for much longer. In addition, the local and international situation in the garment industry, let alone the immigrant role in it, is constantly changing. This chapter reflects my knowledge as of April 1990.

The Los Angeles Garment Industry

Los Angeles is emerging as a major center of garment design, production, and distribution in the United States, second only to New York City. Although the entire U.S. apparel industry has been severely impacted by imports and has suffered major job loss, the Los Angeles industry has grown. Between 1972 and 1988, employment in the U.S. industry dropped 23 percent, but grew by 56 percent in Los Angeles (U.S. Department of Commerce, 1988: 45-3, 1989, 41-11; California Employment Development Department, 1988: 70). In 1989, employment in the L.A. industry was estimated at around 120,000 (Olney, 1989: 28).

The L.A. industry specializes in the "California look," namely, casual wear, sportswear, and swimsuits, especially for women. It occupies a middle segment in the industry, between high fashion and mass-produced goods. This segment is responsive to fashion change and is not easily exportable because of the need for quick response to changes in demand.

Structure of Relationships

Figure 3.1 presents the major institutional actors in the Los Angeles garment industry. In this section I try to lay out the whole system of relationships to provide a context for understanding the role of immigrants in the industry. When explaining parts of figure 3.1, I will refer to the numerated arrows (e.g., "arrow 1").

Manufacturers

Manufacturers are the kingpins of the industry. They are the individuals and business organizations that initiate the production process. The designing of fashion and purchase of textiles occurs under their auspices. Manufacturers vary considerably in size. However, since virtually all you need is a good design idea to enter manufacturing, many manufacturers are small, and there is a high turnover of about 15 percent per year in the business.

FIGURE 3.1
Relationship of Forces in the Los Angeles Garment Industry

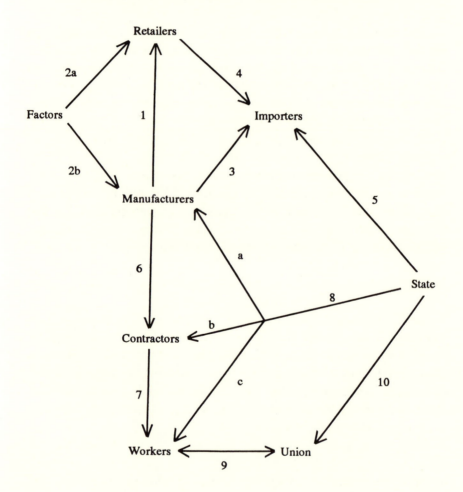

Manufacturers are engaged in bitter competition, sometimes leading to illegal practices. One such practice is "knocking off," (i.e., copying) another company's design. In 1986, the International Trade Commission reported a loss of over $250 million to U.S. textile and apparel firms due to copyright, patent, and trademark infringements. Stealing designs is so common that one lawyer described the industry as an "overall culture of knockoffs," where most firms do not even know it is illegal (Ferraro, 1988).

Retailers

Garments, of course, need to be sold, and the way they are retailed is a major factor in the shaping of the industry. Retailers of apparel are divided into different types. Department stores are probably the most powerful force in the industry. They are in bitter competition with one another, promoting illegality. For example, Nordstrom's was charged with false advertising for putting items on sale that had never been offered at a higher price (Chen, 1989).

Competition also promotes a rapid changing of "seasons," as the old season's garments are swept from the shelves and replaced. Some L.A. industry participants claim that the number of seasons has reached five or six per year. Lot sizes are being reduced, leading to shorter runs of specialized goods. This shift may be the driving force behind the proliferation of small contracting shops.

Mergers

Retail department stores have been undergoing a major merger movement over the last few years (1986-1989), a phenomenon that sends reverberations throughout the industry. Ownership of some of these chains is now international, so that events occurring in London or Canada have ripples that extend all over the world. The case dominating the news at the time of writing concerned a Canadian company, Campeau Corporation.

These leveraged buyouts have important ramifications for the industry. Suddenly Bullocks in Los Angeles gets a different buyer, changing the manufacturers who produce for that store. In addition, the excessive debt of the retailers affects their credit-worthiness and hence the financing that manufacturers can obtain, as we shall see shortly. Finally, the purchasers of these chains treat them as commodities to be bought and sold for quick profits. They may have little interest in merchandizing itself, a fact resented by manufacturers who want to see their wares promoted by expert salespeople.

Relations between Manufacturers and Retailers (arrow 1)

Manufacturers and retailers in the apparel industry have a mutually dependent relationship. Retailers need manufacturers to stock their stores, and manufacturers need retailers to market their products to consumers. Nevertheless there is considerable tension between them, with each party trying to press the other to the wall in maximizing their own benefit. Hard bargaining verges towards illegality, as each party tries to get the most s/he can from the other. Generally, the large retailers are in a better bargaining position than the manufacturers and can squeeze them harder than vice versa.

Retailers use various devices to squeeze manufacturers. One that especially irks manufacturers is known as *chargebacks*. Chargebacks occur when the retailer receives an order and can claim it does meet his specifications precisely, enabling him to charge the manufacturer for the error. In practice, chargebacks can occur for the most trivial reasons, such as whether the order was sent by UPS, whether the list of enclosed items is placed inside or outside of the box, whether hangers were included, etc. A retailer will take off 10 percent for such offenses.

Retailers sometimes simply refuse to pay, claiming they never received the merchandise, and demanding that the manufacturer prove it was sent. Or they will assert it was sent to the wrong branch. This can happen with the largest, most reputable retailers.

In sum, the large retailers are able to bully the manufacturers into making concessions of various kinds because they have the power to do so. The growth of leveraged buyouts among department stores increases this power through consolidation. Manufacturers suffer not only from competition among themselves, but also from the pressure to cut costs imposed by the retailers.

Factors (arrows 2a and 2b)

Garment manufacturing is partially financed through a process known as *factoring*. Forty to 50 percent of U.S. apparel manufacturers use factors. Factoring involves the purchasing of trade debts from manufacturers. The retailer becomes a debtor of the factor, instead of the manufacturer, who is relieved of the risk of non-payment by the retailer. The factor conducts a credit check of the retailer to minimize his own risk, and limits the amount of credit he is willing to extend to the manufacturers accordingly. The typical commission on sales, as this transaction is called, is 1-1.75 percent. As Applegate (1990) points out, this can mean that a manufacturer with sales of $2 million can be spending $25 thousand in commissions.

Factors can also advance up to 80 percent of the value of the product to the manufacturer at the time of the retailer's order. The charge for advances is usually 2-3 percent over the prime interest rate.

Nationally, factors bought about $38 billion in sales in textiles and apparel in 1988. California accounted for about $7-8 billion (20 percent). Advances were worth another $1 billion.

Leveraged buyouts in retailing have affected manufacturers by limiting the willingness of factors to declare certain retailers as credit-worthy. This leaves the manufacturer without a factor, having to assume all the risk of selling to a retailer that might go under.

According to a lawyer who represents dozens of apparel manufacturers in Los Angeles, "a factoring agreement is a Mephistophelean deal. It is very easy to get into and very difficult to get out of." A factor becomes deeply involved in the day-to-day affairs of the company, and can come to exercise tremendous control over the business (Applegate, 1990). This is especially true for small manufacturers that rely on advances.

Manufacturers, retailers, and factors (and banks in general) are the big players in the garment industry. It is here that big money is made (and lost). All three operate in a viciously competitive world, and feel that they must cut costs to the bone. As a result, there is plenty of hard dealing and illegality. As a banker told us, "this industry is not for the faint-hearted." Nevertheless, they wield the power and make the big money, and, in the process, control the fate of the immigrants who work for them.

Importers

The garment industry is undergoing massive international restructuring. It has increasingly moved from developed to developing countries in recent years, with the latter manufacturing clothing primarily for export to developed countries. Imports climbed drastically from 8.9 percent in 1967, to 31.2 percent in 1977, to 57.5 percent by 1987 (Rothstein, 1989: 111-117). Thus, over half of the apparel now bought by U.S. consumers is produced abroad.

Much of the flight of the garment industry abroad can be "blamed" on U.S. capitalists. They have pursued cheaper labor in the Third World through establishing a variety of linkages there. Manufacturers subcontract part of the production process, notably the labor-intensive sewing, abroad (arrow 3), and U.S. retailers produce some of their garments overseas (arrow 4), selling them under their own private labels (Waldinger, 1986: 75-76).

The State and Imports (arrow 5)

The U.S. government also encourages the flight of the industry. An example is Tariff Item 807 and various elaborations of it like the Caribbean Basin Initiative (Jacobs, 1988). Item 807 allows goods assembled abroad to be brought back into the United States with a tariff levied only on the value added, which is low because of low labor costs. It benefits companies that get their sewing done in maquiladoras in Mexico and the Caribbean.

These tariff policies are not based solely on economic factors. They are part of U.S. foreign policy (Rothstein, 1989). The U.S. goal is to get countries in the Western hemisphere to be loyal to the United States by providing them with development aid, jobs, and granting them privileged access to the U.S. market, thereby countering incipient revolutionary movements.

These policies also serve as a mechanism for dealing with Third

World debt by helping U.S. banks to get repaid. The U.S. government and international development agencies actively promote wage-lowering austerity programs, and a manufacturing-for-export development strategy in Latin America and the Caribbean. Thus, the United States not only encourages the production aspect of the flight of the industry, but also fosters the low wages that give Third World countries a competitive advantage. One can question whether such policies lead to genuine development, or only increase working class immiseration and enhance the financial situation of U.S. banks.

While the U.S. government encourages the exodus of the industry, it also makes efforts to control the intense dislocations that occur when a major industry moves abroad. A series of international agreements have been negotiated, notably the Multi-Fiber Arrangement (MFA), to control the flow of imports (Nehmer and Love, 1985). Note that the purpose of MFA is not to stop imports, or to stabilize them, but only to increase them in an orderly fashion. In practice, the MFA has been ridiculously ineffective. Imports keep flooding the country, and the percentage limits are widely surpassed.

Contractors

Although some manufacturers have all of their production done "in house," it is common practice to contract out the sewing, and often the cutting of garments. Getting into contracting does not require much capital. All one needs is a space and a few sewing machines, both of which can be rented. With generous financing terms available, the downpayment can be as little as $6-7 thousand. Ease of entry leads to a proliferation of contractors who are in intense competition with one another. Consequently, the turnover rate is as high as one-third per year.

California requires that all garment manufacturers and contractors register with the state. We obtained a list of the registrants as of 18 April 1989, from the California Department of Industrial Relations, Division of Labor Standards Enforcement. Their computer printout includes names of registrants, names of their businesses, addresses, and zip codes. Out of a total of 4,586 registrants, over 1,000 listed only a corporate name and did not provide the name of an owner. In

73 percent of the cases (3356) we were able to code the ethnicity of the owners.[2] Latinos made up the biggest group, with 28.5 percent. Vietnamese, Chinese, and Koreans accounted for 16.6, 16.0, and 15.4 percent respectively. Other Asians (with unidentifiable names or from other countries) made up 10.4 percent, for an Asian total of 58.4 percent, or the majority of owners. "Others," (i.e., Anglos, Jews, Armenians, Iranians, etc.), made up only 13.1 percent.

Firms are not distributed evenly across the state. Eighty-four percent were located south of the Ventura County line. (Ventura is

TABLE 3.1
Ethnicity of California Garment Factory Registrants, by Location, April 1989

| | | | | | COUNTIES | | | |
| | North | | South | | San Francisco | | Los Angeles | |
	No.	%	No.	%	No.	%	No.	%
Chinese	318	56.1	220	7.9	227	65.6	217	8.7
Korean	26	4.6	492	17.6	18	5.2	480	19.2
Vietnamese	86	15.2	470	16.9	29	8.4	333	13.3
Other Asian	71	12.5	278	10.0	39	11.3	243	9.7
Total Asian	501	88.4	1460	52.3	313	90.5	1273	51.0
Latino	16	2.8	939	33.7	9	2.6	887	35.5
Other	50	8.8	390	14.0	24	6.9	337	13.5
Total ethnic	567	100.0	2789	100.0	346	100.0	2497	100.0
Unknown	179	24.0	1051	27.4	116	25.1	973	28.0
Total	746		3840		462		3470	

Source: California Department of Industrial Relations, Division of Labor Standards Enforcement, List of Registrants in the Garment Manufacturing Industry, 18 April 1989.

immediately north of Los Angeles.) San Francisco housed 10 percent of all licensed businesses, whereas Los Angeles had 76 percent.

Table 3.1 shows the ethnic distribution of firm owners for the northern and southern halves of the state, and for the two centers, San Francisco and Los Angeles. As can be seen, Asians, especially Chinese, predominate in Northern California, especially in San Francisco. In contrast, ownership in the south (and in Los Angeles, where 90 percent of Southern California garment firms are located) is more ethnically diverse. Latinos own over one-third of the shops, and among Asians, the Koreans emerge as the dominant group, followed closely by the Vietnamese.

Table 3.2 divides Southern California into the garment district, the remainder of the city of Los Angeles, the remainder of Los Angeles County, Orange County, and the rest of Southern

TABLE 3.2

Ethnicity of Garment Factory Registrants in Southern California, 19 April 1989

Cntys	Garment District		Other LA City		Other LA County		Orange County		Other SoCal	
	No.	%	No.	%	No.	%	No.	%	No.	%
Chinese	62	6.0	99	12.7	56	8.2	1	0.5	2	1.6
Korean	381	37.0	51	6.5	48	7.0	10	6.0	2	1.6
Vietnamese	66	6.4	111	14.2	156	22.7	102	61.1	35	28.0
Other Asian	86	8.3	94	12.0	63	9.2	25	15.0	10	8.0
Total Asian	595	57.8	355	45.4	323	47.1	138	82.6	49	39.2
Latino	312	30.3	317	40.5	258	37.6	11	6.6	41	32.8
Other	122	11.9	110	14.1	105	15.3	18	10.8	35	28.0
Total	1029	100.0	782	100.0	686	100.0	167	100.0	125	100.0

Source: Same as table 3.1.

California. The garment district contains over one-third of the shops, while over 50 percent are spread around the city and county of Los Angeles. Orange County is the location of only 6 percent of registered shops but apparently is growing fast as a center, and may house more unregistered firms than Los Angeles. Finally, the rest of Southern California has less than 5 percent of firms.

Table 3.2 shows that Koreans are the predominant contractors in the garment district, followed by Latinos. In contrast, both the Chinese and Vietnamese (as well as Latinos) are more dispersed over the city and county. The Vietnamese are the most spread out, and have so far established a predominance in Orange County.

Garment contracting is a viciously competitive business, and there is considerable ethnic rivalry as each new group tries to get a foothold in the industry by undercutting established ones. Jewish contractors complain about the Asians. Koreans and Chinese complain about the Vietnamese, and so on. The degree to which competition among contractors is ethnically structured is probably exaggerated. No doubt undercutting is found among contractors of all ethnicities. The problem is not ethnic but inherent in the organization of the industry. The ethnic diversity of owners, coupled with the tendency for ethnicity to correspond somewhat to time of entry, tends to lead participants to focus on ethnic "traits" as a source of the problem. But the fundamental issue is the intense, cutthroat competition between contractors, and the ability of manufacturers to manipulate it to their advantage.

Relations with Manufacturers (arrow 6)

The contracting system obviously has tremendous advantages for manufacturers. They do not need to maintain a stable workforce, and can pass on to the contractors the problems of recruiting and laying off workers in response to seasonal fluctuations and style changes. The contracting system increases their flexibility. Moreover, contractors have to deal with the problems and anger of the labor force, which the manufacturer can ignore. Even though contractors and their workers are, in every meaningful sense, "employees" of the manufacturer, the contracting system creates a legal fiction that they are not, thereby alleviating the manufacturer of any responsibility for what goes on with his employees.

In practice, manufacturers have all the power of an employer in an employer-employee relationship. They can push contractors to the wall. The contractors I spoke with complained that the prices paid to them by manufacturers had gone down in recent years. Meanwhile contractors' expenses have all increased. The state minimum wage rose to $4.25 an hour on 1 July 1989, but manufacturers were not legally compelled to adjust their prices.

Workers

The estimated 120,000 workers in the Los Angeles garment industry are predominantly Latino immigrants, most of whom are from Mexico. A smaller proportion of Latino workers come from Central America, and about 10 percent are Asians. In a survey conducted in 1979, Maram (1980) found that 81 percent of Latino workers in the industry were undocumented immigrants. L.A.'s garment industry thus relies heavily on "illegal" workers.

Wages and working conditions are notoriously bad. The situation has been described as a reemergence of sweatshops (U.S. GAO, 1988). In 1981, the *Los Angeles Herald Examiner* published a sixteen-part newspaper story entitled "Sweatshop: Undercover in the Garment Industry" (Wolin, 1981). A reporter disguised herself as a Latino immigrant and worked as a seamstress for a while. She found appalling conditions, including exceedingly low wages, and health and safety standards violations. The latter included vermin, filthy eating areas and bathrooms, and exposed wires. A fire in a seventy-six-year-old building in the garment district on 5 December 1989, when forty people were injured, affirmed the dangerous conditions (Malnic and Tobar, 1989; Dunn and Sahagun, 1989).

Most workers are paid on a piecework basis. This serves as an incentive to work quickly, and experienced workers can build up to a reasonably decent level of pay. But piecework also means that inexperienced workers have a hard time coming up to minimum wage. Record keeping to ensure payment of minimum wage is sketchy or downright false in many firms. Needless to say, benefits or paid vacation time are non-existent. In addition, workers are subject to shifting seasons that create a kind of boom or bust. At times they must work day and night to meet rush order, while at other times they face layoffs. Illegal homework is rampant with women and children working at home under unsafe conditions.

A community center in the garment district, Las Familias del Pueblo, reflects the harsh conditions faced by Latino garment workers. The center provides informal childcare, among other services, as hardworking mothers, who cannot afford to pay for childcare, leave off their children while they go to work sewing.

Poor working conditions in the industry were again brought to the public's attention in a three-part story in the *Los Angeles Times* (Efron, 1989). Although it focuses on Orange County, the series reports on widespread labor abuses. Some workers stated they made only $50 a week for working eleven hours a day, five or six days a week. One case involved a Latina homeworker and her three children, ranging in age from seven to fourteen, who were averaging about $1.45 an hour for their labor. In sum, the garment industry in Southern California is the locus of serious labor exploitation and consequent suffering.

Relations between Workers and Contractors (arrow 7)

The contractor is the immediate exploiter of the workers. He/she is the person whom the workers confront, the person who seems to benefit directly from their hardship, the person who imposes that hardship. The workers do not see the hierarchy of exploitative relations that sit on top of the contractor, or at least do not experience it directly. They only experience the contractor as the immediate oppressor. And, relative to the life the workers must lead, the contractor seems like an affluent beneficiary of their hard labor.

There is an inherent antagonism in the contractor-worker relationship. Some contractors try to ameliorate the conflict, by treating the workers in a kindly manner. But no matter how kindly the contractor, the inherent antagonism remains. Contractors are in the business of cutting labor costs to the bone. They must do this in order to stay in business. They do so to serve their employers, the manufacturers.

That is the nature of their occupation. A nonexploiting contractor is a contradiction who will not survive in the system.

In Los Angeles, the antagonism between contractor and workers takes on an ethnic dimension. Although, as we have seen, there are Latino contractors and Asian workers, as well as non-Asians and non-Latinos in both position, the most common configuration is Asian contractors employing Latino workers. At Las Familias del Pueblo, in the heart of the garment district, Latino workers see Korean contractors as the predominant employer. Thus, their antagonism towards contractors has the character of antagonism towards Koreans.

I would like to stress that Asian contractors are not the main exploiters of the workers. They are only the immediate ones. Thus, they become the direct bearers of the (justified) wrath of the workers. This arrangement is, of course, very convenient for the manufacturers and retailers who do not have to soil their hands with labor exploitation. They can feel themselves to be decent, charitable citizens, who have nothing to do with the evils of sweatshops, even though their profits and salaries depend on what is going on in the Asian run shops, and even though they set the terms within which these shops must function.

The State and Labor Standards (arrows 8a, b, c)

The state, both federal and local, regulates the relations between workers and their employers, attempting to curb the worst abuses. The state sets labor standards below which no employee should be permitted to sink. These include setting a minimum wage, extra pay for overtime work, the prohibition of child labor and homework, the payment of Workers' Compensation and Unemployment insurance, and so on. All of these laws are violated in the Los Angeles garment industry.

When Governor Deukmejian took office in 1983 he weakened labor standards enforcement efforts. He abolished a Concentrated Enforcement Program, aimed at enforcing labor standards in industries with known violations, by folding it into the Bureau of Field Enforcement (BOFE), an agency with much broader responsibilities and fewer staff members who can devote themselves specifically to garment inspections. Moreover, evasion of the law is all too easy. When a contractor gets into trouble, he can close the shop and open again under a new name.

Las Familias del Pueblo helps workers file charges against contractors, and they have thick files of cases indicating that such actions are frequent indeed. They include such issues as failure to pay minimum wage and overtime, late payment, or nonpayment altogether, which is quite common. The files also contain evidence of firms changing their names slightly so as to avoid being tracked down. A worker at Las Familias summed up the situation as follows: "The law is so weak it's a joke."

Contractors feel trapped by the laws the state imposes upon them (arrow 8b). One of them complained: "We have to pay time and a half for overtime, but we don't get paid overtime by the manufacturer. The minimum wage goes up, the cost of Workers' Compensation goes up, and the price we get paid goes down." The state, by upholding labor standards, puts them against a wall, which manufacturers have no need to take into account in setting their prices.

The State and Immigration

Another form of state involvement concerns immigration law. In 1986, the federal government passed the Immigration Reform and Control Act (IRCA). The law holds employers accountable for hiring undocumented workers by imposing sanctions upon employers who knowingly hire them. And it grants amnesty to undocumented immigrants who have been stable residents in the United States since 1981. Many Latino immigrant workers in the garment industry were eligible for amnesty. This shift had a potential impact on contractors as employers of the impacted work force.

In practice, IRCA appears to have had little impact on the L.A. garment industry labor force (Loucky et al., 1989). The flow of undocumented immigrants into Los Angeles continues unabated. It is easy, and now cheap, to obtain forged papers, and employers quickly learned that the law does not hold them accountable for the authenticity of immigrant documents. If the Immigration and Naturalization

Service (INS) should raid his shop, the contractor can blame the immigrants for providing false papers. However, such raids are rare to non-existent. Law enforcement is underfunded in this area too. So business proceeds as usual.

The reliance of the industry on oppressed immigrant workers was revealed by the reaction to IRCA. Garment contractors wanted to be permitted to import temporary foreign workers under an urban bracero program (California Legislature, 1987). The industry claims it cannot survive without a special, legally disabled, work force.

Union and Relations with Workers (arrow 9)

Given the Los Angeles focus on the production of women's garments, the main union is the International Ladies' Garment Workers' Union (ILGWU). The ILGWU is extremely weak in Southern California, having dropped from 12,000 members out of 23,000 garment workers in 1946, to about 2,000 members out of 120,000 today (Laslett and Tyler, 1989).

The ILGWU has problems of its own that contribute to the difficulties of organizing garment workers. The L.A. leaders are very hard working and dedicated. Some of the most progressive union activists have been sent by the International to L.A. to see what they can accomplish in what looks like a hopeless environment. However, despite their sincerity, there is still a sense in which they are outsiders to the workers they are trying to organize. Union organizers are trying to get people to join "their" organization. Union dues seem to go to support a stratum of fairly well-paid union bureaucrats, while the underpaid workers are ripped off by yet another sector of American society. Distrust of the union is thus widespread (Soldatenko, 1989).

Union organizing is very difficult in the L.A. garment industry anyway. If a shop is organized it is likely to go out of business. The manufacturer will turn to another contractor and the workers will lose their jobs. The union has no leverage to sign contracts that improve conditions for the workers. And it is too easy for contractors to close shop and move if faced with a unionizing threat.

The State and Unionism (arrow 10)

Under the National Labor Relations Acts (NLRA), the federal government is supposed to protect the rights of workers to form independent unions and engage in collective bargaining. Under the best of circumstances, the law is limited in terms of the ability of workers to develop real social power and bring out the kind of social change that would substantially improve their lives. But even the reformist achievements of the NLRA have been decimated by the Reagan administration.

For example, it is illegal to fire workers for union activity. However, filing a complaint against such a firing is completely useless in the Los Angeles garment industry. Delays in processing due to staff shortages mean that the charged company is likely to have disappeared. Thus, contractors fire union activists with little fear of legal reprisal.

Similarly, holding elections under the NLRA becomes a legal charade in an industry like this. Elections can take place over a year after workers sign cards of intent. The National Labor Relations Board (NLRB) takes months to settle jurisdictional questions, and the Republican-appointed majority generally decides in favor of management. Given the high turnover of workers, by the time the election is held, many of the original union supporters are gone. The union has to expend tremendous resources just to keep the idea of unionism alive among the changing workforce.

Who Benefits?

I have not completed the review of the relationships sketched in figure 3.1. It is clear that among the workers, there is considerable suffering and dehumanizing conditions. Garment workers are obviously exploited, but by whom? Who benefits from their hard lives?

One could argue that the consumers are the ultimate beneficiaries, and that, because garment workers suffer hardship, consumers have access to more affordable clothing. While there may be some truth to this, it is obvious that plenty of money is being made on the production side of the industry. And it is not at all clear that the low wages paid to the workers are significantly passed on to the consumers. Moreover, consumers are manipulated by the fashion aspects of the industry, and by the advertising that supports it. Consumers are teased into spending more money on clothing than they need, in order to keep up with changing fashion trends.

Contractors appear to be the immediate beneficiaries of the poor conditions confronted by garment workers. They are the "exploiters" and appear to establish themselves as immigrant entrepreneurs in the new country at the expense of their employees. However, contractors suffer hardship too. True, their lives are not nearly as pressed as the workers. They can usually afford decent housing and can send their children to college. But their lives are far from easy. Still, despite the fact that contractors are themselves victimized by the system, I do not want to minimize the fact that they bear some responsibility for the exploitation and gain some, albeit relatively small, portion of the surplus taken from the workers (Bonacich, 1987).

As one moves up the hierarchy of the industry, tremendous markups accrue at each level. For example, one contractor said she receives $5 for a skirt that the retailer sells for $85. The skirt contains about $7 worth of fabric, paid for by the manufacturer. Thus, the remaining $73 is split between the manufacturer and retailer. We know the retailer "keystones" his products, (i.e., more than doubles the manufacturer's price), suggesting that he pays the manufacturer around $40. Needless to say, both manufacturer and retailer have major expenses, and must deal with competition and fluctuations in demand. The mark-ups do not reflect pure profits. Nevertheless, money is made by these firms, as indicated in their Annual Reports. The profit rate may not be exorbitant, but given the billions of dollars in sales, the absolute take is huge. And let us not forget that the banks and factors, as well as allied industries such as advertising, rake in their share.

The beneficiaries are not only the stockholders and owners of these firms, and the benefit is not only accrued in the form of profits. It also gets incorporated into salary scales. Manufacturers, retailers, and bankers pay some of their employees handsome salaries, the high levels of which can be attributed in part to the low levels paid to garment workers.

For example, in a study of Macy's, Noyelle (1987: 19-49) not only reports that the company made $221 million in profits in 1984, but their employees are increasingly polarized between low-paid sales, clerical, and service workers, on the one hand, and high-paid, credentialed managers and professionals on the other.

Thus, in manufacturing, retailing, and banking/factoring, there is a stratum of very well-paid employees. Within these sectors are low-paid, increasingly exploited, workers, but that reality does not negate the growth of the well-paid jobs. There is, I am contending, a direct relationship between the below minimum wage and no benefits earnings of garment workers, and the five or six digit salaries plus handsome benefits of retailing, manufacturing, and banking professionals and managers.[3] The widening divide, observed by Ong (1989) is produced and reproduced through the processes described for this industry.

Conclusion

The garment industry reveals starkly some of the horrors of capitalism, and how it helps to construct racial and ethnic antagonisms. The rampant illegality found at all levels of the industry is a product of the system of private ownership and competition that drives people to engage in a ruthless struggle for survival and advantage. Checks on the worst excesses, whether by the state or by opposing forces, are weak or nonexistent, in part because capitalists are able to exert considerable influence over the government, and through it subvert the efforts of the opposition. The result is massive social decay: a dog-eat-dog world in which the unprotected are ravaged by the strong and powerful.

The garment industry raises questions about the goals of economic activity. What is the goal of apparel production, and what should it be? Instead of pursuing a goal of providing decent, affordable raiment for everyone, the garment industry has become a monster, based on the need to sell as much as possible in a system of planned obsolescence. Despite short-term, individual rationalities involved in the construction of this industry, the overall picture is one of social irrationality. The social welfare is not being served.

Finally, we return to the issue of racial oppression. Latino immigrants are severely oppressed in this industry. Asian contractors are their immediate oppressors, but are also partially victims of the system. One group of immigrants is used to keep another group down, to the benefit of higher-ups. The whole edifice depends on keeping workers legally cordoned off, hence powerless.[4] That these workers are also racially distinctive adds to the ease of their targeting. Through the normal workings of capitalism, the United States is increasingly becoming a racially polarized society.

As a society, we need to look at what we have wrought. We need to examine our social system from all perspectives and consider whether it is a sane way to organize human social life.

Notes

1. Thanks go to Patricia Domingues and Jane Bonacich for laboriously punching 4,589 business names, addresses and ethnicities into the computer, and to Phillip Bonacich for assistance in analyzing them. Special thanks to Patricia Hanneman, who conducted the main analysis.

2. In a few cases partners were listed. However, we chose not to do a special analysis of them because database fields were cropped in the state printout to thirty-five characters for names, and the names of partners were sometimes incomplete. We simply coded partners with one ethnic designation. In the rare case where the partners seemed to be of different ethnicities, we arbitrarily chose the clearer one.

    There are no doubt some errors in this coding. However, we were able to check some of the names with a Korean, Vietnamese, and Chinese colleague. (Thanks go to Chris Lee, Yen Esperitu, and Paul Ong for their help.) In addition, we obtained the Los Angeles Chinese and Korean contractors' association membership lists, helping us to verify over one hundred and fifty cases. Using established ethnic names from these two sources, we were able to clear up some discrepancies.

3. Some will argue that the higher paid employees "deserve" their high pay. They are being rewarded for their investment in their education. Their education makes them more valuable to their employers. They are more "productive" workers and are rewarded for their productivity. In answer, I would argue that we are witnessing a social decision about how to allocate reward in this society. Even if one can demonstrate that salary levels are driven totally by market forces, a dubious proposition, the decision to allow the market to drive salaries so high and so low

remains a decision, and not just a force of nature.

4. Of course, the workers are not completely powerless. They always have the potential to become a political force that challenges and overthrows their domination. In this paper I am simply focusing on the ways the system works to try to crush that resistance.

References

Applegate, Jane. 1990. "If Set Up with Care, Relationship with a factor can be Key for Apparel Makers." *Los Angeles Times*, 9 February: sec D.

Bonacich, Edna. 1987. "'Making It' in America: A Social Evaluation of the Ethics of Immigrant Entrepreneurship." *Sociological Perspectives* 30: 446-66.

California Employment Development Department. 1988. Annual Planning Information, Los Angeles-Long Beach, 1988-89. Sacramento, CA: Employment Development Department.

California Legislature, Assembly Subcommittee on Immigration in the Workplace. 1987. A Status Report on California's Garment Industry, Sacramento.

Chen, Edwin. 1989. "Nordstrom to Pay $200,000 to Settle Civil Suit." *Los Angeles Times*, 1 September: pt. IV.

Dunn, Ashley, and Louis Sahagun. 1989. "Fire Heightens Concern About Buildings' Safety." *Los Angeles Times*, 6 December: pt. B.

Efron, Sonni. 1989. "Sweatshops Expanding into Orange County"; "Mother's Plight Turns a Home into a Sweatshop"; "'Hot Goods' Law Revived as Anti-sweatshop Tool." *Los Angeles Times*, 26-28 November: pt. A.

Ferraro, Cathleen. 1988. "Can Design Patents Knock Out the Knockoffs?" *California Apparel News*, 2-8 September.

Jacobs, Brenda. 1988. "The 807 Option: New Trade South of the Border." *Bobbin*, May: 26-33.

Laslett, John, and Mary Tyler. 1989. *The ILGWU in Los Angeles, 1907-1988*. Inglewood, CA: Ten Star Press.

Loucky, James, Nora Hamilton, and Norma Chinchilla. 1989. "The Effects of IRCA on Selected Industries in Los Angeles: A Preliminary Report." Bellingham, WA: Western Washington University. Unpublished manuscript.

Malnic, Eric, and Hector Tobar. 1989. "31 Plucked from Burning Building." *Los Angeles Times*, 6 December: pt B.

Maram, Sheldon L. 1980. "Hispanic Workers in the Garment and Restaurant Industries in Los Angeles County: A Social and Economic Profile". *Working Papers in U.S.-Mexican Studies* #12. San Diego: University of

California.

Nehmer, Stanley, and Mark W. Love. 1985. "Textiles and Apparel: A Negotiated Approach to International Competition." In *U.S. Competitiveness in the World Economy*, edited by Bruce R. Scott and George C. Lodge. Boston: Harvard Business School Press.

Noyelle, Thierry J. 1987. *Beyond Industrial Dualism: Market and Job Segmentation in the New Economy*. Boulder, CO: Westview.

Olney, Peter. 1989. "Some Strategies for Change: The Rising of the Million." *L.A. Weekly*, 24 February-2 March: 28-29.

Ong, Paul M. 1989. *The Widening Divide: Income Inequality and Poverty in Los Angeles*. Los Angeles: University of California, Los Angeles School of Architecture and Urban Planning.

Rothstein, Richard. 1989. *Keeping Jobs in Fashion: Alternatives to the Euthanasia of the U.S. Apparel Industry*. Washington, DC: Economic Policy Institute.

Soldatenko, Maria. 1989. "Who is Organizing Latina Garment Workers in Los Angeles?" Paper presented at annual meeting of the Southwest Oral History Association, 14 April, Los Angeles.

U.S. Department of Commerce, International Trade Administration. 1988. *1988 U.S. Industrial Outlook*. Washington, DC.

U.S. Department of Commerce, International Trade Administration. 1989. *1989 U.S. Industrial Outlook*. Washington, DC.

U.S. General Accounting Office. 1988. "Sweatshops in the U.S.": Opinions on Their Extent and Possible Enforcement Options. Washington, DC.

Waldinger, Roger D. 1986. *Through the Eye of the Needle: Immigrants and Enterprise in New York's Garment Trades*. New York: New York University Press.

Wolin, Merle Linda. 1981. "Sweatshop: Undercover in the Garment Industry." *Los Angeles Herald Examiner*, 14 January-1 February.

4

Immigrants in Garment Production in Paris and in Berlin

Mirjana Morokvasic

The garment industry has always attracted immigrants. It offers jobs to a range of immigrants: those confined at home, those with minimal job opportunities, those capable of mobilizing their co-ethnics, those with sewing skills as well as those with none, those with starting capital and those with none. However, immigrants attracted to this industry share characteristics or often belong to communities already connected with it. The literature treats the garment industry as a sector that requires a flexible, cheap, and nonunionized work force in order to survive. It stresses immigrants and women as the most vulnerable work force. It underscores the exploitative organization of production. A number of studies have investigated workers at the bottom of the scale and also women home workers (Shah, 1975; Hoel, 1982; Labelle, 1987; Saifullah-Khan, 1979; Allen, 1981, 1989; Coyle, 1982). Phizacklea's and my own work have shown that gender and ethnicity, combined with racism, increase the vulnerability of the female work force. Women are naturally paid less and allocated certain jobs because their role as workers is rarely considered paramount (Morokvasic, 1988, 1987b; Morokvasic et al., 1986). Studies of the garment industry in France generally characterize immigrants as illegal labor (Delacourt, 1980; Vincent, 1981; Conseil Economique et Social, 1982; Krieger-Mytelka, 1987) and marginal (Montagne'-Villette, 1987; Dubois, 1987). Rare in France is an analysis of the relationship between formal and informal structures that incorporate illegal labor. The few available studies show that illegal immigrant workers tend to be employed by available co-ethnics or other immigrants (Morokvasic, 1987b), who constitute an important link to manufacturers in the subcontracting chain (Green, 1984, 1986). Some literature does, indeed, focus on immigrants as potential entrepreneurs, and the garment industry provides many opportunities for self-employment. The ethnic business literature has focused on upward mobility of immigrants by access to self-employment, thus, extending current analysis that has focused only on immigrants as workers. It is argued that previous experience of wage employment with a co-ethnic owner enhances the probability of self-employment in the same sector. This approach provides a useful framework, though it does not focus directly on garment industry. Examples include Light's now classic *Ethnic Enterprise in America* (1972), Bonacich's middleman minority theory (1973), Bonacich and Modell (1980), Light and Bonacich (1988), and other works in that field in the United States and Europe (Waldinger et al., 1990). Waldinger (1986) contrasted various explanations for ethnic entrepreneurship, and suggested a theoretical framework based on interaction of opportunity and migrants' characteristics (see also Morokvasic et al., 1990; and Morokvasic, 1987a). Among the most important characteristics of immigrants in this business are skills -- imported or learned on the spot, future-orientation related to the circumstances of immigration (target workers vs. settlers), and the capacity to mobilize ethnic networks and resources. A common obstacle is limited access to the general labor market (Min, 1987). On the other hand, maximum opportunities for self-employment exist in those sectors that have low entry barriers and in which the departure of previous entrepreneurs creates vacancies (Waldinger, 1989). The garment industry is a classic example.

There are, however, numerous controversies about the differential impact of the above on self-employment. Further areas that have not been fully explored include the impact of the circumstances of immigration and the future orientation of immigrants (Waldinger, 1989). Furthermore, gender-specific access to self-employment, and gender differentials in the reliance on ethnic community networks and resources have not been explored sufficiently in any of the occupational sectors in which immigrants have set up their businesses (Morokvasic, 1988; Boyd, 1989). These deserve further attention and analysis.

Another body of literature points to economic restructuring accompanied by the expansion of the informal sector in advanced industrialized countries to explain recent development in the industry. For example, Sassen-Koob (1989) highlights the relationship between the contraction of jobs in formal sectors and the increased reliance in the informal sectors (homes, sweat shops) on subcontracting and job creation in apparel production in New York. Corroborated further by Fernandez-Kelly and Garcia (1989), her views suggest that informal structures are products of the formal economy and state policies. In the case of the garment industry, international competition accentuates this process. It reflects not only employers' strategies to reassert dominance and power, but also the workers' desire to survive and to attain more autonomy (Fernandez-Kelly, 1987).

This chapter draws from my previous comparative work on immigrants in the garment industry in Paris and Berlin (Morokvasic et al., 1986; Morokvasic et al., 1990; Morokvasic, 1987a), from my study of legalized garment workers in Paris (1987c), and from a recent research on immigrant and minority women in self-employment (Morokvasic, 1988). Finally, it incorporates new field data collected in 1989 and 1990.[1]

Paris and Berlin

Paris and Berlin were rival cities in the fashion industry at the turn of the century. Both relied on immigrants' and women's labor (Green, 1984; Klatzman, 1957; Westphal, 1986, Hausen, 1978, etc.) and on flexible production based on subcontracting and homeworkers. Despite rapid industrialization in garment production, that original system has survived the establishment of larger factories and the concentration of capital and production (Guilbert and Isambert-Jamati, 1956; Westphal, 1986). However, while Paris remained a famous fashion center and garment producer, Berlin lost its preeminence after the Second World War. Berlin became an isolated city without a periphery. Its garment industry was transferred to West Germany and Eastern Europe.

Paris and Berlin both have large immigrant populations, with Turks and Yugoslavs in both cities. These two groups have been settled for about the same period of time, and have high propensity towards self-employment. In both cities they have been earning their living dealing with garments: in Paris as labor and as entrepreneur-subcontractors, in Berlin as labor in the remaining industry and as self-employed in repair shops. Let me introduce Milan, a Yugoslav from Paris, and Cihan, a Turk from Berlin:

> Milan produces high quality two piece outfits for a famous haute couture manufacturer of Paris. He came to Paris twenty years ago with his wife from Yugoslavia to seek better opportunities than those available at home where he was a clerk. He had previously studied at the law school for a year. At first, he and his wife were home workers for a compatriot until Milan set up his own business. He had no previous skills related to the industry, but his wife knew how to sew since she had always made clothes for the family. Milan manages to keep a stable pool of seven workers and recruits extra ones, if needed, on a temporary basis. With ups and downs, he has been in business for over fifteen years.

> A Turk from Berlin, Cihan, is a skilled artisan tailor. This was his occupation in Turkey. He remembers, with pride, clients for whom he made suits. He was recruited for a job in the garment industry and put to work as machine operator, which he found humiliating and degrading. However, the only way to enter Germany was to accept unskilled work in manufacturing or construction. When his factory closed, he found another job in a gramophone factory. After another period of unemployment, he started a shop, repairing and altering clothes. This was one of the few niches in which foreigners could be self-employed without too many state formalities. He could, at least, use his skills and his wife could help. "It is a dead end job," he says, "but it is good to survive on." Cihan earns about half of what Milan earns in Paris.

Why could Milan, without any previous skills, do in Paris, what Cihan, with a high level of tailoring expertise, could not do in Berlin? What are the economic circumstances in each of the cities that facilitated the success of the former and not the latter in a similar industry?

Comparative Assessment of Opportunity Structures in the Garment Industry

At first glance, both Milan's and Cihan's chances of success in the garment industry are equally poor, even as workers, let alone as entrepreneurs. In both countries the garment industry is rapidly losing its importance as a major manufacturing employer. Table 4.1 shows, that in the decade 1977-87, there was a loss of approximately ninety thousand jobs in each country, representing one-third of workers. Immigrant workers were the first to suffer from the contraction of jobs.

In contrast to Berlin, the contraction of jobs and the closure of enterprises in France has been accompanied by an increased reliance on subcontracting and on jobs created in the underground economy.

Manufacturers subcontract most labor intensive production to small firms, run by and employing immigrants. This procedure enables them to transfer their own production risks to others. Arguably, industrial segmentation arises when demand falls into stable and unstable portions and which could be separated from

TABLE 4.1.
Declining Employment in Garment Industry 1977-87 in France and Federal Republic of Germany

	1977	1980	1985	1987	Job Loss 77-87
France	279,200	251,334	207,975	189,000	33%
FRG	294,000	282,000	216,000	204,000	31%

Source: France: UNEDIC; FRG: Statistisches Bundesamt

one another (Piore, 1979; Piore and Sabel, 1984). However, interdependence is more important than competition, which is frequently put forward as one of the consequences of segmentation (Taplin, 1989). The secondary segment consisting of small firms have become one of the few economic niches that immigrants can use to enter the countries' labor market.

Subcontracting is steadily increasing in France. The annual survey of enterprises in 1979 recorded that 10 percent of firms contracted out the production. Their numbers doubled in only a few years, and represented 21 percent of the firms in 1984. Their sales constituted over one-third of the total sales in the garment industry. The 1979 survey indicated that 60 percent of all the firms externalized their production (Dubois, 1987). This tendency has been especially marked in the ladies' ready-to-wear sector, in which employment has declined as in other sectors, but in which the number of firms increased at the beginning of the eighties and the number of jobbers almost tripled. At the same time, despite a downward trend in employment, these firms increased their employees: from about three thousand at the end of the 1970s to over six thousand in the mid-1980s. In France, the average size of firms is small, but in Paris, 90 percent of the firms have less than nineteen employees with the majority employing less than nine. Over half of the work force is employed in plants of less than nineteen salaried persons, one-third in plants of less than nine (INSEE, 1986; Morokvasic, 1987c). The closure of plants has affected big firms (of more than 100 employed) more than small ones. The small size of firms lowers risks, reduces tax payments, and enables employers to circumvent labor laws. There results a pronounced tendency toward dispersion and the creation of numerous small units (Weisz and Anselme, 1981). In the meantime, the invisible part of the industry has been gaining in importance. This change enhances the chances of immigrants to become employers because little capital is needed to start working "on one's own" in the garment industry. A petty entrepreneur or contractor can start with one sewing machine only and minimum command of the local language.

The evidence about immigrants as small firm proprietors comes from the lists of registrants at the Chamber de Metiers de Paris. An analysis of the nationality of registrants shows that 54.51 percent of small firm (employing under ten people) proprietors were foreigners. After the French (45.49 percent), the Turks (22.45 percent) and Yugoslavs (8.32 percent) were the most represented nationalities. The Asians accounted for another third of owners (see Table 4.2).

The entry of immigrants into the Parisian garment industry is further facilitated by the absence of legal requirements for garment proprietorships. Anyone who possesses a residence permit can

TABLE 4.2.
Garment Firms of Less Than Ten Employees in Paris by Nationality of the Registrant (March 1990)

	Number	%
French*	1,655	45.49
British	42	1.15
Greek	61	1.67
Total EEC	1,822	50.00
Yugoslav	303	8.32
Other European	314	8.63
Turkish	817	22.45
Pakistan	52	1.42
Chinese	115	3.16
Vietnam	36	1.00
Total Asian	1,234	33.91
Morocan	45	1.23
Tunisian	71	1.95
Algerian	50	1.37
Total African	181	4.87
Total	3,638	100.00

*It is likely that these are to a large extent foreign-born French, naturalized. Unlike the situation in the United States it is not possible to know their "ethnic origin." That is a question one does not ask in France. We know from census data, however, that the tendency to become self-employed is higher among foreign-born French than among foreigners or native-born French (Morokvasic, 1988). "British" are, in fact, the Hong Kong Chinese.

Source: Chambre des metiers de Paris, unpublished data on registrants and my calculations, 1990.

register as self-employed. In Paris, rapid fluctuations in the closure and opening of firms reflect this facility and also indicate the vulnerability of such firms. For instance, in 1989, of the 1,092 firms registered with the Parisian Chamber of Artisans, 658 closed. Of the entrepreneurs who started in this section, 44 percent were French nationals, 31 percent were Turks, 8 percent Yugoslav, and 4 percent Chinese. Of those who closed, French and Turks accounted for 29 percent each, Yugoslavs for 13 percent and Chinese for 7 percent.

In Paris, the subcontracting zone is known as the Sentier after the traditional inner city location of garment producers. Design and showrooms are located here. Fabric is sold and cut here, and manufacturers are linked to a network of immigrant contractors and subcontractors and also to home workers or home-based ateliers, who can deliver finished products at high speed and low cost. In women's ready-to-wear, this parallel structure influences production and retailing in the whole sector. Manufacturers and retailers can satisfy their short-term needs and resupply runs if needed. Sentier can also fill in the dead season. The Sentier structure is being reproduced in the outskirts of Paris and in some cities of the French Provinces (Weisz and Anselme, 1981; Weisz, 1987; Dubois, 1987; Montagne'-Villette, 1987).

This system facilitates the entry of immigrants as subcontractors. Subcontracting externalizes labor intensive functions of production, separating them from creation and distribution. The manufacturer contracts out all production, except for design, model making, and cutting, while giving the assembly to one or more subcontractors. He also markets the garment himself. This strategy enables manufacturers to widen the quality spectrum of their products, to those of high quality, while at the same time specializing in the design of product and in keeping control of its patent. Thus, while remaining in control of the whole process, they transfer *production risks* to contractors.

In competition with one another for economic survival, contractors try to lower their labor costs by further subcontracting work or by engaging in informal activities (Morokvasic, 1987a). Much of this is off the books because "if you are completely legal, you go out of business." The system produces different risk takers involved in activities which include tax violations and other kinds of economic crime. These mask the links between formal, regular activities of manufacturers, and the informal operations of subcontractors (Morokvasic, 1987a). This link is extremely difficult to document. Employers taken to court, in connection with a "false bills" racket, were released because of "lack of evidence." "I knew the outcome from the beginning. They let me go because I knew too much -- and they knew that I could speak," they told me.

In contrast to Paris, the once dynamic system of subcontracting no longer exists in Berlin. As stated earlier, its destruction goes back to the Nazi period, with the boycott and confiscation of Jewish production units, and the exile and deportation of the Jewish producers and workers (Westphal, 1986). After the war, the revival of the German garment industry was based on modernization and mass production. However, the Soviet blockade of 1948 and the Berlin Wall were the ultimate blows to garment production in Berlin. Until 1961, manufacturers could still rely on subcontractors in the eastern part of the city, but the Wall finally isolated Berlin and forced its garment industry to shift its production abroad (mainly to Eastern Europe) and to West Germany, where its new fashion centers of Munich and Dusseldorf are situated, close to rural areas with large supplies of female labor (Figge and Quack, 1989). The economic climate of Eastern Europe encouraged garment production because of low wages, low transport costs, advantageous tariff regulations, and also because of exemption from import taxes for certain types of imports. These strategies of German manufacturers did not produce opportunities for the creation of new small firms, let alone facilitate the entry of newcomer immigrants into them. In the 1960s, at the beginning of migrant labor recruitment period, both industrial firms and artisanal ones were in rapid decline. The system of subcontracting had virtually disappeared. The number of industrial garment firms in Berlin declined from 1,646 in 1965 to 400 in 1977, and is now half that. Artisanal firms declined from 5,616 in 1951 to 1,605 in 1965, a period that coincides with rapid immigration. At present, there are only around two hundred firms left.

To further illustrate my points using my case studies, even if there had been new opportunities when Cihan came from Turkey to Berlin, he would have had to overcome obstacles that Milan did not have to contend with in Paris. These include the legal requirements to produce a German certificate proving his skills in making clothes. He also needed special residence and work permits. The only sector to which entry was possible for him was in clothing alterations. Immigrants, mostly Turks and some Yugoslavs, revived this dying sector in cities all over Germany. In West Berlin, the number of alterations shops increased from only twelve in 1965 to over five hundred at the beginning of the 1980s, employing on average, two to three workers. Immigrants not only created their own demand for this type of service, but also responded to the needs of a population with a limited interest for new garments, by taking over some of the work traditionally done by German women. Morokvasic (et al., 1986) shows that for immigrants who could not find other jobs and were threatened by the loss of residence permits, entering this sector was a survival strategy. Saturation of demand in the 1980s prevented further absorption of immigrants into this sector and also any prospects of upward mobility for them. Some Turkish owners started to diversify their output by offering, for example, leather clothes made in Turkey.

In conclusion, let me reiterate the fundamental differences in opportunities in the two cities which produced different kinds of entrepreneurial behavior among immigrants who had similar starting backgrounds and opportunities. In Paris, a highly flexible organization of garment production, relying on very small units, subcontracting, and increasing informalization facilitated the entry of immigrant entrepreneurs. In Berlin, the dying garment industry absorbed some skilled artisans as unskilled labor, but the artisanal sector rapidly disappeared, too rigid to admit newcomers. Immigrants laid off by the industry created a niche which they reanimated through their own skills. Socioeconomic conditions alone cannot explain this process. Immigrants bring their own skills that are then shaped by the circumstances of the destination economy that enhances certain types of economic behaviors while jeopardizing others.

Immigrant Supply and Characteristics

The differential availability of immigrants in France and in

Germany has depended on different policies of immigration and foreign labor recruitment. Immigrants in France can be aptly described as a "fluid labor supply," a term used by Handlin (1979) for nineteenth-century America. Immigration to France was encouraged by liberal immigration policies. Despite attempts to regulate immigration, it continued unabated, bypassing hiring agencies and the Office National d'Immigration (ONI) established in 1945 to check spontaneous immigration. In the peak period of postwar immigration, the 1960s, approximately 70-90 percent of immigrants had their status legalized. Similar to regularization through IRCA, the procedure of amnesty was adopted as a standard strategy of labor market regulation (Moulier et al., 1987). The amnesty of 1981-82 dealt specifically with the undocumented labor that accumulated in France in the 1970s, and which could not be absorbed by sporadic "admissions to the labor market." Despite the embargo in 1974 on labor migration, the immigration of families, refugees, asylum seekers, and undocumented workers continued and provided certain sectors of the French economy with a flexible, not very demanding work force. A consequence is a considerable labor supply consisting of workers with insecure legal status, who could benefit the garment industry. The data on the French amnesty of 1982 suggest that the total number of regularized workers was 8,820 higher than suggested by the census figures for Paris for the same year (Morokvasic, 1987c).

Based on a random sample of 1,020 immigrants legalized by the 1982 amnesty procedure, my own study provides evidence for the spatial distribution of legalized garment workers. It shows that they were located predominantly in the inner city area of "Sentier" that had most of the garment firms and garment workers and in which immigrants outnumbered the French. Women immigrants and those from Southeast Asia were underestimated. This imbalance suggests that a high proportion of workers were still employed outside the legal sectors (Morokvasic, 1987c). Furthermore, the majority of legalized workers were employed mostly by other immigrant employers, mostly of the same national origin. Co-ethnic employers also provided the employment certificate, a critical prerequisite for legalization, thus emphasizing the solidarity of countrymen.

Some immigrants did use regular procedures of immigration to simplify their entry, though direct recruitment into the garment industry was rare and mostly restricted to factories in the provinces. Parisian garment firms needed flexible labor and the illegal supply was cheapest and most easily mobilized by immigrant subcontractors themselves. These subcontractors were generally recruited among settled immigrants prepared to undertake risks which they would not have accepted as target workers. However, many subcontractors emerged only because of the sector's informalization. Segmentation among subcontractors themselves forced their own workers into self-employment to avoid high social security and health insurance taxes. Thus, entry into self-employment and entrepreneurship was an out-come of power relations established in the subcontracting system, though, it also genuinely reflected a person's desire for autonomy.

In contrast to France, the immigrant population was less available in Germany because immigration channels were more tightly controlled. "Guest workers" were brought in for *specific* purposes to fill vacancies in *specific* German industries. Dependent family members who could have otherwise provided a flexible supply of labor for the informal sector and family-owned firms were kept to a minimum and only increased after labor migration restrictions were lifted in 1973 and when the rationalization of various industries produced redundancies among immigrants. Ever since the unemployment rates of immigrants have been double those of Germans. The trend toward settlement came much later in Germany than in France because, given the official German ideology that the Federal Republic was not an immigration country, insecurity was much greater than in France. A consequence was a great reduction in risk taking in establishing enterprises in Germany.

Thus, the different circumstances of immigration in the two countries determined the availability of immigrants. Whereas Milan in Paris was freely available on the labor market, Cihan in Berlin, had no choice but to be recruited in the official manner for an assigned vacancy. Their personal resources, network connections, and technical skills did not greatly differ. The skills needed to operate in the garment industry are loosely defined and are determined by the job supply because the former can be learned rapidly to meet the demands of the latter. A highly skilled tailor in Berlin, Cihan, was rendered unskilled by his German employers, whereas Milan's lack of skill in Paris was not an obstacle to his becoming a contractor. After all, he could always rely on the skills of his wife. For women, on the contrary, skills were definitely a *sine qua non* of self-employment. Unlike men, women could neither compensate for their lack of skills by mobilizing their husband's resources as unpaid labor nor by mobilizing other labor within the community.

This brings into focus the importance of other resources required to operate in this sector, such as the use of networks for finding work, for obtaining a cheap and cohesive work force, for financial support, and for market transactions. Faced with limited mobility in the labor markets of destination economies, immigrants learned to rely on the informal networks that provided them a competitive edge over nonimmigrants. Their usual ways of finding jobs, workers, and intermediaries, and for establishing connections with manufacturers were word of mouth or advertising in immigrant newspapers. An immigrant employer can also recruit workers directly from his/her place of origin by hiring them on special contracts that, in fact, make these workers directly dependent on him/her.

In such situations, primary relationships blur class relationships because complicity is established between worker and employer through kinship and community solidarity. Both have the impression that they have 'struck a good bargain.' The subcontractor can make them work at a lower price and rely on them for long hours. Workers feel indebted to him for their job, for sympathy with their private worries, and for help if they are in need. For a long time, ethnicity filters out class solidarities which give way to loyalty, based on the shared origin. Conflicts that would otherwise arise in pure market relationships are thereby masked. Eventually, the entrepreneur recruits beyond the immediate family, though relationships with workers are still mediated through kinship, ethnic, and friendship ties within a community that shares common identities and sets of rules and obligations that cement solidarity.

Trust and loyalty are also indispensable for other activities that informalization generates. For instance, the employment of unregistered workers necessitates access to large amounts of cash for their pay. In order to keep this activity invisible and "off-the-books," subcontractors need intermediaries in the subcontracting chain who can provide them with the necessary "pay checks" and "pay slips" for the workers, and also cash for commissions (Morokvasic, 1987a).

Arguably, this flexible organization of work is highly exploitative of workers, in particular women, who often work from 8 a.m. to midnight and also weekends under difficult health and safety conditions. Workers also lack job security and health and pension insurance, thus breaching the labor laws. There are marked gender differences in the upward mobility opportunities. Women are more likely to remain in less visible jobs, either as illegals or as home workers or as assistants to male home workers, all of which literally involves work without pay. Evidence for this was indirectly provided by the legalization figures for the 1982 amnesty. Less than one-quarter of legalized immigrants were women, even in the garment sector where traditionally 80 percent of workers are women (Morokvasic, 1987c). One explanation is the inability of women to fulfill the requirements for legalization which involve the provision of a certificate that documents stable employment for a year preceding legalization. Second, upward mobility through self-employment is much more limited for women because they have to rely on men for their transactions with manufacturers, jobbers, retailers, and wholesalers. Women are also not taken seriously and are subject to sexual harassment. They incur difficulties in getting paid within a reasonable period of time after delivering finished work. They are also unable to mobilize the same resources as men because community networks are not always as supportive of them (Morokvasic, 1988). As a consequence, they are often left to rely exclusively on other female workers.

Despite this, from the perspectives of the workers whose employment alternatives would otherwise be nil, this flexible system is a de facto job creator. Situated in this flexible informal Parisian system, Milan is a provider of opportunities for people he has hired through his networks. Besides, he and his workers operate in an advantageous environment where the requirements of work cross cut those of nonwork and newcomers can be integrated because boundaries between legal and illegal work, between private and public, and between formal and informal, are blurred. Such flexible arrangements defy the conventional wisdom about class structures and class struggles, and the conceptualization of migration as an inevitable process of proletarianization.

Prospects for the Future

Until recently, new technologies were considered to be the only form of future innovation for the garment industry. The prevailing view was that "there is no transformation in this industry without elimination of the traditional sewing operation involving one machine operator to one machine" (Krieger-Mytelka, 1987). However, the highly flexible structure of the Parisian Sentier and its competitiveness seems to be developing into a model for an organi-zational kind of innovation. Whereas only a few years ago, the Sentier was a marginal phenomenon deserving only a footnote in official parliamentary reports, it is now recognized as an innovative adaptation to new consumption demands and to obsolete legislation (Montagne'-Villette, 1990). It is increasingly emphasized that "the future of the whole sector depends on the capacity of enterprises to organize themselves as Sentier" (Dubois, 1987: 66), which is proposed as the only economic model capable of renovating industry to face international competition (Negri, 1990).

The garment industry in Italy (Taplin, 1989), and in the United States (Waldinger, 1986; Fernandez-Kelly, 1987; Bonacich in this volume) and other parts of the world share common features with those of Paris. Internationalization of production has led both to the transfer of production to low-wage countries and also to the alteration of conditions in core countries, due to growing informalization and the demand for cheap labor. On the one hand, this process continues at the expense of workers at the bottom, particularly immigrant women, whose upward mobility in the labor market is extremely limited. On the other hand, garment production also provides opportunities for workers and for new employers. It extends the traditional boundaries between the illegal and the legal, between work and nonwork, and between employer and employee. As a consequence, its effective functioning points to the *obsolescence of traditional class relationships*. An analysis that constructs employers as the exploiters, and employees as the exploited, that is, the winners against the losers, is greatly limited in providing a proper explanation for the most effective strategy for improving equality of opportunity. These new developments are complex and multifold. For example, a recently arrived worker in Milan's atelier in Paris does not consider himself a loser, even though he is forced to abandon his private business at home and migrate to France as a "tourist" to work in the garment industry. He has no other alternatives. Milan's benefits from employing him illegally, and the risk he runs by doing so cannot be explained in strictly market terms, without taking into account the importance attached to solidarity in determining his employment in the garment industry.

Could one, therefore, foresee the revival of garment production in Berlin? Cihan in Berlin belongs to a large settled community with several thousand entrepreneurs specializing in trade and services. Like him, they could easily mobilize resources and rely on established networks. Given the new circumstances it is possible that other niches could open for them or they could themselves create other openings in garment manufacturing. Until recently, Berlin was an isolated city. The conditions in and around Berlin have changed. The Wall no longer exists and the city, east and west together, has a population of 4 million inhabitants. Berlin now has a large periphery and a considerable labor supply. Given the extreme discrepancy in the standards of living in the city and its periphery, Berlin is a likely point of destination for numerous migrants, settlers, and commuters.

As a consequence, the opportunities in the garment sector itself could potentially increase. As stated earlier, West Germany has so far resorted to production in Eastern Europe. Garment factories were operating in Poland and in the former GDR as subcontractors for West German manufacturers for a considerable period. However, there are already informal networks between some Berlin retailers (boutiques) and garment workers in these countries, but on a limited scale, established mostly through informal networks and acquaintances. This whole area needs to be properly researched before any further analysis and comment.

Conclusion

The unification of Germany could produce some further effects. In the past, the GDR employed other foreign workers which included sixty thousand Vietnamese, a large portion of whom worked in the garment industry. The West has only recently learned about the living and working conditions of these "new" migrant laborers (Runge, 1990). Press reports and evidence from our interviews carried out recently point to the existence of informal production and marketing strategies among Vietnamese garment workers who made use of their garment skills at home, to reproduce the patterns made in the factories and to sell them later to private customers. The demand for such output obviously existed because the garments they marketed were replicas of those available only at the hard currency "exquisite shops," for triple the price. In unified Germany, the former GDR mass garment production will undergo major restructuring, thus releasing large numbers of its previous industrial workers (including foreigners) into the labor market for uptake by the informal firms.

As for the former West Germany, in an attempt to overcome the rigidities of current production structures, German garment manufacturers have already sought flexibility domestically by using "atypical" job arrangements (Figge and Quack, 1989). Such a trend has also been observed in other sectors of the economy (Hinrichs, 1989; Buchtemann and Quack, 1989; Lattard, 1989).

Another important dimension of opportunity structures is the vicinity of fashion centers and their markets. There have already been attempts to reestablish Berlin as a fashion center with traditional and alternative fashion shows (Durchreise and Off Line) that have recently been taking place several times a year. This tendency could be further reinforced with garment manufacturers trying to make the most of the new conditions in Berlin through the ready availability of labor, whereas in the same mold, the immigrants will attempt to use these new opportunities to their best advantage.

State policies can encourage these developments in one direction or the another. They should be innovative in their support of activities which are growing and creating jobs. Trying to eradicate the growing informalization through repressive measures and persecution could only produce a counter-effect, and a situation which would be at the expense of those at the bottom.

Note

1. I had access to the files of foreigners legalized in 1982, in the Parisian district. At first, nine thousand files were randomly taken out of the chronologically selected files. Then, all those who were in garment industry were selected and analyzed (1,020). Citizenship, gender, spatial distribution in Paris, type of job, length of stay versus length of illegal stay in France, employer's ethnicity, were among the variables available in the files.

References

Allen, Sheila. 1981. *The Invisible Threads*, IDS Bulletin, University of Sussex Brighton, Britain: 41-47.

Allen, Sheila, and Carol. Wolkowitz. 1989. *Homeworking. Myths and Realities*. London: Macmillan.

Anthias, Floya. 1983. "Sexual Divisions and Ethnic Adaptation: The Case of Greek-Cypriot Women." In *One Way Ticket: Migration and Female Labor*, edited by Annie Phizacklea. London: Routledge and Kegan Paul.

Bonacich, Edna., and John Modell. 1981. *The Economic Basis of Ethnic Solidarity*. Berkeley: University of California Press.

Bonacich, Edna. 1973. "A Theory of Middleman Minorities." *American Sociological Review* 38: 583-94.

Boyd, Monica. 1989. "Family and Personal Networks in International Migration: Recent Developments and New Agendas." *International Migration Review* 23: 638-70.

Buchtemann, Chistoph, and Sigrid, Quack. 1989. "Bridges or Traps? Non-Standard Forms of Employment in the Federal Republic of Germany. The Case of Part-Time and Temporary Work." Discussion Paper FS I 89-6, Wissenschaftszentrum Berlin.

Conseil Economique et Social. 1982. "Le Devenir des Industries du Textile et de l'Habillement." *Journal Officiel*, 25 February.

Coyle, Angela. 1982. "Sex and Skill in the Organization of the Clothing Industry." In *Work, Women and the Labor Market*, edited by Jackie West. London: Routledge and Kegan Paul.

Delacourt, Brigitte. 1980. *Mouvement du Capital et Emploi dans l'Habillement*. Paris: Institut Syndical d'Etudes et de Recherches Economiques et Sociales.

Dubois, Pierre. 1987. *L'Industrie de l'Habillement. L'Innovation Face à la Crise*. Paris: La Documentation Francaise.

Fernandez-Kelly, Maria, Patricia. 1987. "Economic Restructuring in the United States: The Case of Hispanic Women in the Garment and Electronics Industries in Southern California." Paper presented at American Sociological Association Meeting, 18 August.

Fernandez-Kelly, Maria, Patricia, and Ama M. Garcia. 1989. "Informalization at the Core: Hispanic Women, Homework, and the Advanced Capitalist State." In *The Informal Economy*, edited by A. Portes et al. Baltimore and London: Johns Hopkins University Press.

Figge, Karin, and Sigrid, Quack. 1989. *Les Effets de l'Achèvement du Marché Interieur sur l'emploi des Femmes dans l'Industrie Textile et de Confection en R.F.A.* Bruxelles, Belgium: Commission de la Communauté Europeenne.

Frobel, F., et al. 1980. *The New International Division of Labor*. Cambridge Britain: Cambridge University Press.

Green, Nancy. 1984. *Les Travailleurs Immigrés Juifs à la Belle Epoque*. Paris: Fayard.

Green, Nancy. 1986. "Immigrant Labor in the Garment Industries of New York and Paris. Variations on Structure." *Comparative Social Research* 9: 231-43.

Guilbert, Madeline, and Vivianne, Isambert-Jamati. 1956. *Travail Feminin et Travail à Domicile*. Paris: Center National de la Recherche Scientifique.

Handlin, Oscar. 1979. *The Uprooted*. Boston: Little, Brown, and Co.

Hausen, K. 1978. "Technischer Fortschritt und Frauenarbeit im 19. Jahrhendert." *Geschichte und Gesellschaft* 4: 148-169.

Hinrichs, Karl. 1989. "Irregulare Beschaftigung und Soziale Sicherheit." In *Prokla 77*. Berlin: Rotbuch Verlag.

Hoel, B. 1982. "Contemporary Clothing Sweatshops, Asian Female Labor and Collective Organization." In *Work, Women and the Labor Market*, edited by J. West. London: Routledge and Kegan Paul.

INSEE. 1986. *Contours et Caractères. Les Étrangers en France*. Paris: Ministère de l'Economie des Finances et du Budget.

Klatzmann, Joseph. 1957. *Le Travail à Domicile dans l'Industrie Parisienne du Vêtement*. Paris: Armand Colin.

Krieger Mytelka, L. 1987. "Changements Technologiques et Nouvelles Formes de la Concurrence dans l'Industrie Textile et de l'Habillement." *Economie Prospective Internationale* 31: 5-28.

Labelle, Micheline, et al. 1987. *Histoires d'Immigrées*. Montreal: Boreal.

Lattard, A. 1989. "Reduction et Flexibilisation du Temps de Travail en RFA." *Problemes Economiques* 2180: 18-27.

Light, Ivan H. 1972. *Ethnic Enterprise in America*. Berkeley and Los Angeles: University of California Press.

Light, Ivan H., and Edna, Bonacich. 1988. *Immigrant Entrepreneurs*. Berkeley and Los Angeles: University of California Press.

Montagné-Villette, Solonge. 1987. *L'Industrie du Pret-à-Porter en France*. Doctoral Thesis, University of Paris.

Montagné-Villette, Solonge. 1990. *Le Sentier. Un Espace Ambigu*. Paris: Masson.

Morokvasic, Mirjana. 1987a. "Immigrants in the Parisian Garment Industry." *Work, Employment and Society* 1: 441-62.

Morokvasic, Mirjana. 1987b. *Jugoslawische Frauen in Westeuropa. Die Emigration und Danach*. Frankfurt/Main: Stroemfeld-Roter Stern.

Morokvasic, Mirjana. 1987c. "Recours aux Immigres dans la Confection Parisienne." In *La Lutte Contre le Traffic de Main d'euvre en 1985-1986*. Paris: Documentation Francaise.

Morokvasic, Mirjana, et. al. 1986. "Small Firms and Minority Groups: Contradictory Trends in the French, British, and German Clothing Industries." *International Sociology* 1: 397-420.

Morokvasic, Mirjana. 1988. *Immigrant and Minority Women in Self-Employment and Business in France, Federal Republic of Germany, Great Britain, Portugal, and Italy*. Brussels: Commission of European Communities, V/1871/88-FR and V/1871/88-ENG.

Morokvasic, Mirjana., et al. 1990. "Business at the Ragged Edge: Immigrants in the Garment Industry, London, Paris, New York." In *Ethnic Entrepreneurs*, edited by Roger Waldinger et al. London and New York: Sage Publications.

Moulier, Yann, et al. 1987. *Économie Politique des Migrations Clandestines de Main d'Oeuvre*. Paris: Publisud.

Negri, Toni. 1990. *Le Sentier, du Quartier au Modele*. A project proposal, manuscript.

Piore, Michael, and C. Sabel. 1984. *The Second Industrial Divide*. New York: Basic Books.

Piore, Michael. 1979. *Birds of Passage: Migrant Labor and Industrial Societies*. Cambridge Britain: Cambridge University.

Portes, Alejandro, et al., eds. 1989. *The Informal Economy*. Baltimore and London: Johns Hopkins University Press.

Min, Pyong Gap. 1987. "Factors Contributing to Ethnic Business: A Comprehensive Synthesis." *International Journal of Comparative Sociology*. 28: 173-191.

Runge, Irene. 1990. *Ausland DDR: Fremdenhass*. Berlin: Dietz Verlag.

Saifullah-Khan, Verity. 1979. "Work and Network." In *Ethnicity at Work*, edited by Sandra Wallman. London: Macmillan.

Sassen-Koob, Saskia. 1989. "New York City's Informal Economy." In *The Informal Economy*, edited by A. Portes et al. Baltimore and London: Johns Hopkins University Press.

Shah, Amir, 1975. *Immigrants and Employment in the Clothing Industry. The Rag Trade in London's East End*. London: The Runnymede Trust.

Simon, Gildas. 1979. *L'Espace des Travailleurs Tunisiens en France*. Doctoral Thesis, University of Poitiers.

Taplin, Ian. 1989. "Segmentation and the Organization of Work in the Italian Apparel Industry." *Social Science Quarterly*, vol 70: no 2.

Vincent, M. 1981. "Vingt Ans de Textile Habillement." *Economie et Statistique* 138: 21-32.

Waldinger, Roger. 1986. *Through the Eye of a Needle*. New York: City University Press.

Waldinger, Roger. 1989. "Structural Opportunity or Ethnic Advantage? Immigrant Business Development in New York." *International Migration Review* 23: 48-73.

Waldinger, Roger. et al. (eds.): 1990. *Ethnic Entrepreneurs*. London and New York: Sage Publications

Weisz, Roger, and Michel, Ansele. 1981. *L'Industrie de l'Habillement en Region Provence-Alpes-Cote-d'Azur*. Aix-en-Provence, France: CERFISE.

Weisz, Roger. 1987. "L'integration de la Production et de la Distribution: Rationalisation ou Renversement de la Logique Industrielle?" *Cahiers du Centre d'études de l'Emploi* 30. Paris: PUF.

Westphal, Uwe. 1986. *Berliner Konfektion und Mode*. Berlin: Hentrich.

5

Immigrant Entrepreneurs in Israel, Canada, and California

Eran Razin

Entrepreneurship has served as a route of economic advancement and social mobility for many of the more successful immigrant groups. In addition to ethnic and class resources, the formation of small businesses by new immigrants depends as much on character-istics of the host country as on the specific urban area. Furthermore, the interaction of location and ethnicity also influences entrepreneurial behavior of immigrant groups; that is, the role of location may differ for each immigrant group. This issue has only received cursory treatment in previous studies.

This chapter outlines the relation between theories of entrepreneurship among immigrant groups and locational studies of entrepreneurship. It focuses on case studies of self-employment among immigrants in Israel, Canada, and California, using national population censuses from the early 1980s. The analysis examines the role of self-employment among immigrants, in the first decade after arrival in their new countries. Special attention has been paid to the influence of location on the propensity of immigrants to engage in self-employment and their entrepreneurial activities.

Location and ethnicity influence independently and interact with regard to their influence on entrepreneurship among immigrants. On the international scale, the role of location can be attributed to differences in human capital characteristics of immigrants and to differences in opportunities created by the absorbing economies. At an intermetropolitan scale, localized ethnic entrepreneurial enclaves can also be of major significance.

The greater bureaucratization of the absorption process in Israel, as well as its economic attributes and regional policies, have created a less conducive environment for entrepreneurship than that in North America. Canadian attempts to attract entrepreneurs with sufficient capital and proven expertise in business have targeted those with high qualifications. The greater emphasis on family and ethnic ties in the United States might have contributed most to the formation of ethnic enclaves, facilitating entrepreneurial careers for large numbers of immigrants who otherwise lacked qualifications to begin at the top. Still, ethnic entrepreneurial enclaves are influenced more by the differences in metropolitan economies than by those between the national economies of the United States and Canada.

The last two decades witnessed a revival in the role of small businesses in job creation in many Western countries. A new role has been assigned to local entrepreneurs in public economic development efforts, replacing post war strategies that were based on capital-intensive industrialization (Storey, 1988). International migration also reemerged as a political and economic phenomenon of major importance, due to the implementation of liberal immigration legislation in countries of destination during a period of economic growth and prosperity in the 1960s, and due to the economic crises of the 1970s and 1980s in the countries of origin. Thus, the phenomenon of entrepreneurship among immigrant groups has a growing significance for local economic development and social change.

Entrepreneurship among Immigrant Groups

Theories focusing on intergroup variations in entrepreneurial activity stress the role of social networks (Light, 1984; Mars and Ward, 1984; Portes and Bach, 1985). Entrepreneurial immigrant groups tend to preserve ethnic ties and form *enclaves of entrepreneurial activity*, based on family ties, trust relations, language, and culture. These enclaves are characterized by extensive informal ethnic networks and serve as channels for recruiting labor, gathering information, transmitting entrepreneurial skills, and in some cases also forming input and output linkages. Informal ethnic institutions such as rotating credit associations and traditions of enterprise are all elements that characterize ethnic networks. Employment in such enclaves facilitates the acquisition of entrepreneurial skills by immigrants much more than employment in equivalent occupations in the general labor market.

The cultural values and ethnic origin of immigrants also influences their personal inclination toward entrepreneurship. Furthermore, immigrants may favor risk-taking over job security when they consider themselves as sojourners (Bonacich and Modell, 1980). However, human capital and money, termed *class resources* by Light (1984), are the major variables which have to be distinguished from ethnic networks in explaining variations in entrepreneurial behavior. Immigrant groups vary in education, skills, and availability of capital. In a critical examination of the ethnic enclave hypothesis, Sanders and Nee (1987) stress the importance of these variables. Differences in the local opportunity structure can attract immigrants with varying human capital attributes to different locations.

These ethnic influences are termed supply variables in entrepreneurship by Light and Rosenstein (1989). A contextual factor, depending on ethnic origin, which is part of the local opportunity structure, is discrimination. Discrimination can either push immigrants to self-employment by blocking alternative mobility paths in the labor market, or block their way to certain self-employment opportunities. Other factors which influence the opportunity structure for immigrant businesses, termed demand variables by Light and Rosenstein (1989), are discussed in the following section.

Entrepreneurship in Locational Space

Locational studies of entrepreneurship have emphasized locality size, industrial structure, business size composition, and social features of the urban area in order to explain regional variations in business formation (Keeble and Wever, 1986; Razin, 1990). A broader theoretical debate concerned the growth and decline of entrepreneurship-intensive environments, termed *flexible production complexes* or *Marshallian industrial districts*. Entepreneurial agglomerations evolve from industries facing unstable and frag-mented markets, and are characterized by high levels of uncertainty in which the need for flexibility outweighs economies of scale. These businesses have dynamic and complex linkages that lead them to agglomerate locationally in order to reduce the spatially dependent costs of external transactions and face-to-face communications (Scott, 1988).

Storper and Scott (1989) and Piore and Sabel (1984) carry this argument further by suggesting that shifts in the world economy, since the 1970s, have lead to a 'second industrial divide' or a 'post-Fordist era,' characterized by greater instability, uncertainty, frag-mentation of demand, and the introduction of new flexible produc-tion methods. This shift, demonstrated by statistical evidence on the revival of the small-business economy (Blau, 1987; Brock and Evans, 1989; Storey, 1988), has lead to the re-agglomeration of pro-duction and to the resurgence of industrial districts of various types. In high-technology and business services complexes, entrepreneurial networks are dominated by business-oriented cosmopolitan or local ties, whereas local social networks associated with family, commu-nity, or ethnic tradition of skills, are particularly central in revital-ized craft production complexes (Johannisson, 1988). In the most publicized cases, such networks based on trust relations and unwrit-ten business norms have led to the emergence of thriving small-busi-ness complexes in small- and medium-sized towns in central and northeastern Italy, known as the Third Italy (Brusco, 1982).

These arguments have been challenged by Amin and Robins (1990) who argued that there have been significant differences among clusters of small family and craft based firms in Third Italy. A few conform to the ideal model of flexibly organized and interna-tionally competitive Marshallian industrial districts. However, most are little more than small family firms producing the same medium-to-poor quality products for a few large subcontractors or whole-salers. Often, these producers have few entrepreneurial skills and little access to technology. These local businesses are fiercely competitive with each other, and are based on self-exploitation, use of family labor, poor wages, and evasion of tax and social security contributions.

Thus, the role of self-employment either as a significant route for upward mobility of new immigrants or as a no choice retreat (Ladbury, 1984), depends on the type of ethnic entrepreneurial network, reflecting both ethnic attributes and location characteristics. Most ethnic enclaves resemble networks of the less ideal types of industrial districts in Third Italy, and concentrate on various service, trade, and construction activities. Immigrant entrepreneurs who penetrate sectors such as the garment industry, wholesale trade or business services form more advanced networks. Nevertheless, even the least ideal complexes can be significant for the local economy, and can serve as a vital first step in the route toward upward mobility for new immigrants, because it enables capital accumulation and advancement in the labor market for the second generation.

The opportunity structure for immigrant entrepreneurs depends not only on the structure of the local economy, but also on the socio-ethnic composition of the urban area. Multiethnic urban areas create particular opportunities for small businesses to compete: first, by forming fragmented patterns of demand that reduce economies of scale in serving the local population; and second, by offering large niches that serve central city minority slums that attract neither mainstream firms nor the native middle-class population (Light and Rosenstein, 1989).

Location and ethnicity interact to influence entrepreneurship among immigrants. Such interaction effect, termed *specific demand factors* by Light and Rosenstein (1989), was also identified by Razin (1988) in California. Immigrants from a common country of origin who reach different urban areas can vary in their human capital attributes. These variations are an outcome of different opportunity structures that attract immigrants with specific qualifications to each location. They also emanate from family and ethnic networks that lead immigrants from particular regions within the country of origin to concentrate in different urban areas of the destination country. In addition, there is a tendency for ethnic entrepreneurial networks to form only in some locations in which the ethnic group is present, and to differ in their characteristics from place to place. Thus, even when human capital variables are kept constant, the influence of location on entrepreneurship can vary across immigrant groups.

Comparing the Israeli, Canadian, and American Cases

International comparisons of entrepreneurship among immigrants should emphasize two major facets: (1) differences among receiving countries in the attributes of immigrants that, to a large extent, stem from the immigration policies of these countries; and (2) differences in economic characteristics, particularly the political-organizational attitude toward small businesses, and legal requirements and obstacles for starting a business (Ward, 1987). The interaction effects of country of origin and country of destination on entrepreneurship evolve from variations in human capital attributes of immigrants attracted to different destinations. They can also be caused by differing levels of discrimination toward specific immigrant groups, whereas local ethnic entrepreneurial networks can have a more central influence in the intermetropolitan scale.

Immigration and Absorption Policies and Their Impact on Entrepreneurship

The United States, Canada, and Israel are among the few countries that accept permanent settlers. Canadian immigration policies are influenced by, and therefore very similar to, American laws. Prejudices against certain immigrant groups such as Chinese have been common to both countries, and both countries liberalized their immigration policies during the 1960s by eliminating discrimination on ethnic grounds. This liberalization enabled an unprecedented influx of immigrants from Third World countries. However, a closer look reveals some distinctions.

First, European, and particularly British, immigrants have remained more dominant in Canada (Statistics Canada, 1984). Second, the ratio of immigrants per population has been higher in Canada. Thus, immigration influences Canada's economy and demographic composition more than these of the United States (Goldberg and Mercer, 1986). Third, economic development and labor market considerations have played a greater role in Canada. Immigration to the United States, on the other hand, has been based more on precedent and on national tradition than on any recognized economic or demographic needs (United Nations, 1982). Fourth, the share of illegal immigrants has been far greater in the United States. As a consequence of these last two factors, the occupational mix of immigrants in Canada, including nonwhites, has tilted toward the upper rungs of the occupational ladder (Keely and Elwell, 1981; Ramcharan, 1982).

In emphasizing economic considerations since 1978, Canada, has also implemented a program for attracting immigrant entrepreneurs who intend to establish and manage businesses that create or retain jobs for Canadians, and for themselves. A more recent investor program has targeted wealthy people who intend to invest large sums (Nash, 1987) who have a proven record of business, and definite plans for establishing a business in Canada. These are not new immigrants striving for economic success and upward mobility through entrepreneurial activity in an ethnic enclave, but rather, wealthy businessmen who are expected to enter the higher economic strata of Canadian society soon after arrival. This policy has been perceived to have had some positive impact on the Canadian economy but it has lacked close monitoring (Nash, 1987). There is concern about the abuse of this policy by immigrants who do not reside in the province that sponsored them, who have not made the promised investment, and who are "continuing business as usual in Hong Kong, while their families are safely settled in some posh Canadian suburb" (Malarek, 1987).

The Israeli case differs fundamentally from the American and Canadian ones. Immigration policy has been motivated by the maintenance of national identity. The almost sole criteria for granting Israeli citizenship has been a Jewish mother or religious conversion to Judaism. Towards the late 1980s, labor migration of non-Jews from countries such as the Philippines, Portugal, and Poland has become more visible, partly due to deteriorating Jewish-Arab relations, making Arabs less attractive as a pool of cheap unorganized labor. These immigration channels are partly illegal and are perceived as temporary. They have not significantly influenced the self-employed sector, except for household work.

Absorption patterns have varied considerably among the three countries. The strong appeal of the United States has been based on its perception as the land of endless opportunities (Sobel, 1986). Immigrants know that they have to make it on their own and practical assistance has been mainly limited to a network of ethnic voluntary organizations. Canada might not have been that different, but for the government and provincial agencies that assumed more responsibility for the welfare and settlement of immigrants (United Nations, 1982). In Israel, the government took responsibility for the first steps of absorption, and assisted immigrants in the acquisition of language, and other skills, and helped them to search for housing and jobs.

It has been argued that the Israeli absorption system attracted the nonentrepreneurial, elderly, and poor, whereas Jews with capital and entrepreneurial skills preferred the economic opportunities in Western Europe and North America (Inbar and Adler, 1977). The greater dependency of immigrants in Israel on public agencies reduced the probability of forming ethnic subeconomies, although close-knit immigrant groups have a superior capacity to adjust to the new society. Self-employment served, to a limited extent, as an alternative mobility route for Jews of Eastern origins who lacked formal education and who immigrated to Israel in the 1950s and early 1960s (Nahon, 1989; Razin, 1989).

The Canadian emphasis on multiculturalism, which differed from American and Israeli "melting pot" ideologies, probably slowed assimilation, particularly in bilingual localities such as Montreal. However, evidence for this is not definitive. The myth of advancement through the preservation of ethnic ties and culture emerged, paradoxically, in the United States, whereas rapid cultural assimilation was considered beneficial for the promotion of economic mobility amongst immigrants in Israel and Canada.

The Economic Environment and Entrepreneurship

In contrast to Israel, the economic and political environment is most conducive to entrepreneurship in the United States, which is most committed to the free enterprise ideology. Public perception is that the Canadian climate is inferior to that of the United States for investors and entrepreneurs. However, the impression that there is more state involvement in the Canadian economy does not stand close scrutiny. Both Canada and the United States are advanced capitalist economies, and the former is only marginally more regulated than the latter. However, there is a difference in the sentiment toward government, and the Canadian government is more willing to engage in public enterprise. The Canadian economy is also more externally controlled, it offers smaller internal markets, and it is more natural resources-based, attributes that can deter entrepreneurship (Goldberg and Mercer, 1986). According to Peterson (1977), both the merchant and the manufacturing entrepreneur did not enjoy high social status in Canada. He argued that a negative attitude toward entrepreneurship in Canada resulted from being too comfortable in the paternalistic shadow of a great neighbor who, along with other countries, has supported the unearned high standard of living in Canada by buying Canadian natural resources. Without discussing the validity of this argument, it should be noted that these attitudes have been changing. The "quiet revolution" in Quebec has been accompanied by changing attitudes toward small businesses, and Canadian regional policies increasingly promote local entrepreneurship (Savoie, 1987).

Ethnic networks have also been critical in attaining economic success in Canada, as demonstrated in a study of Portuguese immigrants (Anderson, 1974). In the Portuguese case, jobs which served as "stepping stones" were usually unionized. Other groups were more entrepreneurial and, unlike majority group entrepreneurs, minorities typically chose self-employment at first, and could have later changed from one type of business to another, utilizing kinship networks and broader ethno-religious ties (Kallen and Kelner, 1983). Canadian cities lacked the large protected niches of serving central city minority slums, utilized by immigrant entrepreneurs in the United States. However, the Jewish entrepreneurial enclave in Toronto's garment industry, formed during the early twentieth century (Hiebert, 1983), that was later succeeded by the Chinese (Wickberg, 1982) showed close resemblance to the same phenomenon in New York (Waldinger, 1986). Thus, it can be argued that what counts more are not marginal differences between the American and Canadian immigration policies or economic systems, but differences in metropolitan opportunity structures.

The Israeli economy has a large public sector and extensive government intervention (Ben Porath, 1986). It has not been receptive toward small entrepreneurs. This rejection was due to the early socialist bias that favored enterprises owned by the Federation of Labor, and to later policies oriented toward large investors who had the ability to face government bureaucracy. Greenwood (1990) stresses the frustration experienced by immigrant entrepreneurs in Israel, and claims that Israel has been one of few countries where the Jews did not gravitate to small businesses. However, this can not be blamed only on Israel's business climate since Jews form the vast majority of Israel's population, and thus cannot cluster in specific entrepreneurial niches, such as those occupied by Jews in countries where they constitute a small minority. A gradual reorientation of public attitudes toward entrepreneurship has been visible since the late 1970s due to the infiltration of "New Right" ideologies from Britain and the United States, Israel's political change in 1977, and to the stagnation of many of Israel's large industrial corporations (Razin, 1990). However, unlike the reversal of the long-term trend of decline in the proportion of self-employed in the United States (Light and Sanchez, 1987) and Canada (Cohen, 1988), the initially higher rates of self-employment in the less advanced Israeli economy have been declining throughout the early 1980s (Razin, 1990). Israel offers smaller markets, inferior opportunities for financing ventures, and greater legal and bureaucratic obstacles for starting and operating a business. These factors have been stressed by Israeli immigrants starting businesses in the United States (Sobel, 1986), although their role in influencing the decision to migrate to the United States has never been thoroughly examined.

The Role of Regional Policies

Both Canada (Lithwick, 1987) and Israel (Razin, 1991) employ regional policies for supporting their economically backward regions. Although the motivations for initiating these policies differed, the means employed showed resemblance, including the recent interest in promoting the small-business sector in backward regions. The United States lacks clear regional policies, but development efforts pursued by local authorities have traditionally emphasized small businesses and entrepreneurs.

Dispersing new immigrants to peripheral localities has been a corner-stone of Israel's population dispersal policy since 1948 (Shachar, 1971). Measures to direct immigrants to nonmetropolitan development towns were of diminishing effectiveness since the late 1960s. Yet, new immigrants have tended to disperse more than the general population. This has not been the case in Canada and the United States, where immigrants tended to gravitate freely towards the largest metropolitan areas. In Canada, the economic advantages of immigration were emphasized by policy makers. It was stressed that the Canadian entrepreneur immigrant program contributed toward widening the gap between the have and the have-not provinces since its main beneficiaries have been the largest metropolitan areas (Nash, 1987). A Canadian attempt to implement a policy of settling immigrants in places where labor is needed, other than Toronto, Montreal, and Vancouver, faced the problem that employment opportunities and ethnic ties, which assist in economic advancement, have been mainly concentrated in the largest metropolitan areas (Anderson and Frideres, 1981). In the United States, an attempt was made during the late 1970s to influence the resettlement pattern of southeast Asian refugees, so that no state would bear a disproportionate burden of resettlement. However, an initially dispersed pattern soon became concentrated as a second wave of refugees gravitated toward the largest concentrations of earlier arrivals, and as internal migration led to increased clustering of immigrants in a few states (Desbarats, 1985). In Israel, where the government has been more successful in dispersing immigrants, it is worthwhile to examine the extent to which this dispersal affected their prospects for entrepreneurship.

TABLE 5.1

Rates of Self-Employment among New Immigrants in Israel-1983, Canada-1981, and California-1980 by Country of Birth and Urban Area of Residence[1]

Country of Birth	Israel - 1983						Canada - 1981						California - 1980				
	All cities and towns No.	%	Tel Aviv metro.	Jeru-salem metro.	Haifa metro.	Develop. towns[2]	13 CMAs No.	%	Mon-treal CMA	Tor-onto CMA	Van-couver CMA	Other CMAs[3]	Three metro. regions No.	%	Los Ang. SCSA	San Franc. SCSA	San Diego SMSA
USSR	11668	5.1	5.6	6.8	4.1	4.5	113	8.8	::	10.9	::	(0)	240	x	14.2	15.2	7.4
Poland[4]	240	10.0	9.7	(18.4)	::	(5.4)	132	3.0	::	0	::	(2.0)	x	x	x	x	x
Germany[5]	173	13.3	11.0	(23.5)	::	::	206	14.6	::	15.1	(14.6)	14.1	169	8.9	13.2	6.4	::
Britain[6]	x	x	x	x	x	x	1372	5.2	4.0	5.0	8.7	3.9	504	12.7	15.9	8.3	(16.7)
Portugal[7]	x	x	x	x	x	x	765	2.4	0.9	3.3	(0)	1.6	155	1.3	::	1.6	::
Europe-others	2807	7.0	7.0	10.0	4.7	4.8	1277	8.2	8.8	7.9	7.2	8.6	1029	15.3	15.5	15.1	14.5
Iran[8]	675	15.6	18.5	14.0	::	8.5	x	x	x	x	x	x	593	24.6	23.7	24.6	(33.3)
India[9]	287	0.3	0	0	::	0.8	x	x	x	x	x	x	410	9.0	12.6	5.6	::
China[10]	-	-	-	-	-	-	1460	5.1	4.3	5.7	5.3	4.2	1424	15.7	18.3	13.5	(23.5)
Israel[11]	-	-	-	-	-	-	x	x	x	x	x	x	189	28.1	30.5	20.4	::
Middle East-others[12]	458	12.0	15.3	(0)	(9.7)	(2.2)	x	x	x	x	x	x	605	23.6	23.6	23.0	5.3
Asia-others	-	-	-	-	-	-	2693	7.1	8.2	6.9	6.4	7.3	4997	9.7	13.1	5.8	
Africa[13]	1267	10.6	15.2	12.1	7.9	4.4	778	9.4	9.1	8.3	8.8	11.7	323	13.0	14.4	5.5	(34.6)
North America[14]	374	9.8	6.9	12.2	4.8	11.1	563	7.5	7.0	7.3	12.3	5.4	299	17.4	18.3	12.7	(27.3)
Latin America	1592	10.6	12.6	10.3	7.4	8.4	2131	2.6	2.3	2.3	10.3	2.5	11011	3.6	3.5	3.6	5.6
All Immigrants	20541	7.0	8.0	9.9	4.8	5.0	11700	5.9	5.9	5.5	7.4	5.7	22881	8.5	8.4	8.4	9.8
Total pop.[15]		11.6	13.3	10.4	10.1	8.4		6.7	6.1	7.0	8.3	6.4		n.a.	na	na	na

Continuation of Table 5.1

1. *Sources: National census of population. For definitions of populations, see the Data and Methodology section. The table does not give the details for Israeli nonmetropolitan veteran towns in the coastal plain, and for some minor countries of birth. However, these are included in the relevant "total" rows and columns. The figures in the table are of percent self-employed, except for those in bold which are of the total working population. These figures of the total working population refer to the samples used in the analysis (20 percent of the Israeli case, 5 percent in the Californian case, 2 percent in the Canadian case).*

   ( )   *Based on a sample of less than 50.*

   ..   *A sample of less than 25.*

   x   *The country of birth is included in a broader category in the Table.*

   -    *No cases in the sample/irrelevant*

2. Development town: all peripheral towns in Israel, including Beer Sheva, and nonmetropolitan new towns in the coastal plain populated by immigrants after 1948.

3. Halifax, Quebec, Ottawa-Hull, Hamilton, St. Catharines-Niagara, Kitchener, London, Winnipeg, Calgary, Edmonton.

4. Poland: included in "Europe-others" in the California sample.

5. Germany: including Austria in the Israeli sample; including Austria and the Netherlands in the Canadian sample.

6. Included in "Europe-others" in the Israeli sample.

7. Same as note no. 6.

8. Included in "Asia-others" in the Canadian sample.

9. Same as note no. 8.

10. China: - including Taiwan and Hong Kong in the California sample; includes Asian born of Chinese ethnic origin in the Canadian sample.

11. Same as note no. 8.

12. Middle East-others: not including Egypt in the Israeli sample; included in "Asia-others" in the Canadian sample.

13. Africa: not including Egypt in the American sample.

14. North America: including Oceania in the Israeli sample; includes only the United States in the Canadian sample; includes only Canada in the American sample.

15. The rates of self-employment of the total working population refer in the Israeli sample only to Jews.

Self-employment among New Immigrants in the
Three Countries -- A Census Data Analysis

Data and Methodology

The exploratory analysis presented in this section focuses on the influence of location on the propensity of immigrants from various origins to become self-employed, and on the industrial composition of the self-employed immigrants. It is based on the public use files (individual records) of the 1983 Israeli Census of Population, the 1981 Census of Canada, and the 1980 American Census of Population. The Israeli file includes a 20 percent sample of the total population, the California file is a 5 percent sample, but the Canadian census is only a 2 percent sample and lacks detail on some variables. The different sampling, and the fact that the studies on each country were carried out separately, restrict to some extent the level of detail at which comparisons can be made. The present study includes: *(a)* immigrants who arrived in Israel between 1972 and 1983, and lived in 1983 in one of its metropolitan areas or other towns of over five thousand inhabitants; *(b)* immigrants who arrived in Canada between 1971 and 1981, and lived in 1981 in one of its thirteen major metropolitan areas; and *(c)* immigrants who arrived in the United States between 1970 and 1980, and lived in 1980 in one of California's three major metropolitan regions. In addition to basic cross-tabulations, logit models for identifying variables influencing the propensity to become self-employed, and log-linear models for identifying factors associated with the industrial composition of the self-employed, were constructed for the Israeli and Canadian cases. The following is a summary of some of the general findings.[1]

Variations in Rates of Self-Employment

The rates of self-employment among new immigrants were highest in the metropolitan areas of California and lowest in Canada (Table 5.1). Intranational variations were small in California and Canada, but more marked in Israel, where new immigrants in Tel Aviv and Jerusalem possessed high "Californian" rates of self-employment, whereas those in Haifa and in development towns had particularly low rates. Spatial variations in rates of self-employment among immigrants in Israel and Canada, reflected with a few exceptions, those of the general population, although new immigrants showed a lower propensity to be self-employed (Table 5.1). Thus, the local opportunity structure clearly influenced the prospects of immigrants to become self-employed.

In Israel, small development towns offered inferior opportunities for entrepreneurship (Table 5.1), being dominated by externally owned industry. They do not benefit from significant central place functions, as do most Canadian small towns. A relatively high proportion (24.3 percent) of the economically active new immigrants in Israel lived in development towns in 1983, and this might have hampered their prospects for entrepreneurship. In Canada, the rates of nonagricultural self-employment were lower in metropolitan areas than in smaller urban and rural centers, and were particularly low in the provinces of Ontario and Quebec, which have the greatest concentrations of large industrial and public administration establishments (Cohen, 1988). Thus, immigrants to Canada tended to concentrate in localities that proportionally offered more abundant opportunities as salaried employees than as self-employed.

The ethnic composition of immigrants in each of the three countries differed considerably. Immigrants from the USSR were dominant in Israel, Latin Americans in California, and a mix of Asians and Europeans in Canada. However, these major differences in country of origin do not markedly influence the rate of self-employment among immigrants in each country. Immigrants in California, in spite of being dominated by nonentrepreneurial Latin Americans, had the highest rates of self-employment (Table 5.1). Moreover, these rates were equal in San Francisco and Los Angeles despite the far greater concentration of Latin American immigrants in the latter metropolis (Razin, 1988). These findings are indicative of the major role played by local opportunity structures in determining the general extent of entrepreneurial activity among immigrants. The existence of large nonentrepreneurial groups in California, particularly in Los Angeles, merely opened the way for other immigrant groups to reach extraordinarily high rates of self-employment (Table 5.1).

Turning to specific immigrant groups, rates of self-employment among immigrants from the USSR were much lower in Israel than in California and Canada. This could have been due to the initial preference of North America by more entrepreneurial immigrants, and to the different Israeli absorption system and economic environment. However, the latter are not major factors in explaining the above differences since immigrants from the USSR to Tel Aviv had a lower propensity to become self-employed than "average" immigrants or the general population in that metropolis, whereas immigrants to Toronto or Los Angeles had a higher propensity than average to become self-employed (Table 5.1).[2]

Spatial variations in the entrepreneurial behavior of immigrants from specific countries of origin frequently stem from different class and ethnic backgrounds. Thus, Latin Americans immigrating to Israel were middle-class Jews fleeing economic and political instability, whereas most of those immigrating to North America were lower classes possessing few entrepreneurial capabilities. Variations in ethnic backgrounds could account for differences between Poles who immigrated to Israel and Canada, Indians who immigrated to Israel and California, and Middle Easterners who immigrated to Israel and California (Table 5.1). The wide gap in rates of self-employment between Chinese immigrants in Canada and California could be either attributed to the Canadian immigration policy, which is more oriented toward the highly educated and skilled, or to ethnic networks that facilitate the migration of Chinese from different backgrounds to different destinations. Iranian immigrants were more entrepreneurial in California than in Israel. Many Iranian Jews preferred California, or even left for Los Angeles, shortly after immigrating to Israel because of the greater potential of Los Angeles for entrepreneurial ventures and profitable utilization of capital brought over from Iran. However, Iranians were the most entrepreneurial new immigrant group in Israel, and had particularly high rates of self-employment in Tel Aviv (Table 5.1).

Substantial immigration existed among the three host countries included in this study. The rate of self-employment among Israelis in Los Angeles was nearly three times as high as the rate among the urban population in Israel (11.7 percent). This significant difference can be explained in two ways. First, Israelis with entrepreneurial skills are attracted to the more conducive climate for entrepreneurship in the American economy. Second, Israelis in the United States resort to entrepreneurship to realize their high aspirations to surpass the not so low Israeli levels of well-being while lacking professional qualifications and contacts needed to advance in the primary labor market. This second explanation is likely to be of greater significance than the first.

Although Americans showed similar levels of self-employment in American Standard Metropolitan Statistical Areas (7.2 percent -- Light and Sanchez, 1987) and Canadian Consolidated Metropolitan Areas (7.5 percent), Canadians were much more entrepreneurial in California than in their home country. North Americans immigrating to Israel were also more entrepreneurial than the American average, but it should be noted that Jews possessed an above-average rate of self-employment in North America. Furthermore, the rates of self-employment among North American migrants varied substantially across metropolitan regions, Los Angeles, Vancouver, and Jerusalem being the preferred locations by self-employed in each of the host countries.

The influence of country of birth and urban area of residence on the propensity of male immigrants in Israel and Canada to become self-employed was examined by multivariate logit models that included the following additional explanatory variables: age, marital status, years of schooling, knowledge of language of host country, and industry (Razin and Langlois, 1990). Country of birth was identified in both Israel and Canada as a variable of major importance, even when all other explanatory variables were taken into account. Urban area of residence, on the other hand, had a significant impact only in the Israeli case.

Variations in the Industrial Composition of the Self-Employed

Immigrants to the three countries differed in their propensity to become self-employed, and in their industrial choice. Those who turned to self-employment in North America showed a greater propensity to engage in construction, food services, wholesale trade, and business services, whereas those who turned to self-employment in Israel were more represented in public (mainly health and education) services, and in manufacturing (Table 5.2). The differences in the industrial composition of the self-employed immigrants were largely influenced by differences in the general composition of the self-employed sector in each country. An exception was the high propensity of immigrants in Israel to engage in public services, and their low tendency to engage in construction and food services. This was probably due to the middle-class backgrounds of a large proportion of immigrants in Israel during the 1970s.

Intermetropolitan variations in the industrial composition of self-employed immigrants were more marked than variations in the rates

TABLE 5.2
Self-Employed Immigrants by Urban Area of Residence and Industry, Israel-1983, Canada-1981, and California-1980[1]

	Agriculture, Primary	Manufacturing	Construction	Wholesale	Retail	Food Services
Israel-urban						
pop., 1983	0.1	15.6	2.8	4.6	25.8	6.1
Tel Aviv metro.	0.2	18.3	2.1	7.1	26.7	7.1
Jerusalem metro.	0	11.3	3.9	2.7	19.8	3.1
Haifa metro. and veteran towns in coastal plain	0.4	13.4	4.6	3.4	28.1	4.6
Development towns	0	15.2	1.7	1.3	27.3	8.2
Canada-13 CMAs,						
1981	1.9	9.6	8.7	6.0	23.9	9.6
Montreal CMA	0	10.9	5.0	5.9	24.8	14.9
Toronto CMA	1.1	11.4	6.4	8.2	28.6	5.0
Vancouver CMA	6.3	7.9	17.3	7.1	16.5	11.0
Other CMAs	1.1	7.3	8.4	1.7	21.2	12.8
California-two major metro.						
regions, 1980	7.6	10.9	9.3	5.9	19.4	10.3
Los Angeles SCSA	8.1	11.9	9.8	6.5	18.9	8.4
San Francisco SCSA	6.4	8.4	8.2	4.3	20.7	14.8

of self-employment among immigrants. Immigrants had a stronger tendency to establish manufacturing businesses in the largest metropolitan areas like Tel Aviv in Israel, Toronto and Montreal in Canada, and Los Angeles in California. The largest metropolitan centers also offered, as expected, an advantage in wholesale. On the other hand, entrepreneurial opportunities for new immigrants in less central locations, such as Israel's development towns and Canadian smaller CMAs, were relatively concentrated in food services, transportation, and personal services (Table 5.2).

The socio-ethnic composition of a locality is part of the local opportunity structure that strongly influences entrepreneurial

Continuation of Table 5.2

	Transp., storage, communic.	Business Services	Public Services	Personal Services	Total (abs. no.)
Israel-urban					
pop., 1983	5.9	8.4	19.6	10.9	1378
Tel Aviv metro.	4.8	7.1	18.9	8.0	652
Jerusalem metro.	3.1	16.0	21.0	19.1	257
Haifa metro. and veteran					
towns in coastal plain	5.5	8.0	23.1	8.9	238
Development towns	12.6	4.3	16.9	12.6	231
Canada-13 CMAs,					
1981	6.4	12.7	8.7	12.5	687
Montreal CMA	8.9	4.0	12.9	12.9	101
Toronto CMA	6.4	14.3	7.5	11.1	280
Vancouver CMA	2.4	13.4	6.3	11.8	127
Other CMAs	7.8	14.5	10.1	15.1	179
California-two major					
metro. regions, 1980	3.3	10.5	9.9	12.9	1816
Los Angeles SCSA	3.2	10.2	9.2	13.8	1281
San Francisco SCSA	3.7	11.2	11.6	10.7	535

1. The table includes only those who immigrated to the three countries during the decade prior to the census. For detailed definitions, see the Data and Methodology section. Classifications of industries differ slightly in each country. Particularly, services are split in a slightly different way into business, public, and personal services. Also, horticultural services are included in agriculture in the United States and in services in Israel.

behavior of immigrants. The presumptions that the economic conditions (Higgins, 1986) and the bilingual character of Montreal (Ossenberg, 1964) might provide a less compatible milieu for economic and social integration of immigrants than in Toronto, were not supported by differences in rates of self employment among immigrants. However, whereas immigrants in Montreal were slightly more likely to become self-employed than in Toronto (Table 5.1), the data indicate that the bilingual character of Montreal hindered the prospects of immigrant entrepreneurs to engage in business services (Table 5.2). Immigrant entrepreneurs showed a particularly strong tendency toward food services in Montreal and San Francisco, but this was prominently only for certain groups, namely Chinese, Iranians, and Greeks.

Log-linear models for new male immigrants, who were self-employed in Israel and Canada, examined the connections between education, country of birth, urban area of residence, and industries of the self-employed (Razin and Langlois, 1992). Industries were grouped into three categories: (1) distribution -- mainly trade, restaurants, and transportation; (2) blue-collar -- mainly manufacturing and construction; and (3) white-collar -- mainly business, public, and personal services. All three variables were associated with industry, although the significance of urban area of residence was somewhat lesser than that of the other two variables. The less educated and those from Asian and African (and in the Canadian case also Latin American) origins tended to concentrate in self-employment distribution activities. Immigrants who engaged in small distribution businesses tended to cluster in the largest and most diversified metropolitan areas -- Tel Aviv, Montreal, and Toronto. For example, self-employed immigrants in Israel, from Asian and African countries, particularly from Iran, gravitated towards retail (Table 5.3) and concentrated in the Tel-Aviv metropolis, which offered the best self-employment opportunities in retail for immigrants. The more educated immigrants and those from Europe and North America gravitated toward white-collar activities, which were less concentrated in the largest metropolitan areas.

A high proportion of the self-employed immigrants who came to Israel from Europe, North America, and South America were

TABLE 5.3
Self-Employed Immigrants by Country of Birth and Selected Industries,
Israel-1983, Canada-1981, California-1980[1]

	Manu- fac- turing	Con- struc- tion	Retail	Food Ser- vices	Business Services	Public, Personal Services	Total[2] (absol. #s)
Israel-1983							
Iran	8.7	1.9	58.2	6.8	1.9	8.8	103
Asia, Africa[3]	19.0	1.4	36.7	4.2	5.6	18.3	142
USSR	16.5	3.7	25.6	8.2	4.7	28.0	571
Europe[4]	17.3	1.8	17.3	2.6	11.4	43.1	272
North America[5]	7.3	5.7	6.5	3.3	18.7	51.2	123
Latin America	17.4	1.2	25.2	7.8	15.0	28.2	167
Canada-1981							
USA, North- western Europe[6]	8.4	14.3	13.6	3.9	21.4	26.6	154
Southern Europe[7]	10.7	22.6	15.5	11.9	3.6	23.8	84
Europe-others[8]	16.7	14.3	19.0	2.4	9.5	23.8	42
Asia[9]	8.9	3.1	34.9	13.0	8.9	13.5	192
Chinese[10]	8.0	5.3	21.3	18.7	13.3	21.3	75
Latin America	14.5	3.6	21.8	1.8	9.1	25.4	55
California-1980							
Latin America	12.4	12.4	10.3	5.7	10.0	20.4	371
China, Taiwan	11.9	4.0	21.3	25.2	10.9	15.3	202
East and south Asia-others	10.1	6.4	23.8	9.9	9.8	23.9	516
Iran	7.6	12.8	21.8	14.3	12.8	18.9	133
Middle East-others	9.2	5.9	34.4	7.5	7.0	24.7	186
Europe[11]	13.0	15.2	11.2	10.3	13.4	21.0	224

1. See note no. 1 for Table 5.2. The table does not include countries of birth classified as others in the Canada and California samples.
2. Including also industries not specified in the table: agriculture, other primary, wholesale, transportation, storage and communication.
3. Not including Iran and South Africa.
4. Including South Africa.
5. Including Oceania.
6. USA, Belgium, Luxembourg, France, Germany, Netherlands, Austria, Ireland, Britain.
7. Yugoslavia, Greece, Italy, Portugal.
8. Mostly East European countries and the USSR.
9. Not including those of Chinese ethnic origin.
10. Chinese ethnic origin born in Asia.
11. Not including the USSR.

engaged in business, public and personal services (Table 5.3). Jerusalem offered ample self-employment opportunities in these activities, linked with its role as Israel's capital and its extraordinarily large public services sector (Razin, 1990). The concentration of white-collar, self-employed immigrants of Western origins in Jerusalem, cannot be regarded as a typical ethnic entrepreneurial enclave, which is usually dominated by distribution or blue-collar activities. Nevertheless, North American and South African immigrants either come to Israel with a greater tradition of enterprise than that characterizing native Israelis, or are pushed into self-employment because they lack the necessary contacts to compete for the few professional job vacancies in the Israeli labor market, which has high rates of job tenure, and a low turnover of employees.

Detailed data for each metropolitan area, which are not presented here, indicate that the interaction of country of birth and urban area of residence, clearly influences the industrial composition of immigrant entrepreneurs in North America but less so in Israel. Various immigrant groups in Canada and California were more active than in Israel in the typical ethnic entrepreneurial niches, other than retail, such as construction and food services (Table 5.3). Self-employed Iranians, for example, were much less concentrated in retail in California than in Israel, showing greater concentrations in construction, food services, and particularly in business, public, and personal services. Such activities of various groups tended to be relatively concentrated in specific metropolitan areas. For example, Southern Europeans were mainly in construction and personal services in Toronto, and the Greeks gravitated particularly to food services in Montreal. Iranians in California were engaged in a varied range of entrepreneurial activities in Los Angeles, while concentrating more in food services in San Francisco (28.6 percent). Chinese entrepreneurs were heavily concentrated in eating and drinking places in San Francisco (34.3 percent), but were engaged in more diversified activities in their smaller and more entrepreneurial community in Los Angeles (Razin, 1988). These examples indicate the existence of localized ethnic entrepreneurial enclaves of various types in North America, influenced both by ethnic resources and local opportunities.

Conclusions

The rate of self-employment among new immigrants in each country or metropolitan area was more strongly influenced by the local opportunity structure, as reflected by the general size and characteristics of the self-employed sector, than by the ethnic resources of the different immigrants. Thus, Canada's economy, being more advanced than the Israeli one, was characterized by higher levels of organizational concentration, which lowered rates of self-employment. In addition, the Canadian economy did not offer some of the niches available for immigrant entrepreneurs in the United States where the existence of large nonentrepreneurial immigrant groups produced more self-employment opportunities for other immigrants. This has lowered Canadian rates of immigrant entrepreneurship, in comparison with, either Israel, or California. Metropolitan socioethnic characteristics, such as the bilingual character of Montreal, and the concentrations of central city minority slums in American cities, also influenced prospects for using particular self-employment opportunities by immigrants.

Still, ethnic origin, approximated by country of birth, had a more central role than location within the country, in predicting the entrepreneurial behavior of individual immigrants. Whereas the overall entrepreneurial activity of immigrants greatly depended on the local opportunity structure, the entrepreneurial behavior of specific immigrant groups in different locations also depended on their place-specific class resources and ethnic networks. The local opportunity structure could have indirectly attracted the more entrepreneurial immigrants to places that offered more ample opportunities for entrepreneurial ventures. However, it seems that a phenomenon such as the extremely high rates of self-employment among Israelis in Los Angeles, while made possible by ample self-employment opportunities not utilized by other immigrant groups, is mainly an unintended outcome of blocked opportunities for advancement in the primary labor market.

Location and ethnicity interact in their influence on self-employment among immigrants more clearly in North America than in Israel. This indicates the existence of localized ethnic entrepreneurial enclaves in North America specializing in various distribution or blue-collar activities. In Israel, the advancement of immigrants with inferior levels of education through entrepreneurial activity was more limited to retail and also to the Tel Aviv metropolis. The high tendency of self-employed immigrants in Israel to engage in white-collar services, and their relative concentration in Jerusalem, differed from the North American experience. These tendencies can be partly attributed to the local opportunity structure, and partly to the attributes of immigrants from Europe and North America who have been mainly middle-class and frequently had ideological-religious motivations for immigration. Their tendency to engage in white-collar self-employment activities in Jerusalem did not represent typical ethnic enclaves. Nevertheless, difficulties in penetrating attractive jobs in public and private organizations increased their propensity to resort to self-employment. The reemerging debate on where to settle new immigrants in Israel, and the increasing role assigned by demographic trends to immigration in future expansion of the labor force in North America, emphasize the significance of patterns identified in the above for future local and regional development trends.

Notes

The study of the Israeli case was supported by grants of the Israel Foundation Trustees and the Fund for Basic Research administered by the Israel Academy of Sciences and Humanities. The study of the Canadian case was done with Andre Langlois from the University of Ottawa, and was supported by the Programme of Canadian Studies of the Hebrew University.

1. For the complete study of the Israeli and Canadian cases, including formal hypotheses and details of the logit and log-linear models, see Razin and Langlois (1990).
2. It has been argued that the new wave of immigrants from the USSR to Israel, commencing in 1989, is more entrepreneurial than the 1970s wave, because the former includes economically motivated immigrants, some with business experience (Shapiro, 1990). The scarcity of well paying job opportunities in the stagnating Israeli economy may also drive these new immigrants to entrepreneurial ventures.

References

Amin, A., and K. Robins. 1990. "Industrial Districts and Regional Development: Limits and Possibilities," In *Industrial Districts and Inter-Firm Cooperation in Italy*, edited by F. Pyke et al. Geneva: ILO.

Anderson, Alan B., and James S. Frideres. 1981. *Ethnicity in Canada*. Toronto: Butterworths.

Anderson, Grace M. 1974. *Networks of Contact: the Portuguese and Toronto*. Waterloo, Ont: Wilfrid Laurier University.

Ben Porath, Yoram. 1986. *The Israeli Economy, Maturing Through Crises*. Cambridge, MA: Harvard University Press.

Blau, David M. 1987. "A Time Series Analysis of Self-Employment." *Journal of Political Economy* 95: 445-67.

Bonacich, Edna, and John Modell. 1980. *The Economic Basis of Ethnic Solidarity*. Berkeley: University of California Press.

Brock, William A., and David S. Evans. 1989. "Small Business Economics." *Small Business Economics* 1: 7-20.

Brusco, S. 1982. "The Emilian Model: Productive Decentralization and Social Integration." *Cambridge Journal of Economics* 6:167-84.

Cohen, Gary L. 1988. *Enterprising Canadians: The Self-Employed in Canada*. 71-536. Ottawa: Statistics Canada.

Desbarats, Jacqueline. 1985. "Indochinese Resettlement in the United States." *Annals of the Association of American Geographers* 75: 522-38.

Goldberg, Michael A., and John Mercer. 1986. *The Myth of the North American City*. Vancouver: University of British Columbia Press.

Greenwood, N. 1990. "The Nightmares of Israeli Small Business." Jerusalem: Policy Studies, Division for Economic Policy Research.

Hiebert, D. 1993. "Integrating Production and Consumption in the Canadian City: Industry, Class, Ethnicity and Neighborhood," In *The Social Geography of Canadian Cities*, edited by D. Ley and L. S. Bourne. Kingston, Ont: McGill-Queen's University Press.

Higgins, Benjamin. 1986. *The Rise and Fall? of Montreal*. Moncton: Canadian Institute for Research on Regional Development.

Inbar, M., and C. Adler. 1977. *Ethnic Integration in Israel*. New Brunswick, NJ: Transaction.

Johannisson, Bengt. 1988. "Regional Variations in Emerging Entrepreneurial Networks." Paper presented at the 28th European Congress of the Regional Science Association, Stockholm.

Kallen, E., and M. Kelner. 1983. *Ethnicity, Opportunity and Successful Entrepreneurship in Canada*. Toronto: York University.

Keeble, David, and Egbert Wever. 1986. *New Firms and Regional Development in Europe*. London: Croom Helm.

Keely, Charles B., and Patricia J. Elwell. 1981. "International Migration: Canada and the United States." In *Global Trends in Migration*, edited by M. M. Kritz et al. New York: Center for Migration Studies.

Ladbury, Sarah. 1984. "Choice, Chance or No Alternative? Turkish Cypriots in Business in London." In *Ethnic Communities in Business*, edited by R. Ward and R. Jenkins. Cambridge: Cambridge University Press.

Light, Ivan. 1984. "Immigrant and Ethnic Enterprise in North America." *Ethnic and Racial Studies* 7: 195-216.

Light, Ivan, and Carolyn Rosenstein. 1989. "Demand Factors in Entrepreneurship." Paper presented at a Conference on New Forms of Entrepreneurship under the auspices of the Research Committee on Economy and Society of the International Sociological Association, Milan.

Light Ivan, and Angel A. Sanchez. 1987. "Immigrant Entrepreneurs in 272 SMSAs." *Sociological Perspectives* 30: 373-99.

Lithwick, N. Harvey. 1987. "Regional Development Policies: Context and Consequences." In *Still Living Together*, edited by W. J. Coffey and M. Polese. Montreal: The Institute for Research on Public Policy.

Malarek, Victor. 1987. *Haven's Gate, Canada's Immigration Fiasco*. Toronto: Macmillan of Canada.

Mars, Gerald, and Robin Ward. 1984. "Ethnic Business Development in Britain: Opportunities and Resources." In *Ethnic Communities in Business*, edited by R. Ward and R. Jenkins. Cambridge: Cambridge University Press.

Nahon, Yaacov. 1989. *Self-Employed Workers -- the Ethnic Dimension*. Jerusalem: The Jerusalem Institute for Israel Studies (in Hebrew).

Nash, Alan. 1987. *The Economic Impact of the Entrepreneur Immigrant Program*. Ottawa: Studies in Social Policy.

Ossenberg, Richard J. 1964. "The Social Integration and Adjustment of Post-War Immigrants in Montreal and Toronto." *Canadian Review of Sociology and Anthropology* 1: 202-14.

Peterson, R. 1977. *Small Business, Building a Balanced Economy*. Erin, Ontario: Porcepic.

Piore, Michael J., and Charles F. Sabel. 1984. *The Second Industrial Divide*. New York: Basic Books.

Portes, Alejandro, and Robert L. Bach. 1985. *Latin Journey, Cuban and Mexican Immigrants in the United States*. Berkeley: University of California Press.

Ramcharan, Subhas. 1982. *Racism, Nonwhites in Canada*. Toronto: Butterworths.

Razin, Eran. 1988. "Entrepreneurship Among Foreign Immigrants in the Los Angeles and San Francisco Metropolitan Regions." *Urban Geography* 9: 283-301.

Razin, Eran. 1989. "Relating Theories of Entrepreneurship Among Ethnic Groups and Entrepreneurship in Space -- the Israeli Case." *Geografiska Annaler* 71B: 167-81.

Razin, Eran. 1990. "Spatial Variations in the Israeli Small-Business Sector: Implications for Regional Development Policies." *Regional Studies* 24: 149-62.

Razin, Eran. 1991. "Stages in the Development of Israel's Spatial Industrialization Policy," In *Location and Labour Considerations for Regional Development*, edited by F. Dietz, W. Heijman, and D. Shefer. Aldershot: Avebury.

Razin, Eran, and Andre Langlois. 1992. "Location and Entrepreneurship Among New Immigrants in Israel and Canada." *Geography Research Forum* 12: 16-36.

Sanders, Jim M., and Victor Nee. 1987. "Limits of Ethnic Solidarity in the Enclave Economy." *American Sociological Review* 52: 745-73.

Savoie, D. J. 1987. "Establishing the Atlantic Canada Opportunities Agency." Unpublished report, Moncton, NB: Institut Canadien de Recherche sur le Developpement Regional.

Scott, Allen J. 1988. *Metropolis*. Berkeley: University of California Press.

Shachar, A. S. 1971. "Israel's Development Towns, Evaluation of National Urbanization Policy." *Journal of the American Institute of Planners* 37: 362-72.

Shapiro, I. 1990. "The Private Initiative of the Immigrants of 90." *Ha'aretz*, 9 March (in Hebrew).

Sobel, Zvi. 1986. *Migrants from the Promised Land*. New Brunswick, NJ: Transaction.

Statistics Canada. 1984. *Canada's Immigrants, 1981 Census of Canada*. Ottawa.

Storey, David J. 1988. "The Role of Small and Medium-Sized Enterprises in European Job Creation: Key Issues for Policy and Research." In *Small and Medium Size Enterprises and Regional Development*, edited by M. Giaoutzi et al. London: Routledge.

Storper, Michael, and Allen J. Scott. 1989. "The Geographical Foundations and Social Regulation of Flexible Production Complexes." In *The Power of Geography: How Territory Shapes Social Life*, edited by J. Walch and M. Dear. Winchester, MA: Unwin Hyman.

United Nations. 1982. *International Migration Policies and Programmes: A World Survey*. Population Studies, No. 80. New York: Department of International Economic and Social Affairs.

Waldinger, Roger. 1986. *Through the Eye of the Needle: Immigrants and Enterprise in New York's Garment Trades*. New York: New York University Press.

Ward, Robin. 1987. "Ethnic Enterprises in Britain and Europe." In *Entrepreneurship in Europe*, edited by R. Goffee and R. Scase. London: Croom Helm.

Wickberg, Edgar. 1982. *From China to Canada*. Toronto: McClelland and Stewart.

6

Immigrant Entrepreneurs in France

Gildas Simon
Translated by Jeffrey Arsham and Ivan Light

Scientific studies of ethnic entrepreneurship in France got underway fifteen years ago. They coincided with the 1974 economic crisis
and its adverse implications for migration. Naturally this coincidence
was not the result of chance. The economic crisis encouraged the
shift of immigrant employees to self-employment, and so prompted
research on this theme. A thematic reading of this literature reveals
the convergence of three approaches linked to disciplinary affiliations
of geographers, sociologists, and anthropologists. Economists have
shown little interest in immigrant entrepreneurs.

Approach Deriving from Societies of Origin

Some studies proceed from knowledge of the sending country and
its migratory and professional relations with the receiving country
(Simon, 1990). For example, on the basis of our knowledge of
groups of tradespeople originating from Southern Tunisia and now
residing in Paris, we have clarified the process of retail food store
start-ups in Paris commercial space (Costes, 1988; Guillon and Ma
Mung, 1986), the transfer of traditional Maghreb professional and
community practices and their positive adaptation to the commercial
and social environment of large urban agglomerations (Kerrou,

1987; Simon, 1976, 1979). The role of community resources --
"community" is meant culturally and financially -- in the settling in
France of immigrant tradesmen who derive from specific communities of the pre-Saharan regions of Maghreb (Jerbians and Ghomrasni
from Tunisia, Mozabits from Algeria, and Soussi from Morocco),
the practice and mastery of a transnational migration (for example,
concerning investments), the effects of such community migrations in
the countries of origin -- all of these topics were amply developed in
the studies of Boubakri (1984, 1985,) and in the recent thesis of Ait
Ouaziz (1989).

Urban Analysis

The second approach is based upon the ever more visible presence
of foreign shops in the large French agglomerations of the Paris-
Lyons-Marseilles axis, the major triangle of Mediterranean and
Maghreb settlement in France (Alain, 1979). This is the best
explored research path. Of these studies, the case study of a neighborhood or the business fabric in an immigrant neighborhood constitutes the most frequent approach: "La Porte d'Aix" in Marseilles
(Carreno, Hayot, and Lesme, 1974; Dahan, 1985); the old downtown neighborhoods in Lyons (Ariese, 1987); "La Goutte d'Or"
(Khelifa, 1979; Vuddamalay, 1985; Toubon and Messamah, 1988),
"le Temple" (Abeles, 1983), "le Sentier" in the central part of Paris;
and "le Marche d'Aligre" (De Rudder and Guillon, 1986), the Chinese district of the thirteenth arrondissement in the southeast of Paris
(Live, 1989; Guillon and Taboada-Leonetti, 1986). These neighborhood studies have enabled researchers to refine concepts tied to ethnic businesses, to spotlight marking and appropriation of space
(Raulin, 1986, 1988), and to elaborate the modalities of ethnic settlement in cities.

Both public and private agencies have supported social science
research in immigrant entrepreneurship; this support has -- thanks to
the financial and technical resources provided -- paved the way for
multiple investigations of extensive geographic and demographic
scope. So it is that the report of the MIGRINTER team (1986)
financed by the Ministry of Social Affairs is based upon over 300

surveys of establishments in the Paris metropolitan region and the eastern provinces. Recently updated and published (Ma Mung and Simon, 1990), this monograph illuminates Maghrebian and Asian businesses in France (start-up capital, turnover, profits) and the extensive mobility of immigrant business owners within this ethno-economic circuit.

Theoretical Research on the Foreign Artisan Class

The third recent research approach focuses upon the foreign arti-san class, its renewal through contact with the industrial system and the underground economy, its booster role in professional success, and its social integration (Morokvasic, 1988; Pallida, 1988; Auvolat and Bennatig, 1988; Garson and Mouhoud, 1987; Salem, 1981). Although dozens of colloquiums on worker migration have taken place since 1970, it was only at the end of 1987 that the first scientific gathering on "the migrant as economic actor" at long last took place. This meeting and its preparation (ARIESE, 1987) began attempts at theorizing ethnic entrepreneurship in Europe using a cultural and comparative approach analogous to Werbner's studies of Manchester and Light's of the United States.

The relative recency of interest and the lack of critical distance in French research explain the gaps and backlogs of reflection on certain themes in comparison with investigations conducted in Great Britain and the United States, particularly as regards historical analysis of the phenomenon and the role of ethnic communities as middleman minorities.

Entrepreneurs as a New Ethnic Category

The rapid development of foreign entrepreneurship in France has aroused acute interest in political, economic, and social life. The high visibility of foreign (notably Maghrebian) businesses in the little town of Dreux has been perceived by a sizable percentage of the local people as evidence of excessive immigration. Some observers have declared minority domination of the business sector one of the principal factors that explain the success of the rightist National

Front candidate in the 1989 local elections.

French Immigration History

The French have been debating immigration for a century. One hundred years ago, presenting a bill hostile to foreigners, a deputy declared, "The foreigner is everywhere, he invades banks, high finance, and even the liberal professions, he profitably monopolizes certain business, certain industries which up until now, were in the hands of the French." The number of foreign managers in industry and commerce was formerly higher than it is now: 121,000 in 1911, 60,830 in 1982, 89,945 in 1988, and the percentage of self-employed in the active foreign population was four times greater than today's: 20.4 percent in 1911; only 5.8 percent in 1988.

Prior to World War I, the overwhelming majority of craftsmen and foreign businessmen was composed of Europeans generally coming from neighboring countries. About one third were Belgians who generally specialized in hotels and cafés. Another one third were Italians traditionally working in construction. The remaining third consisted of Swiss (hotels, watches and clocks, woodwork), as well as Germans and Eastern European Jews. In the aftermath of the Bolshevik revolution, Russians arrived. Everyone knows that many Russian aristocrats became Paris taxi drivers in the 1920s. The first Chinese also opened Parisian businesses in the early 1920s, contemporaneous with the arrival of Algerian and Moroccan shopkeepers in Marseilles and in the industrial suburbs north of Paris (Haddiya, 1981). These migration waves diversified the ethnic landscape of France between the world wars. Thenceforth, more than half of the foreign entrepreneurs resided in the Paris metropolitan area. And within pluri-ethnic neighborhoods of Paris ("Sentier," "Goutte d'Or") commercial and artisan areas developed, especially garment-manufacture and sale, that profoundly affected the spatial arrangement of these neighborhoods in ways still visible today (Toubon and Messamah, 1988).

The Great Depression, the protectionism it released (the special identity card bearing a "tradesman" designation dates from November 1938), the German occupation, and the anti-Semitic persecutions and deportations hit hard at the business owners and artisans of the Parisian urban district. These successive shocks explain the overall decline in the number of foreign entrepreneurs after World War II. There were only 40,700 in 1968. Two structural factors augmented the effects of the foregoing: the constant decline of self-employed labor relative to salaried labor (the latter has taken on particular importance for immigrants), and also the integrative role of self-employment in French society. Many foreign entrepreneurs have obtained French naturalization before and after World War II.

Revival of and Changes in Foreign Entrepreneurship since the Economic Crisis

The upsurge of foreign entrepreneurship in France was particularly marked in the 1970s and the 1980s; according to official sources, the numbers of industrial and commercial managers doubled (Guillon, 1986). Foreign managers presently represent 5.8 percent of the active non-French population, while 5 percent of industrial and commercial managers are foreign. But if we take into account the projected number of entrepreneurs of foreign origin a generation from now, we had better double the figures just cited. Thus, in 1982 the number of naturalized managers -- whose ethnic origins often remain distinctly perceptible -- was slightly superior to that of foreign self-employed (sixty-eight thousand as opposed to sixty-two thousand). On the basis of this statistic, we estimate that there existed in France as of 1989 around 160,000 entrepreneurs of foreign origin. This category constitutes an incontestably dynamic element in the nation's economic life. If we set aside buyouts or takeovers of agricultural concerns -- a movement that has long since existed in the agriculture of northern and southwestern France, and has taken on new vigor with the imminence of the single European agricultural market -- current estimates attribute 5 to 10 percent of the set-ups and sales of business and artisanal establishments to entrepreneurs who are either immigrants or of recent immigrant origin.

The upsurge of foreign entrepreneurship is particularly impressive at a time when overall employment trends were diametrically opposed. Official statistics illustrate the continued decline in France of the self-employed: 1,995,000 in 1968, but only 1,738,000 in 1982. From the French census of 1982 through 1987, the number of native French entrepreneurs declined by 3.0 percent, whereas that of foreign-born entrepreneurs increased 46.7 percent: 30.2 percent for artisans, 64 percent for businessmen, 88 percent for other services.

Several factors help to explain this revival in France of immigrant entrepreneurship and the consequently increased visibility of the phenomenon, particularly in the most important French cities.

The crisis in immigrant employment. In France as in the other immigrant-receiving countries of the European Economic Community, the economic crisis has reduced the number and quality of salaried jobs traditionally held by immigrants. Areas in which the proportion of foreigners was the greatest are often those in which the economic crisis has been the most serious. Mining, the iron and steel industry, and construction lost hundreds of thousands of jobs between 1975 and 1982, many of which were occupied by foreigners. The continuous restructuring of the automobile industry, due to automation, has also eliminated numerous unskilled jobs. The unemployment of foreigners has become higher than that of the French: 11.7 percent (end of 1988) as opposed to 10 percent. The primary and secondary sectors have emptied out, while tertiary (and particularly independent) activities have waxed into fullness. Severance pay and indemnities in the mines and the automobile industry ("la Regie Renault") have financed Moroccan workers' setting or buying up of a business concern (MIGRINTER, 1986). Our own surveys have shown that for numerous Maghrebian immigrants it was less the loss than the fear of losing a salaried job that triggered the conversion of the salaried to independent work. Prior to setting up on their own behalf, nearly half of the Moroccan businessmen in Paris had been on the payroll in the coal mines of the North (7 percent) and especially in industry (36 percent), for over ten years on the average. No doubt, the realization of a business project in France was often part and parcel of the migratory project of the ethnic group (the Berbers of southern Morocco or the southern Moroccans from Souss), but the crisis in employment accelerated this evolution. The phenomenon is less striking among Asiatics, of whom the overwhelming majority

(83 percent) of interviewed business owners had never received a paycheck in France prior to setting-up on their own.

The role of the regulatory system. The turnaround in French immigration policy -- the replacement of "laissez faire" by strict regulation and the curtailment of worker immigration -- has paradoxically encouraged the installation of immigrants in the independent (or self-employed) sector (Lebon, 1990). Up until the strict regulation stemming from the laws of 17 July 1984 and 22 May 1987, the administrative status of foreign entrepreneurs was especially complex and confusing. No less than fifteen circulars, often mutually contradictory, had been drawn up by the various concerned Ministries (Trade, Justice, Home Affairs, Finances) between 1964 and 1975. If one took subtle advantage of the loopholes in the regulations, it was at times easier to obtain a tradesman's card than a residency permit! This said, such ways of using the rules were especially beneficial to members of groups who already, before leaving for France, had a trading tradition; they were also aware of the "culture" of the French system of administration, that it is to say its intricacies and the areas into which it did not reach (Ma Mung and Simon, 1990).

Following the 1984 law, administration has been simplified; an overwhelming majority of the immigrants no longer need apply for that tradesman's card. Such at least is the case for "residents" under general jurisdiction (for example, Moroccans, Turks, Algerians, EEC nationals, Americans, etc.).

Exercising certain professions remains prohibited for foreigners under general jurisdiction, and nonsedentary business activities are strictly regulated. Nonetheless, this recent evolution of rules and regulations has provided the would-be tradesman with free access to self-employment; it has also favored an increase of requests registered by the "Chambres de Commerce et de Metiers" at the end of the 1980s.

The introduction of new ethnic groups. In comparison with the interwar period, the demographic composition of the self-employed in France has changed profoundly, in conformity with immigration-induced changes in France. Except for the Italians, whose proportion remains considerable (24 percent of the self-employed), the change in nationalities is extreme.

In 1982, about two-thirds of immigrant entrepreneurs were of Mediterranean origin. Southern Europeans (Italians, Spanish, Portuguese) were more strongly represented among artisans. Among the Italians, for instance, there was only one business owner for every four artisans. Maghrebians (Algerians, Moroccans, Tunisians) comprise the majority of business owners. Among Algerians, there were three business owners for each nonbusiness owner (Ma Mung and Simon, 1990; Stora, 1985).

Other groups have only recently come on strong in the self-employed sector: the refugees from Southeast Asia (majority of Chinese origin), and lately, Turks whose business networks are developing with great rapidity in eastern France and the Paris area.

Contemporary Dynamics of Business Start-Ups

The contemporary development of foreign entrepreneurship in France derives from three dynamics that work together, more often than apart:

- the dynamic of Maghrebian tradesman
- the development of foreigner artisanship: the case of Portuguese artisans in the construction industry
- the social dynamic of the second generation

The Community Dynamic of Maghrebian Tradesmen

A community dynamic is at the root of the recent development of small immigrant businesses in France, among Maghrebians as well as Asians. The case of the Maghrebians is particularly telling. Within this group, the overwhelming majority of business owners come from the Berber communities whose regions border the Sahara Desert: Jerbiens and Jebalias from southern Tunisia, the Mozabits of the Algerian Sahara, and the Soussi from southern Morocco (area of Agadir and the Anti-Atlas). Ninety percent of the Moroccan business owners in the urban districts originate from Souss.

These three communities have a long-standing migratory and trading tradition throughout the Maghreb where they have monopolized retail and generally wholesale commerce as well; this activity has in turn impelled and propped up a trade bourgeoisie with strongholds in major metropolitan areas and national capitals. Political (conflict between Morocco and Algeria) or economic (state takeover of businesses in Algeria and Tunisia) reasons brought about their transfer to France in the early 1970s; the uprooted Maghrebians bought the businesses of French family firms which were having trouble competing with large-scale shopping centers. The trades and commerces they opened up are of three basic types:

- Routine neighborhood trade. This is the case with "local" grocery stores whose products are intended for French customers in the wealthy areas (seventh, eighth arrondissements) and western suburbs of Paris (Neuilly, Versailles). Their sales advantages reside in long hours. Maghrebian shops remain open twelve to fifteen hours a day, even during weekends and summer vacation.

- "Intracommunity" trade whose products and services are intended for co-ethnic customers in the neighborhood, for example, "popular" restaurants with North African cooking in old industrial suburbs of Paris (St. Denis, Gennevilliers), Oriental clothes stores in the "Goutte d'Or."

- "Exotic" trade, which offers specific products intended for French customers who want something different. This is the case with ordinary or luxury restaurants mixing Maghrebian with European cooking (Ma Mung, 1989). Spatially speaking, exotic trade can spread into areas with weak foreign colonies and also, conversely, into neighborhoods highly frequented by tourists (for example, the Latin Quarter in Paris).

Taken as a whole, these three trades owe their economic success to the resources of the community system of the business owners. The start-up capital for the purchase of the establishment is essentially raised within the group of origin. Among Moroccans, no less than 77 percent of the tradesmen interviewed in Paris assembled start-up capital with loans from their close relatives or co-ethnics. The would-be enterpreneur seldom has recourse to the bank system; French banks are often reluctant to grant loans to foreigners whose solvency is uncertain.

The functioning of these Maghrebian trades derives in nearly all areas from its community-based dynamic: co-ethnic customers (except "exotic" trades), use of family labor, employment of co-ethnic workers, management of one or several establishments by two or three operators coming from the extended family, resale of establishments into the co-ethnic circuit. To be sure, failures occur (poor location, intracommunity conflicts, competition from super-markets), but generally speaking, economic success is frequent in this type of system, as is proven by reinvestment of profits in France and -- more and more commonly -- in the countries of origin. Thus, the Soussi people, whose business firms are increasing in France, have set up large-scale businesses in their region of origin (financing hotels in Agadir, first seaside resort in Morocco), and likewise in Casablanca, incontestably the leading economic metropolis of this country.

Portuguese Artisans in the Construction Industry

Along with a community system based on solidarity and member-ship, a differing logic of entrepreneurship has also developed; it is founded on an enterprising spirit, the sense of individual success, and the hope for social mobility. We have chosen the example of the Portuguese in the construction industry. This example is not meant to imply that the current upsurge of foreign artisanship is due uniquely to this individualist dynamic. The ethnic system is also quite efficacious in these sorts of activities, as is illustrated by the garment industry circuits in Paris within the Chinese communities of the thirteenth arrondissement (home workshops in the southeast of the city) and, a fortiori, the highly complex case of the "Sentier" (cf. Morokvasic 1987, 1988).

In comparison with the interwar period, the role of construction in foreign artisanship has sharply gone up. Now it has reached 40 per-cent of employed foreign artisans. Southern Europeans represent a clear majority, and the proportion of Portuguese is steadily growing, while that of the Italians and Spaniards is declining because business set-ups do not replace closures.

Survey research led to the conclusion that Portuguese artisanship is attributable more to individual or family considerations than to community-type processes, even though the Portuguese immigrant community in France is known for its networks and vigorous social associations. A study presently underway in the Toulouse region illustrates high scatteration in the provenance of Portuguese of whom 90 percent worked in the construction industry; among three-hundred-thirty artisans, we found at least one-hundred-sixty different places of origin (concelhos) in Portugal (Poinard, 1990).

The individual will to succeed is strongly pronounced but does not suffice. Recent studies (Auvolat and Bennatig, 1988) have insisted on the open-mindedness of these artisans, who are often younger than their French colleagues; emphasis has also been placed on their enduring connections with their industry. Quite often, these ties generate subcontracting. Subcontracting may well result from the continued viability of the relational network that the ex-immigrant worker conserved from his prior employment in large-scale construction concerns (Auvolat and Benattig, 1988), but it can also mask abusive and cavalier dismissal and the reduction of the wage earner to toiler and drudge (Poinard, 1990).

Be that as it may, current prospects for these artisans are favorable inasmuch as, after ten years of crises and slumps, the construction industry which has experienced a phase of recovery and rehiring of personnel since 1987. In this respect, self-employed Portuguese artisans will have little difficulty recruiting Portuguese employees through either seasonal contracts or the networks of clandestine workers that have functioned continuously since the official halt (1974) of immigration in France.

The Social Dynamic of the Second Generation

A third dynamic is emerging in the milieu of foreign entrepreneurship in France. It issues from the will of the second generation immigrants to become integrated into the French social system through economic success. This movement concerns young people of Maghrebian and Portuguese origin. In comparison with the traditionalism of their parents or group of origin, the second generation's determination to modernize is powerful. For example, as entrepreneurs, they look for ways to accommodate the new needs of customers: Tunisians, for instance, are passing from the restaurant-pastry shops to the fast food outlets, and from small business to export-import with Tunisia.

But more frequently there ensues a rupture with the classical life plan of the family or group of origin; the educational level of the young has risen, and they do not wish to reproduce the status quo. They cannot bear the cramped existence of their tradesman or artisan parents. They have innovated frequently in the fields of transportation, business services (supermarket security), computer science, advertising, and mass media. In contrast to their immigrant elders, young people do not hesitate to use banks and especially the different forms of public and private assistance, such as the French Enterprise Foundation, that assist in the setting up of enterprises. Failure is common and yet a dynamic has been launched; prospects of social integration help to ensure its permanence.

Conclusion

Naturally, prospects for the European common market raise many questions about the economic future that these ethnic entrepreneurs face in trade and services (Simon and Ma Mung, 1990). Questions bear upon the migration policy and the administrative regulations that will be applied to these nationals of "third" countries and the capacity of the immigrants to deal with them; the uncertainty also has to do with the economic dynamic of the industries in which these groups play a role, and their ability to adapt to the new givens. One wonders, finally, about the possibilities of associations and articulations between ethnic trade and French trade in the interest of resisting competitive onslaughts from other countries or in exporting.

We hypothesize that, disposing of financial potentials and human resources readily mobilizable in a familial and ethnic framework, these ethnic entrepreneurs are hardly destined to be the latecomers of the 1992 adventure.

Notes

1.   MIGRINTER is a scientific team associated with the University of Poitiers Centre National de les Recherche Scientifique. It specializes in the study of international immigration.

2. INSFF: Institut National de la Statistique et des Etudes Economiques.
3. Sentier, in the central part of Paris.
4. Goutte d'Or: in the northeast part of Paris.
5. From 40,724 in 1968, it increased to 50,185 in 1975; 60,830 in 1982; and 89,945 in 1988: source INSEE. R. G. P. Enquêtes sur l'emploi.

References

Abeles, M. 1983. "Un Espace Marchand à Paris. Le Carreau du Temple." *Revue d'Ethnologie Francaise* 1: 47-60.

Ait Ouaziz, R. 1989. "Les Commercants Soussi dans l'Agglomération Parisienne: Insertion Spatiale et Relations avec le Pays d'Origine (Maroc)." *Thèse de 3e Cycle de Géographie.* Université de Poitiers.

Alain, L. 1979. *Le Commerce Indépendent, le Phenomène Maghrebin: Paris et la Region Parisienne.* Paris: Edition CIGMA.

ARIESE. 1987. *Commerces et Entrepreneurs Ethniques.* Colloquium, Université de Lyon II.

Auvolat, M., and R. Benattig. 1988. "Les Artisans Étrangers en France." *Revue Européenne des Migrations Internationales,* 3: pp. 37-55.

Boubakri, H. 1984. "La Restauration Tunisienne à Paris." *Etudes Méditerraneennes* fasc. no. 7, Poitiers, pp. 51-114.

Boubakri, H. 1985. "Modes de Gestion et Reinvestissement chez les Commercants Tunisiens à Paris." *Revue Européenne des Migrations Internationales* 1: 49-66.

Boubakri, H. 1985. "Le Petit Commerce Immigré du Sud Tunisien à Paris." Thèse de 3e Cycle de Géographie, Université de Strasbourg.

Carreno, J.A., Hayot, F., and F. Lesme. 1974. "Le Quartier de la Porte d'Aix." Aix-en-Provence: CRESM.

Costes, L. 1988. "Les Petits Commercants du Métro Parisien." *Revue Européenne des Migrations Internationales* 4: 57-71.

Dahan, J. 1985. "Le Fonctionnement Commercial du Quartier Belsunce, Marseille." Unpublished paper.

De Rudder, V., and M. Guillon. 1986. *Autochtones et Immigrés en Quartier Populaire: D'Aligre à l'Ilôt Châlon.* Paris: CIEMI-L'Harmattan.

Garson, J. P., and E. M. Mouhoud. 1987. "Sous-traitance et Dévalorisation Formelle dans le Bâtiment et les Travaux Publics." Colloque Européen sur le Travail Non-Salarié, Paris, pp. 135-171.

Guillon, M. 1986. "Les Commercants Étrangers en France." States 1: 1-23.

Guillon, M., and E. Ma Mung. 1986. "Les Commercants Étrangers dans l'Agglomération Parisienne." *Revue Européenne des Migrations Internationales* 2: 105-134.

Guillon, M., and I. Taboada-Leonetti. 1986. *Le Triangle de Choisy; un Quartier Chinois à Paris*. Paris. CIEMI-L'Harmattan.

Haddiya, E. M. 1981. "L'Immigré Marocain sur les Marchés Francais." *Al Asas* 44: 35-38.

Kerrou, M. 1987. "Du Colportage à la Boutique, les Commercants Maghrébins en France." *Hommes et Migrations* 1105: 26-34.

Khelifa, M. 1979. "La Goutte d'Or." *Hommes et Migrations* 970: 19-75.

Lebon, A. 1990. "Le Point sur l'Immigration et la Présence Étrangère en France." *Documents Affaires Sociales*, La Documentation Francaise, p. 119

Light, I. 1972. *Ethnic Enterprise in America*. Berkeley and Los Angeles: University of California.

Live, Y. 1989. "La Diaspora Chinoise en France, Immigration, Activités Économiques et Adaptation." Thèse de Sociologie, EHESS Paris

Ma Mung, E., and G. Simon. 1990. *Commercants Maghrébins et Asiatiques en France*. Paris: Masson.

MIGRINTER. 1986. "Les Maghrébins de la Régie Renault: Solidarités Communautaires et Implications au Maghreb." *Revue Européenne des Migrations Internationales* vol.2, 1: 137-161.

Morokvasic, M. 1988. "Le Comportement Économique des Immigrés dans le Secteur de la Confection." In *Le Recours aux Immigrés dans la Confection à Paris*. Paris: La Documentation Francaise.

Pallida, S. 1988. "L'Immigration Entre l'Économie Ethnique et l'Économie Souterraine," Communication au Colloque International de Vaucresson GRECO 13, Janvier.

Poinard, M. 1990. "Les Artisans Portugais à Toulouse," *Table Ronde Poitiers*.

Raulin, A. 1986. "Mise en Scène des Commercants Maghrébins Parisiens." *Terrain* 7: 24-33.

Raulin, A. 1988. "Espaces Marchands et Concentrations Urbaines Minoritaires, La Petite Asie à Paris." *Cahiers Internationaux de Sociologie* 85: 225-242.

Salem, G. 1981. "De Dakar à Paris, des Diasporas d'Artisans et de Commercants: Etude Socio-Géographique du Commerce Sénégalais en France." Thèse de 3e Cycle EHESS Paris.

Salem, G. 1981. "De la Brousse Sénégalaise au Boul'Mich; le Système Commercial Mouride en France." *Les Cahiers d'Etudes Africaines* no. 81-83, pp. 267-88.

Salem, G. 1983. "Investissements Immobiliers des Travailleurs Migrants et Stratégies de Groupe dans le Grand Dakar (Senegal)." *Etudes Méditerraneennes* 4: 62-70.

Simon, G. 1976. "Une Approche du Petit Commerce Étranger en France:

Exemple des Commercants Tunisiens." *Recherches sur les Migrations*, 1 (Janvier-Mars): 21-31, ERMI-CNRS.

Simon, G. 1979. "L'Espace des Travailleurs Tunisiens en France. Structures et Fonctionnement d'un Champ Migratoire International," Thèse de Géographie, Université de Poitiers.

Simon, G. and E. Ma Mung. 1990. "La Dynamique des Commerces Maghrébins et Asiatiques et les Perspectives du Marché Unique Européen." *Annales de Géographie* 552 (Mars-Avril): 152-172.

Simon, G. 1990. *Les Effets de la Migration Internationale dans les Pays d'Origine: Le Cas du Maghreb*. Paris: CDU, SEDES.

Stora, B. 1985. "Avant la Deuxieme Génération: le Militantisme Algérien en France (1926-1954)." *Revue Européenne des Migrations Internationales* 1: 69-94.

Toubon, J. C., and K. Messamah. 1988. "La Goutte d'Or: Constitution, Modes d'Appropriation et Fonctionnement d'un Espace Pluri-ethnique," IAURIF, Rapport au Ministère de l'Equipement et du Logement, 617 PX (voir "activites commerciales," pp. 214-266).

URA 1145 MIGRINTER. 1985. *Commercants Maghrebins et Asiatiques: Insertion Spatiale et Fonctions Socio-economiques dans les Grandes Villes Francaises*. Rapport au Ministere des Affaires Sociales et de la Solidarité Nationale, Décembre.

Vuddamalay, V. 1985. "La Goutte d'Or, un Pôle Commercial Immigré," Mémoire de l'Institut d'Urbanisme de Creteil.

7

Asian Indians in Southern California: Occupations and Ethnicity

Karen B. Leonard and Chandra S. Tibrewal

The Asian-Indian population of the United States has grown from 70,000 in 1970 to 387,000 in 1980. California is a major destination for Asian-Indian immigrants. These immigrants follow a broad range of occupations (see appendices 7.1 and 7.2), but many run small businesses. According to the Southern California Associations of Governments, the Los Angeles area has the greatest concentration of small businesses in the United States, and Asian immigrants, Indians among them, have contributed heavily to that record.

Desai's (1963) and Bhachu's (1985) work on South Asian immigrants in Britain provide a useful comparative chronology for the experience of South Asians in California. The very earliest South Asian migrants to Britain were seamen who married non-Indian women. These were followed by male Punjabis and Gujaratis, peddlers and industrial workers, who left their families in India and only gradually brought over their wives and children. From the mid-1960s Britain enjoyed a further expansion of this immigrant population, an expansion that initially drew upon India and Pakistan, and then East Africa and Bangledesh in the early 1970s. The East African Sikhs came as family units, old and young together. These East African Asians ranked at the top of Britain's Asian immigrant groups in 1989, with the highest percentage of managerial and professional jobs and the lowest percentage of unskilled workers.

In California, too, the earliest Asian-Indian immigrants were predominantly men who married non-Indian women and followed non-professional occupations, while the later immigrants are urban professionals arriving in family units. Asian-Indian immigrants began coming to California in the early twentieth century. Like other Asians before them, these early immigrants met strong prejudices institutionalized in both law and social custom. Euro-American perceptions of racial difference even subjected the Punjabi men to California's antimiscegenation laws, which prohibited marriage between whites and nonwhites. These discriminatory laws governing citizenship, immigration, and marriage changed only after the Second World War: South Asians became eligible for U.S. citizenship and limited immigration began in 1946; California's anti-miscegenation laws were repealed in 1948.

In the United States, immigration for Asians really opened up with the 1965 Immigration and Nationality Act. The discriminatory laws governing immigration and access to occupations were then removed. The large number of Asian-Indian professional immigrants testifies to the opportunities available here and to their ability to seize those opportunities (they have been educated in English). In 1987, some twenty-five thousand to sixty thousand Asian Indians were settled throughout southern California, with clusters in Cerritos, Norwalk, Artesia, Fountain Valley, and other areas, but without densely populated ethnic enclaves like Southall or Bradford in Britain. In Southern California, the two largest groups are the Punjabi and Gujarati speakers (about 20 percent each), followed by Urdu speakers (18 percent), Hindi speakers (16 percent), and speakers of South Indian languages (12 percent) and Bengali (11 percent) (estimates from Hossain, 1982: 75-76, and Thompson and Yodh, 1985: 59). Unlike the earlier immigrants, few newcomers have gone to rural areas, although there has been a new Sikh migration to Yuba City (La Brack, 1988).

The initial phase of post-1965 Asian-Indian immigration featured professionals and their families, but this situation is changing. In the 1980 Census, Asian-Indian immigrants exhibited a high educational

and income profile, and more than other Asian Americans were concentrated in top professional, managerial, and executive positions
(Gardner et al., 1985: 25-34; Kitano and Daniels, 1988: 169). Since
the mid-1970s, however, an increasing number has started or
invested in small businesses (Lessinger, 1985: 6). Ethnic self-
employment has been more or less equated with an ethnic economic
enclave or an ethnic economy in recent sociological work (Light,
1972: 1980; Bonacich and Modell, 1980; Kim, 1981). The characteristics of an ethnic economy include (Gold, 1989: 8) ethnic economic integration and cooperation; ethnic sources of capital, labor,
and information; restriction of intragroup competition; occupational
specialization; geographical concentration; ethnic solidarity; and
reliance on ethnic-based international networks. A simpler definition
states that an ethnic economy is "a sector of entrepreneurial activity
characterized by family firms operating at the margins in terms of
profitability" (Westwood and Bhachu, 1988: 5). An Asian Indian
ethnic economy has developed in states of heavy immigrant concentration, such as New York and California. Asian Indians have clustered in businesses that employ new immigrants from India, relatives
and nonrelatives, and that cater to the needs and tastes of South
Asians. Examples include Indian grocery stores, sari and yard goods
stores and boutiques, 220 volt electrical appliance stores (for appli-
ances to be taken to India), and the like. Asian-Indian owned insurance and real estate businesses also rely heavily on Indian social
networks for their clientele, in contrast to restaurants, motels, and
travel agencies that typically attract a non-Indian clientele.

Although much research has been done on some immigrant Asian
entrepreneurs (Chinese, Japanese, Koreans), there is virtually nothing available on the Asian Indian entrepreneurs. This situation probably arises because the large numbers of highly educated
professionals who came as immigrants immediately after 1965 are
seemingly poor candidates for "middleman minority" status, the
sociological concept toward which much of the work on Asian
entrepreneurs is oriented. Sociologists have termed some immigrant
entrepreneurs in the United States "middleman minorities" and suggested that immigrant populations cluster in ethnic enclaves in order
to utilize their ethnic resources. Middleman minority theory stresses

socioeconomic disadvantage as the cause of ethnic group movement into small business (Bonacich et al., 1978). That literature associates lack of specialized skills with self-employment and also suggests that the clustering of ethnic group members in the same occupation increases their conspicuousness and vulnerability.

However, it is difficult to theorize when the tendency for Asian Indians to move into self-employment and small businesses is so new that the trend itself is unexplained. It is unclear whether immigrants are sponsoring relatives less skilled in language and professional qualifications, or if there are, indeed, new barriers to entry into the general labor market. This new trend could be explained by the folk wisdom that overseas Indians engaged in business are simply extending their business acumen and kinship networks from India. Yet the Patels who now dominate the motel business in California were not a business community back in Gujarat; they were agriculturalists. And the Sikhs who have done well in business both in India and overseas recently are also largely from agricultural backgrounds.

Our ethnographic work has focused on ethnic identity, entrepreneurship, and ethnic networks. Scholars working on Chinese, Korean, and Japanese immigrants have tended to define an ethnic group by its national origin. For Asian Indians, such a definition is too simple. As Lopez has remarked (1987: 2), there are "multiple levels of identity," ranging from kin and caste through region, language, and religion to the nation or the subcontinent. We made few assumptions beforehand about what "ethnicity" meant for Asian-Indian immigrants, but we did think that co-ethnic clients or customers might include all immigrants of South Asian origin while co-ethnic partners or employees might be more narrowly defined by caste, religion, or regional language. We also thought that associational activities based on these narrower groups would be the most vital expressions of "ethnicity." We expected both pragmatic and personal orientations toward ethnicity, then, when it came to occupational networks, and a somewhat more personal and expressive orientation when it came to associational activities.

Using two standard occupational directories of Asian-Indians, we prepared a comprehensive list of some nine hundred Asian Indian individuals or businesses in self-employment and professional categories in southern California (appendix 7.1). We then developed a continuum of occupations based on degree of dependence on an ethnic clientele as a predictor of strength of ethnicity (appendix 7.2). We focused on grocery store owners, restaurant owners, motel owners, and doctors. We expected these occupations to capture the range of involvement in ethnic businesses and activities: grocery store owners would be most dependent upon an ethnic clientele; restaurant and motel owners, while in occupations characterized by ethnic clustering, would not be dependent upon co-ethnics as customers; and doctors would be least dependent upon co-ethnics as clients.

We contacted seventeen grocery store owners or managers, almost all of them taken from the 1987 India-West Guide: about half were Punjabis and half Gujaratis. Four owners and four managers were women. One of the female store owners was a young, unmarried South Indian, and her store was the only one that was a general, not an ethnic, grocery store. These grocery store owners and managers had diverse economic trajectories. Three owners had worked previously as professionals (engineer, computer programmer, and insurance agent) and had chosen to go into the grocery business instead. Two of the stores were owned by pairs of male, unrelated partners, but more often the stores were family businesses. One owner from the Punjab arrived in the 1980s as a "twice migrant," having worked in Germany in a factory. In California, he worked on a farm, then in a restaurant, and then he married an American woman and established an ethnic grocery store. The women owners included two married women, one single woman, and one widow; the women managers all had husbands who had or had had other jobs.

We looked at eleven restaurants in Orange and Los Angeles Counties, about half of them family-run enterprises. Even in the family-run restaurants, wives and daughters played key managerial roles. In two of the nonfamily ones, women had arranged partnerships with nonrelatives. None of the entrepreneurs had obtained a bank or a small business loan to initiate the enterprise.

In the cases of the ethnic grocery store and restaurant owners, self-employment was due to individual initiative and was not group-based. A number of the businesses have expanded to support relatives, a phenomenon observed among businessmen earlier in East

Africa (Desai, 1989; Zarwan, 1977), but only two cases involved continuity of entrepreneurial background from India to California. One grocery store owner was from a Hindu Khatri family that had fruit and clothing stores in the Punjab, and a restaurant owner's family had six hotels and eight restaurants in India. Even the apparent continuity of entrepreneurial practices and preferences from India in the case of the Khatri family involved, upon closer scrutiny, an initiative by a younger brother and an American wife. These entrepreneurs were not the heads of joint families (Desai, 1989: 24), and women often played important roles in the businesses.

Another way of assessing the continuity in Asian-Indian business activities from India to California is to examine business partnerships. Immigrants are creating partnerships here with non-relatives, and our two most striking examples of this featured women operating restaurants. Sources of loans were unpredictable, and sometimes crossed linguistic and religious lines; here again, banks were seldom utilized.

Similarly, motel owners, frequently Patels (the surname commonly equated with motel owners by Euro-Americans and Indian Americans alike), evidenced diverse trajectories and family patterns. We checked on the equation of Patels with motels by phoning every fourth Patel in the Orange County 1990 Telephone Directory. We discovered that most Patels were professionals. Of the thirty-seven Patels called, nine were engineers, six were doctors, and five were motel owners. Those who did own motels included some with many relatives in that business, while others had been professionals earlier but turned to motel owning because of the promise of a higher income.

Most of the "businesses" make strong marketing appeals beyond the community. Particularly true of restaurants, hotels, and motels, ethnic groceries also attract wider clienteles. The restaurant owners we interviewed estimated their non-Indian clientele at 80 percent to 95 percent. One restaurant has become "Nouvelle Mughlai" by cutting down on grease, adding nutritious foods, and emphasizing food presentation. Hotel and motel owners are conscious of their image and try to avoid public identification with those Indian-owned motels or apartments occasionally cited for code violations. For example, the Southern California chapter of the Indian Hotel-Motel Owners Association recently gave away blankets to the homeless in Orange County. Ethnic grocery stores try to attract wider clienteles, often serving snacks. Their women managers happily conduct market tours and cooking lessons for non-Indian visitors and customers. Two ethnic groceries in West Los Angeles estimated their American clientele at 40-60 percent; in Artesia and Duarte, where many Asian Indians reside, the Indian clientele is about 80 percent at such stores.

Asian Indian businesses also had a greater variety of employees than we expected. In one restaurant's five year history, the only two employees who had remained with it from opening to the present are the spice-maker, an El Salvadorean, and the morning cook, a Mexican woman. Asian Indians frequently employ family members and friends, but they also employ Spanish speakers, even as cooks. Another food preparation business employs an El Salvadorean, and a grocery store that began as an ethnic Pakistani-Indian one adapted itself to its Spanish-speaking neighborhood and has a longtime Guatemalan employee. One motel owner employs a Euro-American woman to manage his motel two weeks of every month. Even when employees are all Indians, the networks responsible for their hiring may be completely new. For example, a waiter at an Indian restaurant obtained his job by telephoning restaurant owners and was hired by a Sikh (he was a Hindu from Haryana) because he had been "a restaurant and hotel man" back in Delhi. Thus, he offered a skill, although current political problems between Sikhs and Hindus back in India's Punjab and Haryana states might be thought to hinder his employment by a Punjabi Sikh.

Since Asian-Indian immigrants are by no means all self-employed, but work in a range of occupations and professions, we explored the extent to which ethnicity is maintained and reinforced by participation in ethnic businesses. Current research on Iranians in Los Angeles, for example, hypothesizes that those Iranians engaged in the ethnic economy tend to cluster in ethnic residential areas, participate more frequently in ethnic associations, and identify more with the ethnic community than those not engaged in the ethnic economy (Sabagh et al., 1986). Following them, we hypothesized that Asian Indians engaged in occupations highly dependent on an ethnic clientele (grocery stores, sari stores, etc.) would be more involved in ethnic networks of all kinds, not only business networks. Confirmation of this hypothesis would be important to a broader theory about immigrants, the labor market, and ethnicity; it would lend support to theories of pluralism by linking occupational patterns firmly to the persistence of ethnicity for yet another immigrant population, one which is considered to be exceptionally occupationally mobile. However, our interviews failed to confirm this correlation. In fact, we found numerous merchants who do not participate in any religious or ethnic business associations (and one of them compared the Indian Merchants' Chamber unfavorably to Korean business associations that conspicuously "serve their community").

The interviews we did with Asian-Indian doctors, who were hypothesized to be at the other end of the scale, low dependence on ethnic clientele and low expression of ethnicity, also failed to fit the expectation. Expressions of ethnicity here could mean investment or charitable giving as well as membership in religious or regional language associations of various kinds. Doctors ranged from those who were very active in pan-Indian and pan-Hindu activities -- the recently constructed Venkateshwar Temple in Malibu could not have been built without their contributions -- to those who were completely inactive. Many presidents of regional and cultural associations are doctors and dentists. In fact, interviews with these professionals lead us to propose an alternative hypothesis that finds ethnicity dependent not upon involvement in ethnically oriented enterprises but upon factors such as length of residence in the United States and the security and status of one's employment. This formulation suggests higher expressions of ethnicity among the earlier, professionally oriented immigrants, rather than among the newer immigrants who are self-employed.

A second set of issues concerns new ways in which ethnic networks are being mobilized by Asian-Indian immigrants in both occupational and social spheres. Here we expected that those least dependent upon the ethnic businesses would be those who crossed "traditional" linguistic, religious, or caste barriers in ethnic activities and memberships. But the reverse hypothesis makes more sense. In the West Los Angeles area, where Pakistanis and Muslims are numerous, we found that ethnic business owners deliberately crossed religious and national boundaries to appeal to a wider clientele on the basis of regional or linguistic commonality. Thus, a Punjabi-Hindu store has leaflets about Hajj trips prominently displayed and gives free food on Id (a Muslim holiday, a time of feasting after a long fast); it routinely advertises mushairas (recitations of Urdu poetry, associated with Muslim culture) along with bharata natyam recitals (classical South Indian dance). Nearby, two Pakistani brothers have named their store Mah Bharat (Mother India).

With none of these occupational categories were we clearly dealing with an "ethnic economy." Westwood's and Bhachu's (1988) definition requires family businesses and low profitability; many of the businesses we looked at were not family businesses and many were doing well. While some of the characteristics specified by Gold's definition are met -- there are geographical concentrations to some extent, at least there are centers of activity, and occupational specialization can be found -- others are not met. Employees can be co-ethnics but a sizable minority are Spanish-speaking (as Gold has found for Vietnamese businesses in California, 1989: 13) and there are others as well. Ethnic sources of capital are utilized since their ethnic identity spans a wider range than hypothesized. That is, those of different religious and national backgrounds were utilized as well as those of the same religious, national, or caste background. International connections seem minimal, although there are some grocery stores that import from South Asia or London and many sari, Punjabi suit, and cloth stores that import from India or Japan. Depending upon the business and its locations, clientele range from 95 percent co-ethnics to only 10 percent or 20 percent co-ethnics. As for a high level of ethnic solidarity, again the definition of the community has broadened in Southern California to include South Asians of diverse religious, national, and caste backgrounds, and the owners of ethnic businesses are by no means the most active in ethnic associations. In short, Asian-Indian businesses are not best analyzed as an ethnic economy, and middleman minority theory does not seem appropriate. For the latter point, Desai's (1989) description of the East African and Australian Asian-Indian entrepreneurs buttresses our position.

The new ways in which occupational and ethnic networks are combined have implications for family and gender issues. The post-1965 immigrants have come as family units, with women equal in numbers to men, a situation far more favorable to family life than in India's own cities. Well placed in the American economy, these new immigrants seem at first glance to be eminently successful in "maintaining" South Asian culture and identity in the United States (albeit an emergent, transnational middle-class culture: Appadurai and Breckenridge, 1986). Yet there is evidence of significant changes, particularly those instigated by women or those that affect the position of women.

Occupational patterns for Asian-Indian men and women in the United States suggest that, as in India, many Asian Indian women are working in professional positions (Desbarats, 1979). For example, in Bakersfield, forty of the ninety doctors from India are married to each other -- that is, the ninety doctors include twenty couples. However, some Asian-Indian women are taking up occupational options that have important implications for the theories about an ethnic economy. From those dealing in clothes and snack products to those working in insurance and computer companies, Asian-Indian women entrepreneurs are often featured in Indian-American newspapers. The prominence of such women, and the highly visible roles of Indian women managers and clerks in South Asian ethnic grocery stores and in motels owned by Gujarati families, demonstrate that Indian women are to be found in a range of economic roles and across local occupational hierarchies.

Westwood and Bhachu emphasize that an ethnic economy is a gendered economy, that family businesses use women's labor power, keeping labor costs and wages low (1988: 5), and the literature in general views women's labor in family businesses as a cheap resource. We did find many women engaged in managing and working in those business enterprises that fell on the high end of our ethnic business continuum, but these were not necessarily family businesses. The model was not that of a "mom and pop store," where both husband and wife worked in the store with the man clearly in charge. Rather, the most characteristic pattern was that found by Gold (1988: 421) for Vietnamese family businesses in

California. Like Gold, we found husbands holding other full-time jobs while their wives ran small businesses: groceries, restaurants, boutiques. Indian grocery stores very often are managed by wives while their husbands work as engineers (or other types of professionals) for American companies. Work on Gujarati motel owners has found women taking important roles in the business (Jain, 1989; Thaker, 1982), while their men sometimes worked elsewhere. This marks a departure from employment patterns back in India, where private businesses, including family businesses, rarely employ women as managers and clerks. Most of these women did not work, or did not work in such jobs, back in South Asia. Gold explains this pattern by referring to Vietnamese tradition, where women were always the money managers for the family. There is no such tradition for South Asians. It seems, rather, that the management of ethnic businesses by wives is a strategy to maximize economic security and family income.

Asian-Indian women in California make desirable, often necessary, contributions to family earnings, and this seems to have brought them a measure of more equal status within the immigrant families. Women make more decisions about spending than do their mothers-in-law back home, or their visiting or even coresiding mothers-in-law in the United States, and parents come to visit or live with their immigrant daughters as well as their sons (Thaker, 1982: 68-73). The contribution of Asian-Indian women to these business efforts is publicly recognized too, for example in crediting the development of new dishes for a restaurant to one's wife, or having a woman make the presentation of blankets to the homeless. Thus, even when the family histories of ethnic entrepreneurs show a continuity of entrepreneurial activity from India to Southern California, there are important changes occurring within families here as new roles are developed through female participation in ethnic businesses.

While there is no space for a full consideration of changing domestic practices, both Desai and Bhachu focus on marriage arrangements and we want to suggest their importance for ethnic businesses in Southern California. Bhachu has postulated that, with regard to marriage arrangements for the Ramgarhia Sikhs in London, there was a time lag -- that is, marriages were arranged with partners in

India or Africa while family units consolidated in Great Britain, the numbers of coresident community members rose, and the establishment of services and goods necessary for the performances of marriages took place (1985: 140-41). Bhachu indicates that these processes took about a decade, from the mid-1960s to the 1970s, before the Ramgarhias began to marry each other within Britain (1985: 39). Clearly this time lag is found in Southern California as well, for marriages are just beginning to be arranged and celebrated within the Asian-Indian population in California (or the United States).

Most Asian-Indians go back to India to perform marriages, where the balance of interested relatives and communities still reside. The Malibu temple priests performed only twelve marriages in 1988, while the two most widely known Southern California priests perform between twenty-five to fifty marriages each per year. These priests are enthusiastic, personable, and travel even beyond California to perform marriage services, but both often perform marriages for non-Indians, using drastically shortened versions of a Vedic or Hindu service. And they are only part-time priests; one is a motel owner, the other is a priest retired from India. The latter, a Punjabi Arya Samajist who publicizes his Vedic wedding services widely, held his own daughter's marriage in India; indeed, he relied upon his son's father-in-law there to select the groom and make all the arrangements.

But the balance is beginning to shift, and the wedding economy is an expanding one for ethnic enterprises. As immigrants bring over older parents and relatives, more Asian Indian weddings are being held in the United States. Providers of goods and services for weddings are springing up. In the spring of 1990, the second annual Indo-Pak Bridal Expo was held in Buena Park. Like the first one in 1989, billed as showing "everything needed for an authentic wedding," this Expo was complete with fashion shows and the displays of some thirty merchants. Ads for wedding pooja items, horoscope matching ("Astro Scan USA"), wedding catering, flower decorations for weddings, Indian style disposable plates for weddings, wedding jewelry, and the like have recently joined other ads in the pages of newspapers like India West. Weddings provide many opportunities for new ethnic businesses or for the expansion of existing ones: a recent and admittedly very lavish wedding in Malibu was an all-day affair providing food and entertainment for some fifteen hundred guests!

Conclusion

The way Asian-Indian immigrants are structuring their occupational networks, whether they are small business people or professionals employed int he larger economy, and their associational activities helps to clarify ideas about the ethnic economy and redefine concepts of gender roles and ethnic identity for Asian Indians in Southern California. Our exploratory findings did not show that Asian-Indian entrepreneurs were typically heads of joint families or representatives of entrepreneurial networks extended from South Asia. We found Asian-Indian women active in ethnic businesses, and women as well as men entered partnerships with non-relatives. These entrepreneurs seldom utilized banks as sources of credit, and the sources of loans were unpredictable, often crossing linfuistic and religious lines. Employees in ethnic businesses included non-relatives and non-South Asian, notably Spanish-speakers. Even when partnerships and employer-employee relationships were between South Asians, these relationships utilized new networks rather than old ones based on caste and community membership in South Asia.

Further, we found that dependence on an ethnic clientele, higher among ethnic grocery store owners than among restaurant and motel owners or doctors, did not correlate well with participation in religious and/or ethnic business associations. In fact, the higher expressions of ethnicity, measured by support of and participation in religious and/or linguistic associations and activities, came from the earlier, professionally-oriented immigrants such as doctors rather than form the more recent self-employed immigrants. And those most dependent upon ethnic clienteles, the grocery store owners, deliberately crossed religious and national boundaries important in South Asia to appeal to wider clienteles in Southern California.

Overall, we found that narrow definitions of an "ethnic economy" failed to capture the diversity and non-traditional nature of the participants in Asian-Indian enterprises in Southern California. Notions of culture have been biased "toward rooting not travel" (Clifford, 1988: 338). Looking at travelers, our exploration of ethnicity and enterprise has shown the importance of context, the continuing importance of family, and an enhanced significance for women in Asian-Indian uses and constructions of occupational and ethnic identity.

Notes

1. Only New York has more than California: 60,505 and 57,901, respectively. We are looking at Asian Indians in Southern California, in the counties of Los Angeles, Orange, San Bernardino, Riverside, San Diego, and Imperial Counties. Within California, Los Angeles County has the largest number of Asian Indians, followed by Santa Clara county in the north, and then Orange County (the numbers in the 1980 Census were 18,562, 5,659, and 4,972, respectively).

2. *The Economist*, 28 October 1989.

3. The earliest Asian Indians came primarily from the Punjab after 1900; the 1917 Barred Zone Act and the 1924 National Origins Quota Act ended the legal immigration of Asians to the United States. They were initially eligible for citizenship, but after the Supreme Court's 1923 Thind Decision, which turned on the question of race, they became "aliens ineligible for citizenship." Technically Caucasian, Asian Indians were nevertheless popularly categorized as nonwhite, and the Thind decision was based on 1790 legislation that used "white" status as entitlement to citizenship. That decision subjected the Punjabis to California's Alien Land Laws, which prohibited aliens ineligible for citizenship from leasing or owning agricultural land. To remain agriculturalists, the men had to make informal arrangements that put them at the mercy of white landowners and shipping companies (Leonard, 1985).

4. In California, about five hundred of the several thousand Punjabis who worked and settled in the agricultural valleys throughout the state, cut off from their families and homeland, married non-Indians, primarily Mexican and Mexican-American women. Exogamy created a large second generation biethnic community of Spanish-speaking Catholics with names like Maria Singh, Jose Akbar Khan, and Rudolfo Chand. Unlike the descendants of the seamen in Britain, these descendants tend to claim "Hindu" ethnicity and have some contact with more recent immigrants from South Asia (Leonard, *Making Ethnic Choices*).

5. Following Ivan Light (1986: 13), we treat entrepreneurship as synony-

mous with business self-employment.

6. Some Asian-Indian business people believe self-employment provides the best opportunity open to them at the present time in this society (Lessinger, 1985; Khare, 1980; Dutta, 1982; Elkhanialy and Nicholas, 1976). This perception may be due to slightly lower educational and occupational qualifications for the immigrants coming since the mid-1970s, but it may also be the result of pressures from the local economy. Evidence comes from the concerted effort to gain "minority group status" for Asian Indians in order to obtain economic benefits: The National Association of Americans of Asian Indian Descent, at the behest of Asian Indian businessmen, petitioned for status as a socially disadvantaged minority in 1982 and got that status from the U.S. Small Business Administration (Fornaro, 1984: 30-31).

7. The so-called Gujaratis, who are one of the dominant business communities in India, are Vaishyas (merchants and bankers), while the Patels are not Vaishyas. For the first Gujarati immigrants to California and how they got into the hotel/motel business, see Jain, 1989: 9 *et passim*.

8. These directories seemed a good starting place since there are no alphabetical directories of South Asians (such as are found for some other Asian immigrant communities), and because South Asians are not residentially clustered to any significant degree. Table 7.2 is based on an interview with Ramesh Murarka, the publisher of *India West*, who estimated the proportion of Asian-Indian practitioners of each occupation listed in his *India-West Guide*, correlating proportions of listings with proportions of practitioners dependent on ethnic clients or customers. Arranging the major occupations listed along a continuum according to Murarka's estimate of their dependence on South Asian clientele, we broke the continuum into three categories of high, medium, and low.

9. This minority group status is controversial within the Asian-Indian community -- the Indian League of America and many individuals do not want "minority" or non-Caucasian status. None of our informants mentioned this status, or when questioned, had utilized it.

10. Johanna Lessinger's preliminary survey of partnership arrangements among New York's South Asian immigrant businesses found that comparative strangers were financing and operating small businesses as partners, creating problems apparently not experienced in India. She hypothesizes that the lack of hierarchical structure and intimate knowledge of each other associated with a joint family business leads Indian businesses here to fail more often than in India because of problems between partners (Lessinger, 1985: 3). Yet, Desai (1989) found that Indian entrepreneurs in East Africa and Australia worked as much for

their nuclear families as for their joint families; he shows internal strife to be characteristic of joint family firms (24-25; this has been found by Leonard and Tibrewal, separately, in unpublished work on Hyderabad and Calcutta, respectively). Commitment to ethnic business could also be assessed by asking Asian Indian business owners what their plans were for the continuity of the business. Since most of our informants had only very young children, such questions seemed premature, but most parents did seem to be encouraging their children toward professional careers. If subsequent generations move away from the small business mode of employment, it remains to be seen if ethnic bonds will weaken (as Bonacich and Modell found in their 1980 study of Japanese Americans).

11. The calls to Patels were made using the Orange County (north and central) Telephone Directory, April 1990, by Tibrewal and Vandana Venkatesh.

12. *India West*, 3 February 1989: 19.

13. The extent to which immigrant entrepreneurs profit from the exploitation of fellow immigrant workers is an important question in the literature (see Lessinger, 1985 on "intraethnic class exploitation"). Here one would look not only for possible exploitation in terms of wages and working hours, but also for indications that family labor is being exploited or abused. Or, conversely, there could be possible advantages that employment by co-ethnics confers upon employees, such as loans, flexible working hours, legal advice and protection, shares in the business, and perhaps sponsorship in setting up businesses (Nee and de Bary, 1972). See Bonacich, 1988, Min's response, 1989, and Bonacich's response, 1989.

14. Tibrewal, who relocated to New York in 1989, senses that there is a mutual acceptance between Asian Indians and Spanish speakers in California that is not paralleled in New York. But Gold (1989) points out that Chinese-Vietnamese businessmen also employ Mexicans frequently in order to exempt themselves from the paternalistic labor relations often expected by co-ethnics and to protect themselves from employees whose inside knowledge could harm store owners!

15. Desai (1989: 21) discusses this issue. He critiques the Bonacich/Modell notion that members of a dominant society have difficulty denying credit to and collecting debts from each other and therefore relegate the running of businesses to immigrants. He claims that within the diverse Asian-Indian community, shared cultural values between businessmen and customers help ensure success, and he proposes that this would be just as true within the dominant society.

16. This point is made by Ghei (1988).

17. There has been little attention to sex or gender as a variable in much of the research on Asian-Indian immigrants in the United States. Exceptions not already remarked on include Rutherford, "Bengalis," Amerasingham, "Making Friends," and work on Indian classical and popular dance by Ghei, 1988 and 1989 papers, and Abramovitch, 1988 paper.

18. An earlier study remarked that "the woman who is running a grocery or restaurant in L.A. would not have done this back in India or Pakistan or Bangladesh" (Hossain, 1982: 78).

19. The marriage ceremonies usually last one or two hours, and, despite astrological forecasts, are scheduled on weekends just prior to a noon or evening meal, for the convenience of attenders. One man uses an English language text, complete with explanations of text and rituals. The other uses a Sanskrit text but translates and explains in English; he has also helped to put *saris* on participants and attenders upon occasion. The men have performed marriages for diverse Euro-Americans, Chinese, Filipinos, and Russians.

20. The Bridal Expo was organized by a young Sikh woman entrepreneur who runs her own beauty shop in Cerritos.

APPENDIX 7.1
Occupation Continuum Based on Dependence on an Ethnic Clientele

High Dependence

Appliance Dealers	100%
Grocery Stores (retail)	100%
Grocery Wholesalers	100%
Jewelers (retail)	100%
Marriage Bureaus	100%
Music Shops and Dealers	100%
Publications	100%
Saree Stores	100%
Video Conversion	100%
Video Tape Dealers	100%

Medium Dependence

Periodicals and Book Dealers	90%
Priests and Astrologers	90%
Restaurants	90%
Attorneys	90%
Gift Stores	80%
Travel Agents	75%
Investment, Financial Consultants	75%
Insurance Agents	65%
Doctors and Dentists	65%
Importers and Exporters	65%

Low Dependence

Accountants	50%
Real Estate Agents	50%
Miscellaneous Businesses	50%
Computer Dealers	35%
Yoga Centers	35%
Video Rentals	25%
Engineers, Architects, Contractors	10%

Source: India-West Guide and Business Directory, India-West Publications, Inc., Fremont, California, 1987. Table of Contents, with interview comments by Publisher Ramesh Murarka.

APPENDIX 7.2
Distribution of Asian-Indians in Selected Occupations in Southern California*

Business

Hotels and Motels	174
Other Businesses	97
Restaurant	75
Grocery Stores	73
(Retail and Wholesale)	
Real Estate Agents	48
Travel Agencies	45
Importers - Diamond and	44
Precious Stones	
Insurance Agents	42
Investment and Financial	31
Consultants	
Engineers, Architects,	28
Contractors	
Jewelers	24
Saree Stores	22
Exporters/Importers	18
Appliance Stores	17
Computer and Related	16
Business	
Garment and Boutique	6
Stores	
Prints and Typesetters	5
Books and Magazine	4
Distributors	
Manufacturers	3
Crafts and Gift Stores	2
Construction Firms	1

Professional Practitioners

Doctors and Dentists	108
Insurance Consultants	18
Real Estate Consultants	7
Attorneys	13
Engineering Consultants	5
Media Consultants	2
Computer Consultants	1
Professional Financial	1
Planning	
Psychologist	1
Tax Shelter Consultant	1

*Sources: North American Directory and Reference Guide of Asian Indian Businesses and Independent Professional Practitioners. Compiled and edited by Dr. Thomas Abraham. Published by India Enterprises of the West, Inc., Bronx, New York, 1984, pp. 87-111; India-West Guide and Business Directory, Published by India-West Publications, Inc., Fremont, California, 1987.

References

Abramovitch, Ilana. 1988. "Flushing Bharata-Natyam: Indian Dancers in Queens, New York." Paper presented at the 17th Annual Conference on South Asia at the University of Wisconsin, Madison.

Amerasingham, Lorna Rhodes. 1980. "Making Friends in a New Culture: South Asian Women in Boston, Massachusetts." In *Uprooting and Development*, edited by George Coelho and Paul Ahmed. New York: Plenum Press.

Appadurai, Arjun, and Carol Breckenridge. 1986. "Asian Indians in the United States: A Transnational Culture in the Making." Paper presented at the Asia Society symposium, April, New York.

Bhachu, Parminder. 1985. *Twice Migrants*. New York: Tavistock.

Bhachu, Parminder. 1988. "Apni Marzi Kardhi. Home and Work: Sikh Women in Britain." In *Enterprising Women: Ethnicity, Economy and Gender Relations*, edited by Sallie Westwood and Parminder Bhachu. London and New York: Routledge.

Bonacich, Edna. 1988. "The Social Costs of Immigrant Entrepreneurship." *Amerasia Journal* 14:1, 119-28.

Bonacich, Edna. 1989. "The Role of the Petite Bourgeoisie within Capitalism: A Response to Pyong Gap Min." *Amerasia Journal* 15:2, 195-203.

Bonacich, Edna, and John Modell. 1980. *The Economic Basis of Ethnic Solidarity: Small Business in the Japanese American Community*. Berkeley: University of California Press.

Bonacich, Edna, et al. 1978. "Small Business Among Koreans in Los Angeles." In *Counterpoint: Perspectives on Asian America*, edited by Emma Gee. Los Angeles: Asian American Studies Center, University of California, Los Angeles.

Clifford, James. 1988. *The Predicament of Culture*. Cambridge: Harvard University Press.

Desai, Rashmi. 1963. *Indian Immigrants in Britain*. New York: Oxford University Press.

Desai, Rashmi. 1989. "Kinship of Business: An Account of the Indian Entrepreneurs." Paper presented at the Immigration Conference, December, Toronto.

Desbarats, Jacqueline. 1979. "Thai Migration to Los Angeles." *Geographical Review* 69:3, 302-18.

Dutta, Manoranjan. 1982. "Asian Indian Americans -- Search for an Economic Profile." In *From India to America*, edited by S. Chandrasekhar. La Jolla, CA: Population Review.

Elkhanialy, Hekmat, and Ralph W. Nicholas. 1976. *Immigrants from the Indian Subcontinent in the U.S.A.: Problems and Prospects*. Chicago:

India League of America.

Fornaro, Robert J. 1984. "Asian Indians in America: Acculturation and Minority Status." *Migration Today* 12: 28-32.

Gardner, Robert W., et al. 1985. "Asian Americans: Growth, Change and Diversity." *Population Bulletin* 40: 4. Washington, DC: Population Reference Bureau, Inc.

Ghei, Kiren. 1988. "Hindi Popular Cinema and the Indian American Teenage Dance Experience." Paper presented at the 17th Annual Conference on South Asia, Madison, WI.

Ghei, Kiren. 1989. "From Bhangra to Kuchipudi: Movement Dimensions of Indian Public Events in Los Angeles." Paper prepared for the Western Conference of the Association for Asian Studies, October 1989, at California State University, Long Beach.

Gold, Steven J. 1988. "Refugees and Small Business: The Case of Soviet Jews and Vietnamese." *Ethnic and Racial Studies* 11:4 (November), 411-438.

Gold, Steven J. 1989. "Chinese-Vietnamese Entrepreneurs in Southern California: An Enclave with Co-Ethnic Customers?" Paper prepared for the American Sociological Association, San Francisco.

Hossain, Mokerrom. 1982. "South Asians in Southern California: A Sociology Study of Immigrants from India, Pakistan, and Bengladesh." *South Asia Bulletin* 2:1 Spring 1982: 74-82.

India-West Guide and Business Directory. 1987. Fremont, CA: Ramesh Murarka.

Jain, Usha R. 1989. *The Gujaratis of San Francisco*. New York: AMS Press.

Khare, Brij B. 1980. "Cultural Identity and Problems of Acclimatization: Three Areas of Concern." In *Political Participation of Asian Americans: Problems and Strategies*, edited by Yung-Kwan Jo. Chicago: Pacific/Asian American Mental Health Research Center.

Kim, Illsoo. 1981. *New Urban Immigrants: The Korean Community in New York*. Princeton: Princeton University Press.

Kitano, Harry H. L., and Roger Daniels. 1988. *Asian Americans: Emerging Minorities*. Englewood Cliffs, NJ: Prentice Hall.

La Brack, Bruce. 1988. *The Sikhs of Northern California 1904-1975: A Socio-Historical Study*. New York: AMS Press.

Leonard, Karen. 1985. "Punjabi Farmers and California's Alien Land Law." *Agricultural History* 59:4 October: 549-62.

Leonard, Karen. 1991. "Ethnic Identity and Gender: South Asians in the United States." In *Ethnicity, Identity, and Migration*, edited by N. K. Wagle and Milton Israel. Toronto: South Asian Studies, University of Toronto.

Leonard, Karen. 1991. *Making Ethnic Choices: California's Punjabi Mexican Americans*. Philadelphia: Temple University Press.

Lessinger, Johanna. 1985. "Painful Intimacy: The Establishment of Trust in Business Partnerships among New York's Indian Immigrants." Houston: University of Houston.

Light, Ivan. 1972. *Ethnic Enterprise in America*. Berkeley: University of California Press.

Light, Ivan. 1980. "Asian Enterprise in America." In *Self-Help in Urban America: Patterns of Minority Business Enterprise*, edited by Scott Cummings. Port Washington, NY: Kennikat Press.

Light, Ivan. 1986. "Ethnicity and Business Enterprise." In *Making It in America: The Role of Ethnicity in Business Enterprise*, edited by M. Mark Stolarik and Murray Friedman. Lewisburg, PA: Bucknell University Press.

Lopez, David. 1987. "The Organization of Ethnicity: Asian Indian Associations in the United States." SSRC Submission, January 1987. (Available from UCLA Sociology Department.)

Min, Pyong Gap. 1989. "The Social Costs of Immigrant Entrepreneurship: A Response to Edna Bonacich." *Amerasia Journal* 15-2: 187-94.

Nee, Victor, and Brett de Bary. 1972. *Long Time Californ': A Documentary Study of an American Chinatown*. New York: Pantheon Books.

Rutherford, Dorothy Angell. 1984. "Bengalis in America: Relationship, Affect, Person, and Self." Ph.D. diss. American University, Washington, DC.

Sabagh, Georges, et al. 1986. "Emergent Ethnicity: Iranians in Los Angeles." *ISSR Quarterly* 3-1: 7-10.

Thaker, Suvarna. 1982. "The Quality of Life of Asian Indian Women in the Motel Industry." *South Asia Bulletin* 2: 68-73.

Thompson, Gordon, and Medha Yodh. 1985. "Garba and the Gujaratis of Southern California." In *Selected Reports in Ethnomusicology* VI, edited by Nazir A. Jairazbhoy and Sue Carole De Vale. Los Angeles: University of California, Los Angeles, Department of Music.

Westwood, Sallie, and Parminder Bhachu, eds. 1988. *Enterprising Women: Ethnicity, Economy and Gender Relations*. London and New York: Routledge.

Zarwan, John. 1977. "Kinship, Community, and Business: A Study of Indians in Kenya." Paper presented at the joint meeting of the Latin American Studies Association and African Studies Association, Houston.

8

Twice and Direct Migrant Sikhs: Caste, Class, and Identity in Pre- and Post-1984 Britain

Parminder Bhachu

The twice-migrant East African Sikhs form one part of the total Asian Indian population in the United Kingdom from East Africa. This population is estimated to be around 206,000, of which slightly over half are men.[1] The majority of East Africans arrived in the United Kingdom from the mid-1960s onward, their pattern of migration being different from that of direct migrants from the Indian subcontinent and Pakistan (Ballard, 1973; Ballard and Ballard, 1977; Saifullah Khan, 1976, 1977; Helweg, 1979; Anwar, 1976; Dahya, 1973, 1988; Jeffrey, 1976; Robinson, 1984; Eade, 1989; Shaw, 1988; Werbner, 1990). These settler Sikhs are twice removed, having left the Punjab during the early part of the twentieth century as indentured labor to build the Kenya-Uganda railway (Mangat, 1969: 32) and thence to the United Kingdom in the 1960s, having been affected by post-independence Africanization policies.

The twice-migrated community[2] of East African Sikhs in the United Kingdom, constitute a single group of urban through traditionalist settlers with a common history of migration from India to Africa to Britain, and who: (*a*) belong predominantly to one caste group, that of the Ramgarhias (the artisan caste)[3]; (*b*) were already part of an established community in East Africa, where they had developed considerable community skills prior to migration; (*c*)

163

moved from urban East Africa to urban Britain (Ghai, 1965: 93) having been concentrated in a handful of towns in East Africa; (*d*) were mainly public sector workers[4] forming the middle level of the three-tier system in the plural society of East Africa (Mangat, 1969: 131; Ghai, 1965: 94); (*e*) were technically skilled because of early recruitment policies that only allowed skilled labor into Africa (Morris, 1968: 62); (*f*) have maintained many of the values and traditions they migrated with in the early twentieth century despite their absence from India and the lack of home orientation; and (*g*) arrived in Britain with employable skills, command of English and also some capital. These advantages render them relatively prosperous and one of the most progressive of the non-European migrants.

In the following, I shall refer to salient features of the East African Sikh community to put them into the context of the wider minority of directly migrant Sikhs and other South Asians in Britain of whom they are a part, but from whom they differ in certain fundamental ways.

Twice versus Direct Migrants

Outsiders view South Asian migrants in Britain as a homogenous community, yet there are clear differences among them of class, caste, experiences of migration, origins (from urban to rural areas), and so on. These differences affect their orientation and settlement. The complexity of internal ethnicity among South Asians does not receive due weight because all are supposed to share 'South Asian Culture.' Yet there are direct migrants for whom migration to Britain has been their first move from the Indian subcontinent, often from rural areas to urban ones, and there are twice migrants like the East African Sikhs, who have moved from India to Africa, and from there to metropolitan Britain.

In Britain, East Africans, mainly Ramgarhia Sikhs, constitute a minority within a larger minority of Sikhs consisting of other caste groups with a large number belonging to the Jat Sikh caste. The Jats have mostly migrated from the Indian subcontinent and have been in Britain longer than the East Africans. The East Africans' residence in Africa for over sixty years resulted in the loss of their ties with

India, unlike the direct migrants, who maintain them more intensely. East Africans anticipated permanent settlement in the United Kingdom, right from the point of entry. This expectation was in contrast to other sojourning South Asian migrants (Saifullah Khan, 1977; Dahya, 1973, 1988; Aurora, 1967; Anwar, 1979; Helweg, 1979; Jeffrey, 1976) who were home-oriented in the 1960s and 1970s and who made and still make frequent visits to the subcontinent for reinforcement of their cultural values. East Africans based abroad belonged to a community that lacked a crucial feature common to South Asian minorities: the myth of return.

The myth of return refers to the desire by migrants to return to a "homeland," to a country of origin, even though the return may never take place. It remains, however, a powerful imperative that drives migrants to view their return home as either imminent, or even delayed, despite constant postponement or even the eventual abandonment of return itself. The myth remained critical in structuring the attitudes of direct migrants and their orientation toward settlement in the United Kingdom, especially, in the early decades of their residence in Britain. In spite of increasing lengths of stay and after reuniting families, the myth of return was often still retained by direct migrants as "a central charter for the maintenance of Sikh ethnicity in Britain" (Ballard and Ballard, 1977: 41-42). Brooks and Singh (1978: 22) further declare that "the myth of return is of overriding importance when considering the perspectives and actions of migrant workers, particularly those from the Asian ethnic groups. The retention of the myth of return is necessary for the emphasis on the minimizing or prevention of contact with the wider society."

Dahya (1973: 241) makes similar points in classifying Pakistani migrants as "transients" and as economically motivated immigrants. "Like Indians, Pakistanis emigrate not in order to earn a livelihood but to supplement the economic resources of their families of origin . . . to improve their existing landholding and/or to extend them, to improve their family homestead by building a pakka (literally, solid) house." South Asians in Blackburn, have "restricted aspirations while in the UK, centered upon the myth or reality of an early return to the sending society. This factor, when allied to structural constraints, has ensured that the group remains encapsulated in its neighborhood, in its place of work and in its place of learning" (Dahya, 1974: 82).

Eventual repatriation remained the ultimate goal, even though the final return might either have been constantly postponed or indeed might never have taken place. Migration was seen as an interlude, the country of origin and kinsmen resident there acting as a controlling influence on the motivations, actions, and attitudes of the directly migrant South Asian minorities. For example, in describing Muslim Pakistanis in Bristol, Jeffrey (1976: 145) stated that "values carried over from Pakistan influence patterns of interaction in Bristol, links with kin at home contain obligations and necessitate a constant orientation in the direction of Pakistan on the part of migrants, and their investment patterns and intentions to return have an impact on the lifestyles they choose." Features mentioned above are consistently salient in descriptions of the settlement patterns of South Asians in Britain at the time. Similarly, Dahya (1988: 444), describing the "economically motivated" direct migrants, states that "Asians regard Britain as -- *pardes Vilayat* (foreign country) -- and distinguish it from *des/sada mulk* (homeland or own country)." Such characteristics, however, do not apply to East Africans, who do not fit into a number of commonly held stereotypical assumptions about minorities. They are neither home orientated nor view their stay in Britain as a sojourn, since their migration to Britain was always of a permanent nature.

Despite their absence from India for a long period and their lack of ties to a home country, East Africans have remained traditionalist. This generalization also applies to other East African Asians like the Gujaratis who have remained culturally conservative and intensely religious (Tambs-Lyche, 1980; Michaelson, 1979; Shah, 1979). They are almost "Victorian Sikhs" as an Indian Sikh informant suggested, having maintained some of the traditions with which they migrated from India. Of course, their cultural values have changed in response to their foreign sojourns and localities of settlement. But they do observe many traditions stringently, more so than newly established migrants. Their conservatism manifests itself in the ritual elaboration of their marriages, in the gift exchanges that take place according to traditional rules, and in the injection of the wages of

brides into their dowries, thus converting female wealth into a traditional framework, and so on (see Bhachu, 1985b, 1985a: 86).

The perpetuation of some central cultural values has occurred,
despite changes since migration in domestic organization such as an
increasing tendency toward nuclear families, the high rate entry of
women into the labor market,[5] the dispersal of the community, the
lack of a myth of return on arrival, and also the absence of long distance control exercised by a kinship group.

Arrival in Family Units: Balanced Age and Sex and Structure

East Africans' intention to stay in the United Kingdom permanently is obvious from other features of their social organization.
For example, they arrive in complete family units, often consisting
of three generations, of grandparents, parents, and children.
Complete families make them unique in relation to international
migration in general, which is of a much younger age group.[6] In the
majority of cases, even if the households' heads arrived first,
families were united within a couple of years. The phases of
settlement described by Ballard and Ballard (1977) for Sikhs and
most other migrants from the subcontinent are not relevant to them
since the community has not gone through the early stages of
bachelor households to full family life. The arrival of East Africans
as family units has led to their rapid settlement in the United
Kingdom as well as the reproduction of strong communication links
established during their stay in Africa. The longer process of
settlement applicable to South Asians who had migrated directly was
automatically telescoped for them. Together with their strong
communications network, this contraction of phases of settlement has
catalyzed the establishment of ethnic services within a short period
of their arrival, even though in comparison to direct migrants East
Africans were latecomers, arriving first in the late 1960s. Direct
migrants have been in Britain since the labor shortage period
following the Second World War; and they only started the process
of consolidated families in the late 1950s and early 1960s, with
people of Bangladeshi origin doing this even later, in the early
1970s, even though their men have been in Britain since the earliest

days of South Asian migration. This period also coincides with the arrival of Ugandan Asians in 1972 as refugees ousted by General Idi Amin. I shall not discuss their settlement here since it has already been well documented (Kuepper et al., 1975; Humphrey and Ward, 1974). Because they were mainly public sector workers based in Nairobi, East Africans in my study are either from Kenya, or have arrived prior to the 1972 Amin episode. Some of the features attributed here to East African Sikhs are also of relevance to other East African Asians in general, whether they be refugees from Uganda, Kenya, or Tanzania; and whether they are Hindus, Muslims, or Gujaratis (Fernando, 1979; Tambs-Lyche, 1980; Michaelson, 1979; Robinson, 1981, 1984; Shah, 1979). Their past experiences and common position in East Africa as middlemen gives them a large number of shared characteristics (Brooks and Singh, 1978).[7]

Strong Community Ties and Expertise

Despite their late arrival in the United Kingdom, their common experiences have given them skills that they are able to utilize in the establishment of communities in Britain. In East Africa they were concentrated in a few towns, and were highly urbanized; they were employed by an equally small number of organizations, their children attended select "Asian" schools in the main towns, and so on. Since they were already part of an established diaspora before migration to the United Kingdom, they have been able not only to reproduce common ties and skills, but also to establish institutions like temples (*gurdwaras*) and caste associations rapidly on arrival. Their skills have helped them to establish themselves more rapidly than direct migrants who have not possessed the same expertise, linguistic facility, and communications network. All this community-building has reaffirmed their East African identity.

In East Africa, they had maintained their community through traditionally-arranged endogamous marriages (Bharati, 1967: 284; Morris, 1967: 267). Endogamy helped group formation and the development of the community along caste lines, and also led to the perpetuation of the traditional values. Cross-cutting kinship ties developed through marriage alliances in East Africa, and the great overlap of contact through concentration in urban areas encouraged the building of a powerful network there, which is now to be found in the United Kingdom. This network mobilizes the community for specific projects.

East Africans were also skilled technically prior to arrival in Britain as a result of the selective recruitment to the colonial British government in East Africa. The colonial government only admitted in the skilled labor needed to build the Kenya-Uganda railways (Morris, 1968: 62; Mangat, 1969: 61; Ghai, 1965: 96).   Morris (1968: 62) states that immigration rules in East Africa were so difficult that "no alien was admitted unless he could fill a post that was for the benefit of everybody."

Since those who have arrived in Britain have mainly been public sector workers, they have not necessarily occupied low-grade jobs or semi or unskilled industrial work (Dahya, 1988; Eade, 1989; Phizacklea and Miles, 1980; Rex and Tomlinson, 1979; Castles and Kosack, 1973; Brooks, 1975a/b), being more occupationally dispersed in different spheres of work than is suggested by the general literature on migrant workers. The emphasis on working-class and "underclass" migrants (Rex and Tomlinson, 1979: 275) is also not always relevant to East Africans as a whole, though it clearly applies to some. In London, East Africans have pursued the occupations they had in Africa, filling administrative civil service jobs as well as factory and professional ones. In the Midlands, in relation to the local employment situation, East Africans are to be found in heavy industrial work though not on the same scale as migrants coming direct from the Indian subcontinent (Duffield, 1988). East Africans do not conform to the employment patterns portrayed in the existing literature, being much more diversified throughout the United Kingdom, though with a strong tendency toward occupying public sector employment niches, as in East Africa.

Geographical Dispersal and Cultural Conservatism

Unlike other minorities, the East African community is geographically dispersed. A feature of minority settlement frequently mentioned is residential segregation and concentration in inner city areas, that leads to the formation of "ethnic ghettos" (Eade, 1989; Anwar, 1979; Castles et al., 1984; Rex and Tomlinson, 1979; Dahya, 1973, 1974). East Africans are residentially dispersed even though they reside in areas of high immigrant population. Despite this dispersal, a strong communications network operates within the community. However, the community ties that have helped perpetuate cultural values and religiosity have further catalyzed the revival of Sikhism, especially in the pre-1984 phase, among the general Sikh community residents in Britain for much longer. The injection of a more culturally conservative, though progressive (that is in their attitudes toward residence in the United Kingdom and their command over mainstream skills), community with a clear East African identity, into a much less developed and more diverse home-orientated one, has precipitated over the last decade the militant resumption of Sikh symbols. This resumption has led to a stricter organization of temples and the establishment of ceremony along more defined lines, with a stronger emphasis on their Sikh identity. It has been helped by their tight community links, which are useful in mustering support by setting up internal community organizations. Ballard and Ballard, (1977: 47) have also referred to this trend among the Sikhs, attributing the conservatism of East Africans to their lowly Ramgarhia status.[8] They state that since they are "traditionally ranked lower than the Jats, the Ramgarhias have long sought to improve their status by following the rules of religious orthodoxy more closely and they continued their strategy both in East Africa and Britain." However, the Ramgarhias are also highly organized, and able to maintain common East African Sikh identity, which is not entirely based on religious orthodoxy but is secular in nature, a product of residence and consolidation in East Africa as a Sikh community. This overt observance of their religious and cultural practices also reflects their confidence accrued from their middle-class status in comparison with the predominantly working-class situation of direct migrants, who were less confident about openly projecting their "Sikhness" in earlier stages of settlement. These factors partly account for greater conservatism despite more westernized urban ways, and also, the market skills that make them successful settlers. They are thus a traditionalist twice migrant community that possess community skills as well as those needed for operating within urban institutions in the United Kingdom. They have in the past acquired such experiences through having worked within the British East African administration, employment, education, social services sectors, and so on. Familiarity with colonial British institutions and urban life prior to migration in conjunction with their greater command of the English language facilitated the dispersal of East Africans all over the United Kingdom, away from areas of concentrated Asian population. In this respect, they differ from direct migrants who have lacked experience with European institutions, having migrated from rural areas in the subcontinent in which they had considerable familiarity with traditional social organizational values and hierarchies (Saifullah Khan, 1979).

Caste and Class: Internal Differentiation versus External Identity — pre-1984

Of the traditional features that have gained prominence in the United Kingdom, caste has become a definitive principal of organization of many minorities of Indian origin, and one which is gaining in importance. The increasing significance of caste, and the projection of exclusive caste identities among Gujarati communities from East Africa in the United Kingdom has also been described by Michaelson (1979), Shah (1979), and Tambs-Lyche (1980).

Caste differences have always been important in the arrangement of marriages. They still apply stringently in Britain to the criteria of spouse selection, even though there are minor changes in the rules of marriage arrangement as a result of settlement. On the whole, Jats marry Jats, Chamars marry Chamars, Ramgarhias from East Africa marry other East African Ramgarhias. However, these caste divisions have been accentuated and reflected in the British Sikh diaspora institutionally, for example, in the formation of separate caste associations and temples, which have executive committees restricted exclusively to caste members. Overtly this may not seem the case because of the open entry to anyone who cares to worship within Sikh temples. In fact, in a number of cases caste has crystallized as a feature of organization in Britain and has manifested itself in the establishment of caste-based institutions, precisely because of the interaction of the different caste groups with varying orientations. This is most obvious in areas of high concentration like the Midlands and London. In such places, there are exclusive Jat temples, Ramgarhia Caste Associations, separate Chamar and Bhattra temples and so on, contrary to the egalitarian Sikh religious ideals that in theory deny caste divisions.

The caste status of East Africans has been emphasized in the United Kingdom, not because of their own consciousness of it, even though in East Africa it was crucial in marriage arrangements and in the maintenance of caste endogamy. Since they themselves were the majority Sikh group in East Africa, which was almost 90 percent Ramgarhia Sikh (Mcleod, 1974: 87; Bharati, 1972: 34-39), caste position was not a defining marker of their intra-Sikh ethnicity because their status as Sikhs assumed greater importance. The homogeneity of their caste group rendered their caste status irrelevant as a defining feature of their interaction with other Sikhs who were mostly other Ramgarhias. Their caste boundary has been defined in the United Kingdom, as a result of their interaction with direct migrants from the subcontinent who, as Ballard and Ballard (1977: 54) have also mentioned, are more conscious of their caste and village ties, being more familiar about functioning caste hierarchies. The East Africans' position in Britain is a new one. They became a minority caste within the majority Sikh population of Jat Sikhs, even though there are other minority castes such as the Khatris, Ahluwalias, Ravi Dasis, Bhattras. In a way, the caste consciousness of East Africans, (i.e., their Ramgarhianess), is interactive ethnicity (Wallman, 1979: 6), produced as a result of contact with a more diverse range of caste groups within the United Kingdom, who have different experiences of migration and settlement from their own East African ones.

However, even though caste has become a powerful organizing principle for the British Sikhs, equally important is class position within the British class hierarchy. Class already has assumed, and will further assume, increasing importance as a defining feature of internal differentiation within the Sikh community, in common with other ethnic minorities (Robinson, 1988: 456). For example, the division between the Jat and Ramgarhias which expresses itself in the maintenance of separate marriage circuits and community institutions, is a reflection not only of their different caste positions and experiences of migration, but also of their different class positions. The Jats are predominantly working-class, having entered the British hierarchy as industrial workers from rural Punjab, while the Ramgarhias entered as middle-class public sector workers. So, the expression of their differences is not only produced by their different caste positions, but also by their different class positions in Britain. However, the definition of these two positions is also dependent on the context reflecting their class position. "East Africaness" manifests itself most clearly vis-`a-vis interaction with the indigenous British to stress their difference from the mainly working-class, home-orientated, and directly migrant Sikhs; "Ramgarhianess," reflecting their different caste positions, is expressed most saliently during interaction with the dominant Jat Sikh community. In areas of high Sikh concentration, caste and class positions amalgamate to define the East African separateness from the direct migrants, the projection of differences being a joint product of caste and class. Hence, their caste status is of especial relevance to the ethnic context, but not in relation to interaction with the indigenous British who do not perceive internal differences between the different caste groups, and between the twice and direct migrants.

However, racism and the lack of awareness by the white British of the different South Asian groups land them in the very groups from which they seek exclusion. Thus, the East African exclusion of the directly migrant South Asian groups is only effective within, and relevant to, the internal organization of the community. Conversely, even though caste and class divisions have become more salient than ever in the past, there is also increasing strategic unity for effective political action in conjunction with other "black" and "Asian" groups. This is the result of the growing sophistication of the community, especially among the younger generation of East Africans and "British Asians" who are British products and who are forming overreaching and more inclusive identities for collective action and political mobilization of common interests.

External Threat, Internal Coalescence:
Reaffirmation of a Sikh Identity -- post-1984

Boundaries between twice and direct migrants are continuously redefined -- weakened and strengthened -- according to the national and international forces to which the Sikhs are subject. For example, the otherwise important boundaries of class and caste between the various Sikh groups blur on specific issues that affect the Sikhs generally, and during times of crisis. An example of a crisis was the assault on the Golden Temple in Amritsar in June 1984. This assault angered the Sikhs everywhere. During this crisis there developed increased consciousness of a more universal Sikh identity, regardless of caste, class, and histories of migration. The reaffirmation of a more cohesive Sikh identity was a consequence of a most serious external threat to the Sikhs and their religion and that generated unprecedented emotion from the British Sikhs. This horrendous event and also the Delhi riots after the assassination of the former prime minister Indira Gandhi during which Sikhs were massacred, remain in the present and will do so in future, the most critical forces in the generation of an exclusive and internally inclusive Sikh identity, irrelevant of the country of residence in the diaspora, and of caste and class divisions.

In Britain, this effect was also obvious from the support mustered by British Sikhs, during the much-publicized Mandla versus Lee[9] case that resulted in successful classification of the Sikhs as a "race" in 1983. The protest marches that took place in central London included Sikhs of different origins and caste and class groups, even though East Africans were prominent as initiators of the case and the ensuing demonstrations. Community support was mobilized on the basis of common Sikh identity because these issues angered the Sikhs as a group.

Thus, in such cases boundaries coalesced for particular purposes and when posed by an external threat, to include people who in other circumstances would have been excluded (Wallman, 1979: 4-5). During times of difficulty, a consolidated Sikh identity evolved, ignoring the twice- and direct-migrant differences and caste and class divisions that otherwise divide Sikhs. A more united Sikh identity became paramount as represented by the post-1984 period, in which Sikh consciousness peaked. This heightened consciousness was reflected in the generous donations given to reconstruct the Golden Temple, in rehabilitating the victims of the Delhi riots, in gathering support to present the Sikh case to the international organizations, and so on.

But, even though boundaries dilute in relation to particular national and international issues of universal concern to the Sikhs, on the whole, these internal boundaries remain key features of the internal organization of the Sikhs in Britain. In the current phase, the different orientations of the Sikhs have reestablished themselves, though some of the forces that impinge on them are different. For example, the home orientation of the directly migrant Jat Sikhs is reflected in their greater interest in an establishment of Khalistan -- a homeland in the subcontinent and in Sikh politics in the Punjab. On the other hand, the Ramgarhia Sikhs, being twice migrants and urbanite Khatri and Arora Sikhs, are more distant from these particular concerns. However, their common interests remain latent, and ever-ready to coalesce, when their religious institutions, symbols, and values are subject to external attack.

Whereas in the above, I discussed the impact of external forces on Sikh identities, other forces are equally critical. These forces include the construction, not only by the international media, but also by other agencies, of Sikhs as terrorists regardless of their caste position, citizenship, political inclinations, or interest in the Punjab and Indian affairs. This treatment imposed on them a derogatory identity, beyond their control or management, relegated to realms of public perceptions and media constructions of them.

A parallel situation is pervasive racism that applies equally to all Sikhs and "lumps" them together with other South Asian minorities referred to as "Pakis" and "Hindus," by sections of the white majority regardless of their internal differences. However, their negotiation of racism is dependent on their class position and the skills that accrue from it. The more middle-class twice-migrant Sikhs were, for example, more efficient at maintaining their external Sikh symbols because of their confidence and familiarity with urban processes and skills, which made them more "ethnically assertive" -- as opposed to working-class Sikhs who were more willing to forgo them in order to obtain jobs. As a result, working-class Sikhs were less efficient in perpetuating their Sikh identity overtly in the pre-1984 period, when the external threats were not in existence in the same fashion, as in the post-1984 period. Since this period, a different situation applies in which young and old Sikhs have donned turbans (often orange colored ones) and become more conscious of their Sikh roots. Thus, religious and cultural values have been revived as a consequence of processes that differ from those operative on the Sikhs prior to this phase. Just as they remain familiar with the internal differences within the Sikh community, which continue to persist as a principle of Sikh social organization in times of relative peace, they are equally conscious of their common religious and cultural values that have been serious threatened and misconstructed since 1984.

Conclusion

This chapter has dealt with twice-migrant South Asians to show that their experiences of settlement and also orientations are different from those of the direct migrants in quite fundamental ways. Contrary to existing stereotypes of migrants in Europe, East Africans possessed technical, community, and urban skills necessary for operating effectively in urban Britain; they were relatively prosperous on arrival to Britain, lacked a "myth of return," were occupationally dispersed, and have remained traditionalistic, despite their urbanized and "westernized" ways.

Their relationship to the directly migrant groups has also been explored to refer to the internal dynamics of the community, both in the pre-1984 and the post-1984 phases, to show that their intragroup identities articulate along the axis of caste, class, and experiences of migration. Equally important is the impact of racism on the twice and direct migrants, and also the national and international forces that the Sikhs are and have been subject to.

Finally, this chapter also examined some of the dynamics within the British Sikh communities after the dramatic post-1984 phase, which has seen developments that are quite different from that of the pre-1984 period.

Research Methodology

This chapter is a product of research undertaken from 1976 to 1980, fieldwork for which was conducted between 1977 and 1978 in London, updated during 1981-1985 and 1987-1989 in London and the Midlands. It is based predominantly on two anthropological research studies: doctoral research that focused on the East African Sikhs, and the second, postdoctoral, one that dealt with the educational aspirations of Asian parents, in particular the Sikhs.

The East African study on which this paper is based has been reported in *Twice Migrants* (Bhachu, 1985a). I lived in Southall (London) for a year during my doctoral fieldwork and relied on participant observation. A number of my sample families lived in other parts of London, though Southall acted as my main base. My fieldwork was a "network of study," since this was the most practicable way of working in an urban area with a population as geographically dispersed as the East African Sikhs. Also, methodologically, this approach helped to get the right criteria included in a manageable number of households.

I concentrated on thirteen families who acted as my "core" group, though I operated more peripherally with a wider group of another twenty families. The latter were referred to as "wedding families,"[1] with whom I was more involved during the wedding season. In choosing to concentrate on these families, I looked for features that partly represented the general background of the East African Sikh community and that were also related to a key theme of the research, marriage and dowry patterns.

My fieldwork experiences, the joys and difficulties of working as a young Sikh woman within my own community in urban Britain and also within a geographically dispersed minority, have been described in greater detail in a forthcoming article "The Resocialization of an Anthropologist: Fieldwork within One's Own Community" (Bhachu, 1991).

Notes

1. The Labor Force Survey of 1984, conducted by the Office of

Population Censuses and Surveys, reveals a total Asian population from the New Commonwealth of approximately 1,011,000, of which the Pakistani and Bangladeshi groups constitute 462,000, and the Indian, 805,000; and in all included 206,000 Asians of East African origin.

2.   I have used the word "community" loosely through the article to refer to Asians of Sikh origin who have migrated from East Africa. They share with other East African Asian groups from their experiences as "middlemen" in the plural setting in East Africa, where they formed settled communities with developed community institutions, cross-cutting kinship links, and close neighborhood and work ties. Therefore my usage of the term "East African community" does not refer to a bounded geographical group resident in one area in the United Kingdom and from a particular region of the subcontinent, but to a population that has shared past experiences and has a strong East African identity that has been reproduced in the United Kingdom. During their considerable stay in Africa, the East African Sikhs consolidated to form an endogamous group that is perpetuated in the United Kingdom.

3.   East African Sikhs belong predominantly to the Ramgarhia caste group (Mcleod, 1974; Bharati, 1967), consisting of three artisan groups: Lohars (blacksmiths), Tarkhans (carpenters), and Raj (bricklayers). This caste ranks above the scheduled castes, but below the Jats (landowners) and Khatris (the mercantile group) in the traditional caste hierarchy. Their move to East Africa consolidated this group much more so than on the Indian scene. Within the Sikh society in East Africa there was no intermarriage between the Ramgarhias and Jats (Bharati, 1967). From the marriages in my sample, regional endogamy was also more intact than it is in Britain at present.

4.   In the 1960s, East Africans moved to the United Kingdom, especially from Kenya, which had the largest number of wage earners of the three East African countries. There was a preponderance of employees working for the public sector, which was especially highly developed in Kenya, since Nairobi, its capital, had the headquarters of all the government and major private concerns. These included the Railway and Harbors, Posts and Telecommunications, and Public Works departments, and the banks. Government enterprise was not as developed among Kenyan Asians as it was among the Ugandan and Tanzanian communities. Ghai (1965), commenting on the occupational distribution of Asian employees in the three-tier system of East African countries, states that 36 percent of Asian workers performed executive, administrative, and managerial functions; about 25 percent were involved in skilled manual jobs; another 20 percent in secretarial and clerical jobs; and 15 percent in professional and technical occupations. As in previous

decades, Asians provided the "middle level" manpower, though by the late 1950s and early 1960s a number was obtaining higher-level executive positions, thus denting the three-tier system.

5. The higher rate of entry into the labor market by East African Asian women is borne out by statistical surveys. For example, the Unit of Manpower Study (DOE, 1976) demonstrated that, in comparison with indigenous women born in the United Kingdom, a larger percentage of full-time female workers are migrant women born overseas: 81 percent of those born in the New Commonwealth (of which East African Asian women are a part), as compared with 62 percent of U.K.-born women (quoted in Allen, 1980). When the category of South Asian women in full-time employment between the ages of 16 and 59 years is examined separately, East African women constitute 67 percent, as compared to 58 percent of women of Indian origin, and 17 percent Pakistani and Bangladeshi women. In the Southeast of Britain, which has a higher rate of female employment than any other region, there is hardly any difference in the employment percentages of East African Asian women and indigenous British ones -- East African women constitute 67 percent, in comparison to 66 percent indigenous white women. Afro-Caribbean women have a higher rate, at 77 percent, than both white indigenous and Asian women (Labor Market Survey, 1986).

6. The balanced age and sex structure of the East African Sikhs also applies to other East African communities (Robinson, 1982), giving them enormous advantage of settlement abroad as communities with a sufficiently large pool of people who can marry endogamously. It also makes them unique in relation to the international migration of minority groups that tend to have a younger age profile and a more restricted range of people within them.

6. The balanced age and sex structure of the East African Sikhs also applies to other East African communities (Robinson, 1982), giving them enormous advantage of settlement aboard as communities with a sufficiently large pool of people who can marry endogamously. It also makes them unique in relation to the international migration of minority groups that tend to have a younger age profile and a more restricted range of people within them.

7. Brooks and Singh (1978) say "we accept obviously that East African Asians come from a number of ethnic groups. Nevertheless, it is apparent *to us that the East African experience is so important that it cuts across ethnic divisions* and, for the purposes of our argument, it is appropriate to group East African Asians together . . . whilst recognizing their ethnic 'identity'" (my and authors' emphasis).

8. Paul Ghuman (1980: 315) describes a similar process for the Bhattra

Sikhs who, he suggests, have remained "ultra conservative and traditional" because of their lower caste position. He states "that the Bhattras
want to adhere rigidly to their religious and social way of life to compensate for their low status; they pride themselves on being pukka Sikhs
and consider themselves the custodians of the Khalsa traditions."

9. The Mandla versus Lee case was sparked off by the refusal of the
    headmaster of a private Catholic school, Mr. Dowell-Lee, to allow an
    East African Sikh boy, Gurinder Mandla, the permission to wear a tur-
    ban as part of his school uniform. The main Sikh actors involved in the
    case, the boy himself, his solicitor father, and the main prosecuting bar-
    rister are all East African Sikhs. Similarly, Sikh religious leaders who
    gave it impetus, and the community organization that initiated the
    demonstrations that ensued (especially after the Denning ruling, which
    refused to classify the Sikhs as a "race," but which was later overturned
    by the House of Lords) were all largely East African Sikh in origin.
    This case demonstrates particularly well not only the organizational
    abilities and strong community ties of the East African Sikhs, but also
    their religiosity and staunch adherence to external opposition to their
    maintenance. The complex procedures involved in the case, and their
    ability to succeed, albeit with the expertise and resources of the com-
    mission for Racial Equality, also reflects their urban skills and familiar-
    ity with British institutions, which they were able to mobilize
    effectively.

References

Allen, Sheila. 1980. "Perhaps a Seventh Person." *Women's Studies International Quarterly* 3: 325-38.

Anwar, Muhammad 1976. *Between Two Cultures: A Study of Relationships
Between the Generations in the Asian Community.* London: Community
Relations Pamphlets.

Anwar, Muhammad. 1979. *The Myth of Return: Pakistanis in Britain.* London: Heinemann.

Aurora, Gurdip Singh. 1967. *The New Frontiersmen.* Bombay: Popular
Prakashan.

Ballard, Roger. 1973. "Family Organization among the Sikhs in Britain."
The New Community 2: 12-24.

Ballard, Roger, and Catherine Ballard. 1977. "The Sikhs: The Development
of South Asian Settlements in Britain." In *Between Two Cultures:
Migrants and Minorities in Britain*, edited by James Watson. Oxford:
Basic Blackwell.

Bhachu, Parminder Kaur 1985a. *Twice Migrants: East African Sikhs Settlers in Britain*. London: Tavistock Publications.

Bhachu, Parminder Kaur. 1985b. "Parental Education Strategies: The Case of Punjabi Sikhs in Britain." Research Paper in Ethnic Relations, 3. Centre for Research in Ethnic Relations, University of Warwick, Coventry, Britain.

Bhachu, Parminder Kaur. 1986. "Work, Dowry and Marriage among East African Sikh Women in the United Kingdom." In *International Immigrants: The Female Experience*, edited by Caroline Brettell and Rita Simon. Totowa, NJ: Rowman and Allenhead.

Bhachu, Parminder Kaur. 1988. "Apni Marzi Kardhi. Home and Work: East African Sikh Women in Britain." In *Enterprising Women: Ethnicity, Economy, and Gender Relations*. London and New York: Routledge.

Bhachu, Parminder Kaur. 1991. "The Resocialization of an Anthropologist: Fieldwork Within One's Own Community." In *From the Female's Eye: Researchers Working in their Own Communities*, edited by M. N. Pannini. Delhi: Hindustan Publishing Corporation.

Bharati, Agehananda. 1967. "Ideology and Content of Caste among the Indians in East Africa." In *Caste in Overseas Indian Communities*, edited by B. M. Schwartz. San Francisco: Chandler Publishing Corporation.

Bharati, Agehananda. 1972. *The Asians in East Africa: Jayhind and Uhuru*. Chicago: Nelson-Hall.

Brooks, Dennis 1975a. *Race and Labour in London Transport*. London: Oxford University Press for the Institute of Race Relations.

Brooks, Dennis. 1975b. *Black Employment in the Black Country: A Study of Walsall*. London: Runnymede Trust.

Brooks, Dennis, and Karamjit Singh. 1978. "Ethnic Commitment Versus Structured Reality: South Asian Immigrant Workers in Britain." *New Community* 7-1.

Castles, Stephan. 1984. *Here for Good: Western Europe's New Ethnic Minorities*. London: Pluto Press.

Castles, Stephan, and Godula Kosack. 1973. *Immigrant Workers and the Class Structure*. London: Oxford University Press for the Institute of Race Relations.

Dahya, Badr. 1973. "Pakistanis in Britain, Transients or Settlers?" *Race* 14: 246-277.

Dahya, Badr. 1974. "The Nature of Pakistani Ethnicity in Industrial Cities in Britain." In *Urban Ethnicity*, edited by A. Cohen. London: Tavistock.

Dahya, Badr. 1988. "South Asians as Economic Migrants in Britain." *Ethnic and Racial Studies* 11-4: 439-55.

Duffield, Mark. 1988. *Black Radicalism and the Politics of De-Industrialization: The Hidden History of Indian Foundry Workers*. Avebury: Aldershot, Britain.

Eade, John. 1989. *The Politics of Community: The Bangladeshi Community in East London*. Avebury: Aldershot, Britain.

Employment Gazette. 1985 (December). *Ethnic Origin and Economic Status*. Office of Population Censuses and Surveys. London: Her Majesty's Stationery Office.

Employment Gazette. 1987 (January). *Ethnic and Economic Status*. Office of Population and Surveys. London: Her Majesty's Stationery Office.

Fernando, T. 1979. "East African Asians in Western Canada: The Ismaili Community." *New Community* 7-3.

Ghai, Dharam. 1965. *Portrait of a Minority: Asians in East Africa*. Nairobi: Oxford University Press.

Ghuman, Paul. 1980. "Bhattra Sikhs in Cardiff: Family and Kinship Organization." *New Community* 8-3.

Helweg, Auther W. 1979. *Sikhs in England: The Development of a Migrant Community*. Delhi: Oxford University Press.

Humphrey, Derek, and Michael Ward. 1974. *Passports and Politics*. Harmondsworth, Britain: Penguin Books.

Jeffrey, Patricia. 1976. *Migrants and Refugees: Muslims and Christian Pakistani Families in Bristol*. Cambridge: Cambridge University Press.

Kuepper, William, et al. 1975. *Ugandan Asians in Britain: Forced Migration and Social Absorption*. London: Croom Helm.

Mcleod, W. Hew. 1974. "Ahluwahlias and Ramgarhias: Two Sikh Castes." *South Asia* 4: 78-90.

Mangat, J. Singh. 1969. *A History of the Asians in East Africa, 1886-1945*. Oxford: Clarendon Press.

Michaelson, Maureen. 1979. "The Relevance of Caste Among East African Gujeratis in Britain." *New Community* 7-3.

Morris, H.S., 1967. "Caste among the Indians in Uganda." In *Caste in Overseas Indian Communities*, edited by B. M. Schwartz. San Francisco: Chandler Publishing Company.

Morris, H.S., 1968. *Indians in Uganda*. London: Weidenfeld and Nicolson.

Phizacklea, Annie, and Robert Miles. 1980. *Labour and Racism*. London: Routledge and Kegan Paul.

Rex, John, and Sally Tomlinson. 1979. *Colonial Immigrants in a British City: A Class Analysis*. London: Routledge and Kegan Paul.

Robinson, Vaughan. 1981. "The Development of South Asian Settlements in Britain and the Myth of Return." In *Ethnic Segregation in Cities*, edited by C. Peach, et.al. London: Croom Helm.

Robinson, Vaughan. 1982. "The Assimilation of South and East African Asian Immigrants in Britain." In *Demography of Immigrants and Minorities in the United Kingdom*, edited by D.A. Coleman. London: Academic Press.

Robinson, Vaughan. 1984. "Asian in Britain: A Study in Encapsulation and Marginality." In *Geography and Ethnic Pluralism*, edited by C. Clarke, D. Ley, and C. Peach. London: Allen and Unwin.

Robinson, Vaughan. 1988. "The New Indian Middle Class in Britain." *Ethnic and Racial Studies* 11, 4.

Saifullah Khan, Verity. 1976. "Perceptions of a Population: Pakistanis in Britain." *New Community* 5: 222-229.

Saifullah Khan, Verity. 1977. "The Pakistanis: Mirpuri Villages at Home in Bradford." In *Between Two Cultures: Migrants and Minorities in Britain*. Oxford: Basil Blackwell.

Shah, Samir. 1979. "Who are the Jains?" *New Community*. Britain: Macmillan Press, 7-3.

Shaw, Alison. 1988. *A Pakistani Community in Britain*. New York: Blackwell.

Tambs-Lyche, Harald. 1980. *London Patiders: A Case in Urban Ethnicity*. London: Routledge and Kegan Paul.

Wallman, Sandra, ed. 1979. *Ethnicity at Work*. London: Macmillan.

Werbner, Pnina. 1990. *The Migration Process: Capital, Gifts & Offerings Among Overseas Pakistanis*. Oxford: Berg Press.

9

Korean Immigrants in Los Angeles[1]

Pyong Gap Min

During the period 1903 to 1905, about seven thousand two hundred Koreans immigrated to Hawaii to work for sugar plantations.[2] The mass immigration of Korean workers to the United States almost ended after 1905, and did not resume until 1965 when the U.S. Congress amended the immigration law. Some two thousand additional Koreans came to the United States between 1906 and 1923, and almost all were picture brides of the 1903-1905 labor immigrants or students. The 1924 national origins quota system put an end to influx of any Koreans, whether labor immigrants or family members of U.S. residents. The immigration of Koreans resumed during and after the Korean War as the United States maintained close political, military, and economic relations with South Korea. More than three thousand Koreans were admitted as legal immigrants during the period of 1950-1964; the vast majority were Korean wives of U.S. serviceman stationed in South Korea and Korean children adopted by U.S. citizens.

The U.S. Congress passed a new immigration law in 1965. This law abolished discrimination based on national origins, ending the legal exclusion of Asians. The new law allowed aliens to be admitted to the United States as legal immigrants based on three criteria: (1) if they had occupational skills useful for employment in the United States (occupational immigrants); (2) if they had relatives already settled in the Unites States (family unification); and (3) if they were vulnerable to political persecution (refugees and asylees). The new immigration law set a quota of twenty thousand per country each year. However, each country can send more than twenty thousand immigrants per year, since spouses, fiancees, parents, and unmarried children of U.S. children can be admitted as legal immigrants exempt from the national limitation.

The passage of the new immigration law had a great impact on the Korean American community. Although the immigration of Koreans to the United States had started in 1903, the Korean community was tiny in 1970. Even allowing for a great undercount, the Korean population of the United States in 1970 may have been no more than a hundred thousand. However, more than six hundred thousand Koreans immigrated to the United States between 1970 and 1990. The number of annual Korean immigrants steadily increased in the early 1970s. In 1976 it exceeded thirty thousand; and it maintained that level throughout the 1980s. Korean immigrants have accounted for 6 - 8 percent of total immigrants to the United States over the last fifteen years. In this period, Korea has sent more immigrants to the United States than any other country, except Mexico and the Philippines. The 1990 census estimated the Korean population in the United States to be about 800,000. Adding Korean students, visitors, illegal residents, and children born since 1990, the true Korean population may be close to one million in 1992.

Like other Asian immigrants, the Korean immigrants have largely hailed from the middle class. The U.S. Bureau of the Census (1984:1-12) shows that of the Korean immigrants admitted between 1970 and 1980, 32 percent had completed four years of college education. In contrast, only 6.8 percent of adults in Korea received a college education (The Korean National Bureau of Statistics, 1983:164-165). This discrepancy suggests that Korean immigrants are an educational elite in their homeland. Only 16.2 percent of adult Americans were college graduates in 1980. Therefore, Korean immigrants also surpass the U.S. population by a significant margin in college education. Consistent with their high levels of education, the vast majority of Korean immigrants held professional and white-collar occupations prior to immigration. Hurh and Kim (1984:105) found that 90 percent of Korean respondents in Los Angeles had held professional and white-collar occupations in Korea.

Few Koreans had already settled in the United States in 1970. For this reason, few Korean immigrants admitted in the early 1970s were admitted on the basis of family unification; many came as beneficiaries of occupational preferences. Occupational immigrants constituted more than 30 percent of Korean immigrants admitted in the early 1970s. About one-third of Korean occupational immigrants in the early 1970s were medical professionals. The proportion of Korean occupational immigrants gradually decreased after 1975, accounting for less than 10 percent of annual Korean immigrants over the last several years. This reduction reflects the general reduction of occupational immigrants in the United States since the mid-1970s. When the general unemployment rate rose in 1976, the U.S. Department of Labor denied labor permits to many prospective occupational immigrants. The Health Manpower Act of 1976 required that alien medical professionals obtain a job offer from a U.S. employer before being admitted to this country. This revision of the 1965 Immigration Act almost put an end to the immigration of Korean medical professionals.

Korean Immigrants' Concentration in Los Angeles

The Immigration and Naturalization Service indicates that approximately 20 - 30 percent of annual Koran immigrants chose California for residence and 7 - 9 percent chose Los Angeles. The proportion of Korean immigrants who chose California as the state of intended residence steadily increased from 20 percent in the early 1970s to almost 30 percent in 1979. The proportion of Korean immigrants who chose Los Angeles has consistently ranged from 7 percent to 9 percent. The number of Korean immigrants in Hawaii, the oldest center of Korean immigration, has decreased relative to other states since the 1970s.

Approximately 260 thousand Koreans had settled in California by 1990. These settlers accounted for 32.5% of the Korean population in the United States (U.S. Bureau of the Census, 1992). One hundred fifty thousand Koreans, 55% of Koreans in California, resided in Los Angeles County, and another 36 thousand Koreans lived in Orange County (U.S. Bureau of the Census, 1992). Both the state of California and Los Angeles County achieved a higher rate of increase in the Korean population between 1970 and 1990 than did the United States as a whole. Although Korean Americans heavily concentrate in California, other Asian ethnic groups concentrate even more highly in the Golden State. The U.S. Bureau of the Census (1992: 125) reveals that 50 percent of Filipino Americans, 43 percent of Chinese Americans, 37 percent of Japanese Americans, and 46 percent of Vietnamese Americans resided in the state. There were also more Japanese, Filipino, or Chinese Americans than Korean Americans in Los Angeles County in 1990.

Koreatown

Los Angeles is the American capital of Korean immigrants not merely because it has the largest Korean population in the United States, but also because it has Koreatown, the only Korean residential and commercial center in the United States. Located about three miles west of downtown Los Angeles, Koreatown covers approximately 16 square miles, four miles from the east to the west and another four miles from the north to the south. Koreatown is bounded by Beverly Boulevard on the north (North 200), Pico Boulevard to the south (South 1,400), Hoover Street to the east (East 2,000), and the line connecting Crenshaw Boulevard and Plymouth Boulevard to the west (West 4,200). The north-south line covers fifteen blocks and the east-west line covers 26 blocks. Koreatown includes twenty census tracts, ten of which constitute its core.

Koreatown initially developed around Korean stores. Yu (1985) claims that the establishment of the Olympic Market at the corner of Olympic Boulevard and Hobart Street in 1969 was the origin of Koreatown. Following the Olympic Market, many other Korean restaurants, gift shops, and other ethnically oriented stores opened up along Olympic Boulevard. The increasing number of Korean stores paralleled the residential concentration of Koreans in Koreatown. Koreatown became the residential and commercial center for Los Angeles Koreans. Koreatown has extended its boundary to the north since 1980. Not only Olympic Boulevard, but also Eighth and Seventh Streets, covering fifteen blocks between Hoover street and Western Avenue, have been the core of Koreatown since the mid-1980s. Many ethnically oriented stores such as Korean restaurants, boutiques, and bakery stores have been recently established several blocks north of Beverly Boulevard, which Korean residents called the northern boundary of Koreatown just a few years ago.

Table 9.1 shows the racial composition of residents in twenty Koreatown census tracts and ten Koreatown core census tracts based on the 1980 census. Koreans constituted 10.5 percent of the total Koreatown population in 1980. Nonwhites made up the vast majority of Koreatown residents, with whites constituting only 27 percent of total population. The largest group in Koreatown is Mexicans, who serve as customers and frequent employees of Korean-owned

TABLE 9.1
Ethno-Racial Composition of Koreatown Residents

Racial Group	Koreatown		Koreatown Core	
	N	%	N	%
Korean	11,675	10.5	8,840	14.4
Other Pacific/ Asian	15,693	14.1	8,837	14.6
Black	10,962	9.9	6,103	10.1
Hispanic	40,780	36.7	23,376	38.5
Indian	519	0.5	312	0.5
White	29,852	26.9	12,475	20.5
Others	1,626	1.4	973	1.4
Total	111,107	100.0	60,716	100.0

Sources: Adjusted from 1980 Census of Population and Housing, Census Tracts, Los Angeles-Long Beach, California, PHC 80-2-226, Table P-7, Tracts 2111, 2112, 2113, 2114, 2115, 2117, 2118, 2119, 2121, 2122, 2123, 2124, 2125, 2126, 2127, 2129, 2131, 2132, 2133, and 2134.

businesses. Only 14.4 percent of Koreatown's population, Koreans constitute a minority even in the core of Koreatown. Since many more Koreans have moved to Koreatown since 1980, Koreans will comprise a larger proportion of Koreatown residents in the 1990 census.

Although Koreatown's Koreans comprise a minority of its residents, they account for a large proportion of Koreans in Los Angeles. The 1980 census shows that Koreans settled in Koreatown constituted 35 percent of Koreans in the city of Los Angeles, 19 percent of Koreans residing in the Los Angeles-Long Beach metropolitan area, and 15 percent of those in Southern California. Partly because of the heavy residential concentration of Los Angeles Koreans in this area, people called it "Koreatown." With the exception of Chinese, no other recent Asian immigrant group maintains so much residential concentration. A large proportion of recent Chinese immigrants have settled in existing Chinatowns in Los Angeles and other cities. Los Angeles Koreatown and Miami's Little Havana are the only immigrant enclaves created in the post-1965 era (Portes and Rumbaut, 1990).

Many fresh Korean immigrants, who have difficulty with English, settle in Koreatown, seeking employment in Korean-owned stores. Koreatown also attracts many temporary visitors and illegals, who find employment in Korean restaurants, garment factories, and stores. Most Korean immigrants, however, consider Koreatown, which has a high crime rate and poor schools, at best a temporary home. Once having lived in Koreatown long enough to acculturate, many Korean immigrants move to suburbs. In the 1986 survey, 28 percent of Koreatown respondents reported that they had been in this country for three years or less, in comparison to 13 percent of Korean respondents in other areas of Los Angeles (Min, 1989).

Koreatown is not only a residential but also a commercial center for Los Angeles Koreans. The level of Koreans' commercial concentration in Koreatown is reflected in my 1986 survey of Los Angeles. Koreatown contained 26 percent of total Korean-owned businesses in Los Angeles and Orange Counties. This result does not mean that a higher proportion of Koreatown Koreans are business owners than are Koreans in other Los Angeles neighborhoods. In fact, my 1986 Los Angeles survey showed that Koreatown's Koreans were self-employed in smaller proportion than were Koreans outside of it (Min, 1989). This disproportion suggests that many Koreans who live outside of Koreatown must own a business in Koreatown. In fact, the 1986 study indicated that 59 percent of Korean-owned businesses located in Koreatown were owned by Koreans who lived outside of it.

The vast majority of Korean businesses located in Koreatown meet the special consumer demands of co-ethnics. That is, they serve Korean food, Korean groceries, Korean books/magazines, and personal services with distinctive Korean cultural tastes. Approximately 73 percent of Korean firms located in Koreatown declared Koreans the majority of their customers, compared to 21 percent of Korean firms in other areas of Southern California (Min, 1989). This imbalance makes a good contrast with Chinatown and Little Tokyo, whose business firms mainly serve out-group members. Only 13 percent and 23 percent of Korean businesses located in Koreatown serve blacks/Mexicans and whites, respectively, as the majority of their customers. Many Koreans, especially the elderly, live in Koreatown mainly because all kinds of services are available there in a culturally congenial setting.

Table 9.2 shows the types of Korean businesses that concentrate in Koreatown. Koreatown has many restaurants and night clubs. Koreatown restaurants and night clubs account respectively for 43 percent and 48 percent of those in Southern California, although only 15 percent of Koreans in Southern California live in Koreatown. Since Korean restaurants in Koreatown confront strong competition, they provide better service for lower prices than do Korean restaurants located outside. Koreans even claim that they dine better and more cheaply in Koreatown than in Seoul. Many Koreans regularly drive to Koreatown for meals. Koreatown also has many Oriental grocery stores in proportion to its Korean population. Moreover, Oriental grocery stores located in Koreatown are generally larger than those outside of it.

Many Korean immigrants speak English poorly. They depend upon co-ethnics for professional services. Most Korean accounting firms are located in Koreatown. Korean lawyers and medical doctors also partly depend upon co-ethnic customers, and a large proportion of their professional offices are located inside or near

TABLE 9.2
Major Korean Businesses Located in Koreatown

Business Line	Total Businesses	Businesses Located in Koreatown	% of Total Business
Boutiques	67	37	55.2
Korean restaurants	231	100	43.3
Night clubs	90	43	47.8
Oriental grocery stores	113	27	23.9
Korean bakery	29	20	70.0
Accounting services	109	82	75.2
Medical services	424	110	25.9
Law firms	69	40	58.0
Insurance	49	29	59.2
Real estate	114	42	36.8
Beauty salons	141	59	41.8
Barber shops	15	11	73.3
Travel agencies	64	48	75.0
Video shops	64	28	43.8
Recreation centers	23	16	69.6
Ethnic newspapers and magazines	32	20	62.5
Ethnic book stores	32	15	46.9
Oriental herbs and acupuncture	130	69	53.1
Fortunetellers	17	10	58.8
Total	1,813	806	44.5

Sources: Keys Advertisement and Printing Company, The Korean Directory of Southern California, 1986-87.

Koreatown. Insurance and real estate agencies are the other professional service businesses in which Korean entrepreneurs service a Korean clientele. Therefore, the concentration of these two industries in Koreatown is natural. Approximately ten large multistory Korean-owned buildings line Wilshire Boulevard. Many Korean medical professionals, lawyers, accountants, insurance, travel, and real estate agents rent offices in these buildings. Koreatown also houses numerous businesses that peddle traditional Korean products and services. Fifty-three percent of a hundred and thirty Korean herbs and acupuncture services and ten of seventeen fortune tellers have offices in Koreatown.

Koreatown mixes commercial and residential areas. Zoning restrictions severely hampered Koreatown business development. Although several shopping malls have been established in Koreatown, they lack parking space. Traffic congestion, scant parking, and a lack of English language signs have made it difficult for non-Korean customers to visit Koreatown for shopping and sightseeing. For these and other reasons, Koreatown is not well known to non-Koreans. In a marketing survey only 11.5% of respondents reported that they knew the location of Koreatown whereas 76.9% and 61.7% of them knew the locations of Chinatown and Japan Town respectively (*Sae Gae Times*, 1992). Non-Korean residents of Koreatown have complained about Korean commercial encroachment into their residential areas. Koreatown leaders have tried to persuade the city government to rezone some residential areas in the heart of Koreatown for commercial and public use. However, they have had little success. Until a major renovation involving demolition of several residential areas is achieved, Koreatown may not draw many non-Korean customers from outside of its area.

Koreatown is also a social and cultural center for Los Angeles' Koreans. The central organization of the Los Angeles Korean community, the Korean Federation of L.A., and all eight major Korean business associations, including Koreatown Development Association and Korean Chamber of Commerce of L.A., have their offices in Koreatown. The Korean Youth Center, the Korean Family Legal Counseling Center, and other Korean social work organizations are also located in Koreatown. Twenty of thirty-two Korean ethnic newspapers and magazines in Southern California, including all three ethnic dailies, have their offices in Koreatown. Koreatown also houses nearly half of thirty-two Korean language book stores in Southern California. Korean business associations, social service organizations, alumni associations, and other social clubs hold regular seminars, meetings, and parties at offices and restaurants in Koreatown. Many Korean families settled in other parts of Southern California often come to Koreatown restaurants for a wedding reception, a birthday party, a New Year dinner, or other events. Koreatown holds its annual "Koreatown festival" in October. This event introduces traditional Korean dances, songs, dresses, games, and food to non-Korean residents and visitors. There are eight Korean-owned hotels and motels in Koreatown, and two of them house a Korean professional convention on the national level almost every month. The Koreatown hotels also accommodate visitors and entertainers from Korea.

Concentration In Small Business

Although well educated, Korean immigrants probably have more language problems than other comparably educated immigrants. For example, Filipino and Indian immigrants spoke English in their native country prior to immigration. Although almost all Korean immigrants studied English as a second language in Korean schools, few spoke English fluently prior to immigration. The difficulty Korean immigrants have with spoken English is well reflected in the 1986 pre-departure survey conducted in Seoul. Only 9.2 percent of departing immigrants did not need an interpreter for the visa interview in English (Park et al., 1990). Mainly because of this language difficulty and partly because of nonrecognition of diplomas and professional certificates earned in Korea, many educated Korean immigrants cannot find jobs comparable to their education. As a result, a large majority of college educated Korean immigrants have to accept blue-collar jobs.

As an alternative to undesirable blue-collar occupations, a large proportion of Korean immigrants become self-employed in small businesses (Min, 1984b). Results of survey studies in several major

Korean communities suggest that 40 percent to 60 percent of Korean immigrant households own at least one business (Hurh and Kim, 1988; Min, 1988a, 1989, 1992a). Koreans' small-business activities are particularly strong in Los Angeles. A survey conducted in 1973 showed that 25 percent of Korean household heads in Southern California were self-employed (Bonacich et al., 1976). The self-employment rate of household heads in the Los Angeles Korean community increased to 40 percent in 1977 (Yu, 1982). A 1986 survey indicated that 53 percent of Korean male household heads and 48 percent of all Korean workers in Los Angeles were self-employed. Thirty percent of Korean workers in Los Angeles were also employed in Korean firms. Thus, only one quarter of Los Angeles Korean workers worked in the general labor market (Table 9.3). Households that owned at least one business accounted for 52.5 percent of total Korean households in Los Angeles in 1986 (Min, 1989).

Table 9.4. shows that the major industries of Koreans in Los Angeles. Trade businesses dealing largely in Korean-imported items such as wigs, handbags, jewelry, and clothing constitute approximately 15 percent of Korean-owned businesses in Los Angeles.

TABLE 9.3
Los Angeles Korean Immigrants' Self-Employment Rate and
Segregation by Sex

	Male		Female		Total		Spouses & Others	
	No.	%	No.	%	No.	%	No.	%
Self-employed	179	53.0	57	35.8	236	47.5	374	45.1
Employed in ethnic firms	88	26.0	49	30.8	137	27.6	248	29.9
Employed in general labor market	71	21.0	53	33.3	124	24.9	207	25.0
Total	338	100.0	159	100.0	497	100.0	829	100.0

Sources: My 1986 Survey of Koreans in Los Angeles.

Table 9.4
Korean Industries in Los Angeles, 1986

Industry	N	%
Wigs and Other Fashion Items	44	14.8
Professional	38	12.8
Restaurants and Related	32	10.8
Grocery and Liquor Stores	31	10.4
Gas Stations	29	9.8
Garment Factories	16	5.4
Maintenance	13	4.4
House Painting	11	3.7
Others	83	27.9
Total	297	100.0

Sources: *My 1986 Survey of Koreans in Los Angeles.*

They include a large number of import and wholesale businesses. The 1986 Directory of Southern California listed three hundred and twenty Korean-owned import-export companies (Keys Advertisement and Printing Company, 1986). Koreans' concentration in businesses dealing in Korean exports depends on and expands trade between the United States and South Korea (Min, 1984a). Korean exports to the United States substantially increased after the early 1970s, when the influx of Koreans to the United States also started. By virtue of the advantages associated with their language and ethnic background, many Korean immigrants have established import businesses dealing in Korean exports. Korean importers distribute Korean-made consumer goods mainly to co-ethnic wholesalers, who in turn distribute them mainly to co-ethnic retailers. As a result, Korean immigrants have nearly monopolized wigs and several other import products.

Five professions (medical, legal, accounting, real estate, and insurance services) comprise almost 13 percent of Korean businesses in Los Angeles. As previously indicated, the majority of these professional businesses are located inside or near Koreatown, serving mainly Korean customers. My 1986 survey reveals that 76 percent of Korean-owned professional businesses depended on Koreans as the majority of their customers whereas only 17 percent of nonprofessional businesses did so. Restaurants and food related businesses constitute the third ranking Korean industry in Los Angeles. Whereas overseas Chinese usually serve Chinese food to non-Chinese customers, Korean immigrants in the United States mainly serve American fast food to American customers. Many Korean restaurants mainly serve Korean customers a true Korean cuisine.

Another industry in which Koreans concentrate is the grocery/liquor business. Requiring long work hours, the grocery business does not interest native-born people. But, it has proved acceptable to many immigrants with labor market disadvantages. Korean immigrants are no exception. The President of the Korean-American Grocers' Association of Southern California told me that there were approximately 1,500 Korean-owned grocery stores in the Los Angeles-Long Beach metropolitan area and 2,250 Korean-owned grocery stores in Southern California as of March 1990. The grocery business is the single most significant industry of the Los Angeles Korean community. In many other Korean communities, the American grocery business is also the major Korean industry. In Atlanta, for example, grocery stores constituted 31 percent of total Korean-owned businesses in 1982 (Min, 1988a).

Gas stations, garment manufacturing, and building maintenance services are the other major businesses of the Los Angeles Koreans. Gas stations and garment manufacturing are connected directly to U.S. corporations. That is, Korean immigrants franchise gas stations and subcontract garment manufacturing from U.S. corporations. The direct connection between Korean small businesses and U.S. corporations is possible mainly because Korean owners use family members and new immigrants as cheap labor. Korean gas station owners and garment manufacturers help U.S. corporations by providing cheap labor, to which the corporations have no access. This is why Bonacich argues that Korean small businesses serve the interests of big U.S. corporations (Light and Bonacich, 1988:

chapter 15). However, only 20 percent of Korean-owned business in Los Angeles are franchised or subcontracting businesses (Min, 1989). Moreover, fewer Korean immigrants in other Korean centers are engaged in gas station franchise or garment industry subcontracting.

Does self-employment help Korean immigrants to achieve economic mobility? Table 9.5 helps to answer this question. The median household income for all U.S. households in 1986 was $24,897 (U.S. Bureau of the Census, 1987:422), and over 70 percent of Korean immigrant households in Los Angeles reached that income level in the same year. Whereas only 16.8 percent of U.S. households earned $50 thousand dollars or more in the year, 30.6 percent of the Los Angeles Korean immigrant household achieved this income. These figures suggest that Korean immigrants in Los Angeles have done well economically relative to other groups.

More important is the income gap between self-employed and employed Koreans. We find a significant differential in family income between self-employed and employed Koreans. Approximately 19 percent of self-employed workers, in comparison to 36 percent of employed workers, reported that their annual family income was below $25 thousand. At the high end, 43 percent of self-employed respondents reported $50 thousand or more in comparison to only 20 percent of employed respondents. Moreover, other indicators such as home ownership, bedrooms, and cars owned suggest

TABLE 9.5
Korean Income by Class of Worker

Annual Family Income	Self-Employed		Employed		Total	
	N	%	N	%	N	%
Below $25,000	47	19.4	108	36.7	155	28.9
$25,000 - $49,000	90	37.2	127	43.2	217	40.5
$50,000 or more	105	43.4	59	20.1	164	30.6

X2 = 39.032 p. < 0.001

Sources: My 1986 Survey of Koreans in Los Angeles.

that Korean business families enjoy a higher standard of living than wage-earning families (Min, 1989). However, self-employed and employed respondents were similar in educational level, English skills, length of residence in the United States, and number of workers per family. Thus, the differences in family income and standard of living between self-employed and employed workers were mainly a product of self-employment itself. Small business is the main avenue of economic mobility among Korean immigrants.

Ethnicity

The extent to which members of an ethnic/immigrant group maintain their native cultural tradition and social interactions with co-ethnic members is "ethnic attachment" or "ethnicity" (Hurh and Kim, 1984; Reitz, 1980; Yinger et al., 1980). Korean immigrants in the United States maintain high ethnic attachment. That is, the vast majority of Korean immigrants speak the Korean language, eat mainly Korean food, and practice Korean customs most of the time. Most Korean immigrants are affiliated with at least one ethnic organization. They are involved in ethnic social networks. Hurh and Kim (1988) reported that 90 percent of Korean immigrants in Chicago mainly spoke Korean at home and that 82 percent were affiliated with one or more ethnic organizations. Koreans are joiners. A comparative study of Koreans, Chinese, and Filipinos indicates that a much larger proportion of Koreans (75 percent) than of Filipinos (50 percent) or Chinese (19 percent) joined one or more ethnic associations (Mangiafico, 1988: 174).

Korean immigrants maintain high ethnic attachment for three reasons (Min, 1991). First, Korean immigrants come from a small and culturally homogeneous country. Cultural homogeneity at home provides a firm basis for Korean ethnicity overseas. Second, the vast majority of Korean immigrants are affiliated with Korean Christian churches (Hurh and Kim, 1990; Min, 1992a). The churches facilitate immigrants' fellowship and preservation of Korean traditions. In addition, as noted in the previous section, Korean immigrants concentrate in small businesses; this ethnic occupation provides an economic basis of ethnic solidarity (Bonacich, 1973; Bonacich and

Modell, 1980; Reitz, 1980). When cultural and economic boundaries coincide, "ethnic solidarity is doubly reinforced" (Olzak 1986; see also Bodnar et al., 1982). Korean immigrants in the Unites States maintain high ethnicity because of this coincidence of cultural and economic boundaries.

Residential segregation encourages ethnicity (Lieberson, 1963; Yancy et al., 1974), and Koreans in Los Angeles maintain a higher level of ethnicity than co-ethnics elsewhere because of their residential concentration. First of all, the Koreatown territorial community enhances Korean ethnic attachment on the part of not only Koreatown Koreans, but also of those in other areas of Los Angeles. Of course, Koreatown Koreans maintain more frequent social interaction with co-ethnics, and thus speak Korean with their neighbors more often than co-ethnics elsewhere. The Koreatown Koreans are also likely to speak Korean at home more often than Koreans in other Los Angeles areas. Asked about the frequency of speaking English at home, 68 percent of the Koreatown respondents reported speaking English rarely or never in comparison to 47.5 percent of Koreans settled elsewhere in Los Angeles. This means that two-thirds of Koreatown Koreans speak Korean at home most of the time whereas less than half of Koreans in other Los Angeles areas do so. The Koreatown residents also eat Korean food more often and preserve other Korean customs more strictly.

As a Korean social and cultural center, Koreatown reinforces ethnic attachment and ethnic identity not only for Koreatown Koreans, but also for those in other Los Angeles areas. Moreover, a large concentration of Koreans in Los Angeles encourages social interaction among Koreans, thereby facilitating maintenance of the Korean language, food, and customs. For these reasons, Koreans in Los Angeles maintain a higher level of ethnic attachment than do those in other parts of the United States. The census report provides the percentage of the foreign-born five years old and over who speak their native language at home. It shows that 92.1 percent of foreign-born Koreans residing in the Los Angeles-Long Beach metropolitan area speak Korean at home; in comparison only 83.8 percent of total foreign-born Koreans in the United States spoke Korean at home (U.S. Bureau of the Census, 1988: table 43).

Conclusion

Korean immigrants constitute one of the major new immigrant groups that have emerged since the revision of the U.S. immigration law in 1965. Los Angeles has received more Korean immigrants than any other city in the United States. The Los Angeles Korean community includes Koreatown, the Koreans' residential, commercial, and cultural center. Together with Little Havana in Miami, Koreatown is probably the only nationally prominent ethnic enclave developed by any of the post-1965 immigrant groups. Another unique feature of Korean immigrants' adjustment is that many are self- employed because of low English proficiency and other labor market disadvantages. Korean immigrants maintain a higher level of ethnic attachment than do other Asian immigrant groups. The affiliation of the majority of Korean immigrants with Korean churches, their cultural homogeneity, and their concentration in small businesses contribute to their high ethnic attachment. Korean immigrants in Los Angeles preserve an even higher level of ethnicity than they do in other parts of the United States partly because of the existence of Koreatown as a territorial base and partly because of a large concentration of Koreans in the city.

Notes

1. This chapter is based on works supported by the National Science Foundation under grant number SES-8098735. Any opinions, findings, conclusions, or recommendations expressed in this chapter are those of the author and do not necessarily reflect the views of the National Science Foundation. Detailed information on data collection is provided in Min, 1989b.
2. Between August and September 1986, 557 Korean immigrants in Los Angeles were personally interviewed. The interviews provide major data source for this chapter. Public documents, articles from Korean ethnic newspapers published in the Los Angeles area, the Los Angeles Korean ethnic directory, my personal observations, and other published materials will also be used as data sources. For detailed information on the Korean labor immigrants to Hawaii between 1903 and 1905, see Patterson, 1988.

References

Bodnar, J.R., et al. 1982. *Lives of Their Own: Blacks, Italians, and Poles in Pittsburgh, 1900-1960*. Urbana: University of Illinois Press.

Bonacich, Edna. 1973. "A Theory of Middleman Minorities." *American Sociological Review* 38: 583-594.

Bonacich, Edna, et al. 1976. "Small Business among Korean Immigrants in Los Angeles." In *Counterpoint: Perspective on Asian America*, edited by Emma Gee. Los Angeles: University of California Press.

Bonacich, Edna, and John Modell. 1980. *The Economic Basis of Ethnic Solidarity: Small Business in the Japanese American Community*. Berkeley: University of California Press.

Hurh, Won Moo, and Kwang Chung Kim. 1984. *Korean Immigrants in America: A Structural Analysis of Ethnic Confinement and Adhesive Adaptation*. Madison, NJ: Fairleigh Dickinson University Press.

Hurh, Won Moo, and Kwang Chung Kim. 1988. "Uprooting and Adjustment: A Sociological Study of Korean Immigrants' Mental Health." Final Report Submitted to the National Institute of Mental Health, U.S. Department of Health and Human Services.

Hurh, Won Moo, and Kwang Chung Kim. 1990. "Religious Participation of Korean Immigrants in the United States." *Journal for the Scientific Study of Religion* 29: 19-34.

Immigration and Naturalization Service. 1970-1986. *Annual Reports*. Washington, DC: U.S. Government Printing Office.

Keys Advertisement and Printing Company. 1986. *The Korean Directory of Southern California, 1986-1987*. Los Angeles: Keys Advertising.

Kim, Illsoo. 1981. *New Urban Immigrants: The Korean Community in New York*. Princeton, NJ: Princeton University Press.

Korean National Bureau of Statistics. 1983. *1980 Population and Housing Census Reports, Vol.1: Complete Enumeration*. Seoul, Korea: Economic Planning Board, Korean Government.

Lieberson, Stanley. 1963. *Ethnic Patterns in American Cities*. New York: Free Press.

Light, Ivan, and Edna Bonacich. 1988. *Immigrant Entrepreneurs: Koreans in Los Angeles 1965-1982*. Berkeley and Los Angeles: University of California Press.

Mangiafico, Luciano. 1988. *Contemporary Asian Immigrants: Patterns of Filipino, Korean, and Chinese Settlement in the United States*. New York: Perager.

Min, Pyong Gap. 1984a. "A Structural Analysis of Korean Business in the United States." *Ethnic Groups* 6: 1-25.

Min, Pyong Gap. 1984b. "From White-Collar Occupations to Small

Business: Korean Immigrants' Occupational Adjustment." *The Sociological Quarterly* 25: 333-352.

Min, Pyong Gap. 1988a. *Ethnic Business Enterprise: Korean Small Business in Atlanta*. New York: Center for Migration Studies.

Min, Pyong Gap. 1989. "Some Positive Functions of Ethnic Business for an Immigrant Community: Koreans in Los Angeles." Final Report Submitted to the National Science Foundation, Washington DC.

Min, Pyong Gap. 1991. "Cultural and Economic Boundaries of Korean Ethnicity: A Comparative Analysis." *Ethnic and Racial Studies* 14: 225-241.

Min, Pyong Gap. 1992a. "Immigrant Entrepreneurship and Wife's Overwork: Koreans in New York City." *Korea Journal of Population and Development* 21: 23-36.

Olzak, Suzan. 1986. "A Competition Model of Ethnic Collective Action in American Cities, 1877-1889." In *Competitive Ethnic Relations*, edited by Susan Olzak and Joane Nagel. New York: Academic Press.

Patterson, Wayne. 1988. *The Korean Frontier in America: Immigration to Hawaii, 1896-1910*. Honolulu: University of Hawaii Press.

Park, In-Sook Han, et al. 1990. "Koreans Immigrating to the United States: A Pre-Departure Analysis." Paper no.114. Honolulu, Hawaii: Population Institute, East-West Center.

Portes, Alejandro, and Ruben G. Rumbaut. 1990. *Immigrant America: A Portrait*. Berkeley and Los Angeles: University of California Press.

Reitz, Jeffery G. 1980. *The Survival of Ethnic Groups*. Toronto: McGraw-Hill.

Sae Gae Times. 1992. "Koreatown is Not Known to LA Residents." 29 July 1990.

U.S. Bureau of the Census. 1984. *1980 Census of Population*, PC80-1-D1-A. Washington DC: U.S. Government Printing Office.

U.S. Bureau of the Census. 1987. *Statistical Abstracts of the United States, 1988*, 108 edition. Washington DC: U.S. Government Printing Office.

U.S. Bureau of the Census. 1988. *1980 Census of Population*, PC80-2-1E. Washington DC: U.S. Government Printing Office.

U.S. Bureau of the Census. 1992. *1990 Census of Population*, PC90-1-C6. Washington, DC.: U.S. Government Printing Office.

Yancy, William L., et al. 1974. "Emergent Ethnicity: A Review and Reformulation." *American Sociological Review* 41: 391-402.

Yinger, Milton. 1980. "Toward a Theory of Assimilation and Dissimilation." *Ethnic and Racial Studies* 4: 249-264.

Yu, Eui-Young. 1982. "Occupation and Work Patterns of Korean Immigrants." In *Koreans in Los Angeles: Prospects and Promises*, edited by Eui-Young Yu et al. Los Angeles: Center for Korean-American and Korean Studies, California State University.

Yu, Eui-Young. 1985. "'Koreatown' Los Angeles: Emergence of a New Inner-City Ethnic Community." *Bulletin of Population and Development Studies* 14: 29-44.

10

Koreans in Japan and the United States: Attitudes toward Achievement and Authority

George A. De Vos and Eun-Young Kim

In the United States, various minority groups have had different responses to educational adaptation. A number of the Asian groups are doing relatively well, having taken to the school system positively and are much overrepresented, at the major American tertiary educational institutions. Other groups, such as Mexican Americans and blacks, have done relatively poorly. How have ethnic minorities with long histories of discrimination within majority dominated school systems, adapted in other systems? Research on this topic has recently been initiated in a number of countries.[1]

The present generation of Korean youths in Japan suffers particular personal alienation because of the degradation of their parents and grandparents since their arrival in Japan. Most of these individuals speak no Korean and are culturally, but not socially, assimilated within contemporary Japanese society. De Vos (1973) has earlier reported their high rates of delinquency and other behavioral symptoms of the alienation.

Degradation and Exploitation: Koreans in Japan

When Japan formally colonized Korea in 1910, it subjected the Koreans to Japanization. Throughout the thirty-five year history of direct colonization, the Japanese intended to eradicate not only Korean political autonomy, but also their separate ethnic and cultural identity. A coercive governmental policy periodically attempted to force Koreans to become Japanese culturally without full social acceptance in mainstream Japanese society as partial compensation.

The Japanese defeat in World War II allowed the Korean state to reestablish itself in 1945. Its remarkable progress toward modernization and industrialization leading to its postwar success has surprised the Japanese. After being colonized and subordinated to an alien government, problems about authority still persist among individual Koreans, especially during youth, and in their social dissension as adults.

During the colonial period many Koreans migrated to Japan to avoid poverty and later to replace the troops used to fight the Chinese. After the surrender of the Japanese in 1945, two-thirds to three-quarters of the Koreans in Japan eventually repatriated (Lee and De Vos, 1981), and almost a million remained, some of whom now "pass" as Japanese.

The sad history of this Korean minority in Japan has been described elsewhere (Lee and De Vos, 1981). The four generations of Koreans in Japan originate from unskilled and uneducated farmers imported for unskilled jobs during the Japanese industrial development in the late 1920s and 1930s. As a result of increased manpower demands due to the Japanese incursion into China in the 1930s, Koreans replaced the remaining Japanese unskilled and semiskilled labor, which was at that time being drafted into the war effort. Their lowly status was felt particularly strongly by the million or so Koreans who did not repatriate at the end of World War II.

In contrast to this history of Koreans in Japan has been the recent history of immigration to the United States. Since 1965, there has been an influx of over nine hundred thousand Koreans. Their success in establishing themselves in the United States has been remarkable, and is reflected in their rapid upward mobility in educational and economic spheres. This is not to say that Koreans are not subject to discrimination directed toward Asians generally by a white majority culture in the United States, though, compared with their previous history, Koreans in the United States have attained a high level of social acceptance. This is in complete contrast to their negative experiences in the Japanese colonial context. The younger Koreans who migrate to the United States have already benefited from their concerted interest in education and educational achievement in the newly independent postwar Korean state.

The Maintenance of a Korean Identity in Japan

Dilemmas of Achievement Motivation among Minority Koreans

Instrumentally based definitions of social, occupational, economic, and political success or achievement are found in every society. In any pluralistic society that emphasizes the ascendancy of one group, social success may require one to disguise one's minority class or ethnic origins. Lee and De Vos (1981) have discussed why and how some Koreans changed their behavior and disguised their background, to succeed in the world of entertainment. Passing, a term first used by light-skinned American blacks, is a universal phenomenon found in any hierarchical setting in which an individual's ethno-racial or class background may disadvantage him or her. Passing occurs in social settings in which escape from community surveillance is possible. Complex urban environments facilitate passing in modern societies. The problem, however, is more difficult for Koreans in Japan where intermarriage is vigilantly interdicted. In passing from one class or caste to another in a rigidly controlled society, the individual is continually subject to exposure. An inadvertent linguistic usage, or an inappropriate behavior can easily betray past affiliations.[2]

A Korean background is ostracized even today in Japan. Korean intermarriage is extremely rare with other than Burakamin outcastes. Even an entertainer of Korean background, who would otherwise be socially acceptable, remains an anomaly. Koreans who choose not to pass are ambivalent toward those who attempt it. Covert contacts or signs of allegiance are maintained, though such individuals feel personally alienated. For this reason, most Koreans attempt *not* to pass.

Frustrated efforts to achieve within contemporary Japanese society result in five predictable results. *First*, there is political dissidence, some of which is illegal and violent. *Second*, there are various forms of innovative social behavior, some of which lead to individualistically achieved professional and even business success, within the heavily group-oriented Japanese society. *Third*, there is goal-oriented criminal activity. The Japanese criminal underworld contains many relatively successful Koreans, but even here, there is a great deal of passing practiced. *Fourth*, many Koreans, especially the youth, incur difficulties in making future plans. They deviate and reject family and public expectations. The rate of delinquency among Korean youth is seven times higher than that found among the Japanese. *Fifth*, there are cases of social and psychological alienated withdrawal as reflected in school failure, which is especially high.

The social protest of Koreans in Japan displays a spectrum of socially adaptive and psychologically adjustive reaction patterns. These range from infantile destructiveness rationalized as social purpose, to the espousal of radical political causes, which derive from their commonly felt injustice. In our empirical work in the field of delinquency in Japan (De Vos and Wagatsuma, 1969; De Vos, 1980; Wagatsuma and De Vos, 1981), we documented an uncommonly high rate of delinquency among Korean youths and the social degradation of Koreans from marginal slums and broken families. The direct, as well as indirect, effects of social disparagement have generational consequences for family life. Delinquent behavior is not only a reaction to external discrimination, but also a product of damaged parental authority, which has often been further undermined by alcoholism and disrupted families. Thus, Korean families in Japan have become generationally vulnerable to social disparagement.

Koreans in Japan find it difficult to draw on their group identity to counter periods of individual uncertainty about their ability. Instead, self-hate because of negative group experience leads to introjection of some of the prejudice directed at the Korean group. In contrast, the situation for Koreans is quite different in the United States. The performance of the present generation of Koreans on psychological tests (Table 10.2) resembles that of Japanese immigrants of the past two generations. The Confucian emphasis on social hierarchy within the family is more easily practiced in the United States, than in Japan.

Koreans who migrate to the United States do so voluntarily to seek personal and family advancement. Their families are intact in the United States and they escape from Korean degradation and unemployment. However, these Koreans are selective of a class, having already achieved professional status in many cases, prior to migration. Even though many work in occupations much below their professional training and capabilities, they do so with the conviction that their children will be more successful in the future. This expectation is amply demonstrated by present statistics. For example, as stated earlier, Koreans are overrepresented in major American universities and are also rapidly mobile in the educational system.

In comparing responses to the Thematic Apperception Test (TAT) in small samples taken in Japan, with those obtained in Korea and in the United States, the differences in futuretime orientation between the Japanese sample of Korean youth and Korean Americans are particularly clear. The former show little future orientation and avoid projecting into the future with optimism, while the latter, in contrast, view the future in positive terms.

Social Dissension

The lives of Koreans in Japan are characterized by disruption and inherited hostilities. Long-standing political alliances are split between the North and South; between progovernment and antigovernment supporters, between Christians and non-Christians, and so on. Koreans blame these cleavages on their pawnlike status in power games that are controlled by the Soviet Union, China, the United States, and Japan. However, discordance is also caused by intragroup factionalism and by internal animosities among Koreans, which are *generationally* sustained.

The most effective group mechanism for achieving intragroup harmony is by deflecting socially disruptive behavior onto individuals outside the core group of Koreans. Displacement of internal tensions onto an outside enemy is basic to ethnocentrism, wherever it operates, and is a well researched phenomenon in social psychology.

Unfortunately, for many Koreans, the "outgroups" often constitute other Korean factions. For example, in Japan, North Koreans in schools and other social institutions have strengthened their internal group solidarity by expressing discord toward other "less virtuous" factions among the Korean community.

Both at home and in Japan, Koreans often label the Japanese collectively as "the enemy" to attain internal group harmony. It is easier to hate all Japanese rather than to differentiate between those who are prejudiced and those who may be helpful. Hence, Koreans are hostile toward all Japanese. This negative attitude further contributes to animosity on both sides.

Most Koreans apply stiff sanctions against group members who take up Japanese citizenship. Since they are rejected by the Japanese, naturalized citizens of Korean origin in Japan have set up the Seiwa Club for their own group, a name that can be roughly translated as "the realization of harmony." In this group, naturalization is openly acknowledged and the Korean background of individuals is celebrated to avoid passing, while at the same time, there is a positive assertion of their Japanese citizenship, even though they are in a precarious and socially isolated position.

Discrimination is a potent force in disrupting Korean families. The destruction of Korean males' occupational prowess and dignity through discrimination results in spasmodic acts of compensatory masculine chauvinism at home. It also leads to the disparagement of the husband by his wife within the domestic sphere. Confucianist values, which dictate that the wife "ideally" plays a subordinate role to the household head, ensuring that the children are obedient to authoritative elders, are not well exercised in many Korean homes. Family relationships, themselves, become bonds of aggressive displacement and result in alienation and delinquent behavior among Korean youths, which later leads to criminal careers.

Korean-Japanese children perform poorly in school for reasons similar to those found among American minorities (De Vos, 1980). This presence in "alienated" peer groups discourages conformity to the dominant values of educational institutions and of the majority society. These peer groups constitute important arenas for the demonstration of male prowess and also appreciative judgment.

Attitudes toward Authority and Group Loyalty

Korean-Japanese youths disregard family or adult authority more strongly, simply because of lower gratification from interdependent family relationships. Affiliation with delinquency-oriented groups antagonistic toward social authorities — including teachers and other officials in Japanese administrative agencies — leads to attitudes of protective association and antagonism toward the outside. These attitudes survive right into adulthood.

Korean-Japanese seek out individualistic affiliations and couple oriented companionship in marriage, even though their Confucian tradition emphasizes the supremacy of family authority. Indeed, romantic love today, in some cases, transcends social barriers between Koreans and lower status Japanese. Such marriages, however, compound problems of identity for the Korean partners who are faced with the dilemma of affirming, or denying their Korean affiliations outside of marriage, while maintaining solidarity with their spouses.

A Comparison of Attitudes on the
Thematic Apperception Test:
The United States and Japan

To further illustrate the issues discussed above, the results of our study are reported here using a projective test, the TAT (Thematic Apperception Test). Korean youths adapt differently in Japan than in the United States, two host societies characterized in the former case, by harsh discrimination, and in the latter case, by relative acceptance. Underneath these patterns of adaptation, are attitudinal and behavioral differences, which are revealed in our test results and which demonstrate the validity of the TAT results. Latent attitudes are captured in different cultural settings to demonstrate that projective tests can be used cross-culturally, despite opinions held to the contrary, by many social scientists who are generally sceptical about the validity of TAT tests, especially when used cross-culturally.

The Use of the TAT in Social Science Research

The first publication that drew attention to what became known as the Thematic Apperception Test appeared in 1938 in Henry A. Murray's volume, *Explorations in Personality*. Subsequent psychologists, recognizing the research or clinical potential of analyzing stories given to a standardized set of pictures or drawings, developed similar related tests. Anthropologists in the 1940s and 1950s, used them to make cross-cultural comparisons of "culture and personality."[3] Thus, the Murray set of TAT cards became the most frequently employed thematic projection tests to be used outside the West.

TAT projective analysis used cross-culturally was characterized by three approaches. In a number of instances, cards taken from the Murray series were used without modification. Concern about the cultural unfamiliarity of some users led to the development of cards that were thematically similar, but which were modified for suitability to culturally-specific situations. These changes involved the inclusion of different facial features, clothing, and the addition of new cards more appropriate for the cultures studied. However, in some other studies, any attempt at direct comparison of themes was abandoned, though the idea of social or personal themes reflecting personality was retained. Other cards were also developed that bore little resemblance to the drawings and interpersonal situations used in the original Murray series.

A uniform approach and methods of analysis for the use of TAT did not develop either among psychologists or anthropologists, nor were the series of twenty cards used in fixed sequence, as suggested in the manual accompanying the published set. Murray and Christina Morgan, the originators of the set, suggested that it was easier to identify with a figure of one's own sex and approximate age. They developed specific adult and child cards of both sexes to be used alternatively as part of the series. However, most subsequent research and clinical application has not differentiated between cards designated specifically for men, women, boys, or girls. They have been gender-free and chosen for the thematic material to be elicited. Whereas clinicians have selected cards from the series that suited their particular diagnostic purposes, other practitioners have found it easier to create a story with a personally significant theme using a figure of the opposite sex.

The use of the Murray cards (Murray, 1943) by anthropologists has been varied. They have used TAT as one of the preferred testing devices that could elicit culturally relevant content and have favored particular cards, especially those from eight to twelve. Although Murray's original trait lists of internal "needs" and external social "presses" were largely ignored, some motivational factors such as "need achievement" were used with greater interest.

Comparative Research Concerning Achievement Motivation and Social Adaptation

Research eliciting projections on achievement motivation became central to many of the nonclinical research studies attempted with the Thematic Apperception Test, both in the United States and elsewhere. Beginning in 1948, William Caudill and De Vos[4] had used respectively the TAT and the Rorschach tests as part of a more general attempt to investigate the postwar adaptation of Japanese Americans in the Chicago area. A strong achievement drive was evident throughout the projective test materials, as well as in the interviews conducted with the Issei immigrants and their second generation Nisei children (Caudill and De Vos, 1956).

McClelland (et al., 1953; 1961), with other colleagues, also developed extensive systematic work, specifically with what Murray had termed "need achievement." McClelland considered "need achievement" a motivation socialized differently in different social contexts, and he developed a precise and elaborate series of criteria for scoring. His colleagues used similar methods to create specific scales for measuring needs for "affiliation" (Atkinson, 1958) and "power" (Shipley and Veroff, 1952; Veroff, 1958). They applied these measures to an analysis of the fantasies of children and adults in the context of economic development (McClelland 1961).

The obvious need to achieve, and the culturally induced motivational patterns underlying this need had become a central concern for Caudill and myself, in understanding patterns of adaptation among the Japanese Americans in Chicago. However, McClelland and his associates' quantitative focus was limited to three basic concerns and ignored other salient themes that recurred continuously in the sequential logic embedded in the Japanese TAT stories. For example, the McClelland approach did not allow for complex examination of achievement stories that were continually dramatized in the Japanese data, as related to repayment for family nurture and other familial roles and duties.

McClelland and his associates also did not tabulate several specific conflictual themes that could be used for comparison of cultural differences. For example, the Japanese were continually concerned with problems of inadequacy that might have interfered with achievement goals. In contrast, American control samples were concerned with more individualistic issues, of whether "one wanted to apply oneself to a task or not," or "how one should deal with the force of parental pressure inducing the assumption of future goals" (De Vos, 1973). De Vos, therefore, developed categories for scoring that would allow for more exhaustive quantification.[5]

A System of Scoring Interpersonal Concerns

As a means of reporting the Japanese data, De Vos established some basic categories to compare the relative saliency of the achievement stories with other interpersonal concerns.[6] Rather than discarding material not directly relevant to the categories of achievement, affiliation, and power, he developed a set of basic categories that would allow for an inclusive classification of all the story material in a more complex fashion. He has developed categories that include basic human emotional states such as love, hate, anxiety, guilt, and shame, drawn from the psychodynamic literature. He has also included virtues and vices recognized as desirable or undesirable in various cultures (i.e., harmony, endurance, etc.).

He separated stories into instrumental and expressive emphases, a distinction he borrowed from the work of sociologists Parsons and Bales (1955) who examined "pattern variables" in small group research. Rather than repeating Murray's distinction between needs and presses, he focused on the active or passive stance of the stories' central characters and the positive or negative evaluation attributed to the social acts depicted in the story material by the individual narrating the story. De Vos was equally concerned with developing categories that reflected personal perceptions of status differentials, marking horizontal and vertical social relationships, and also socially evaluative considerations that could be either internalized, or remain an external to the subject.

Instead of focusing on the concept "personality," per se, he considers social concerns and their attendant attitudes to be a reflection, both of socialized motivation and of socialized perception, of how interpersonal roles are enacted in particular social or cultural settings. In so doing, he has been able to include almost every story taken from a stratified sample of 728 rural and urban Japanese within ten basic interpersonal categories, and two sets of impersonal ones, each further elaborated into a number of subcategories (De Vos, 1973). These categories have been successfully applied to samples of interview and projective data taken from a variety of cultural or social groups.[7]

Interpersonal concerns (considered "values" in some contexts) are placed in categories that I consider universally applicable and found in one form or other in every culture. The content or context may differ, but human interpersonal concerns in most cultures are basically *self-oriented*, *vertical* in respect to status and power differentials, or basic *horizontal* peer level relationships. Some relationships are marked by concern with the *evaluations* or *judgments* of self and others, or with concord or discord in human relations. Others are concerned with what are perceived as internalized standards or as directives governing social behavior. Status and role considerations influence processes of nurture, appreciation, harmony, achievement, and so on.

Thematic fantasy, therefore, is self, interpersonal (dyadic or group) oriented, in horizontally or vertically structured situations. These categories are represented in basic or complex forms in all interview materials, as well as on specially devised projective tests directed toward specific theoretical concerns. Fantasies about personal behavior in the social world are either focused on the "self," excluding the awareness of others from immediate concerns, on "group" processes, or on "dyadic" relationships. Behavior takes place in "vertical," unequal status relationships, or, in "horizontal" situations between individuals of equivalent status. Interpersonal concerns in their social contexts are socially judged implicitly or explicitly, as either positive, negative, unresolved, or ambiguous, in accordance with established norms. They divide into concerns that are essentially expressive in nature, contrasting with instrumental goal-oriented concerns. Since interpersonal concerns grow out of the basic inherited interaction patterns of humans as social animals, they are elemental and appear in every social group. They are universally inherent in child socialization in one form or other. Cultures differ, however, as to how they are relatively emphasized, interrelated or blended with one another in molecular patterns that may be culture-specific. This difference in emphasis is what we are demonstrating in our comparisons of the present sample of Koreans in Japan and those in the United States.

Results

We used the same Murray set of TAT cards with a sample of immigrant Koreans tested in Los Angeles and another located in the Kyoto-Osaka area in Japan. In previous work with the TAT in Japan, De Vos noted that the original Murray and the Japanese sets with special cards produced similar results with Japanese informants. For comparative purposes, the original set can be used as identical stimuli with several different cultural groups. No serious difficulties in these comparative analyses has arisen.

In the following, only the partial results obtained through a brief analysis of three cards are considered, as they reveal attitudes of achievement and alienation. A fourth card dealing with attitudes toward authority is also used. Results obtained by systematic comparisons of a sample of one hundred records from Korea, with a small sample of thirty-one from Japan, and also a sample of fifty Koreans from Los Angeles are reported here. Findings on the Korean sample, compared with previous samples of immigrant Japanese done by William Caudill in 1947 (Caudill and De Vos, 1956) are reported elsewhere (De Vos, 1983). The similarity in attitudes and concerns about achievement, reflected in the thematic

Table 10.1
Basic Thematic Concerns in Human Relations[1]

EXPRESSIVE BEHAVIOR				
Thematic Concerns	Positive (Socially Sanctioned)	Passive or Indeterminate	Negative (Socially Unsanctioned)	
	Active initiated and/or resolved	Passive or unresolved	Active, initiated and/or resolved	Passive, withdrawal and/or resolution
SELF				
Pleasure (within oneself) self-expression(E)	Satisfaction sense of curiosity, creativity, enjoyment	Indifference boredom	Masochistic behavior, ascetism	Suffering
VERTICAL				
Nurturance (for some-one) (V)	Donor Nurturance care, help, comfort, succor, security	Recipient Dependency	Withholding	Sense of personal, social, or economic deprivation; Some "egocentric" suicides; Insecurity; Lack of protection
HORIZONTAL				
Affiliation (toward someone) (H)	Affiliation intimacy union, re-sponsiveness contact	Isolation loneliness, alienation	Rejection of another	Sense of loss due to rejection or separation; Some "egoistic" suicides; Distrust

Continuation of Table 10.1

	EXPRESSIVE BEHAVIOR			
Thematic Concerns	**Positive** (Socially Sanctioned)	**Passive or Indeterminate**	**Negative** (Socially Unsanctioned)	
	Active initiated and/or resolved	**Passive or unresolved**	**Active, initiated and/or resolved**	**Passive, withdrawal and/or resolution**
STATUS EVALUATIVE				
Appreciation (of from someone)	Awe, Deference, Respect			
others: (H-V)	Recognition of achieved or ascribed status	Feeling ignored unappreciated	Disdain, disparagement	Sense of degradation; Some "anomic" suicides
self: (S)	Self-respect	Doubt about worth, sense of shame	Self-abasement self-depreciation	Sense of worthlessness Some "egoistic" suicides
STATUS AND CONCORDANCE				
Harmony (with, emotionally) (H-V)	Harmony peaceful relationships	Jealousy, fear of threat, emotional discord	Violence injury revenge; Some "egocentric" suicides	Withdrawal into hostility and resentment; Fear

Continuation of Table 10.1

INSTRUMENTAL BEHAVIOR				
Thematic Concerns	**Positive** (Socially Sanctioned)		**Negative** (Socially Unsanctioned)	
	Active initiated and/or resolved	**Passive or unresolved**	**Active, initiated and/or resolved**	**Passive withdrawal and/or resolution**
SELF				
Achievement (will do) internalized goals (S)	Goal-oriented activity	Internal conflict, over commitment role diffusion, daydreaming	Goal-oriented criminal activity	Anomic withdrawal alienation from social goals
VERTICAL				
Control-Power (must do) external power				
superordinate: (V)	Legitimate authority, power-mastery persuasion	Defensive insecurity	Authoritarian dominance security, control through destruction	Failure to assert proper, authority (spineless, gutless)
subordinate: (V)	Liberation, autonomy or compliance	Ambivalence about authority or power	Rebellion trickery	Submission

Continuation of Table 10.1

	INSTRUMENTAL BEHAVIOR			
Thematic Concerns	**Positive** (Socially Sanctioned)	**Passive or Indeterminate**	**Negative** (Socially Unsanctioned)	
	Active initiated and/or resolved	**Passive or unresolved**	**Active, initiated and/or resolved**	**Passive withdrawal and/or resolution**
HORIZONTAL				
competitive: (H)	Regulated competition, games, contests	Envy	Unethical competitive behavior	Capitulation withdrawal from competitive situation
cooperative: (H)	Concerted behavior (mutual trust)	Distrust, disagreement	Plotting, deception of a cohort	Sense of betrayal distrust
EVALUATIVE				
Competence (can do) internalized standards of excellence (S)	Avowal of capacity	Doubt about capacity, worry, diffuse anxiety, chagrin	Failure due to personal inadequacy	Sense of incapacity and inadequacy
STATUS INTERNALIZED				
Responsibility (ought to do) internalized moral standards and controls	Sense of duty, assumption of obligation Some forms of "altruistic" suicide	Remorse, guilt regrets over acts of commission or omission	Profligacy irresponsibility	Avoidance, escape; Some forms of "anomic" suicide

1. Additional categories scored were the impersonal concerns of "concern with fate, impersonal force events" and "concern with objects".

fantasy of both the Korean and Japanese samples, was quite remarkable. The contrast between minority Korean youth and recent samples of majority Japanese youth, who continue to exhibit strong motivation for achievement, is not considered here (see De Vos, 1973).

Achievement Themes

The examiner's standard initial request asks for themes that interpret, not only the present, but also the past, and future, as suggested by the specific pictures shown. Comparison of the American and Japanese-Korean samples strongly contrasts their stories in respect to any future time orientation.

The boy with the violin (card 1), a farm scene (card 2), and a man on a rope (card 17 BM) all evoke, for most samples, some percentage of stories related to achievement motivation projected into the future. In the following, we illustrate the glaring differences reported in accompanying tables. Illustrative material is frequently more revealing than the bare presentation of statistics.

Card 1: the boy with the violin. Card 1, the boy with the violin, has proven to be extremely useful in comparative studies. In my past work this card was used with North American Indian cultures, as well as samples of Japanese and Chinese. Doctoral students have used the card with individuals from Kenya, Central America, and the Philippines. Colleagues have also used this card with Moroccans, Turks, Sicilians, and Martiniqueans in Europe. In each instance, the card elicits a concern with self-motivated ambition in some percentage of those tested. Such stories, by and large, have a future time orientation that depicts either optimism or a lack of resolution of fantasies about possibilities of successful achievement.

Compared with American counterparts, the sample of Koreans from Japan suggests much less incentive to resolve stories toward a self-motivated positive view of the future. Of the fifty sampled in Los Angeles, twenty-five gave stories of eventual success, in contrast with the Japan sample from Kyoto and Osaka, wherein only two of thirty-one gave such stories.

Stories of parental pressure are an element in some of these narratives. Parental pressure appeared in 42 percent of the Korean

Table 10.2
Summary Comparison of Card 1 – Los Angeles Koreans and Korean Japanese

Groups Total Cases	Los Angeles 50		Japan 31	
Themes				
1. Questions of motivation and competence	29		14	
Percentage of total sample	58%		45%	
Positive direction	25	(86%)	2	(14%)
succeeds - or studies hard	5		0	
studying in process	2		0	
concern with ability but succeeds	9		1	
blind man studying to improve his attitude	1		0	
concern with broken object, fixes it, succeeds	2		0	
receives violin, will learn to play well	3		1	
ambivalent about motives resolved positively	3		0	
Negative or unresolved	4	(14%)	12	(86%)
receives violin - unresolved (physical complaint)	0		2	
ambivalent about motives, unresolved or quits	1		6	
concern with ability, unresolved	0		4	
no ability, gives up	2		0	
not concentrated, falls asleep	1		0	
2. Questions of parental pressure	16		13	
Percentage of total sample	32%		42%	
Positive	5	(31%)	2	(15%)
complies and continues positively	4		2	
changes task and succeeds	1		0	
Negative or unresolved	11	(69%)	11	(85%)
forced, results not indicated	5		3	
complies but results no good	1		0	
complies only temporarily	2		3	
refuses to study	3		5	
3. Other	5		4	
Percentage of total sample	10%		13%	
Resolved	2	(40%)	0	(0%)
instructs the feeble minded	1		0	
receives toy, throws it away	1		0	
Unresolved	3	(60%)	4	(100%)
sad son seeking mother	1		0	
scolded by father or teacher	1		1	
cripple studying instrument to assist himself	1		0	
accident trouble	0		3	
Total unresolved and negative results		(36%)		(87%)

Japanese sample. However, in only two of these thirteen stories was there a positive compliance. Parental pressure also appeared in 32 percent of the Los Angeles sample, in which five of sixteen were resolved positively.

Overall, 87 percent of the Osaka-Kyoto sample gave stories with no resolution or with negative outcomes, compared with, 36 percent among the American Koreans. The Koreans in Japan do not give stories like the majority Japanese, who worry about possible incompetence, though the directly migrant Koreans from Korea to the United States do give stories similar to those of majority Japanese. For example, in the Los Angeles sample of Koreans we obtained the following replies:

L.A. (Los Angeles Korean) Female, age 22: The boy hopes to be a good violinist. Today he played the violin badly before his violin teacher. He would practice the violin harder. He will eventually be a good violinist.

L.A. Male, age 25: The boy is a pupil who learns to play the violin. He practiced the violin concerto several times but his performance was not very good. He thinks now how he will be able to master the tune. He will practice very hard and he will eventually master this concerto.

Although concerned with competence in 26 percent of their stories in Los Angeles, they fantasize overcoming incompetence and gaining eventual mastery in all but two of these stories. It is the single most prevalent theme dealing with personal motivation. In brief, the fantasies elicited on card 1 show that Korean immigrants, by and large, maintain positive attitudes toward future achievement. They are aware of the necessity to have a strong will, to overcome individual weaknesses and disabilities in attaining a long-range goal. Contrast this with these illustrative stories from the Koreans in Japan:

JK (Japanese Korean) Male, age 25: He was bought and given a violin. But he does not know how to play the violin, so he is watching the instrument. He is worrying

> if he will become a violinist. I wonder if he has a toothache. That's all.

> JK Female, age 25: He is bemused by an accident that has no relation to this violin. If this scene were after his violin practice, the accident might be related to the violin.

> JK Male, age 18: Well, he is practicing the violin, and it seems that he is tired of playing the violin. And now he sighs, looking at the violin. He is completely fed up with it . . . And after all, when he is asked if he wants to quit the violin, he cannot decide. I don't know.

The next large category of stories are those in which there is some mention of parental insistence on learning the violin. Both groups give stories of compliance. However, among the Japanese Koreans, 25 percent of their total stories (compared with 10 percent of the L.A. group) depict a boy complying only temporarily, or rejecting parental insistence outright. This result is similar to that reported by William Caudill for a lower-class American sample where the rate of refusal was even higher. To illustrate:

> JK Male, age 23: Parents had hoped this boy would have a lot of musical skill. But now he is thinking he should do otherwise. He will probably quit music although I can't guess what he will do. I don't know what he will do next but now he is being lazy.

> JK Female, age 25: He was scolded by his mother once because he quit playing it. He feels gloomy because he has to go practice again. He will not be a violinist.

What differs from American samples generally is that among the Japanese or the Koreans, there are rarely stories of the desire to play baseball, as is often the case with either lower- or middle-class American youths. Such individualistic interests in play are not readily depicted by youth from a Confucian family tradition.

Card 17: a man on a rope. Let us turn now to card 17, which is another symbolic measure of achievement concerns. There is a kinesthetic response to this card that results in the individual on the rope either being perceived as climbing up and resting, or climbing down. This card can be used as an indication of a relative amount of spontaneous vitality and upward surge, projected spontaneously by particular individuals. The content elicited is also symbolic of attitudes of self-confidence, the awareness of performance before an audience, or concern in some instances with possible illegal or sexual activities.

Expressions of confidence and vitality reflect interest in active accomplishment. By and large, the Korean stories are highly imaginative compared to some other samples studied. Out of the fifty stories, most of those sampled in Los Angeles view this activity as that of an energetic nature. Their stories are much more positive than those of Koreans in Japan.

> L.A. Male, age 21: He is an acrobat. He climbs up the rope. He seems to be an old man but he is healthy. He is a veteran acrobat. He is full of confidence in climbing on the rope. He is looking at somebody. He has a slight feeling of repugnance for his job but he will climb to the end of the rope.

> L.A. Female, age 29: He climbs the rope. He must be climbing up a mountain. Maybe he will go to the top of the mountain easily. He is a person who enjoys mountaineering. He enjoys rock climbing.

> L.A. Female, age 21: This man is a circus performer. He wants to demonstrate his talents to his friends so he goes up a castle wall. He will climb to the top of the castle.

The Los Angeles and the Japanese groups show contrasting attitudes toward these stories of performance and sportlike activity. In contrast to the American Koreans who have positive attitudes, the

Japanese Koreans gave stories in which the performer is constructed as malformed, or as clownish.

Table 10.3
Summary Comparison of Card 17 - Los Angeles Koreans and Korean Japanese

Groups Total Cases	Los Angeles 50		Japan 31	
Themes				
1. Climbing	27		14	
Percentage of total sample	54%		52%	
climbing positive tone	20	(74%)	3	(21%)
going to the top (mountains, sportsman, etc.)	4		0	
competing in contest	0		1	
circus expert performing well	11		1	
practicing, exercise	4		1	
escape (very positively toned)	1		1	
climbing, performing, ambiguous tone	5	(19%)	5	(36%)
searching, watching, dreaming	1		2	
escape from danger	4		1	
performing (flat tone)			2	
performing, but with negative tone	2	(7%)	6	(43%)
performing, but with despair	0		1	
refugee or orphan must earn living in circus	0		1	
playing a fool, clown, (Hunchback 2)	0		3	
drunk	0		1	
just a blue-collar worker, not so good	2		0	
2. Climbing for unsanctioned activity	8		2	
Percentage of total sample	16%		8%	
mischievous	3		0	
sexual	4		2	
thief	1		0	
3. Escaping, climbing down or falling	13		10	
Percentage of total sample	26%		37%	
escaping from prison, etc.	2		4	
unsuccessful escape (recapture by police, etc.)	5		0	
falls in escape from hell	0		2	
running away, mad	4		1	
accident, falls into alcoholism	0		1	
falls to death (in circus 1)	2		1	
self destruction in elevator shaft	0		1	
4. Other	2		0	
Percentage of total sample	4%		0%	

JK Male, age 25: Should I look at picture lengthwise or crosswise? He is playing a fool. His face is playing a fool. He is playing a show for a show booth. He is masculine. This is more cheerful one than the other pictures. I don't mind if he is naked or not. This is the most masculine and cheerful picture.

JK Female, age 20: This reminds me of a hunchback of Notre Dame. He may be a clown in a circus. Is he naked? He may wear a tight suit. He is very masculine. He seems to be opposed against the law of gravity. This is the poorest picture that I've seen.

However, among the American Koreans it must also be noted that in eight of the active stories, the climbing is done positively but for illegal or unsanctioned activity. Here are examples of vigor being put to questionable purposes.

L.A. Male, age 25: The man is an inquisitive person and he likes to see games. He is climbing on a rope to see a game free. He will enjoy seeing the game and will satisfy his risky attempt.

L.A. Male, age 31: The place is a public bath. On the other side of a window is the woman's bath. This fellow tries to climb on the rope because he wants to look. He satisfies himself looking at many naked women's bodies. He will then come down on the rope without any accident. He is not a sincere man, but may be someone like a bad drunk.

Both groups have a number of reactions to the seeming nudity of the performer. A small number (four in the American and one in the Japanese group) see the figure as insane or demented. In the negative stories given by the Kyoto-Osaka group, there is a tone of despair and degradation found in none of the American sample.

JK Male, age 23: This is a monotonous wall, isn't it? [past] Probably he might have been a hero of a circus but he was once discouraged by a physical accident like breaking a bone or by a mental shock. Then he become afraid of going up high, was kicked out of the circus and indulged in drinking heavily. [present] This could be a prison. Anyway he is trying again, recalling his past. [future] He will not be able to go back to the colorful world that he was in before. Like in this picture, he will fall low. And probably he will find no release from his drinking. His face is gloomy. He has a recollection of the past, but reality is coming upon him . . . least he should do so.

Both groups give a number of escape stories, but the American-Koreans are more apt to see an escapee apprehended by the police. Negative scenes of escape, climbing down, or some form of failure occur in 28 percent of the American Korean stories, as opposed to the past samples of Caudill of 30 percent among the first generation Issei and 22 percent of the American Nisei, the second generation Japanese. This contrasts with 40 percent among Koreans in Japan.

Two of the Japanese-Korean stories refer to a short story by Akutagawa Ryunosuke evoking the sad plight of an alienated man doomed to hell. Glancing down a well, the Buddha sees him. Compassionately he has a spider send down a filament to allow the sufferer to climb. In his anxiety to prevent others from following up the delicate strand, he kicks at his fellow sufferers, causing the thread to break, dooming him to hell once more.

JK Male, age 23: This one reminds me of the "Thread of a Spider" by Akutagawa. And this man is the first one climbing, and there are some others following him, and he is telling them to stop. Well, so the story goes, a spider's thread is coming down . . . and when he says something, it is cut suddenly . . . The thread is cut suddenly, and he will return to hell . . . This picture reminds me of that story. But if so, his body . . . His masculine body bothers me . . . the rope. He is not climbing a tree. But he may be competing in a rope climbing contest . . .

Twenty-five percent of the L.A. sample responses involved an audience and a confident performer.

L.A. Female, age 29: He climbs on the rope. He must go up a mountain. Maybe he will go up that mountain easily. He is a person who enjoys the mountaineering. Now he enjoys rock climbing.

L.A. Female, age 30: This picture is a circus performance. The man is climbing on the rope. He is full of pride before an audience. He is satisfied with his occupation in the circus. He will continue in this job.

This was true for only 12 percent (three) of the Korean-Japanese cases. Instead, they gave such stories:

JK Female, age 25: He is not a primitive man because he has a long hair. He may begin something after getting drunk. After getting drunk, he said, "I can do everything." He was unclothed and began climbing up the wall.

JK Female, age 25: I wonder if he is going upwards or downwards. Maybe he is going upwards. He is searching for something desperately. This does not let me feel any fear. I don't know.

In sum, even when symbolically climbing, the Koreans in Japan give negative or disparaging stories compared with the L.A. Korean sample.

Card 2: the farm scene. Card 2, of the Murray series shows a man working with a horse. It is used and generally interpreted as a representation of rural life everywhere. Though the horse is not used for plowing in Japan, out of hundreds of records, De Vos has only

TABLE 10.4
Summary Comparison of Card 2 -- Los Angeles Koreans and Korean Japanese

Groups Total Cases	Los Angeles 50		Japan 31	
1. Mission or social welfare work (% of Total)	5	10%	1	3%
succeeds	5		0	
fail		0		1
2. Harmony emphasized (% of Total)	15	30%	4	13%
family role	5		2	
pioneering	4		1	
improve conditions	1		0	
guilty about school	1		0	
ambitious, returns (help to parents, etc.)	4		0	
unresolved about farm or school	0		1	
3. Leaves farm without discord (% of Total)	7	14%	3	10%
parental sacrifice	0		1	
likes city or study more	1		1	
does not return from city, marries	2		0	
ambitious, but does not return (guilty)	1		0	
returns, but dislikes farm	0		1	
dislikes farm life	3		0	
4. Interpersonal difficulty (% of Total)	16	32%	6	19%
loneliness	1		2	
sexual involvements				
waiting for lover	0		1	
return to native land	1		0	
(triangularity)-responsibility	4		0	
triangularity/competition	4		1	
discord				
discord resolution	2		0	
dislike farm/discord/leaves	1		0	
discord separation	3		0	
discord religion	1		0	
discord, no resolution	0		2	
5. Other (% of Total)	7	14%	17	55%
Neutral tone				
unrelated activities or motives	5		3	
passer-by or observer	1		4	
picture description	0		3	
dream	0		1	
Negative tone				
exploitation of workers	0		1	
dissatisfied life	0		4	
male lack of opportunity	0		1	

documented one or two comments to this effect. Generally speaking, people accept the card and project willingly into it according to their attitudes. The girl with the book in the foreground, represents for many, concerns for social change or achievement. Responses to this card typically either put emphasis on the internal family dynamics and the need for work on the farm, a rural context, or, on the future concerns of the young woman with the books. Results on this card can be rather complex to analyze, since themes can vary considerably. There are crosscutting themes of family harmony and disharmony, as well as themes of personal ambition, that conflict with concerns about the fulfillment of social obligations or other roles.

Among the Japanese Issei in Caudill's original sample, 43 percent of the stories emphasized negative feelings about the poverty inherent in farm life and compensatory activities toward a better life. The second most prevalent theme among them was the concern of 38 percent with ambition. In the recent Korean sample, 43 percent of the stories focus on problems of family harmony. The story content varies, however, and no particular issues become paramount.

> L.A. Female, age 28: The picture describes a scene showing that people live in the world naturally. They live in a warm atmosphere. The pregnant woman looks at a distant mountain, and she thanks God for his creation of the beautiful world. The girl on the left walks along thinking that she has to study hard. She attends school. The man works hard to protect his family. The man and the woman on the right are a couple, or brother and sister.

> L.A. Female, age 31: They work on a farm. The three persons are a couple and their daughter. The daughter thinks, "How can we do farming more easily?" and, "How can we sell the crops for a high price?" She also thinks about farming a modern way. The daughter is a student. She hopes to marry a good person who is talented in farming, and that she and her future husband modernize the farming.

In another 18 percent of the Korean stories, a daughter is seen leaving for personal ambition. Out of these nine stories, five depict a daughter's return home to help her parents, revealing her obligations to her family.

> L.A. Female, age 19: The woman comes back home from school. She looks at her parents working hard on their garden. She thinks how she will serve her parents after graduation from school. After arrival she will rest for a little while, and then she will study very hard.

> L.A. Female, age 21: The three persons are in a triple love affair. The woman on the left and the man were close in past days. But the man got married to the woman on the right. The left woman came here to meet her old lover. The left woman will live alone while waiting for her old lover.

In other stories, Koreans depict sexual triangles causing conflict between two women. Such stories were totally absent among the Japanese, but present in the Korean-American samples. In these stories, the American Koreans, in effect, depict situations in which the man is forced to choose between two women, and it is the younger woman who invariably loses out to a wife. These stories illustrate the ultimate duty of the man to his wife whatever his straying sexual interest. Confucian emphases on propriety and legitimacy are still explicit moral imperatives among Koreans. A second unusual theme found in the Korean sample can be explained by the self-consciousness of Koreans about missionary work in their rural villages. In our sample of fifty, there are nine stories mentioning missionary work as the activity of the protagonist. The missionary is the protagonist in nine stories, represented by the woman with the books. In these stories the mission work is seen, in effect, as another form of achievement theme. Farmers initially resist her missionary efforts but ultimately succumb to her persistence. In Japan, there is only one such story and her effort fails.

> L.A. Female, age 22: This is a country in a pioneer stage. The woman with the books did missionary work in rural villages. Many rural people did not listen to her but the woman must have succeeded finally in her mission work.

These stories attest to the fact that Christians have played an important part in Korean modernization. They played and continue to play a forceful role in contemporary Korean society.

There is more consciousness among the L.A. Koreans than in the previous Japanese sample of the girl as a player of a woman's role, rather than as representer of an abstract concept of individual achievement. The Koreans are more self-conscious about the necessity to continue the woman's role than the Japanese, and the situation of the young girl suggests potential problems of how she will marry, as well as what she will study. Any conflict between the two is resolved by forefronting the woman's role. In this respect, Koreans remain more Confucian than do the Japanese.

> L.A. Male, age 19: They are parents with their daughter. The daughter goes to school and the parents are peasants in the countryside. The parents want to be helped in their agricultural work by their daughter. The daughter cannot assist them. She is conflicted in her mind. "What shall I choose between studying and farming?" Sometime later she will assist her parents farming.

> L.A. Male, age 25: The young woman student on the left is in deep thought. In the past she was eager to study in school. Now she goes to school, she thinks, "If I did not study hard, I will have to work hard on the garden like those others. If I marry somebody, I will also be pregnant like that woman. After marriage, I will be a good wife and good mother."

We note how this respondent, throughout his story, makes the girl self-conscious of the alternative decisions to be made by young women. In fact, more of these stories or roles are given by men than by women in our sample. In the stories given by the Japanese, there was less concern with the specific dimension of women's roles.

Among Koreans in Japan, their alienation is represented by their withdrawal from the family implications of the card. American-Koreans see family life in 86 percent of their stories. They directly depict both harmony (30 percent) and discord (32 percent) in many of their stories. In others, the girl is torn between ambition and family continuity. In sharp contrast, the Japanese Koreans in 55 percent of their stories see the characters in the picture in unrelated activities or in some state of general dissatisfaction.

> JK Male, age 23: What is this? Naked man is disagreeable! I feel as if I have come to a world of different era. [past and present] This is a society that male is tortured and female can go to school and have more opportunity than males. A man is required to engage in physical work and a woman is not required to do anything. [future] But it became a male-centered world after all in the result of males showing their ability.

> JK Male, age 31: Which one shall I talk about? I don't get a clear image. Well, the present of the woman leaning against the tree is that she is pregnant, isn't she? So her future is that she is going to have a baby. I don't know her past . . . The person in the middle looks like a Caucasian. But what does it mean that he is pulling his horse? He looks like a manual laborer. In the future, he will continue to work (laugh). The past, I don't know. The woman with the book here does not have much expression. She is a student, and in the future she will have a mediocre marriage. Her present and past are mediocre . . . That's all.

> JK Female, age 20: This woman is a daughter of an owner of a farm. She is a student. I don't know when (what era) it is. Exploitation. They use these people. She

is thinking about the exploitation of workers. She is after all the daughter of a landlord, and she is thinking what she should do in this position. The future is, it is difficult to say. Maybe she will feel comfortable in such a life. Or, she will leave home, and live independently. Or she will involve herself in this kind of . . . (movement against exploitation).

Card 7: attitudes toward authority. A second set of attitudes that influence adult adaptation differentially in minorities has to do with authority relationships as observed from responses to card 7, a picture depicting an older man and a younger man in conversation. The Japanese interpret this picture most often as some form of mentorship. The Koreans interpret it as a conspiracy (38 percent in the L.A. group compared with 55 percent in Japan). Compared with majority Japanese, relatively less attention is given to the age and status differentials of the two figures. Among Japanese Issei immigrants (De Vos 1983), 94 percent depicted compliant attitudes as did 68 percent of Nisei. In 28 percent of the Nisei, however, there was rebellion or assertion of autonomy. Only one Issei gave such a story. Among the majority Japanese in Japan, this age disparity also remains central to the story (De Vos, 1973). However, in the present sample, only 16 percent of the Koreans in Japan view age and differential status as a significant consideration of the themes of the stories, whereas, among the L.A. Koreans, a status differential is important in 52 percent of the stories.

Distrust is an immediate reaction of Japanese Koreans to a picture of two individuals with their heads together. Over half (55 percent) immediately thought of a conspiracy, either by politicians, businessmen, criminals, or simply friends. Such stories appear in the Los Angeles sample, in 42 percent of all cases. Koreans in Japan are less conscious of status differentials than are those in L.A., especially as related to conspiratorial situations. The remaining Japanese-Korean stories show almost no positive themes. In contrast to the L.A. sample of Koreans, who see positive younger-older situations in 24 percent of their stories, the Japanese sample gave only four such stories (13 percent). Thus, these distrustful propensities are present in both

TABLE 10.5
Summary Comparison of Card 7 -- Los Angeles Koreans and Korean Japanese

Groups Total Cases	Los Angeles 50	Japan 31
1. Younger - older: cooperate, advice, comfort	12	4
Positive or autonomous	24%	13%
Positive older-younger relationship	3	2
son's acceptance of father's advice or comfort	3	2
son's acceptance of a scolding	1	
son succeeds father's business, but son doesn't		
give good impression	1	
discord resolved in eventual harmony	3	
son does not follow father's advice	1	
2. Mutual Cooperation and conflict	10	8
No status diff.	20%	26%
cooperative or positive exchanges	8	4
dispute or negative exchange	2	4
3. Conspiracy and evil or negative activity	13	1
Status diff. (older-younger)	26%	3%
evil advice	0	1
businessmen conspiring (age difference		
secondary)	7	
older and younger conspire	2	
older man deceives younger man	1	
debauched son does not correct behavior	1	
father bends to strong-willed son	2	
4. Conspiracy and evil activity	11	16
No status differences	22%	52%
friends together in a plot	2	2
two conspire against another	0	1
politicians conspiring	4	3
businessmen conspiring	3	6
evil thing going on nonspecific	0	1
lawyer and criminal	0	1
Mafioso types	1	1
hired to kill for money	1	0
5. Other	3	2
Percentage of total sample	6%	6%
lawyer advises client	1	0
man pressured to become son-in-law	1	0
"discussing" -- no elaboration	0	2

samples, but are higher among those in Japan. Moreover, the problems of distrust toward authority, strongly evident in those who migrate to the United States, are compounded among the Japanese Koreans by an expectation of a bleak future in which there is hope for success only if they are favored by patronage of a corrupt and powerful individual:

> JK Female, age 22: The two are in high posts of a large company, president or executives. They are planning something evil. About Peanut [a name in the Lockheed bribery incident] (laugh). Well something about the work, or about a woman. They are plotting something evil. The future is . . . They are discussing that they don't have much hope of success in plot.

> JK Female, age 25: They seem to be doing something evil. They are directors of a company or politicians. This older man is saying, "How is that business going? You have to manage successfully by using a bribe." So, younger one answers, "Yes, sir. I'll do it skillfully." This older man is talking calmly, this younger man (points to the right) is carefully listening to him. He is trying desperately to gain his favor.

Contrast these stories with the more positive tone of the L.A. stories.

> LA Female, age 23: They are discussing business. The person on the left is the other man's boss. The topic they are discussing is about the sales strategy of the company. The plan which will be produced from their discussion will be successful because they seem to be very bright men.

> LA Male, age 52: The young man on the right has a cause of anxiety. The old discusses the cause of anxiety with the young and he comforts the young. The old

seems to be the young man's father or teacher. As they do not find an appropriate solution to the problem, they only worry about the problem together.

However, distress about conspiracy is not absent in L.A.

LA Male, age 76: The two people are conspiring. They are very close and they trust each other. They will endeavor to work out their conspiracy but I cannot forecast the result. Maybe their conspiracy is in a legal strategy of some sort.

LA Female, age 22: They are friends. Their facial expression is not so good. They are concocting a plot. But the plot will be not be successful.

Conclusion

Koreans in Japan demonstrate traits of alienation and lack of resolution toward either future accomplishment or a positive destiny in interpersonal relationships. Indirect evidence of the effect of degradation over several generations on any minority population has been discussed above to show that Koreans in Japan are not genetically inferior from the sample obtained from new Korean immigrants in the United States. Therefore, their social history and the history of Japanese domination have had a more critical impact on Koreans as a discriminated minority, a situation in complete contrast to that of voluntary immigrants to the United States, who display positive social and economic aspirations.

Notes

1. For example, anthropologists and other social scientists in Belgium and Sweden are beginning studies of children of migrants in North European industrial states (see De Vos and Suarez-Orozco, chapter 8).
2. In class hierarchies of British or French societies, for example, certain individuals delight in exposing upwardly mobile pretenders.
3. The Rorschach test was used by several investigators attempting

research on modal personality structures in different cultural settings (see De Vos and Boyer, 1988).

4. De Vos began his detailed research with the TAT in 1953. As a clinical psychologist he had utilized the test as part of clinical diagnostic work since 1948. His first training with the test as part of cultural analysis was under the guidance of William E. Henry at the University of Chicago in 1947. Henry (1947) had begun to apply the test both to research in industrial psychology and cross-culturally as part of a comparative psychocultural study of American Indian child development.

5. This work, related to the personality of Japanese Americans, came to the attention of Professor Tsuneo Muramatsu of Nagoya National University in Japan. In 1952, the fulbright Scholar Exchange Program was initiated for Japan. Muramatsu asked me to come to Japan and participate in organizing and carrying out a program of research on Japanese personality and culture at Nagoya University. I accepted and journeyed to Nagoya in 1953.

From the inception of joint work in Nagoya on the cultural psychology of the Japanese, I was faced with the necessity of developing some systematic methods for analyzing the large amount of data that was to be gathered from a basic sample of approximately twenty-four hundred rural and urban Japanese. Caudill had examined the stories obtained from Japanese Americans in Chicago empirically, using no apriori scoring system to order his data. I concluded that some more systematic quantification would be necessary to handle the very large amount of data being assembled at Nagoya 1953-1954.

6. This section draws directly on the EMIC interpersonal categories presented in detail in De Vos and Suarez-Orozco, 1990, Chapter 1. It also draws on material discussed more fully in my *Social Cohesion and Alienation*, chapter 4.

7. With some of my former students, I am, at present, preparing a volume on the use of the TAT in Japan, Korea, the Philippines, Brazil, Argentina, and Kenya. See especially the recent large scale comparison of nine hundred high school students in Japan with nine hundred American students (Vaughn, 1988) matched on TAT, "field independence," and the CPI (the California Psychological Inventory test of Harrison Gough).

References

Atkinson, John William. 1958. *Motives in Fantasy, Action, and Society: A Method of Assessment and Study*. Princeton: D. Van Nostrand.

Caudill, William and George A. De Vos. 1956. "Achievement, Culture and

Personality: The Case of the Japanese Americans." *American Anthropologist* 58: 1102-26.

De Vos, George A. 1973. *Socialization for Achievement*. Berkeley: University of California Press.

De Vos, George A. 1980. "Deliquency and Minority Status: A Psychocultural Perspective." In *Crime and Deviancy: A Comparative Perspective*, edited by Graeme Newman. Beverly Hills: Sage Publications.

De Vos, George A. 1983. "Achievement Motivation and Intra-Family Attitudes in Immigrant Koreans." *Journal of Psychoanalytic Anthropology* 6-2: 125-62.

De Vos, George A. 1984. "Ethnic Identity and Minority Status: Some Psycho-Cultural Considerations." In *Identity: Personal and Socio-Cultural*, edited by Anita Jacobson-Widding. Stockholm: Almquist and Wiksell International.

De Vos, George A. 1992. *Social Cohesion and Alienation: Minorities in the United States and Japan*. Boulder, CO: Westview Press.

De Vos, George A, and Hiroshi Waqatsuma. 1969. "Minority Status and Delinquency in Japan." In *Mental Health Research in Asia and the Pacific*, edited by William Caudill and Tsong Y. Lim. Honolulu University of Hawaii.

De Vos, George A., and L. Bryce Boyer. 1988. *Symbolic Analysis Cross-Culturally: The Rorschach Test*. Berkeley: University of California.

De Vos, George A., and Takeo Sofue, eds. 1986. *Religion and the Family in East Asia*. Berkeley: University of California.

De Vos George A., and Marcelo Suarez-Orozco. 1990. *Status Inequality: The Self in Culture*. Newbury Park CA.: Sage.

De Vos, George A., and Kwang-Kyu Lee. 1981. "Dilemmas of Authority in Post Colonial Korean Modernization." In *Modernization and the Impact of the West*, edited by Changsoo Lee. Los Angeles: University of Southern California Press.

Lee, Changsoo, and George De Vos. 1981. *Koreans in Japan: Ethnic Conflict and Accommodation*. Berkeley: University of California Press.

McClelland, David C. 1961. *The Achieving Society*. Princeton: D. Van Nostrand.

McClelland, David C., et al. 1953. *The Achievement Motive*. New York: Appleton-Century-Crofts.

McClelland, David C., et al. 1943. *Thematic Apperception Test Manual*. Cambridge, MA: Harvard University Press.

Parsons, Talcott, and Robert Bales. 1955. *Family Socialization and Interaction Process*. Glencoe: The Free Press.

Shipley, T., and J. Veroff. 1952. "A Projective Measure of Need for Affiliation." *Journal of Experimental Psychology* 43: 349-56.

Vaughn, C. 1988. "Cognitive Independence, Social Independence, and Achievement Orientation: A Comparison of Japanese and U.S. Students." Ph.D. diss. University of California, Berkeley.

Veroff, J. 1958. "A Scoring Manual for the Power Motive." In *Motives in Fantasy, Action, and Society*, edited by J. W. Atkinson. Princeton: D. Van Nostrand.

Wagatsuma, Hiroshi, and George A. De Vos. 1981. *Heritage of Endurance*. Berkeley: University of California.

11

Subethnicity: Armenians in Los Angeles

*Claudia Der-Martirosian, Georges Sabagh,
and Mehdi Bozorgmehr*

Subethnicity refers to the presence of nationalities within an ethnic group, and is analytically distinct from "internal ethnicity," which applies to ethnic groups within an immigrant group (Bozorgmehr, 1992). Internal ethnicity exists among ethnically diverse immigrant groups such as Iranians, who are further divided into subgroups (Armenians, Bahais, Jews, Muslims). On the other hand, subethnicity, refers to ethnic groups such as Armenians of different nationalities, for example, Iranians, Lebanese, and the native-born. Subethnicity results from successive influx of an ethnic group from different countries of origin, and may also include native-born offspring of earlier immigrants. Even though these groups share an all-encompassing ethnicity, each subgroup has a different national identity and heritage. Subgroups may also differ in social and economic characteristics.

In common with Armenians, Jews and Chinese are two major ethnic groups in the United States, who, originating from diverse lands, offer historical and contemporary examples of subethnicity, respectively. Jewish immigration from different countries spans three centuries, whereas Chinese national origin diversity is more recent. Sklare (1971: 5-6) emphasizes this issue: "Among Jews such diversity has been ever sharper than with most other groups, for Jews originated in different countries, frequently with contrasting traditions." The experience of Jews and Chinese in the United States provides further evidence that diverse migration waves produce subethnicity.

There have been four distinct waves of Jewish immigration to the United States. The first consisted of a small number of Spanish-Portuguese Jews in the seventeenth and eighteenth centuries. The second brought a more sizable number of German Jews in the nineteenth century. The third was the massive influx of Eastern European Jews in the late nineteenth and early twentieth centuries (Sklare, 1971), and the fourth consists primarily of today's Russian and Israeli Jews (Goldscheider and Zuckerman, 1984). First-generation Jewish immigrants have established associations and voluntary organizations based on nationality, which has been an important organizational factor for the second and third waves (Sklare, 1971), and still continues to be a factor among the fourth wave (Goldscheider and Zuckerman, 1984).

Several studies of the earlier Chinese settlers highlight the significance of provenance in the organization of social and economic life of these communities (Lai, 1988; Light, 1972; Lyman, 1986; Nee and Nee, 1972). The influx of Chinese from many countries at present has superseded these earlier regional distinctions. The two major waves of Chinese migration to the United States represent completely different migration streams. The first wave in the late nineteenth to early twentieth centuries originated in the rural areas of Southern China. The current wave (post-1965) consists mainly of Chinese from cities in China and Chinese from Taiwan and Hong Kong (Kwong, 1987; Zhou and Logan, 1989). For example, New York's Chinatown, one of the oldest in the nation, consisted mainly of the Cantonese from China, and the Chinese from Hong Kong before the 1970s. New York's Chinatown now contains "Chinese from all parts of the world" including those from Southeast Asia and even from several Latin American countries. These Chinese subgroups bring different occupational specializations, dialects, and cultural traditions. They tend to settle in parts of Chinatown that correspond to their countries of origin (Kwong, 1987: 39-42). Similar patterns of diversity based on national origin exist in San Francisco's

Chinatown, and in Chinatown and Monterey Park in Los Angeles. To our knowledge, however, no published studies document subethnicity in these major Chinese centers. Although a few historical accounts of subethnicity among Jews are available (Rischin, 1962, 1986), current research on subethnicity among Jews, and especially Chinese, is missing. The lack of research on subethnicity is due mainly to the concentration of most studies on one subgroup (e.g., the Israeli Jews, the mainland Chinese) instead of on intragroup differences.

In Los Angeles today, in addition to Jews and Chinese, Armenians are a sizable, visible, and rapidly growing ethnic group containing subgroups. Representing the most recent example of an ethnically diverse minority, Armenians enable us to study this important historical phenomenon. Armenians in Los Angeles have co-ethnic counterparts of different national origins such as Lebanon, Iran, and the former Soviet Union. By treating Armenians as a homogenous category, however, ethnic stratification researchers have masked important socioeconomic differences among Armenians in the United States (Farley and Neidert, 1990; Treiman et al., 1986-87).

A population in diaspora, Armenians in Los Angeles are a distinctive ethnic group. Foreign-born Armenians have had a long history of settlement as a minority in various Middle Eastern countries such as Iran, Lebanon, Turkey, Syria, and Egypt. For instance, in prerevolutionary Iran, ethnic Armenians spoke Armenian as a mother tongue, practiced the Christian religion, attended Armenian schools, and participated in exclusive Armenian associations (Amurian and Kasheff, 1986). Christian religion and distinctive Armenian language differentiated Armenians from the Muslim majority in the Middle East. Armenian communities in most of the Middle Eastern countries have resisted assimilation. Unsurprisingly, Armenians carry over their premigration experience as a minority to the United States.

Subethnicity plays an important organizing role among Armenians in Los Angeles. In some facets of life (e.g., social ties), Armenians cluster along the lines of national origin. Armenians from Iran are, for example, referred to by other Armenians and they identify themselves, as "Iranian Armenians". In Iran, Armenian ethnic identity was constructed in a social context that only emphasized Armenian ethnicity. In the United States, however, the term Armenian is no longer a sufficient differentiator because of the presence of different Armenian subgroups. Instead, national origin (American, Iranian, Lebanese, Turkish, etc.) is used by the Armenian community members to define subgroups. Non-Armenians are largely unaware of these internal distinctions.

Subethnicity among Armenians is not limited to Los Angeles -- it occurs wherever Armenians of different national origin backgrounds congregate. For example, Talai (1989) observes that the Armenian community in London consists of recent immigrants from Armenia and various Middle Eastern countries, as well as Armenians born in England. As in the United States, Armenians are not the only internally differentiated ethnic group in England. Bhachu (1985, 1993) observes a similar phenomenon among Sikhs and Hindus.

Although subethnicity exists within the Armenian community in Los Angeles, a sense of being Armenian transcends subethnic divisions. A common Armenian history, use of the Armenian language despite its Eastern and Western dialects, the Christian religion, the proliferation of voluntary ethnic associations, the availability of several Armenian newspapers, and even an Armenian telephone directory all point to a thriving Armenian community in Los Angeles. In this sense, Armenians are an all-encompassing ethnic group that contains distinct national origin subgroups.

Sources of Data

Armenians are a distinctive ethnic minority in the United States, but until the 1980 census provided data on ancestry it was not possible to identify them separately (Sabagh and Bozorgmehr, 1986). Our data set examines the Armenian population in Los Angeles. We developed it from the 5 percent sample of the 1980 census. The data set is based on two criteria: (1) persons who reported Armenian as either their first or second ancestry, and (2) persons who spoke the Armenian language at home. These criteria yielded a sample of 2,619 cases, representing 52,400 Armenians in Los Angeles in 1980.

The census data provide no information on the ethnicity of social and economic ties of Armenians. This information is necessary fully to document Armenian subethnicity. In the absence of available data on all Armenian subgroups, we have relied on our own survey of a random sample of 195 Armenian-Iranian heads of household who took part in the study of Iranians in Los Angeles in 1987-88 to illustrate subethnic social and economic networks (Bozorgmehr and Sabagh, 1989).

Armenian Migration to Los Angeles

In order better to understand ethnic diversity among Armenians in Los Angeles, we examine first their migration patterns into this region. Armenian immigration to the United States has been primarily triggered by political pressures rather than determined by economic forces. The two major waves of Armenian immigration correspond to the pre-1920s and post-1960s periods. The earliest wave of Armenian migration consisted of refugees who fled the Ottoman Empire in the late nineteenth and early twentieth centuries. The second wave of Armenian immigration began after 1965 when the restrictive U.S. Immigration Act of 1924 was finally lifted (Mirak, 1980, 1983). The second wave was also caused by political turmoil in Egypt, Turkey, Lebanon, and Iran, and more recently in the former Soviet Union. Thus, an unusual mix of countries of origin and generations are represented among Armenians in Los Angeles. One group includes the survivors of the first wave of immigrants and their descendants who are now a middle-aged second generation, and a young or a very young third and even fourth generation. By contrast, Armenian immigrants who arrived after 1965 are mostly a first generation with a wide variation in age, so that there are both first-generation and third-generation Armenians of the same age.

Most of the earlier Armenian immigrants settled in the Eastern United States, though some later migrated to the West to places such as Fresno, California to work in agriculture. The new wave of Armenian migration targets California, and especially Los Angeles, which has attracted both native-born Armenians from Fresno and from the Eastern states, as well as recent immigrants from Middle Eastern countries and the former Soviet Union. As a result, Los

Angeles is now one of the most ethnically diverse Armenian centers in the world.

National Origin Diversity

Table 11.1 gives the sample size and the population estimates of different Armenian subgroups in 1980. According to the census, there were an estimated 52,400 Armenians in Los Angeles, accounting for nearly one-quarter of all Armenians in the United States. The actual population size of Armenians in Los Angeles was probably larger in 1980 because of an undercount in ancestry data (Lieberson and Waters, 1988). This population has increased dramatically since 1980 after the massive influx of Armenian

TABLE 11.1
Country or State of Birth of Armenians, Los Angeles, 1980

Country or State of Birth	Sample Size	Population Size	Percent Distribution
Native-born population			
California	508	10,200	19.5
Other states	224	4,500	8.6
Total	732	14,700	28.1
Foreign-born population			
Iran	386	7,700	14.7
Former Soviet Union	376	7,500	14.3
Lebanon	297	6,000	11.5
Turkey	256	5,100	9.7
Other Middle East	311	6,200	11.8
Other countries	261	5,200	9.9
Total	1,887	37,700	71.9
Total Population	2,619	52,400	100.0

Source: Public-Use Microdata Sample File (5 percent) from the 1980 U.S. Census of Population.

TABLE 11.2
Year of Immigration of Foreign-Born Armenians, Los Angeles, 1980.

Year of Immigration	Percent Distribution						
		Country of Birth					
	Foreign-Born	Iran	Lebanon	Other Middle East	Turkey	Former Soviet Union	Other Countries
Before 1950	6.1	1.8	0.9	1.2	17.1	15.1	7.0
1950-59	5.1	2.2	3.0	5.3	4.9	7.0	14.6
1960-64	2.5	2.8	3.0	2.1	2.9	1.7	5.8
1965-69	6.9	4.9	8.5	7.8	9.8	3.3	15.5
1970-74	12.8	13.5	13.2	21.0	12.2	6.0	16.4
1975-80	66.6	74.8	71.4	62.6	53.1	66.9	40.7
Total	100.0	100.0	100.0	100.0	100.0	100.0	100.0

Source: See Table 11.1.

immigrants into Los Angeles. More than two-thirds of Armenians in Los Angeles are foreign-born, indicating the importance of Los Angeles as a magnet for immigrants. By comparison, in the United states as a whole, only 40 percent of Armenians are foreign-born (Sabagh et al., 1988). Since national origin differences may disappear, the preponderance of the foreign-born makes subethnicity more applicable to this ethnic group. Among Armenian immigrants in Los Angeles, those from Iran and from the former Soviet Union constitute the largest groups (29 percent of all Armenians). The massive influx of Armenian refugees from the former Soviet Union in the 1980s has further increased the number of Armenians from Armenia (County of Los Angeles, 1989). Armenians from Lebanon are almost as numerous. These three subgroups account for four out of every ten Armenians in Los Angeles. Turkey accounts for only 10 percent of Armenians in Los Angeles, even though it was the predominant place of origin of the first wave of Armenian immigrants to the

United States.

On the whole, Los Angeles has attracted the newest Armenian immigrants. Table 11.2 shows that two-thirds of all foreign-born Armenians residing in Los Angeles in 1980 arrived in the United States between 1975 and 1980. About seven out of ten immigrants from Iran, Lebanon, and the former Soviet Union arrived during this five-year period. Migrants from Lebanon fled from a war and those from Iran fled from a revolution. Although the earliest migrants were mainly from Turkey, six out of ten of these immigrants arrived between 1970 and 1980. However, Armenians from Turkey in other parts of the United States make up a much higher share of the old Armenian migration (Sabagh et al., 1988). Because Turkish Armenians have resided longest in the United States, they are distinctly older than any of the other Armenian subgroups. Thus, in Los Angeles the median age of Turkish Armenians was about sixty-four years, compared to a median age in the range of twenty-six to thirty-six years for other foreign-born Armenians. Native-born Armenians had a median age of twenty five years.

Geographical Distribution

The geographical distribution of Armenians within Los Angeles varied by country of origin. Armenians from Armenia concentrated in East Hollywood, Armenian Iranians were predominantly in Glendale, and many native-born Armenians resided in Montebello and Pasadena. According to the 1980 U.S. census, the vast majority of Armenians were concentrated in four major areas: Glendale (including the adjacent Burbank area), Pasadena, East Hollywood, and Montebello. In 1980, Armenians in East Hollywood, in Glendale, and in Pasadena constituted 56, 25, and 9 percent respectively of the total Armenian population of Los Angeles County. Together, these three areas included 90 percent of the Armenian population of Los Angeles County. The Armenian population in each of these areas has increased since 1980. In East Hollywood, there has been a substantial increase of Armenians from Armenia (County of Los Angeles, 1989). In the Glendale Unified School District, Armenians constituted the largest immigrant group who spoke an ethnic language at home (Glendale Unified School District, 1990). Until recently, the Armenian community of Pasadena consisted primarily of native-born Armenians, but recent Armenian immigration has changed its demographic composition. In 1989, Pasadena commissioned a special census of Armenians it considers a legal minority. According to this Pasadena census, only 17 percent of Armenians are native-born and the rest are immigrants. The largest foreign-born Armenians in Pasadena are the Lebanese (33 percent), Armenians from Armenia (16 percent), and the Syrians (12 percent) (Pasadena Armenian Census, 1990).

Socioeconomic Differences among Armenian Subgroups

The significance of subethnicity is reflected in socioeconomic differences among Armenian subgroups. Although the general level of education among all Armenians in Los Angeles was fairly high, there were more who did not go beyond elementary school than who obtained a postgraduate college education (Table 11.3). This profile indicates vast educational differences among Armenian subgroups. Nearly half of Turkish Armenian men, and about one-quarter of Lebanese and other Middle Eastern Armenian men, had a limited elementary school education (Table 11.3). The noticeably lower levels of educational achievement among Turkish Armenians can be partly attributed to their older age. By contrast, less than one out of ten Iranian-Armenian and Armenian men from Armenia, and almost none of the native-born Armenian men, had a comparably low level of education. Although women, generally, had a lower educational achievement than did men, internal differences among subgroups were comparable to those of the Armenian men. Modal educational categories were lowest for Turkish Armenians (elementary school for men and women) and highest for Iranian and native-born Armenians (college for men but not for women). For all other men and all women, the modal education was senior high school. Even though Lebanese-Armenian men were part of the new immigration, their educational profile differed from that of Iranian-Armenian men. Clearly, an aggregated level of education for all Armenians masked significant subgroup variations.

The occupational profile of all Armenians also masked subgroup variations (Table 11.4). Approximately one-quarter of Armenian men worked in the two highest occupational categories of executives and professionals, but the subgroups ranged from 15 percent for

TABLE 11.3
Educational Distribution of Male and Female Native-and Foreign-Born
Armenians, Ages 16 Years and over, Los Angeles, 1980.

Education by Sex	Percent Distribution							
	All Arme- nians	Native- Born	Foreign-Born					
			Iran	Lebanon	Turkey	Other Middle East	Former Soviet Union	Other Coun- tries
Males								
Element'y	15.2	0.9	8.0	23.9	45.8	25.6	9.8	10.7
Jr High	9.2	1.1	5.5	10.3	21.7	12.2	13.6	8.8
Sr High	34.7	35.2	31.9	33.3	19.2	29.1	52.6	38.1
College	29.4	45.6	40.5	25.4	8.3	20.9	14.9	33.6
College 5 yrs +	11.5	17.2	14.1	7.1	5.0	12.2	9.1	8.8
Total	100.0	100.0	100.0	100.0	100.0	100.0	100.0	100.0
Sample size	(1,085)	(261)	(163)	(126)	(120)	(148)	(154)	(113)
Females								
Element'y	17.9	0.8	14.2	18.5	48.0	32.6	11.1	13.5
Jr High	10.5	1.8	8.0	19.4	13.4	13.3	12.4	13.6
Sr High	39.9	48.7	43.8	34.3	29.1	28.9	44.8	41.5
College	24.6	35.3	28.4	24.1	7.1	18.5	26.9	22.9
College 5 yrs +	7.1	13.4	5.6	3.7	2.4	6.7	4.8	8.5
Total	100.0	100.0	100.0	100.0	100.0	100.0	100.0	100.0
Sample size	(1,019)	(224)	(162)	(108)	(127)	(135)	(145)	(118)

Source: See Table 11.1.

Armenians from Armenia to 32 percent for Iranian and native-born Armenians. At the other end of the occupational scale, 44 percent of Armenians were craftsmen and operators, but this proportion ranged from a low of about one-third for native-born and Iranian Armenians to two-thirds for Armenians from Armenia.

Armenians in Los Angeles consisted of immigrant subgroups with a strong proclivity toward entrepreneurship. Therefore, self-employment has been included in our analysis of their economic activities. The rate of self-employment among all Armenians was twice as high as that of the general population of Los Angeles (18 as compared to 9 percent). But even this figure masked important variations among subgroups, especially, between the native- and the foreign-born. The rate of self-employment was 32 percent for Turkish Armenians, whereas native-born Armenians had the lowest rate of self-employment (11 percent), only slightly higher than the general rate for the Los Angeles population. The rate of self-employment for other subgroups was close to that of Armenians as a whole.

Since Armenians from Armenia were not allowed to extricate money from the former Soviet Union, they arrived with little or no capital. Also, the tradition of entrepreneurship may not have been as strong in the Soviet socialist economy as it remained in Middle Eastern market economies. Therefore, relative to other foreign-born Armenians, Armenians from Armenia have been less inclined to start their own businesses, especially in the early phases of settlement.

Subethnic Social and Economic Ties

Subethnicity is characterized not only by marked differences in socioeconomic characteristics, but also by the predominance of exclusive social and economic ties within subgroups. Our survey of Iranians in Los Angeles provides evidence on the networks of Iranian Armenians (Der-Martirosian, 1989). The close friends of more than 80 percent of these respondents and their spouses were Iranian Armenians, as were the people at their social gatherings. The children of these respondents had fewer Armenian friends, suggesting the broadening of social ties among the second generation. The small size of the Iranian-Armenian labor force relative to

TABLE 11.4
Occupational Distribution of Male and Female Native- and Foreign-Born
Armenians, Ages 16 Years and Over, Los Angeles, 1980.

Occupation by Sex	Percent Distribution							
	All Armenians	Native-Born	Foreign-Born					
			Iran	Lebanon	Turkey	Other Middle East	Former Soviet Union	Other Countries
Males								
Executives	14.1	18.9	16.8	10.2	12.5	14.6	8.4	9.4
Professionals	10.4	12.8	12.8	11.1	8.3	6.5	7.4	10.4
Technical	24.7	26.9	32.8	23.1	25.0	22.0	14.8	25.0
Services	6.5	7.9	4.8	6.5	5.6	6.5	4.6	8.3
Farming	0.5	1.2	0	0	1.4	0	0	0
Crafts	27.3	17.8	20.0	35.2	25.0	35.0	39.8	30.2
Operators	16.5	14.5	12.8	13.9	22.2	15.4	25.0	16.7
Total	100.0	100.0	100.0	100.0	100.0	100.0	100.0	100.0
Sample size	(874)	(242)	(125)	(108)	(72)	(123)	(108)	(96)
Females								
Executives	8.5	10.5	8.0	7.3	6.2	10.9	4.4	6.9
Professionals	14.5	21.4	9.7	13.0	12.5	13.8	10.3	11.3
Technical	46.2	53.2	48.4	42.6	43.8	36.9	38.2	49.3
Services	13.0	10.4	14.5	13.0	12.5	13.8	16.2	14.1
Farming	0	0	0	0	0	0	0	0
Crafts	6.3	1.3	6.5	5.6	12.5	12.3	7.4	8.5
Operators	11.5	3.2	12.9	18.5	12.5	12.3	23.5	9.9
Total	100.0	100.0	100.0	100.0	100.0	100.0	100.0	100.0
Sample size	(506)	(154)	(62)	(54)	(32)	(65)	(68)	(71)

Source: See Table 11.1.

the general labor force of Los Angeles has resulted in complex economic networks. Iranian Armenians operated an ethnic economy that is distinctive from either an all-encompassing Iranian or Armenian ethnic economy (Light et al., 1992). Co-ethnics constituted the vast majority of business partners of self-employed Iranian Armenians, but their employees or customers were non-Armenians and non-Iranians. Also, most salaried Iranian Armenians had co-workers who were non-Iranians and non-Armenians. Interestingly, the tendency for co-ethnic economic ties was greater among Armenian Iranians than among any other Iranians (i.e., Bahais, Jews, and Muslims), reflecting the special strength of Armenian Iranian ethnicity. Although no comparable information is available for the other Armenian subgroups, the data on Iranian Armenians is indicative of the exclusive social and economic networks that existed among the various subgroups.

Conclusion

In this chapter, we introduced and defined the concept of subethnicity and applied this concept to Armenians. Subethnicity is not limited to Armenians; it also applies to many other ethnic groups, notably Jews and Chinese in the United States. Armenians in Los Angeles consisted of foreign-born from several Middle Eastern countries and from the former Soviet Union, as well as the native-born. With the exception of Armenian immigrants from Armenia, foreign-born Armenians were already an ethnic minority in their countries of origin. Upon resettlement in Los Angeles, nationality distinctions have emerged within the Armenian community in spite of a strong attachment to an overarching Armenian ethnicity.

We used census data on all Armenians and survey data on Iranian Armenians in Los Angeles to document the significance of subethnicity. Successive Armenian migration streams from various countries, and the presence of the native-born, have created ethnic diversity among Armenians in Los Angeles. The older immigration before 1950 was mainly from Turkey, whereas the new immigration after 1975 is primarily from Iran, Lebanon, and Armenia. These distinctive immigration waves have resulted in a complex age distribution. The overall Armenian socioeconomic profile masked significant internal differences in the characteristics of subgroups. Native-born and Iranian-born Armenians had the highest socioeconomic status, whereas those from Turkey had the lowest levels. Conversely, Armenians from Turkey had the highest rate of self-employment, and native-born Armenians had the lowest rate.

Survey data show the exclusivity of the social and economic ties of Iranian Armenians, supporting the argument that subethnicity is more salient than an all-encompassing Armenian ethnicity in Los Angeles. Future research on Armenians in Los Angeles, and on other ethnically diverse ethnic groups such as Jews and Chinese, should take subethnicity into account.

This chapter is based on research supported, in part, by grant #SES-8512007 from the National Science Foundation, and by grants from the International Studies and Overseas Programs and from the Academic Senate of the University of California, Los Angeles.

References

Amurian, A., and M., Kasheff. 1986. "Armenians of Modern Iran." In *Encyclopedia Iranica*, edited by Ehsan Yarshater. London and New York: Routledge and Kegan Paul.

Bhachu, Parminder. 1985. *Twice Migrants: East African Sikh Settlers*. London and New York: Tavistock.

Bhachu, Parminder. 1993. "Twice and Direct Migrants: Caste, Class, and Identity in Pre- and Post-1984 Britain". This volume.

Bozorgmehr, Mehdi. 1992. "Internal Ethnicity: Armenian, Bahai, Jewish, and Muslim Iranians in Los Angeles." Ph.D. Diss., University of California, Los Angeles.

Bozorgmehr, Mehdi, and Georges Sabagh. 1989. "Survey Research among Middle Eastern Immigrants in the United States: Iranians in Los Angeles." *Middle East Studies Association Bulletin* 23: 23-34.

County of Los Angeles. 1989. "The Impact of Soviet Armenian Immigration on Los Angeles County." Los Angeles: Commission on Human Relations.

Der-Martirosian, Claudia. 1989. "Ethnicity and Ethnic Economy Among Armenian Iranians in Los Angeles." Master's thesis, University of California, Los Angeles.

Farley, Reynolds, and Lisa Neidert. 1990. "Racial and Ethnic Stratification in the 1980s: An Appraisal of Melting Pot, Conflict, and Emergent Ethnicity Theories." Paper presented at the Annual Meeting of the American Sociological Association, 11-15 August, Washington, D.C.

Glendale Unified School District. 1990. "Language Census Report." *Informational Report* no. 1. Glendale, CA: The Board of Education.

Goldscheider, Calvin, and Alan Zuckerman. 1984. *The Transformation of the Jews*. Chicago: University of Chicago Press.

Kwong, Peter. 1987. *The New Chinatown*. New York: Hill and Wang.

Lai, David. 1988. *Chinatowns*. Vancouver: University of British Columbia Press.

Lieberson, Stanley, and Mary C. Waters. 1988. *From Many Strands: Ethnic and Racial Groups in Contemporary America*. New York: Russell Sage.

Light, Ivan. 1972. *Ethnic Enterprise in America*. Berkeley and Los Angeles: University of California Press.

Light, Ivan, et al. 1992. "Los Angeles: l'Economie Ethnique Iraniene." *Revue Europeenne des Migrations Internationales* 8: 155-169.

Lyman, Stanford M. 1986. *Chinatown and Little Tokyo*. Millwood, NY: Associated Faculty Press.

Mirak, Robert. 1980. "Armenians." In *Harvard Encyclopedia of American Ethnic Groups*, edited by Stephen Thernstrom. Cambridge, MA: Harvard University Press.

Mirak, Robert. 1983. *Torn Between Two Lands: Armenians in America 1880 to WWI*. Cambridge, MA: Harvard University Press.

Nee, Victor, and Brett de Bary Nee. 1972. *Longtime Californ'*. New York: Pantheon.

Pasadena Armenian Census. 1990. "The Armenian-American Population in Pasadena: A 1989 Survey." Whittier, CA: SC Communications Group.

Rischin, Moses. 1962. *The Promised City: New York Jews, 1870-1914*. Cambridge, MA: Harvard University Press.

Rischin, Moses. 1986. "Germans versus Russians." In *The American Jewish Experience*, edited by Jonathan Sarna. New York: Holmes and Meier.

Sabagh, Georges, and Mehdi Bozorgmehr. 1986. "The Usefulness of Ancestry Data: The Case of Middle Easterners." Paper presented at the Annual Meeting of the Population Association of America, 3-5 April, San Francisco.

Sabagh, Georges, et al. 1988. "Socioeconomic and Demographic Characteristics of Armenians in the United States in 1980." Paper presented at the "International Migration of Middle Easterners and North Africans: Comparative Perspectives" Conference, 19-21 May, University of California, Los Angeles.

Sklare, Marshall. 1971. *America's Jews*. New York: Random House.

Talai, Vered A. 1989. *Armenians in London*. Manchester, England: Manchester University Press.

Treiman, Donald, et al. 1986-87. "Occupational Status Attachment among Ethnic Groups in Los Angeles." *Working Papers in the Social Sciences*.

Vol. 2, no. 1. Institute for Social Science Research, University of California, Los Angeles.

U.S. Bureau of the Census. 1980. Census of Population and Housing 1980: Public-Use Microdata Sample A. [MRDF]. Washington, DC: U.S. Bureau of the Census [producer and distributor].

Zhou, Min, and John R. Logan. 1989. "Returns on Human Capital in Ethnic Enclaves: New York City's Chinatown." *American Sociological Review* 54: 809-20.

12

Armenians in Moscow

Yuri Arutyunyan

Like other republican nations of the Soviet Union, the Armenians have a bifurcated sociocultural center.[1] Armenia and Nagorniy Karabakh are the main ethnic territory of Armenians in the Soviet Union. Yerevan is the capital of Armenia. However, Moscow shares political, social, and cultural centrality with Yerevan. The Armenians' situation in this respect is quite different from that of the Russians whose capital city, Moscow[1], is the center of their nation and of Russian cultural life as well as the capital of the Soviet Union. In ethnic terms, Moscow is a Russian city. As the capital of a huge centralized state, Moscow offers attractive economic and cultural opportunities to Armenians who must, however, relocate in order to obtain them.[3]

In the past, Tbilisi and Baku had many Armenian residents, too. However, these cities' share of Armenian population has declined in the last thirty years as Russia's has grown. Deteriorating ethnic relations caused this change. Competitive intergroup relations in Georgia and Azerbaijan led to the gradual exclusion of Armenians from some social roles and to the numerical reduction of their populations in the trans-Caucasian capitals. Table 12.1 shows that between 1959 and 1989, the percentage of Armenians declined in the Georgian and Azerbaijan zones of their local residence.[4] In the same thirty year period, the number of Armenians grew and their percentage of total population increased in zones of their dispersed residence.[5] In the Russian Socialist Republic, including Moscow, Armenians increased from 348.7 thousand in 1959 to 576.3 thousand in 1989. Their percentage of the total population increased from 11.5 to 15.6 in the same period. Armenians represent a substantial and significant ethnic minority in Russia.

Armenians In Moscow

The Soviet Census of 1979 found only thirty-one thousand Armenians residing in Moscow. These Moscow Armenians were only about 0.4 percent of the approximately 8 million Moscow residents. They also represented less than 1 percent of the approximately 4 million Armenians in the Soviet Union. Of the Armenians in Moscow in 1987-88, three-quarters were internal migrants. Only one-quarter were born in Moscow. Of the migrants, only 44 percent came from Armenia, even though Armenia always contained more than 60 percent of the total Armenian population of the Soviet Union (Table 12.1). On the other hand, the proportion of Moscow Armenians from Georgia and Azerbaijan was 1.5 times higher than those two republics' share of the Armenian population of the Soviet Union. We conclude that ethnic troubles caused some Armenians in the trans-Caucasian capitals to migrate to Moscow.

Armenians migrated to Moscow as young adults. Of Armenians twenty-five to twenty-nine years old, 76 percent had lived in Moscow nine or fewer years; among those forty to forty-nine years old, only 10 percent were newcomers.

Essentially those of the Russian Republic, Moscow's selection rules determined not only the provenance of the Armenian migrants there but their socioeconomic characteristics as well. It is not accidental, for example, that among the Armenian migrants to Moscow, there were absolutely no people from rural localities. Moscow's selection rules simply excluded rural people. Most migrants to Moscow came from capitals of the various Soviet Republics. "All-Union" selection also favored migrants who had graduated from Russian secondary schools, and who had a good command of the Russian language. As young people, the Armenian

TABLE 12.1
Dynamics and Distribution of the Armenian Population in the USSR

	In Thousands			In Percent		
	1959	1979	1989	1959	1979	1989
Main ethnic territory:	1661.7	2848.1	3209.1	59.7	68.6	69.3
Armenia	1551.6	2725.0	3083.6	55.7	65.6	66.6
Nagorniy Karabakh	110.1	123.1	145.5	4.0	3.0	(2.7)
Zone of mostly local residence:	774.0	810.3	682.3	20.8	19.5	15.1
Georgia	442.9	448.0	437.2	15.9	10.8	9.4
Azerbaijan (without Nagorniy Karabakh)	332.0	362.3	245.1	11.9	8.7	5.7
Zone of mostly dispersed residence:	348.7	492.8	711.9	11.5	11.9	15.6
RSFSR,	256.0	364.6	532.0	9.2	8.8	11.6
Including Moscow	18.4	31.1	426.0	0.7	0.8	
Baltic Area,				(0.66)	(0.75)	
Ukraine, Byelorussia, Kazakhstan, Central Asia Republics	64.3	128.2	179.5	2.3	3.1	4.0
Totals	2786.9	4151.2	4623.3	100.0	100.0	100.0

Source: "Itogi Vsesoyuznoj Perepesi Naseleniya 1959 Goda SSSR" (1959 USSR Census Results) (Moscow, 1962), 184, 207, 210; ibid., Russian Soviet Federal Sovelist Republic (Moscow, 1963), 316; "Itogi Vsesoyuznoj Perepisi Naseleniya 1970 Goda," vol. 4 (Moscow, 1973), 103, 272, 263; Chislennost' i sostav naseleniya SSSR po dannym perepisi naseleniya 1979. (Size and composition of the USSR's population according to the 1979 Census data) (Moscow, 1984), 126, 141; Sojuz 1990.

migrants rapidly adapted to the Russian culture of Moscow. However, despite their command of Russian language, this adaptation to Russian or, at least, to a polyethnic culture unavoidably affected their way of life.

As another result of initial selection rules, Armenian migrants stood out conspicuously among Muscovites by their educational achievement; at least one-half of the young Armenian new arrivals had university diplomas. However, in the cohort aged eighteen to nineteen years, the number of students among the Armenians was only slightly higher than among the Russians. Among the Russians, a significant proportion of whom are Moscow-born, the younger the people, the higher their average level of education. Among the Moscow Armenians, the *older their age-group*, the higher their average educational attainment (Table 12.2).

TABLE 12.2
Percent of Moscow Residents With University Diplomas by Age Cohorts

	Armenians	Russians
18-29 age cohort	57%	53%
30-39	62%	[
		[51%
40-49	66%	[
50-59	72%	41%
60 years and older	76%	26%

These data become more vivid if we analyze the educational standards of the Armenians in relation to duration of their residence in Moscow. Among the "new arrivals," (i.e., Armenians living in the capital for nine years or less), half had university diplomas; among old settlers, 69 percent; and among Moscow-born Armenians, 72 percent. On the whole, among the adult Armenians in Moscow two-thirds had university diplomas compared to 46 percent of Russians. These data suggest the comparatively high social status of the Moscow Armenians.

An analysis of the careers of the Moscow Armenians confirms this conclusion. Table 12.3 shows the career indices of Russians and Armenians in Moscow. The career index is the difference between the shares of those with the higher and those with the lower career status. On the whole, Armenians had higher career indices than did Russians in both the five-year and ten-year review periods. However, two reservations are in order. First, among the newly arrived

Armenians, the career index is slightly lower than the Russian average. Second, high career indices were most typical of Armenian men, a product of the traditional differentiation of career roles between men and women.

The Armenian occupational structure in Moscow offers some signs of ethnic specialization. In this case, immigration cohort defined two groups of Armenians, each of which had different modal occupations. Thus, 40 percent of the newly arrived Armenians engaged in industry, transport, and construction. Some were the so-called *limitchiki* who work in these short-handed industries, and after some time earn the right to reside in Moscow. On the other hand, among the old settlers and the Moscow-born, the modal occupational cluster was scientific and creative arts organizations. Taken together, the two clusters show that Armenians were not randomly spread among the industries of Moscow.

Table 12.4 offers further evidence of the Armenians' occupational clustering and of its connection to migration cohort. Of course, the socioprofessional differences between the Russians and the

TABLE 12.3
Career Indices of Russians and Armenians in Moscow

	Last five years work status has			Last ten years work status has		
	Higher	Lower	Career Index	Higher	Lower	Career Index
Russians	30.7%	5.4	25.3	44.0	5.9	38.1
Armenians,	33.5%	2.8	30.7	52.2	5.0	47.2
including:						
New arrivals				41.9%	6.4	35.5
Old settlers				52.8%	5.7	47.1
Moscow-born				55.6%	2.2	53.4

*Career index is the difference between the shares of those with the higher and lower statuses.

Armenians in Moscow reflect the unique features of the migrant Armenian population, molded, as it was, by legal selection norms. These intergroup differences are not a product of nationality traits since the immigrant Armenians in Moscow are not representative of their nation. Whatever the causes, the Armenians in Moscow had distinct occupational niches. On the whole, they were underrepresented as workers, but overrepresented in the intelligentsia and leadership professions. In this aggregate sense, Armenians were an elite. However, upon closer inspection, we observe that the old settlers and the Moscow-born Armenians had a completely different occupational profile than did the Armenian new arrivals. Compared to Russians, the newly arrived Armenians had twice their statistical share of workers and about half their statistical share of intelligentsia and leadership occupations.

The same interesting patterns of internal differentiation appear when we desegregate Armenians by age cohort rather than by migration cohort. In Armenia, as in Russia, younger workers normally have higher average educational attainments than do older workers, and more of the younger workers engage in skilled labor, including mental labor. Such is exactly the situation we observe among Russians in Moscow. Younger Russians more frequently engaged in

TABLE 12.4
Moscow Armenians by Professions (Percentages)

	Workers	Intelli-gentisia	Leaders	Not in Labor Force	Total
New arrivals	45%	28%	5%	22%	100%
Old settlers	15	52	15	18	100
Moscow-born	9	55	10	26	100
Total:					
Armenians	20%	47%	12%	21	100
Russians	32	43	4	21	100

skilled or comfortable mental labor than did older Russians. Those engaged in manual labor accounted for 20-25 percent of employed Moscow Russians up to twenty-nine years old; among those thirty years of age and older, manual workers represented 25-33 percent of the employed. However, the situation among Moscow's Armenians was almost the reverse. True, among the younger cohort, the percentage of Armenians engaged in manual labor was 32 percent, about the same as among Russians of the same age. However, among those thirty to forty-nine years old, manual workers were 23 percent, and in the oldest group of workers, those fifty and older, it was only 12 percent. Thus, the oldest Armenians in Moscow were most likely to perform skilled mental labor, a trend at variance with both Russian and Armenian national results.

Naturally, these socioprofessional advantages of the Armenian population in Moscow had economic correlates. Among the Armenians, 76 percent earned more than two hundred roubles monthly. Among Muscovites, only 42 percent earned that much. The Armenians also reported more influence on the job than did Russians (Table 12.5). Again, however, the difference depended on migration cohort. Older settlers and Moscow-born Armenians reported more on the job influence than did Russians; newly arrived Armenians reported less influence than did Russians.

Comparing Russians and Armenians in respect to their evaluation of the conditions of cultural and everyday life, we found no difference between the nationalities. One's evaluation depended upon the duration of one's residence in Moscow, not upon one's nationality. Appreciating the advantages of Moscow compared to their town of previous residence, new arrivals offered the highest evaluation of everyday life in Moscow. Old settlers and those born in Moscow were less enthusiastic.

However, ethnic differences appeared in certain attitude questions. Seventy percent of the families of Moscow Armenians were nationally mixed, and they were mostly Armenian-Muscovite ones (60 percent). We asked: "Should one ask his/her parents' consent to get married?" Thirty-eight percent of Russians replied yes, as did 46 percent of Armenian-Russian families and 69 percent of purely Armenian families. Such national differences were

TABLE 12.5
Self-Evaluation of One's Influence on the Job (Percentages)

	Exert Some Influence	Exert Much Influence
Armenians,	27.5%	8.5%
including:		
New arrivals	16.0	6.5
Old-settlers	34.0	9.0
Moscow-born	26.0	9.0
Russians	18.0	4.0

reflected too in attitudes toward the employment of women, and in the evaluation of the men's engagement in household work. The Armenians seemed more conservative. However, these attitudes were speculative and had little to do with behavior. Even in purely Armenian families we found no real difference in the distribution of family duties compared to Russian families. Thirty-five percent of Russians claimed to have an egalitarian distribution of family responsibilities; among the Armenians only 25 percent made this claim. Nevertheless, some ethno-national differences appeared in the family life sphere. Otherwise it is difficult to explain why, despite their higher social status, Moscow Armenians had larger families. Fifty-one percent of purely Armenian families in Moscow had four or more members, whereas the majority of Moscow Russians (55 percent) had one child only. In the case of mononational families the Armenians more frequently had at least two children (58 percent).

Families with husband, wife, and children were a little above one-half (54 percent) of the Russian families. Among the Armenians, who have fewer divorces, such families represented 80 percent of all families and, in the case of the mixed Armenian-Russian families, 73 percent.

Ethnic traits were more distinctive in the sphere of arts and culture. Traditional customs, ceremonies, holidays, family rites, weddings, funerals, and so on, were not in evidence among the Armenians whatsoever, and there was practically no difference in this respect between the Russians and the Armenians. For instance, in nine cases out of ten there were no elements of national wedding rites present at all during marriage. The only exception was presented by new Armenian migrants, among whom national wedding rites were observed in 29 percent of the cases.

Ethnic features were much more manifest in cultural life, the latter being understood in its broad sense. But here too, international forms predominated. We learned, for example, which artists were most popular among the Armenians and among the Russians, but the difference proved insignificant. Artists and scholars of Russian culture were chosen by the Armenians almost as frequently as by other Muscovites. True, every set of such workers was invariably supplemented with the names of their "own" Armenian scholars, actors, and so on. We noted that an increase in the emotional coloration of a sphere was followed by an increase in the numbers of their "own" ethnic choices (Table 12.6). Thus, among all Armenians, 45 percent preferred co-ethnic composers, but only 16 percent preferred co-ethnic scholars, a difference we attribute to the emotional warmth of music. However, the data for all categories show a clear trend toward cosmopolitanism among the Armenians. In every aesthetic category, newly arrived Armenians were more likely than old settlers to select co-ethnic cultural workers, and the old settlers were, in turn, more likely than the Moscow-born to do so.

Judging by our data, ethno-national tastes were stable and strong in literature, art, theater, and music. These tastes encouraged preference for co-ethnics in these cultural fields. However, our data also attest to the wide cultural interests of the Moscow Armenians, whose artistic tastes were cosmopolitan, not ethnocentric. Armenians selected Russian artists and writers as frequently as did other Muscovites. Armenians selected foreign artists and writers more frequently than did other Muscovites. Indeed, 30 percent of the Armenian respondents selected foreign scholars.

We performed a close analysis of musical taste, giving our respondents an opportunity to express a preference for ethnic or

TABLE 12.6
Mention of Armenian Workers of Culture Among Moscow Armenians

	All Armenians	New arrivals	Old settlers	Moscow-born
Scholars	16%	35	16	2
Writers	19	34	19	9
Painters	29	41	30	16
Actors	28	52	21	16
Composers	45	60	46	27

TABLE 12.7
Musical Tastes (Percentages)

	All Arme-nians	New Arrivals	Old Settlers	Moscow-born	Russian
Music Preferred					
Russian folk music	15%	14%	17%	14%	48
Armenian folk music	46	60	49	24	10
Symphonic music	53	35	55	67	38
Light music	64	70	60	68	63
Dances Preferred					
Russian folk dances	11%		42		
Armenian folk dances	39	52	42	21	13
Ballet	55	32	59	68	50
Modern dances	46	55	37	57	46

classical forms of dance and music (Table 12.7). Fifty-three percent of Armenians liked symphonic music compared to only 38 percent of Muscovites, mostly Russians. Unsurprisingly, Russians liked Russian folk music more than did Armenians, and Armenians liked Armenian folk music more than did Russians. We found the same pattern in preference for folk dance. Russians liked Russian dance, and Armenians liked Armenian dance. Examining the Armenian data more closely, we find decreasing liking for Armenian music and folk dance with length of residence in Moscow. Moscow-born Armenians expressed much less liking for ethnic dance and music than did newly arrived Armenians. However, the Moscow-born Armenians liked ballet and symphonic music more than did other Armenians.

Language knowledge, use, and skill indicate the stability of ethno-national elements of culture as well as respondents' international interests. Naturally, the Moscow Armenians had a perfect command of Russian. Many indicated that Russian was their mother tongue. However, the Armenians exceeded the Muscovites in their knowledge of foreign languages. Among Russians, 10 percent had a free or good command of a foreign language, usually English. Among Armenians, fully 19 percent did so. Of all the Armenians, the Moscow-born were most skilled in foreign languages.

Knowledge of the Armenian language clearly distinguished the migration cohorts (Table 12.8). More than half of Moscow Armenians knew some Armenian, but 64 percent of the Moscow-born Armenians professed no knowledge of Armenian. One-third of Armenians "thought" in Armenian, but only 7 percent of the Moscow-born did so. One-fifth spoke Armenian freely, but only one-tenth of the Moscow-born. In general, knowledge and use of Armenian declined with duration of residence in Moscow.

Taken together, these data point to a wide and cosmopolitan range of cultural interests among the Moscow Armenians coupled with a rapid eclipse of Armenian culture. In these processes we perceive persistent differences between Armenians in Moscow and Armenians in Armenia. Armenia reanimates the Armenian cultural attachments of her children abroad. Real reproduction of waning Armenian traits in the Armenians of Moscow would require a permanent influx of Armenian immigrants from Armenia. Short of that, no superficial

TABLE 12.8
Armenians' Knowledge of the Armenian Language (Percentages)

	Total	New Arrivals	Old Settlers	Moscow-born
"Think" in their "own" language	34%	54%	36%	7
Speak rather freely	21	20	27	10
Speak with difficulty	14	9	16	13
Speak with great difficulty	7	5	7	7
No knowledge	24	6	14	64

efforts to stimulate national consciousness in the culture of Moscow's Armenians will prevent the erosion of their cultural heritage.

Ethnic identity has a loose connection to acculturation. Despite the rapid deethnicization of their Armenian culture, the Moscow Armenians retained a lively ethnic identity. Ethnic identity was not only ubiquitous; it was almost independent of level acculturation. Those who knew the Armenian language and those who did not, those who treasured the culture of "their own" people and those who were not connected to it in any way, whether they had any contacts with co-ethnics or not, almost all the Moscow Armenians preserved some sense of national identity. Their reasons are neither obvious nor open to direct observation. A feeling of kinship with one's own nationality is natural and spontaneous. This is a psychological feeling. The causes that form and stimulate that feeling reflect needs for solidarity, which, in the present case, has an ethnic origin and expression. Among Armenians abroad, this feeling, which is independent of acculturation, had survived and, sometimes, had even grown stronger.

Only 11 percent of the Moscow Armenians found any difficulty in answering the question: "What makes you feel kindred with the people of your nationality, if anything?" Among the respondents, 97 percent of the "new arrivals" reported a feeling of kinship; among the old settlers 90 percent, and among those Moscow-born, 88 percent. In other words, the feeling of ethnic "kinship" was almost universal in its intensity even though Moscow Armenians differed in their knowledge of Armenian, their national culture, their length of residence in Moscow. Now, what is behind this stable feeling of kinship? The answers obtained were mostly situational (Table 12.9). Among the recent migrants, many of whom speak Armenian, language occupied an important place among the "uniting" traits. In the case of the Moscow-born Armenians, the majority of whom did not speak Armenian, its loss is compensated by the "historical fates and destiny."

That is, people almost always found some reasons to explain "kinship," but these reasons were, of course, very conventional. Ethno-national identity, (i.e., the feeling of kinship), is not a Soviet or an Armenian phenomenon but a human universal inherent in different peoples, and in different national and social media. However, in this general feeling of identity, which is caused by the psychological need to belong to a social or, more exactly in the present case, to an ethnic community, different combinations of causes are possible. National identity varies in the intensity of its manifestation, and it is

TABLE 12.9
What Makes Moscow Armenians Feel Kindred With Their People

	Moscow-Armenians	New Arrivals	Old Settlers	Moscow-born
Armenian culture, customs, traditions	52	65	53	38
Armenian language	31	48	30	15
Historical fate and destiny of Armenians	32	27	31	38
Character, psychology of Armenians	16	19	14	16

*In their sum total the answers are much in excess of 100 percent because many respondents supplied multiple answers to kinship factors at the same time.

very important to acknowledge such variation. This variation affects social behavior and, when intense, is capable of precipitating inter-group conflicts, or nationalist movements or, on the opposite side, can promote humanistic expression of national feelings that do not undermine the solidarity among peoples.

Used in Old Soviet Union (OSU) was a set of means with whose help it is possible to assess not only identity, but also its qualitative characteristics and hierarchy. It is even possible to some extent to determine the aggressive or sympathetic attitude of a given identity to other nationalities, whether it affects the real behavior of the Moscow Armenians and if so, to what extent.

To have enough grounds for such important conclusions we should consider concrete manifestations of national identity in various spheres of life. One can distinguish territorial, legal, psychological, and ethno-cultural forms and spheres of national identity. Such a method helps to deepen and to concertize the feeling of kinship with one's nationality, which is characteristic of Moscow Armenians. To determine the intensity of ethnic identity in the legal sphere, we asked about "the necessity to register one's nationality in the documents." As to the "territorial" border of identity, we asked respondents what each considered his/her fatherland -- the Soviet Union, Russia, or "something else," this "something else" usually "a republic of one's nationality."

The conventional ethnic elements of identity were registered by the question about "one's own language." The language of one's nationality is "one's native tongue" even when the knowledge of a language is poor or absent, but sometimes the situation is reversed, one's language fluency is excellent but the language is not one's "native tongue." Forty-three percent of the Moscow Armenians knew the Armenian language and considered it their native tongue; 6 percent did not know it or knew it poorly, but called it native; 13 percent knew it well and even thought in it, but did not consider it native. The remaining 38 percent neither knew Armenian nor considered it their native tongue.

The ethno-psychological aspects of identity are reflected in the questions about the human traits typical of their own and other peoples. Both among the Armenians and among the Russians, the attractive humanistic traits of "one's own people" were evaluated almost one and a half times higher than those of foreign peoples. In contrast to the general manifestation of identity, the intensity of its expression in the distinguished spheres (territorial, legal, ethnic, and psychological) depended on the degree of the Moscow Armenians' real unity with their own ethnicity. Hence, as acculturation of the Armenians in Moscow proceeds, rapid changes take place in the ways national feelings are expressed in the four spheres distinguished above (Table 12.10).

TABLE 12.10
Moscow Armenians' Identification with Their People (Percentages)

Intensity of Self-Identification	All Armenians	New Arrivals	Old Settlers	Moscow-born
General feeling of "kinship" with their own people[1]	91	97	90	88
Identity in concrete manifestations:				
"Legal" (necessity to register one's nationality in documents)	58	66	57	39
"Ethno-cultural" (native language -- the Armenian)	49	80	52	13
"Geographical"[2] (what is fatherland)	30	67	20	30
"Psychological"[3] (superior qualities of one's own people)	30	63	20	30

1. Those with positive or negative answers. Not included here are those who found it difficult to answer, some 10 percent among all the Moscow Armenians.

2. Discarded from our calculations have been those who indicated the USSR and the Russian Soviet Socialist Republic as their fatherland. Sixty-five percent of all the Moscow Armenians indicated the USSR as their fatherland, while an overwhelming majority of the others indicated "their own republic" as their fatherland.

3. The percentage of positive evaluations of the Armenians by individual traits (the questionnaire contained nine of them -- "kindness," "hospitality," "cleanliness," "industry," "business-like attitude," "talent," "unselfishness," "steadfastness") is summed up and compared with the respective evaluations of the Russians. The table presents differences obtained through the comparison of the general evaluations of the peoples.

Of course, differentiation in the spheres of social consciousness is artificial because real-life interests are intertwined. They each carry a more or less equal psychological burden independently of their relation to a "territory," "psychology," or "ethnic culture." Thus, one's "native" language is a conventional ethnic category because the recognition of a native language does not depend on knowledge of it so much as a simple assertion that it is one's native language. Two prominent American-Armenian writers, William Saroyan and Michel Orlen offer examples. "Any Armenian in the world," said Michel Orlen, "who writes, writes as an Armenian, no matter in which language he puts down his thoughts. For you are speaking about the family of Armenian writers and not about the family of those writing in Armenian. The linguistic barriers are conditioned by the fates of each of us, while the family ties are those of bloodship." Michel Orlen does not know the Armenian language at all, although he recognizes it as his native tongue.

Of course, language "knowledge" and "recognition" can be "independent" of the medium of "origin" but not yet unconditionally, a situation distinctly reflected in the materials on the Moscow Armenians. Eighty-two percent of the Moscow Armenians who came from Armenia had a good or even a free command of the Armenian language and 75 percent recognized it as their native tongue. Among the "Caucasian" Armenians from Georgia and Azerbaijan, only 63 percent were in command of "their own" language; 50 percent thought of it as their "native language." For other republics, the respective figures are 42 and 24 percent, and among the Moscow-born Armenians the figures are only 28 and 19 percent. Such data indicate that despite the preservation of national identity, acculturation is a reality. Acculturation must become manifest in various spheres of social life in the actual behavior of people.

Our study has registered a connection between ethnic identity and behavior. This result is understandable. If identity is not only and not simply a passive feeling, then it affects behavior. Our study permits us to observe a number of indicators that reflect such a connection. Not to drown in facts, let us distinguish two indicators of the effect of identity, conditionally speaking, mostly in Moscow and outside it. As the first indicator, consider the influence of identity upon informal social contacts. Among one-fourth of the Moscow Armenians, their closest friends were Armenians, too. Moreover, according to the data, culture, language knowledge, traditions, customs, and rites had no effect here; the friendship community was created independently of these traditional and purely ethnic traits. However, in the process of acculturation and assimilation of the Armenians in Moscow, their "ethnic" ties became weaker. Compare, for example, the intensity of contacts of the "recent Armenian migrants" to Moscow and those "Moscow-born" (Table 12.11).

With the passage of time, an Armenian's social life in Moscow gradually disconnected from other Armenians. In many respects the relation becomes inverse: the more active the social life, the less national traits influence the life and the behavior of the Armenian people. The laconic and distinct independence of the social and the national present in the life of the Armenians in Moscow is vividly reflected by the model of their socioethnic life, as reconstructed on the basis of the Old Soviet Union data.

Conclusion

To perpetuate the ethnic life of Moscow Armenians in Moscow, permanent "injections" of their national culture from the outside are

TABLE 12.11
Intraethnic Contracts of Moscow Armenians (In Percent)

Armenian Groups	Close Armenian friends	Visits to Armenia		
		Annual	Once in a	No Visits
All Armenians	24	33	35	32
Including:				
Recent migrants	46	66	19	15
Old settlers	22	27	44	29
Moscow-born	8	11	31	38

necessary; it is necessary to support the natural ties between this group and the Armenian nation. It follows then that for all the conventionality of the borders of nations within the USSR, even such a developed ethnicity as the Armenian has no prospects for self-reproduction as an ethnic group in Moscow if its ties with Armenia are severed or general injections of the national culture are undermined.

Our analysis indicates, on the one hand, that we should not ignore the differences between people of the same nationality residing in their own nation and abroad. On the other hand, there is a danger of absolutizing the specificity of an ethnic group, of underestimating its flexibility and limits of its culture, which are largely dependent on the socioethnic features of the relevant locale.

The real needs and possibilities of ethnic groups require objective evaluation to realize a flexible and effective nationality policy. Equally unacceptable would be any centralized decisions from no matter what sources, all-Union or republican. National groups residing in alien ethnic locale, unique in their own way, require unique approaches and unique solutions every time such problems arise.

Notes

1. This paper was composed in 1990.
2. Passport registration rules are particularly strict in Moscow. To get his/her passport registered, a person must work there, but to get a job he/she must have housing and be registered. The circle is vicious but there are ways to break out. They require much effort and the intervention of some authorities. Apart from such official exceptions, one can get one's passport registered in Moscow through marriage to a Muscovite.
3. Another cohort of Armenians arrived in Russian cities in 1989-90. These were refugees fleeing earthquake disasters and genocide. We are unable to shed any light upon this most recent cohort of Armenians in Moscow.
4. For methodological details, see Yuri Arutyunyan, "Sotsialnokulturniye Aspecti Razvitiya i Sblizheniya Natsij v SSSR (Rogra a, Metodika Issledovaniya)." in *Sovietskaya etnografiya*, 1972, no. 3, ed. Yuri V. Arutyunyan, et al. *Etnosotsiologiya: Tseli, Metodi i Nekotoriye resul'tati.* (Moscow, 1984), 3-18.

5. The notion of the dispersed residence of a people and, most importantly, empirical analysis of such dispersed groups in a large city began with the work of Starovoitova. See Y. V. Starovoitova, *Etnicheskaya Gruppa v Sovremennom Sovetskom Gorode* (Leningrad, 1937), 30-31.

But while the geographical scale of the analysis of dispersed groups waxes, the relevant concepts should be corrected and specified. The compactness of dispersed groups differs from one area or settlement to another. Compactness affects inevitably the place of an ethnic group in the surrounding alien locale and influences relevant socio-ethnic processes. Highly compact dispersed groups lose their "dispersed" qualities even if found within an alien ethnic locale. For example, in Tbilisi even now and more so in the past, when the Armenians there were more numerous than the Georgians, the point was not about dispersal but about the so-called local pattern in settlement and about local ethnic groups, with their own cultural and social services, not only with their schools, own theater, and own churches, but even their own national informal representations in the organs of control.

13

Critical Issues in the U.S. Legal Immigration Reform Debate

Demetrios G. Papademetriou

Introduction: The Reform Context

The passage of the Immigration Reform and Control Act of 1986 (IRCA; P.L. 99-603) completed the first act in what is often regarded as a three-act play on immigration reform. The 1986 law focused primarily on illegal or undocumented immigration.[1] The play's remaining two acts are intended to focus on reforming legal permanent immigration and legal temporary immigration.

As in the past, the initiative for reform of legal immigration in the 101st Congress came from the Senate. There, Massachusetts Democratic Senator Edward Kennedy, the Immigration Subcommittee's chairman, and Wyoming Senator Alan Simpson, the Subcommittee's ranking Republican and that party's whip, were successful in having passed in successive Congresses a joint immigration bill, S. 358. The House, however, did not formally enter the fray until early in 1990. At that time, Connecticut Democrat Bruce Morrison, chair of the House Immigration Subcommittee, with the assistance of an Immigration Taskforce composed of members of the House Education and Labor Committee proposed and, after several resubmissions, gained Subcommittee and full Judiciary Committee approval for his bill, H.R. 4300.

Still under debate in 1990, when this paper was written, the two bills made different core assumptions about the proper role, future size, and composition of immigration to the United States. However, both addressed the same two questions:

(a) How many immigrants should be admitted into the United States annually and who they should be?

(b) How many economic/labor market/employment-related immigrant visas[2] should be made available, and under what circumstances?

Although each bill gave different answers, they addressed these questions within a common framework. Folded into the first question, for instance, were the following issues: (1) overall immigration levels; (2) family immigration and visa backlogs; and (3) immigration source-country diversity. The second question involved two interrelated issues: (1) how to evaluate an employer's claim that a foreign worker is needed; and (2) how to balance responsiveness to the manpower needs of business and labor's concerns that foreign workers might hurt the wages and job opportunities of U.S. workers.

Visa Numbers and Distribution

IRCA was in many respects Congress' response to an ideology of limits. The 1970s and early 1980s had encouraged perceptions of U.S. vulnerability to foreign political and economic events. This perception reinforced a self-image of a nation unable to control its destiny. This self-image resulted in a defensive approach to immigration reform that highlighted "law and order" initiatives offset only partially[3] by a legalization program.

In contrast, immigration reform in 1990 reflected a more confident attitude. A more self-assured United States was rethinking its legal immigration policy in the two major pieces of legislation discussed in this chapter.

Immigration Levels

One of the key themes driving immigration reform has been the question of overall immigration numbers. Underlying this theme are questions about the ability of the United States to "absorb" -- in cultural, social, and particularly labor market[4] terms -- constantly increasing numbers of immigrants (Miles, 1992).

In the 1980's, the United States admitted about half-a-million immigrants per year[5]. The Senate bill would increase that number by about 25 percent; the House bill would augment it by more than 50 percent plus an additional 20 percent for programs that would be phased out after three to five years (Table 13.1). The differences in overall numbers reflect contrasting views about immigration.

The House bill demonstrates an optimistic attitude about the ability of the United States to benefit from higher immigration. Much of its authors' optimism stems from the findings of two bodies of research literature: (a) the universally positive findings of more than a decade of intensive research on the economic effects of immigration (Papademetriou et al., 1989; Council of Economic Advisors, 1986, 1990; Muller and Espenshade, 1985; Papademetriou and Muller, 1987; Borjas, 1990; and Simon, 1989); and (b) the inability of that literature to identify more than isolated instances of immigration affecting adversely either the wages or the job opportunities of U.S. workers (Papademetriou et al., 1989; U.S. General Accounting Office, 1986, 1988a; Bailey, 1986; Waldinger, 1987). These research results explain the House bill's commitment to accelerating the reunification of families.

On the other hand, the Senate bill exhibits a more cautious approach toward growth in immigration. Allowing measured increases in overall levels, the Senate bill would link increases to periodic reviews and readjustments. This more conservative orientation toward immigration is reflected most directly in one of the bill's hallmark ideas: the establishment of an overall U.S. immigration "national level," popularly known as a cap.

The concept of an immigration cap entered the U.S. immigration debate in the early 1980s. It is a variation of the Canadian practice of setting biennial numerical targets (Papademetriou, 1988) and reflects concern about the effects of unrestricted growth in the category of "immediate relatives of U.S. citizens" on overall immigration levels (see Table 13.2). That category has been growing at an annual pace of about 6.2 percent, but is expected to grow at much higher rates by

TABLE 13.1
Legal Immigration Levels Under Current Law, S. 358, and H.R. 4300
Projected to Fiscal Year 1992

Preference System	Current Law	S. 358	H. R. 4300	
Family Stream	480,000	480,000	564,000	
Immediate relatives of U.S. citizens[1]	264,000	264,000	264,000	
Family preferences	216,000	216,000[2]	300,000	
1st preference	54,000	19,440*	55,500	
2nd preference	70,200*	123,120*	150,150*[3]	
4th preference	27,000*	19,440*	29,600*	
5th preference	64,800*	51,840*	64,750*	
Independent Stream	54,000	150,000	158,500	
Special immigrants[4]	Unlimited	4,050	Unlimited	
Medical workers	N/A	4,950	N/A	
Employment-based workers	54,000	80,400	158,500[5,6]	
a) Professionals	(27,000)	(40,200)		
b) Skilled and unskilled workers	(27,000)	(40,200)*[7]		
Investors	N/A[8]	6,750	N/A	
Point system immigrants	N/A	53,850*	N/A	
Diversity	N/A	N/A	55,000[9]	(begins in 1994)
Transitional Visas[10]	N/A	N/A	146,000	
Adversely affected countries	N/A	N/A	25,000	(1991-93)
Displaced aliens (East Europe and Tibet)	N/A	N/A	15,000	(1991-93)
Africa	N/A	N/A	15,000	(1991-93)
2nd preference backlog	N/A	N/A	10,250	(1991-95)
5th preference backlog	N/A	N/A	40,750	(1991-95)
3rd & 6th preference backlog	N/A	N/A	25,000	(1991-95)
Employees of U.S businesses operating in Hong Kong	N/A	N/A	15,000	(1992-94)
Grand Total (excluding refugees)	534,000	630,000	868,500	

Continuation of Table 13.1

1. Immediate relatives remain unlimited under all scenarios; projected to reach 264,000 by FY 1992.

2. The minimum floor for family preferences is 216,000. For at least two years, when visa use by immediate relatives falls below 264,000, unused visas would be provided to this group of preferences.

3. H.R. 4300 splits the current second preference into two categories: (1) spouses and minor children (115,000 visas), and (2) other children (35,150 visas).

4. The current system and H.R. 4300 exempt "special immigrants" from numerical limitations. This category includes certain former employees of the U.S. government abroad, children born abroad to legal permanent residents, and aliens who have continuously resided in the United States since 1972. An annual average of approximately 3,500 immigrants entered the United States through these exempted categories during the 1980s.

5. For FY 1992-96, employment-based immigration is set at 65,000 principal workers per year. Based on recent data, it is estimated that an additional 93,500 accompanying spouses and children would be admitted. In FY 1997, the ceiling will be raised to 75,000 principal workers with an estimated accompanying 104,250 spouses and children.

6. Employment-based preference immigrants under H.R. 4300 include "priority workers" and "other employment-based aliens." Priority workers comprise: (1) aliens with extraordinary ability, (2) outstanding professors and researchers, (3) certain executives and managers of multinational corporations, and (4) aliens with business expertise. (This last category is limited to 2,000.) Any visas not used by priority workers become available for "other employment-based aliens," (i.e., immigrants "performing specified labor, not of a temporary or seasonal nature, for which a shortage of employable and willing persons exists in the U.S."). Both skilled and unskilled labor would qualify an alien.

7. S. 358 would eliminate access to U.S. independent immigrant visas by unskilled aliens.

8. Theoretically available under the current nonpreference category.

9. This number is not used to calculate the total for FY 1992 because the program begins in 1994. At that time, the first three transitional visa programs will have lapsed: those 55,000 visas would be used for the diversity program.

10. The dates in parentheses denote the years during which each set of visas would be available.

Source: The first column is based on the Immigration and Nationality Act; the last two columns on proposed legislation.

1995-1996. The primary reason is the approximately 3 million persons who are expected to receive permanent resident status through IRCA (U.S. Immigration and Naturalization Service, 1990) -- a process that is expected to spill over into the next century.

Underlying this concern is uncertainty about the likely petitioning behavior of that cohort of immigrants. The U.S. General Accounting Office (1988b) reported the results of a statistically significant sample of fiscal year (FY) 1985 petitions for such relatives. Nearly two-thirds of all such petitions were filed by native-born U.S.

TABLE 13.2
Worldwide Numerically Limited Immigrants (270,000 Annually)

Preference	Provision	Percent and number of visas	Actual Visa Use – FY 1989
First	Unmarried sons and daughters of U.S. citizens and their children	20% or 54,000	13,259
Second	Spouses and unmarried sons and daughters of permanent resident aliens	26% or 70,200*	112,771
Third	Members of the professions and aliens of exceptional ability in the sciences and arts and their spouses and children	10% or 27,000	27,798
Fourth	Married sons and daughters of U.S. citizens and their spouses and children	10% or 27,000*	26,975
Fifth	Brothers and sisters of U.S. citizens (who are at least 21 years of age) and their spouses and children	24% or 64,800*	64,087
Sixth	Workers for permanent employment in skilled or unskilled occupations in which U.S. workers are in short supply, and their spouses and children	10% or 27,000	25,957
Nonpreference	Other qualified applicants	Any numbers** not used above	0

* Numbers not used in higher preferences may be used in these categories.

** Unused numbers become available to immigrants coming for employment purposes (if they have labor certification but no preference status) and immigrants not entering the labor market (i.e., investors, retirees, and other nonworkers). Nonpreference numbers resulting from undersubscription in previous categories have been unavailable since late 1978.

Source: INS Statistical Yearbook, 1989.

Litizens -- most often on behalf of a spouse. Only Asians and Europeans deviated from the norm. The majority of the Asians were naturalized U.S. citizens seeking to bring their parents to the United States; those petitioning for Europeans were overwhelmingly native-born.

Related research reinforces the view that the "immediate relative" visa category benefits U.S. natives. The immigrant "multiplier" is the number of additional immigrants generated by a new immigrant. An immigrant entering through the family preference categories petitions at a rate that "never reach[es] one as n [the number of years since immigration] approaches infinity" (Jasso and Rosenzweig, 1986: 308). The chain migration effect of immigrants entering under the labor market categories is somewhat stronger: 1.44 additional immigrants for males and 1.33 for females.

These and additional findings (see Fawcett et al., 1990; Goering, 1989; Jasso and Rosenzweig, 1989) suggest the following:

(a) Most petitioners for immediate relative visas are U.S. natives.

(b) Most chain migration involves a principal immigrant's immediate family members, takes place at the time or soon after one immigrates (the law requires that the relationship to the beneficiary must be preexisting), and can be calculated relatively easily.

(c) The size of the long-term immigrant multiplier is vastly exaggerated.

Yet, anecdotes about a few immigrants who have sponsored forty or more relatives continue to animate the U.S. immigration debate and to dampen interest in expanding immigration.

Family Immigration and Visa Backlogs

Family reunification is almost universally recognized as the appropriate centerpiece for U.S. immigration policy. A family reunification-based immigration policy recognizes that families buffer and mediate the individual immigrant and the unfamiliar environment. Families facilitate immigrants' social, economic, and political integration and enhance their ability to make a successful transition to the new society. A successful transition, lays a solid foundation for the economic success of the immigrants' children.

The United States demonstrates its commitment to family unification through the following policies: (*a*) by offering immediate immigration to the parents, spouses, and minor children of U.S. citizens; (*b*) by allowing the immigration of families (spouses and minor children) in all preference categories; and (*c*) by allocating more visas for closer family relatives over more distant ones (see Tables 13.1 and 13.2).

At the political level, the most contentious issue has been how to respond to delays in second and fifth family preference reunification. At issue is the commitment to family members that is appropriate and possible absent an explicit decision to increase U.S. immigration substantially.

The second family preference. Both bills now before Congress would increase the number of visas available to second preference applicants. The Senate bill would guarantee a minimum of about 123,000 visas per year to that category. This number amounts to an approximately 80 percent increase over the visa numbers currently allocated but only a 20 percent increase over those currently available to it *de facto* (Table 13.2). These additional visas, however, would be more than offset by petitions of those legalized under IRCA. These petitions would join a second preference visa backlog that currently stands at about 420,000 persons[7]. Given these additional pressures on the category, one can predict the imminent onset of much larger second preference backlogs.

The House bill takes a longer-term view of the second preference and its backlog. Aware that nearly 60 percent of that category's backlog is made up of spouses and minor children, the House bill addresses that backlog in two ways. First, it splits the preference into two subcategories: (*a*) spouses and minor children (whom it would make immune to the Immigration and Nationality Act's [INA] prohibition against any single country obtaining more than twenty thousand preference system visas in any fiscal year); and (*b*) "other children" (who would continue to be subject to that prohibition). Second, it would offer about fifty thousand additional visas over five years for reducing the category's backlog by targeting for relief those who have waited the longest regardless of country of origin.

The fifth family preference. Changes to the fifth family preference arouse even stronger feelings despite the fact that, for the nationals of some countries, the present system's commitment to the reunification of siblings is already a partly empty promise because of visa unavailability.[8] Yet, efforts to curtail or eliminate the fifth family preference have been resisted strenuously by virtually all immigrant group advocates.

Much of the resistance stems from the proposals' take-it-or-leave-it attitude. The unwillingness to compensate affected groups has not encouraged the search for compromise. Paradoxically, the mood has been most uncompromising among those for whom the promise of reunification is most distant. And while most people declare the Hispanic lobby the most prominent on this issue, the most effective lobbying may in fact have come from Asian-American organizations.[9] The debate concerns not only the withdrawal of a privilege, but also an attempt by the majority culture to impose their definition of a family on Asians.

The Senate and House bills come out on different sides on this issue too. The House bill contains neither a cap nor limitations in eligibility/visa allocations in this (or any other) preference categories. In fact, it proposes a "backlog reduction program" that would distribute an additional 40,750 visas annually to fifth preference applicants for five years.

The Senate bill's original approach was to restrict severely both the category's eligibility criteria and available visas[10] under an overall family stream cap. Under that cap, the growth in the numerically exempt immediate relative category would have gradually exhausted all visas from the other family categories. The full Senate rejected this attempt. As a result, the category would remain largely[11] unchanged in the Senate bill.

Immigration Source-Country Diversity

The third focus of legal immigration reform responds to four facts. First, nationals of only seven countries[12] receive the majority of exempt (i.e., numerically unrestricted) immediate relative visas.

Second, Mexico and the Philippines account for nearly two-thirds of these visas. Third, pretty much the same seven countries account for about the same proportion of all numerically restricted immigrant visas. Fourth, the European presence has now fallen to less than 10 percent of total U.S. immigration, fueling a perception that the current immigration system hampers access to the United States by Europeans. This fourth fact is portrayed as an unintended consequence of the 1965 amendments to the U.S. Immigration and Nationality Act -- without any critical examination of the assumptions underlying this assertion.

This concentration of visas preoccupies both Senate and House attempts at legal immigration reform. In response, each bill develops formulae designed to enhance source country "diversity"[13] by creating conditions for better access to the United States by Europeans.

The reforms seem unaware that nationals from a handful of countries have always dominated immigration to the United States. For instance, long before 1924, when the United States instituted quota restrictions, the composition of the immigration flow to the U.S. reflected as much the adverse political, religious, and economic conditions of the immigrants' home countries as the opportunities offered by the United States. Well into the second half of the nineteenth century, nationals of Northern and Western Europe dominated the U.S. immigration flow.

Increasingly, however, and primarily in response to the labor needs of U.S. industry, this passive approach to immigration gave way to aggressive recruitment by U.S. employers. This recruitment shifted the sources of immigration to the United States not only toward Eastern and Southern Europe, but also toward Mexico and several Caribbean island nations (Papademetriou et al., 1989: chap. 1).

Obstacles to the immigration of Eastern and Southern Europeans, nationals of Western Hemisphere countries, but especially Asians, were not removed until the 1965 immigration amendments to the INA (P.L. 89-236). These amendments created an outlet for the pent-up demand for immigration from these countries. What is almost uniformly ignored, however, is that the resulting dramatic reorientation in the source-country composition of U.S. immigration reflects as much this legislative opening as the fact that, in recent years, Europeans have been uninterested in immigrating to the United States.

Immigrants from Asia and the Western Hemisphere have simply filled the void created by this lack of European interest. The 1965 amendments created a system in which, unless a country's demand for immigrant visas remains stable -- and at high levels relative to other countries -- its future immigrants are deflected by immigrants from higher demand countries. Only by being inhospitable to intermittent demand for family visas has the 1965 law disadvantaged Europeans and any others (primarily Africans) who lack adequate numbers of recent "anchor" relatives in the United States. The changed country-of-origin profile of post-1965 U.S. immigration has been shaped only in small part by that law's family unification provisions.

The Senate bill proposes to diversify the immigrant flow primarily by creating a "point-system" for selecting independent immigrants without regard to family relationships and by reducing and recalibrating the maximum numbers of visas available for each country under both family and labor market immigrant tracks.

The House, however, proposes several concurrent initiatives that address the issue more directly. These initiatives include offering additional visas for certain Eastern Europeans and Africans, a new legalization program geared toward illegal Irish immigrants, and a preference for nationals of "adversely affected" countries in some of the visas allocated to the labor market categories.

In addition to these indirect programs, however, the House bill proposes a complex permanent system of allocating 55,000 visas per year to regions and countries "underrepresented" in recent immigration flows to the United States. No country would be able to obtain more than 3,850 visas under this diversity formula that would divide visas among six designated world regions, and all countries within each region, on the basis of whether the region/country is a "high" or "low" admission one. In this formula, the proportion of diversity visas allocated to low admission regions/countries would equal the proportion of all immigrant visas from high admission regions/countries. In other words, the higher the proportion of U.S.

immigrants from high admission regions/countries, the greater the number of diversity visas going to low admission regions/countries and, as a result, the lower the number of diversity visas available for high admission regions/countries.

Labor Market Immigration

The second key question of legal immigration reform focuses on the numbers of employment-related visas, their relative weight in relation to family visas, and the circumstances under which such visas would become available to U.S. employers. Both bills would accommodate much larger numbers of employment-based immigrants and would provide more balance between the family and employment-related streams.[14] Both bills also recognize, however, that larger employment-based visa numbers are tied to two overarching issues. First, they require a reliable methodology for making key labor market immigration decisions consonant with an area's human resources' needs (Briggs, 1984, 1990). Second, they require a regulatory mechanism that conditions initial employer access to foreign workers to evidence of U.S. worker unavailability and additional access to efforts to prepare, attract, and retain U.S. workers for such jobs.

Obtaining satisfactory solutions to these two problems, in turn, requires reflecting on two other, antecedent questions. First, how does one establish that a foreign worker will neither displace nor affect adversely the wages and working conditions of employed U.S. workers? And second, how does one become reasonably certain that the labor market intervention to which employment-based immigration amounts will not lead U.S. business into dependence on foreign workers?

Evaluating the Need for Foreign Workers

The impetus for reforming labor market immigration has come from the system's "unresponsiveness" to employers' needs for alien workers with skill characteristics otherwise unavailable among U.S. workers.[15] Both the discussion's tone and terms of reference have been set primarily[16] by business within the framework of U.S. competitiveness in the global marketplace.

The discussion's economic context is the a demand for labor that grew by approximately 2 percent per year between 1976 and 1988 (Fullerton, 1987, 1989). That rate of increase moved to the front of the immigration discussion on a number of relatively new issues of which two have played a particularly important role: (*a*) "demographic deficit" issues and their implications for the adequacy of the pool of U.S. workers in meeting the economy's need for workers (see Wattenberg, 1990); and (*b*) questions about the adequacy of the educational and vocational preparation of U.S. workers as it relates to the ability of U.S. businesses to compete successfully in a global economy (Papademetriou et al., 1989).

The discussion about both demographic and educational/skill deficits has been fueled by a recent Hudson Institute report (1987). The report focused the attention of policymakers, educational and training leaders, as well as of many key professional associations, on the widening gap between the preparation of U.S. workers and the demands of the economy of the future. However, it has also obscured several other issues that are probably best considered in a more rational framework.

Intervening in the Labor Market through Immigration

Clearly, the Hudson Institute Report has heightened awareness of the magnitude and consequences of projected skill mismatches and shortfalls. At the same time, however, it has encouraged the drawing of many questionable inferences from the very same projections about emerging labor shortages.[17]

Remarkably, the fundamental difference between projections and facts -- the former relying on several demographic, economic, and labor demand/supply "wild-cards" -- seems to have been lost on most policy influencers and policymakers alike. As a result, a chorus of Congressional witnesses issued persistent calls for acting now to meet impending "shortages" by streamlining business access to foreign workers. In particular, these witnesses argued, the law should encourage the immigration of aliens with educational and labor market characteristics that build up the U.S. reservoir of qualified workers in areas likely to experience skill shortfalls.

Absent from this discussion have been systematic analyses of either the nature of the labor market or the role of employment-based immigration in it. Even more notably absent has been an appreciation of the fact that tying immigration policy too closely to predicted events may prove unwise if projections prove wrong (Lutz, 1990). This reckless course shows an inadequate appreciation of the market's complexity -- and its ability to adjust to changes in the labor supply (Papademetriou, 1990; Bach and Meissner, 1990).

Congressional Responses

Intellectually and philosophically, the Senate and House bills offer two radically different answers to the dilemmas outlined in this section. Both bills would increase the labor market immigration by nearly a fourfold. Each, however, would obtain that increase differently.

The Senate bill proceeds from two assumptions. First, it assumes that although business should be allocated some additional visas, the more important reform is to develop a methodology that allows the independent assessment of an employer's need for foreign workers. If the need is upheld, an employer's access to the foreign worker should be timely. Second, it assumes that in light of the nation's global competitive woes, immigration should replenish the U.S. reservoir of needed skills.

The Senate bill addresses the first concern by directing the Department of Labor to explore ways of assessing the accuracy of employer claims that they were unable to find U.S. workers willing, able, and available at the time and place needed. It accomplishes its second goal by ensuring that all labor market immigrants enter in occupations requiring higher qualifications. The bill would offer 4,950 visas to "medical personnel for rural areas,"[18] plus 40,200 visas each to (a) alien professionals with "advanced degrees or aliens of exceptional ability,"[19] and (b) skilled workers with two years of training or experience, and professionals with baccalaureate degrees (Table 13.1).[20] In addition, and more significantly in terms of its second objective, the Senate bill would create a new category of "independent immigration" whereby foreigners would gain access to the U.S. labor market through a competitive worldwide lottery.

Independent immigrant visas would be distributed in accordance with each applicant's score on a "point-assessment system" (Table 13.1). Twenty percent of these visas would go to those with the highest scores. The remaining ones would be distributed randomly to those with a minimum of sixty points. The criteria would be as follows:

- age (up to ten points);
- education (up to twenty-five points);
- occupational demand (up to twenty points);
- occupational training and work experience (up to twenty points); and
- prearranged employment (fifteen points).

The House bill's approach to these issues is sharply different in that, although it attempts to answer the same difficult questions, it does so in a more provocative manner. While the House bill shows no interest in a point system,[21] it would increase total employment stream visas by an amount roughly equal to the Senate's. These visas would be made available first to foreign nationals of exceptional skills and abilities called in the bill "priority" workers. The pronounced majority of the House bill's employment-based visas, however, would be available to employers who can demonstrate that they have been unable to locate U.S. workers for a specific job opening.

In assessing the accuracy of employer claims of worker unavailability, the House bill breaks with both current law and the Senate's approach. As the Judiciary Committee's Bill Report notes, the bill's authors intend the role of the Department of Labor to change from that "of a processing instrument [of employer requests for foreign workers] to a complaint-driven investigative and adjudicative agency, one which can serve as *a labor resource for employers and workers alike*" (emphasis added, U.S. House of Representatives "Family Unity and Employment Opportunity Immigration Act of 1990", 1990: 61). In this new role, the Department of Labor would use both existing data and new data gathering schemes[22] to identify national, regional, and, to the degree possible, local labor needs on which it would then base its decisions about employment-based immigration.[23]

In addition, however, the bill would simultaneously impose on prospective employers of foreign workers extensive requirements for the recruitment of U.S. workers and require employers to pay foreign workers the higher of the area's prevailing or the firm's actual wages for the occupation. Most significantly, employers would have to attest that they have met these requirements. Such attestations would be subject to challenge both prior and subsequent to an immigrant's entry by "interested parties" that would include unions.[24]

Finally, rather than simply rely on immigration to fill skill gaps, the House would require employers to pay a fee significant enough to give pause to employers who might not have deliberated their need for a foreign worker sufficiently and create a substantial fund to educate and train U.S. workers. Clearly, this provision rests on the assumption that upgrading the skills of U.S. workers provides the best long-term protection against further erosion in our international competitiveness.

These are not the only areas in which H.R. 4300 offers novel answers to important questions about employment-based immigration policy. The bill also bridges the artificial gap that has separated permanent from temporary labor market immigration. That separation has allowed much of the temporary policy to be made on an ad hoc basis -- and without much thought to the central economic and labor market role that temporary immigration plays. In linking the two types of migration, H.R. 4300 recognizes that the labor market cannot differentiate between the effects of permanent and temporary employment-based immigration. This is particularly the case since in all but the nonagricultural[25] unskilled labor visa category, "temporary" immigrants are routinely allowed to work in the United States for at least five years, and substantial proportions use the temporary visa of route while waiting to obtain permanent U.S. immigration status.[26] In view of these twin realities, the House bill correctly argues that comprehensive reform of the labor market-based component of immigration must examine both permanent and temporary visa categories.[27]

In sum, both pending immigration bills have made a compelling case that decisions about employment-related immigration must take into account both the results of an assessment of the quality of our present workforce and the larger, and less certain, discussion about future labor market trends. The House bill, however, goes one step further, arguing that decisions about employment-based immigrants must be integral parts of initiatives designed to enhance the qualifications of U.S. workers. In that bill's approach to reform, labor market immigration becomes a supplement, one response in the reservoir of possible policy responses to those labor market anomalies to which the market mechanism is either too slow or unable to adapt.

The House bill's counsel is thus clear: unless U.S. labor market immigration policy heeds these principles, a national commitment to lifetime education and training -- the widely acknowledged *quid pro quo* to long-term international competitiveness and social progress -- will be much more difficult to achieve.

Conclusion

In a nation of immigrants, immigration is inextricably interwoven not only with the economy's historical evolution, but also with the society's social, cultural, and political ethos. Understanding this reality, and acting on that basis, however, does not reduce the tensions that always underlie discussions about immigration policy. As a result, realistic immigration "reform" legislation must reconcile diverse and often competing cultural, social, political, and economic interests.

In its attempt to manage the delicate dynamic among these interests, the House bill is the more interesting from the vantage point of the social scientist. Of particular interest is its authors' conscious decision to reject contentious and partisan solutions to questions about which intelligent and honest people can disagree -- whether regarding immigration's overall impact on the labor market and social and physical infrastructure, its effects on the society's social goals, or its meaning for the future ethnic and cultural composition of the country.

In that regard, both bills recognize that true immigration reform requires a farsightedness that transcends narrow interests. Immigration's economic effects may be positive. It is immigration's noneconomic effects that have always made "reform" and the successful passage of major legislation difficult tasks.

Epilogue of November, 1992

The two approaches to immigration reform embodied in the two bills discussed here reflect not only different philosophies but also different levels of ambition about how deep reform should be. On October 27, in the waning moment of the 101st session, the Congress passed the Immigration Act 1990. The President signed the new act into law on November 29. Considering the timing of the final act (the reconciliation of the two bills did not really begin until the 101st Congress was already past its originally scheduled time for adjournment), it should not be a surprise that the P.L. 101-649 is a compromise. And while detailed discussion of the new law's provisions goes beyond the scope of this effort, it would be useful to outline its major provisions (see also Table 13.1, columns 4 and 5).

Numerically, the Act of 1990 comes out about midway between the House and Senate bills. A lot of the tough decisions about relative preference immigration have been left for another day. P.L. 101-649, however, does make a number of clear statements. Family immigration receives a resounding reaffirmation as the defining feature of U.S. immigration policy through an allocation of four-fifths of total visas. And together with compassionate ideals (as expressed in refugee immigration), non-employment-based immigration will account for about five-sixths of total immigration to the United States.

The Immigration Act of 1990 streamlines the decision-making process on employer petitions to import foreign workers while simultaneously establishing additional safeguards against adverse effects on the wages and job opportunities of the U.S. workers -- particularly in the nonimmigrant system. In further opting for the middle road between the two source bills, the Immigration Act of

1990 requires the testing of new mechanisms in search of one method that might allow the independent assessment of an employer's claim that he/she needs a foreign worker.

Finally, the new immigration act links permanent and temporary legal immigration reforms. In an approach similar -- though not identical -- to that followed in the Immigration Nursing Relief Act of 1989 (INRA), P.L. 101-649 changes the way foreigners coming to the United States for temporary work gain access to the labor market. The 1990 Act restricts the number of such workers and requires employers to give U.S. workers preference in employment. In addition, and in order to prevent the erosion of the wages of U.S. workers, the Act also requires that employers compensate foreign workers at the higher of the prevailing rates for the job classification. More importantly, however, the Act interposes the Department of Labor as the resolver of disputes arising from the terms and conditions of the employment of temporary foreign workers. Although these steps do not go as far as some of the more ambitious ideas the the House bill had advocated, they are much closer to these ideas than to the Senate's.

In the end, it might be appropriate to say that in 1990, the U.S. Congress, after considerable soul searching, agreed on a bill that takes some of the Immigration and Nationality's Act's more outdated and flawed provisions. In the years ahead, many of the ambitious ideas found in both INRA and the Immigration Act of 1990 will form the basis for more comprehensive -- even definitive -- reforms. To assure this, the Act wisely sets up a long-term monitoring and evaluation system administered by a Commission with a mandate broad enough to guarantee that the Congress will not shy away from regularly revisiting immigration policy.

Notes

The views expressed herein are the author's and may not represent those of the Department of Labor or the U.S. Government.

1. The key provisions of IRCA include the following: (a) legalization programs for several types of aliens, (b) requirements that employers hire only individuals who could establish their right to work in the

United States (or risk substantial civil and criminal penalties known as "employer sanctions"), (c) a program guaranteeing a supply of legal foreign workers to perishable-crop agricultural growers between fiscal years 1990 and 1993 in the event of worker shortages in that industry, and (d) significantly enhanced border controls. See Meissner and Papademetriou (1988) for a discussion of IRCA's provisions and underlying assumptions; see Papademetriou (et al., 1991) for an evaluation of the effectiveness of the law's implementation.

2. These terms will be used interchangeably to denote immigrants who gain entry into the United States through the labor market, rather than the family stream.

3. I am not taking issue here with the generosity of offering legal immigration status to approximately 3 million persons (U.S. Immigration and Naturalization Service. 1990. "Provisional Legalization Application Statistics." Statistics Division. Office of Plans and Analysis. Washington, DC). Nor am I insensitive to the fact that the main legalization program's eligibility date of 1 January 1982, a date five years removed from the date of the law's passage, reflected what proponents of legalization considered politically viable at the time. What I mean is that little thought was given to the government's ability to control illegal immigration absent draconian control measures. Legalization programs in other countries had chosen eligibility dates much closer to or concurrent with such laws' passage. See Meissner et al., 1987.

4. As usual, the debate uses a vocabulary of labor markets. Even when the issue is about race/ethnicity, language, immigrant "quality" (i.e., education and skills), and immigrant use of social and physical infrastructure, as it usually is, the debate in Washington is couched in terms of the ability of the labor market to incorporate immigrants. This debate occurs despite widely accepted evidence that the economic effects of immigrants -- even of illegal immigrants -- are positive and that U.S. workers do not suffer significant or prolonged adverse effects. See Papademetriou et al., 1989.

5. This figure excludes refugees. Refugee admission levels are determined annually through consultations between Congress and the administration.

6. Families also provide important private social and childcare services that improve a household's economic opportunities (Gurak, 1988; Perez, 1986; Tienda and Angel, 1982). Research also shows that success in the labor market is often linked directly to the social and institutional environment in which a worker functions (see Wial, 1988a, 1988b). Information and social networks are essential to an immigrant's successful incorporation into the host economy. See Papademetriou and

Muller, 1987, and Papademetriou et al., 1989, for a discussion of the extensive literature on this subject.

7. Three countries: Mexico, the Philippines, and the Dominican Republic account for 46 percent of the persons on this waiting list. Respectively, the waiting period for each of them is projected to be twenty, nineteen and seven years (U.S. Department of State, *Visa Bulletin*, 1989; U.S. General Accounting Office, 1989)! Considering that Mexican nationals comprised more than 70 percent of those receiving legal status under IRCA (U.S. Immigration and Naturalization Service. 1990. "Provisional Legalization Application Statistics." Statistical Division. Office of Plans and Analysis. Washington, DC), and absent some policy initiative to address this issue, the waiting times for these Mexicans' reunification with their spouses and children will become even less defensible -- and will continue to contribute to illegal immigration.

8. Backlogs in the fifth family preference now stand at more than 1.4 million persons (see U.S. Department of State. 1989. *Visa Bulletin*. Monthly). Five countries account for 54 percent of the persons on this waiting list: the Philippines (16 percent), India (13 percent), Mexico (10 percent), Korea (8 percent), and China (7 percent). In a recent report, the U.S. General Accounting Office (1989) estimated that fifth preference relatives from low visa-demand countries can expect average delays of twenty years. Delays for high visa-demand countries are projected to reach fifty years.

9. The Asian-American community's emergence as a powerful political group makes its views extremely relevant. That community's power in this regard stems from the following facts: (a) Asian immigrants as a group have comprised nearly half of the total immigrant population to the United States in the 1980s -- thus recording the fastest rate of growth of any U.S. minority, (b) the Asians' aggregate education and economic success are higher than those of U.S. natives (Papademetriou and DiMarzio, 1986), and (c) their geographic concentration in a few states (California, New York and Illinois) where they make up substantial shares of the electorate.

10. That proposal would have basically eliminated the reunification prospects for most recent and virtually all current and future beneficiaries of that preference category by stretching average waiting times to more than fifty years. See U.S. General Accounting Office, 1989.

11. In fact, the category would lose about 12,000 visas annually. This would occur because the bill splits numerically limited immigration into family and employment-based streams. By guaranteeing the current limit of 216,000 visas to the family preference stream, the category's allocation of 24 percent computes to 51,840 visas -- rather than the

64,800 visas now available to the category (24 percent of 270,000).

12. These countries are, in descending order, Mexico, the Philippines, South Korea, the Dominican Republic, India, China (mainland-born Chinese), and Great Britain and dependencies (including Hong Kong).

13. This is another among the many euphemisms trying to disguise the fact that what is being attempted is a fundamental retreat from the 1965 Act's decision to make U.S. immigrant selection source-country-neutral (Papademetriou and Miller, 1983).

14. That ratio now stands at approximately nine-to-one in favor of family visas. Both bills would change that ratio to about four-to-one.

15. The political discussion adds an ingredient that has been often notable by its absence: the concerns of U.S. workers. It is the essence of these concerns that underlies the concept of "labor certification" whereby employers petition the U.S. Department of Labor for a specific alien. Employers must demonstrate first, that there are no U.S. workers who, at the time and place of the job offer, are able, willing, qualified, and available for the job in question and second, that the wages offered to the alien would not affect adversely the wages and working conditions of similarly employed U.S. workers (U.S. House of Representatives. Committee on the Judiciary. 1989. Immigration and Nationality Act [as amended through 1 January 1989] 8th ed: 212 [a] [14]). The challenge has as a result become one of how to make employment-based immigration more responsive to the long term economic interests of the nation without being insensitive to the legitimate interests of U.S. workers.

16. After ceding the political and policy center stage on this discussion to business interest throughout most of the latter half of the 1980s, organized labor's views began to be felt again in the drafting of the House bill, particularly through the involvement of the House Education and Labor committee.

17. Among the Hudson Institute's most relevant projections in this regard are that 82 percent of the net increase in the labor force between 1985 and 2000 will go to women, minorities, and immigrants -- with immigrants representing the largest share of the increase in the "population and the workforce since the first World War" (1987: x). In reality, the 22 percent immigrant share in net new workers projected by the report to occur in 2000 was already reached by the late 1980s (see Papademetriou et al., 1989: Table 2.7). Notably, the BLS projections on many of the issues tackled by the Hudson Institute Report paint a much less somber picture (see Kutscher, 1987, 1989).

18. Of these visas, 3,960 would be allocated for nurses and 990 for medical doctors willing to perform medical services in Health Manpower

Shortage Areas designated by the Department of Health and Human Services.

19. Under current law, the third preference, after which this category is fashioned, does not require an advanced degree.

20. This preference category is a hybrid of the current law's third and sixth preferences (see Table 13.2). Under the Senate bill, however, unskilled workers would no longer be able to immigrate to the United States.

21. Despite this system's earlier appeal among policy analysts and policy-makers, its current reception ranges from tepid and ambivalent (even on the part of the Administration and employer groups) and outright opposition (on the part of organized labor and ethnic groups). Concerns include the lack of protections and potentially adverse effects on the wages and upward mobility opportunities for U.S. workers, as well as practical considerations (such as verifying the academic, professional, and training credentials of lottery winners), and the costs for administering a worldwide lottery system with an expected applicant pool in the millions.

22. Both avenues promise more than they are likely to deliver in that they are ultimately not as reliable as they may appear at first. See Norwood, 1990.

23. No such data are used now. Instead employers petition the Department of Labor for an immigrant if they have engaged in an open search for and have been unable to fill a job opening with a U.S. worker.

24. If the ensuing Department of Labor investigation bears out the plain-tiff's complaint, the employer would not be allowed to import the requested foreign worker (if it is a pre-entry challenge) or would be disqualified from obtaining additional foreign workers for a period of one year (if it is a post-entry challenge). In either case, fines and other administrative remedies could also be imposed.

25. Most temporary visas for foreign seasonal agricultural workers (H-2As) go to individuals with whom the U.S. growers already have long-standing relationships.

26. Recent research sponsored by the Department of Labor indicates that in FY 1988, two-thirds of all successful permanent labor certifications were issued to foreign workers who were already employed by a U.S. employer in the United States -- usually in the position for which a "job vacancy" was advertised. In only 0.5 percent of the cases was a U.S. worker "selected" by the employer. See Research and Evaluation Associates, 1990: 49, 64.

27. There is widespread recognition of this reality. However, the complexity of linking these two reform processes, and the pronounced data and analytical voids that surround the temporary visa categories,

have raised the concern that inclusion of reforms in the temporary system might interfere with the successful enactment of legal permanent immigration legislation in the 101st Congress. The contentiousness that has surrounded some of the House bill's proposals in that regard appear to reinforce the position of those who oppose the linkage.

References

Bach, Robert, and Doris Meissner. 1990. "America's Labor Market in the 1990's: What Role Should Immigration Play?" Washington, DC: Immigration Policy Project, Carnegie Endowment for International Peace.

Bailey, Thomas. 1986. *Immigrant and Native Workers: Contrasts and Competition*. Boulder, CO: Westview Press.

Borjas, George. 1990. *Friends of Strangers: The Impact on Immigrants on the U.S. Economy*. New York: Basic Books.

Briggs, Vernon M., Jr. 1984. *Immigration Policy and the American Labor Force*. Baltimore: Johns Hopkins University.

Briggs, Vernon M., Jr. 1990. "Experts Debate Response to Labor Shortages." *Immigration Policy and Law* 14: 4-5.

Council of Economic Advisors. 1986. *The President's Economic Report to the Congress*. Washington, DC: USGPO.

Council of Economic Advisors. 1990. *The President's Economic Report to the Congress*. Washington, DC.

Fawcett, James, et al. 1990. "Selectivity and Diversity: The Effects of U.S. Immigration Policy on Immigrant Characteristics." Annual Meeting of the Population Association of America, 3-5 May, Toronto.

Fullerton, Howard, Jr. 1987. "Labor Force Projections: 1986 to 2000." *Monthly Labor Review* 110: 19-29.

Fullerton, Howard, Jr. 1989. "New Labor Force Projections, Spanning 1988 to 2000." *Monthly Labor Review* 112: 3-12.

Goering, John. 1989. "The Explosiveness of Chain Migration: Research and Policy Issues." *International Migration Review* 23: 797-812.

Gurak, Douglas. 1988. "Labor Force Status and Transitions of Dominican and Colombian Immigrants." Paper presented at the U.S. Department of Labor Conference on Immigration, September, Washington, DC.

Hudson Institute, The. 1987. *Workforce 2000: Work and Workers for the 21st Century*. Indianapolis, IN: The Hudson Institute.

Jasso, Guillermina, and Mark Rosenzweig. 1986. "Family Reunification and the Immigrant Multiplier: U.S. Immigration Law, Origin-Country Conditions, and the Reproduction of Immigrants." *Demography* 23: 291-311.

Jasso, Guillermina, and Mark Rosenzweig. 1989. "Sponsors, Sponsorship

Rates and the Immigration Multiplier." *International Migration Review* 23: 856-88.

Kutscher, Ronald. 1987. "Overview and Implications of the Projections to 2000." *Monthly Labor Review* 110: 3-9.

Kutscher, Ronald. 1989. "Projections Summary and Emerging Issues." *Monthly Labor Review* 112: 66-74.

Lutz, Wolfgang. 1991. *Future Demographic Trends*. Vienna: International Institute for Applied Systems Analysis.

Meissner, Doris, and Demetrios Papademetriou. 1988. *The Legalization Countdown: A Third Quarterly Assessment*. Washington, DC: Carnegie Endowment for International Peace.

Meissner, Doris, et al. 1987. *Legalization of Undocumented Aliens: Lessons from Other Countries*. Washington, DC: Carnegie Endowment for International Peace.

Miles, Jack. 1992. "Blacks Vs. Browns." *The Atlantic* 270: 41 ff.

Muller, Thomas, and Thomas Espenshade. 1985. *The Fourth Wave: California's Newest Immigrants*. Washington, DC: The Urban Institute.

Norwood, Janet. 1990. "Testimony before the House Subcommittee on Immigration, Refugees, and International Law." U.S. House of Representatives. March. Washington, DC.

Papademetriou, Demetrios. 1988. "The Canadian Immigrant Selection System: A Technical Report." U.S. Department of Labor, International Labor Affairs Bureau. October. Washington, DC.

Papademetriou, Demetrios. 1990. "Immigration Reform: Key Issues for the Department of Labor." Keynote address at the U.S. Department of Labor Conference on Legal Immigration and Early Impacts of IRCA. May, Washington, DC.

Papademetriou, Demetrios, et al. 1989. *The Effects of Immigration on the U.S. Economy and Labor Market*. U.S. Department of Labor, International Labor Affairs Bureau. Washington, DC.

Papademetriou, Demetrios, et al. 1991. *The Effects of Employer Sanctions on the U.S. Labor Market*. U.S. Department of Labor, International Labor Affairs Bureau. Washington, DC.

Papademetriou, Demetrios, and Nicholas DiMarzio. 1986. *Undocumented Aliens in the New York Metropolitan Area*. New York: Center for Migration Studies.

Papademetriou, Demetrios, and Mark Miller. 1983. "U.S. Immigration Policy: International Context, Theoretical Parameters, and Research Priorities." In *The Unavoidable Issue: U.S. Immigration Policy in the 1980's*, edited by Demetrios Papademetriou and Mark Miller. Institute for the Study of Human Issues. Philadelphia, PA.

Papademetriou, Demetrios, and Thomas Muller. 1987. *Recent Immigration to New York: Labor Market and Social Policy Issues.* A Report Prepared for the National Commission for Employment Policy, February. Washington, DC.

Perez, Lisandro. 1986. "Immigrant Economic Adjustment and Family Organization: The Cuban Success Story Reexamined." *International Migration Review* 20: 4-20.

Research and Evaluation Associates. 1990. "Study of the Permanent Alien Certification Program." Employment and Training Administration. U.S. Department of Labor. Washington, DC.

Simon, Julian. 1989. *The Economic Consequences of Immigration.* London: Basil Blackwell.

Tienda, Marta, and Ronald Angel. 1982. "Headship and Household Composition among Blacks, Hispanics, and Other Whites." *Social Forces* 61: 508-29.

U.S. Department of State. 1989. *Visa Bulletin.* Monthly. Washington, DC.

U.S. General Accounting Office. 1986. "Illegal Aliens: Limited Research Suggests Illegal Aliens May Displace Native Workers." (GAO/PEMD-86-9BR). Washington, DC.

U.S. General Accounting Office. 1988a. "Illegal Aliens: Influence of Illegal Workers on Wages and Working Conditions of Legal Workers." (GAO/PEMD-88- 13BR). Washington, DC.

U.S. General Accounting Office. 1988b. "Immigration: The Future Flow of Legal Immigration to the United States." (GAO/PEMD-88-7). Washington, DC.

U.S. General Accounting Office. 1989. "Immigration Reform: Major Changes Likely Under S. 358." (GAO/PEMD-90-5). Washington, DC.

U.S. House of Representatives, Committee on the Judiciary. 1989. *Immigration and Nationality Act (As Amended Through January 1, 1989).* 8th ed. Washington, DC.

U.S. House of Representatives. 1990. "Family Unity and Employment Opportunity Immigration Act of 1990." (H.R. 4300) Report 101-723. Washington, DC.

U.S. Immigration and Naturalization Service. 1978-1990. *Statistical Yearbook.* Statistical Division. Office of Plans and Analysis. Washington, DC.

U.S. Immigration and Naturalization Service. 1990. "Provisional Legalization Application Statistics." Statistical Division. Office of Plans and Analysis. Washington, DC.

U.S. Senate. 1989. "Immigration Act of 1989." (S. 358) Report 101-55. Washington, DC.

Waldinger, Roger. 1987. "Changing Ladders and Musical Chairs: Ethnicity and Opportunity in Post-Industrial New York." *Politics and Society* 15:

369-401.

Wattenberg, Ben. 1990. "Dispelling America's Gloom: Why Not?" *The American Enterprise* 8, 2: 32-37.

Wial, Howard. 1988a. "Job Mobility Paths of Recent Immigrants in the U.S. Labor Market." Paper presented at the U.S. Department of Labor Conference on Immigration, September, Washington, DC.

Wial, Howard. 1988b. "The Transition from Secondary to Primary Employment: Jobs and Workers in Ethnic Neighborhood Labor Markets." Ph.D. diss., Massachusetts Institute of Technology.

14

New Zealand's Immigration Policies and Immigration Act (1987): Comparisons with the United States of America

Brian Wearing

As in the United States, the colonial period in New Zealand was one of rapid influx from distant lands and an overwhelming of the population present at the time of European discovery. The Maori population of New Zealand at the time of Captain Cook's first voyage in 1769 has been estimated at between 150,000 and 200,000 (Bedford, 1986). In 1840, when, by the Treaty of Waitangi, New Zealand became a British colony, that figure still exceeded 100,000 compared to some 1,500 European settlers. Even acknowledging an undercount of the Maori in the first national census of 1858, 48.5 percent out of a total population of 115,462, there is no denying that a pattern of a predominant non-Polynesian population had been established (Pool, 1977) (Table 14.1).

The steady growth of migrants from Britain throughout the nineteenth century, with small contributions from France, Scandinavia and Yugoslavia, reflected the same economic, religious, and social motivations as did transatlantic movements to the United States. In similar fashion, from time to time, unusual circumstances created surges in the flow. The first was the discovery of gold in the South Island of New Zealand. Following the arrival of Chinese prospectors

TABLE 14.1
New Zealand Population Growth: Total and Maori Population

Census	Total Population	NZ Maori Population (Incl. in Total)
1858	115,462	56,049
1874	344,984	47,330
1878	458,007	45,542
1881	534,030	46,141
1886	620,451	43,927
1891	668,651	44,177
1896	743,214	42,113
1901	815,862	45,549
1906	936,309	50,309
1911	1,058,312	52,723
1916	1,149,225	52,997
1921	1,271,668	56,987
1926	1,408,139	63,670
1936	1,573,812	94,053
1945	1,702,330	116,394
1945	1,747,711	100,044
1951	1,939,472	134,842
1956	2,174,062	162,458
1961	2,414,984	202,535
1966	2,676,919	249,867
1971	2,862,631	290,501
1976	3,129,383	356,847
1981	3,175,737	385,524
1986	3,307,084	405,309

Source: New Zealand Census, various years.

from Australia, the Gold rush opened the debate over Oriental migration to New Zealand (Price, 1974). In contrast to the United States, the New Zealand government operated a subsidized immigration scheme that accelerated influx from Britain in the 1870s. World War II produced an increase in refugees. These included Jews fleeing the Nazis and Chinese and Dutch fleeing the Japanese in Southeast Asia. In a drive for new migrants following the end of the war, and failing to secure sufficient applicants from Britain, the New Zealand government established an agreement with the Netherlands that introduced a significant Dutch element into New Zealand. There was a dramatic upsurge in immigration, both from Britain and the islands of the South Pacific in the early 1970s. Meanwhile, refugees continued to enter New Zealand displaced by such disparate events as nationalist movements throughout the British Empire, oppressive dictatorships as in Chile after 1973, and the dislocations in Southeast Asia stemming from the Vietnam War. Finally, the 1987 Immigration Act has resulted in a major increase in applications for residence with significant contributions from Southeast Asia and the islands (Table 14.2).

New Zealand's immigration has, like that of the United States, been influenced by foreign policy. For the United States, the war with Mexico (1848), the war with Spain (1898), the Korean War, the Vietnam War, and more recent involvement in Central America have led to special immigration connections with Mexico, Puerto Rico, Cuba, Korea, the Philippines, South Vietnam, and Nicaragua. New Zealand's special relationship with Australia, and less obvious ties with Fiji and Tonga, are a legacy of the British Empire and Commonwealth. Within that overall relationship New Zealand has developed close bonds with Western Samoa, the Cook Islands, Niue, and the Tokelauan Islands.[1]

Immigration Legislation

The record of immigration policy and legislation in New Zealand, both in thrust and timing, evidences some interesting similarities with the United States until the 1960s. Suspicion and fear of Chinese immigration produced specific restrictive Chinese Immigration Acts in 1881, 1886, and 1896. An added fear of migrants from India resulted in legislation in 1890 and 1910 that used language and literacy tests effectively to exclude Asian migrants (Roy, 1970).

In 1920, foreshadowing the United States' restrictive legislation based on the concept of national-origins quotas, New Zealand also introduced legislation designed to maintain and foster the predominance of a Northwest European ethnic stock. The principle applied was to grant free entry to all persons of exclusively British, including Irish, birth and descent. All others needed to obtain entry permits from the Minister of Customs, and later from Labour and

TABLE 14.2
Numbers of Persons Granted Residence Visas and Permits

Country	1985	1986	1987	1988	1989
Afghanistan					1
American Samoa	1	7	4	2	11
Argentina	5	5		2	59
Austria	11	26	45	53	47
Bahrein		1	1		
Bangladesh	3	6	3	5	11
Barbados	2			4	2
Belgium	6	11	6	11	25
Brazil	3	1	5	7	11
Brunei				1	8
Bulgaria		3	4	1	1
Burma	3	5	1	2	9
Canada	274	347	527	386	354
Chile	11	32	35		62
P.R. of China	121	118	175	256	686
Colombia	2	3	4	17	6
Cyprus	1	2		1	1
Czechoslovakia	15	11	4	5	8
Denmark	16	21	21	37	45
Ecuador					1
Egypt	6	1	3	9	15
Fiji	154	127	605	1942	3987
Finland	1	5	6	3	11
France	58	44	28	61	64
French Polynesia	3	4	3	4	14
German D. R.	2	5		5	19
German F. R.	210	204	292	242	420
Greece	18	5	9	18	25
Guyana				6	7
Hong Kong	143	162	188	512	1016
Hungary	12	1	13	8	21
Iceland	2	4	7	7	7
India	107	108	204	369	695
Indonesia	26	34	44	31	74
Iran	29	26	62	187	107
Iraq	1	8	14	2	28
Ireland	52	79	148	186	207
Israel	6	7	14	25	37
Italy	25	16	10	17	20
Jamaica	2	1		1	3
Japan	53	47	52	57	290

Continuation of Table 14.2

Country	1985	1986	1987	1988	1989
Kampuchea	432	417	87	96	413
Kenya	2	1	2	2	6
Kiribati		4	5	5	
(North) Korea		1	1		20
South Korea	8	20	23	23	28
Laos	82	129	73	80	26
Lebanon	7	5	9	36	20
Liechtenstein			1		
Malawi					8
Malaysia	122	86	529	755	1824
Maldives	1				2
Malta		4	3	10	3
Maritius	7	1	4	14	6
Mexico		5	2	2	6
Morocco		1			
Nauru				1	1
Nepal		3			4
Netherlands	510	397	468	543	756
New Caledonia	6	3	15	4	6
Nigeria				4	3
Norway	14	6	6	16	23
Oman					48
Pakistan	6	7	3	15	51
Papua New Guinea	6	9	12	9	15
Peru	2	2		6	24
Philippines	145	296	487	587	658
Pitcairn Island					3
Poland	45	25	34	27	91
Portugal	6	6	3	14	16
Romania	1	7	4	3	7
Saudi Arabia					1
Singapore	38	54	168	157	257
Solomon Island	2	3	3	2	10
South Africa	91	101	311	311	400
Spain	6	7	5	8	11
Sri Lanka	38	64	92	212	354
Sweden	11	19	64	99	113
Switzerland	82	90	87	78	124
Taiwan	26	12	25	95	1640
Tanzania	3		4	2	9
Thailand	19	28	21	32	46
Tonga	444	200	688	371	2080

Continuation of Table 14.2

Country	1985	1986	1987	1988	1989
Trinidad/Tobago		3	2	2	5
Turkey	4	5	1	5	9
Tuvalu	2	1	4	1	20
United Arab Emirates	1				
United Kingdom	7201	2966	4712	4272	4881
United States (USA)	392	367	527	444	686
Uruguay	2		1	1	6
Vanuatu	1	1	1	4	1
Venezuela	1	7		1	7
Vietnam	158	91	134	164	135
Western Samoa	1706	1560	2096	1753	4982
Yugoslavia	10	13	8	14	43
Zanzibar	23	6	22	33	47
Other	47	162	50	53	97
Totals	8097	8680	13335	14893	27462

Source: Department of Labor. Immigration Permit Statistics, various years. Wellington, New Zealand.

Immigration. It gave a flexibility of control, not available to the U.S. government, and its discriminatory rigidity ensured that New Zealand would be a nation of predominantly British settlers and their descendants.[2]

By requiring all non-New Zealand citizens to obtain an entry permit, the 1974 Immigration Act apparently paralleled the U.S. abolition of the quota system in 1965. However, New Zealand continued to practice discrimination in favor of certain countries both by official bilateral agreements and administrative practice. The most obvious example of discrimination is the Trans Tasman Travel Agreement (TTTA) (Hurrelle, 1988). This agreement allows Australian citizens, together with other British and Commonwealth and Republic of Ireland citizens who have permission to reside in Australia exception from the need to obtain a permit to enter New Zealand. Until February 1986 the Department of Labour maintained a policy of giving preference to persons from "traditional source countries." Skilled persons from developing countries were specifically excluded, ostensibly to prevent "brain drain" from those counties. Perhaps the most uniquely New Zealand restriction, which remains fundamental to the New Zealand attitude toward immigration, was that despite membership in some preferred group, the basic requirement, save for those entering under the TTTA, was to possess useful skills and qualifications in sufficient demand to warrant recruitment overseas (Ministry of Foreign Affairs, 1983).

The 1987 Act perpetuated and even further emphasized the priority given to "occupational" entry.[3] However, in the light of U.S. practice, it is of interest to note the following points in the legislation. The new Labour government maintained that the legislation provided only the legal basis for administering immigration activities.[4] The decision as to who may reside in New Zealand remains that of the government of the day, delegated to the appropriate minister. Mindful of past experience, and aware of the problems connected with the legal technicalities of entry documents in immigration cases in many countries, including the United States, the New Zealand Act discarded the previous emphasis on permission to enter New Zealand in favor of the simple concept of status within New Zealand. In addition, offenses against the immigration laws were no longer to result in criminal prosecution, deportation, and consequent permanent prohibition from entry into New Zealand.

New Zealand's Immigration Categories

From colonial times, but especially since the 1960s, an acknowledged priority has been the encouragement of the immigration of people with skills and experience needed in New Zealand. Present policy is based on three categories. The first is economic. A regularly updated Occupational Priority List (OPL) is produced by the Department of Labour in consultation with employers and labor unions. This list provides a clear, if restricted, guideline to officials. In addition, a prospective employer may make a case for employing a foreigner on the grounds of the impossibility of filling a position from the local labor market. The standard requirements relate to health, character (lack of a criminal record), ability in the English language, and proof of the means to provide accommodation. There is no limitation on the number of children in a family, the definition of which takes into account the cultural practices of neighboring South Pacific nations. Family income must be sufficient to guarantee that a household will place no demand upon social services. The normal age limit for migrants to New Zealand is forty-five years. A firm offer of a job by a New Zealand employer remains the prime factor for permission to reside in New Zealand. In contrast to the U.S. law, New Zealand law discriminates in favor of the citizens of two very different countries of origin, in addition to the very fundamental one implicit in the TTTA. A quota of up to eleven hundred per annum has been available to Western Samoans who, having met the standard requirements, need only to have a guaranteed job with no level of skill to be proven. A further quota of one thousand per annum exists for citizens of the Netherlands with a guaranteed position or an assurance, from the Netherlands Emigration Office, that such entrants will not become a public charge. Netherlands immigrants must comply with all other conditions.

The New Zealand situation also provides a comparison with Puerto Rico. Because of their being former New Zealand dependencies, Cook Islanders, Niueans and Tokelauans are entitled to settle in New Zealand with all the rights and privileges of citizenship. Between 1965 and 1975 the New Zealand government, recognizing the problems of rapid population growth on atolls resettled about five hundred Tokelauans in New Zealand, arranging both employment and accommodation. Resettlement is a distinctive aid program. As a result of these special relationships, the majority of the populations of these islands, especially Niue, now reside in New Zealand. In an almost farcical situation, stemming from a decision of the Privy Council of the United Kingdom in 1982, a similar citizenship by virtue of a former dependency relationship was conferred upon some one hundred thousand Western Samoans for a matter of weeks (Macdonald, 1986).

Since 1979 New Zealand has had a second economic category of business migrants. After evaluation of their business record and credit worthiness, screened entrepreneurs have been allowed entry regardless of age, occupation, and national origin. They do have to meet general requirements of health, character, and knowledge of English.

New Zealand's social immigration policy stresses family reunion. There are few formalities for spouses and children of New Zealand

TABLE 14.3
Short Term Visitors from Countries for Which New Zealand has Visa Exemption Arrangements - Year Ended 31 March 1989

Austria	2,395
Belgium	852
Canada	36,999
Denmark	3,449
Finland	1,218
France	8,304
German Federal Republic	23,523
Greece	376
Iceland	182
Indonesia	3,825
Ireland	3,061
Italy	3,235
Japan	99,916
Kiribati	127
Liechtenstein	18
Luxembourg	61
Malaysia	10,043
Malta	157
Morocco	---
Nauru	207
Netherlands	8,246
Norway	1,481
Portugal	477
Singapore	12,124
Spain	667
Sweden	9,928
Switzerland	8,942
Thailand	3,686
Turkey	198
United Kingdom	91,176
United States of America	160,745
Total	495,623

Source: New Zealand Immigration Service.

citizens. Parents may be approved if they are alone in their home country or have at least the same number of adult children resident in New Zealand as are resident in any other country. An adult child resident in New Zealand must sponsor the applications and meet the general requirements. Brothers and sisters may be approved if they are the last member of a family in the home country, are under forty-five years old, are sponsored by a New Zealand sibling resident, and possess a "worthwhile" skill.

New Zealand's humanitarian category is somewhat different from the refugee programs in the United States. First, any relative of a New Zealand resident who does not meet the standard criteria may apply for consideration based on the intrinsic merit of the appeal. Again New Zealand demonstrates selectivity in the country of origin of refugees. Currently, special rules apply to applications from Sri Lanka and Lebanon. Subject to continuing community sponsorship, the present government is following a program, adopted in 1987, of admitting up to eight hundred refugees per year in association with the United Nations High Commissioner for Refugees. However, in 1989, at the Geneva Conference on Indo-Chinese Refugees, the Minister of Immigration made a commitment that New Zealand would accept at least one thousand Indo-Chinese refugees beginning on 1 April 1990. This figure will include two hundred Vietnamese per year and will limit the number of admissible refugees from other areas over the next three years.

There are four categories of temporary admission into New Zealand. The largest is that of tourism and the visiting of kin. Some 57 percent of short term visitors enter visa free (Table 14.3). Students require visas if their course lasts longer than three months. Since 1990, foreign students may enter only on the basis of full cost recovery. Cost recovery regulations also apply to the category of temporary entry for medical treatment.

NZIA (1987) versus IRCA (1986)

The New Zealand Immigration Act (1987) makes an interesting comparison with the U.S. Immigration Reform and Control Act (1986) because it was similarly the result of attempts to control illegal migration and offered amnesty. The roots of the New Zealand legislation lie in the late 1960s. These circumstances were again present in New Zealand in 1990; thus, it is important that current attempts to link planned economic growth with a policy of increased immigration be based on a knowledge of the results of a similar policy in the past. It appears all the more of a replay when it is noted that the present government's ideal annual immigration figure of ten thousand persons is the same as it was twenty years ago.

New Zealand experienced an economic recession between 1967 and 1969. Associated with this were the first migration losses since the 1930s (Farmer, 1979). The National Development Conference of 1969, realizing that its economic growth target could not be met without a recruitment of manpower, put forth the case for another period of active encouragement of migrants. In a reversal of traditional unease over competition for jobs and resources, political and public opinion favored extensive immigration. The aim was to recruit from Great Britain, the traditional source of skilled migrants. With the target achieved by 1972 the scheme was judged a success, but there were misgivings when the flow reached thirty thousand only two years later (Bedford and Lloyd, 1982). Soon, even the migrants from Europe were subjected to widespread criticisms for the shortage they were creating in the supply of housing.

More significant, however, to the creation of future demands for amnesty was that the New Zealand's government's desire to see a rapid expansion of the manufacturing sector coincided with two other events in the South Pacific region. The first were improvements in the efficiency of transportation between the South Pacific islands and New Zealand. The second was a great push from the other islands to New Zealand.[5] The result was a rapid influx of migrants from several island communities. Just as many poor Mexicans dreamed of going to "El Norte," so did unemployed Pacific islanders aspire to go to "Godzone."[6] Overstaying became a problem. Many visitors and those on short-term permits stayed on in New Zealand after the expiry of their permits. The growing number of "illegal" migrants was tolerated at first because of the need for labor. The situation changed dramatically following Britain's entry into the European Economic Community and the Oil Crisis of 1973. These two events were a body blow to the New Zealand economy, which suffered a severe downturn from which it has yet to recover. Many Pacific islanders were put out of work and their racial visibility made them subject to widespread criticism. As in the United States, politicians responded to the public demand that "something be done about" the problem. However, unlike the situation in the United States, since New Zealand is a small unitary parliamentary nation, the government could respond quickly. The immigration department was instructed to be more rigorous in its regulation of short-term entry into New Zealand. Also, police embarked on a policy of identifying those who had "overstayed" and began proceedings for their deportation.

In March 1974, publicity about the infamous "Dawn Raids" caused an outcry against procedures that were "alien to our way of life," and the government had to change its policy. Determined to respond to the public outcry about overstayers, the government received requests from Pacific island communities in New Zealand. These ranged from total amnesty to being allowed to return home with dignity and without penalty. The first amnesty/stay of proceedings was announced in April 1974 for Tongans only. Over three thousand Tongans came forward to register and gain immunity from prosecution. They were given an extension of time to make the necessary arrangements before leaving. In an attempt to meet both the demands of the employers and the special relationship that New Zealand strives to maintain with the South Pacific islands, a work permit scheme was introduced. In order to make it uneconomical for visitors to work in New Zealand, visitors permits from the islands were restricted to one month. This restriction was another example of discrimination. However, there was continued concern about the social and employment pressures, and media coverage reinforced popular fears with "silent invasion" headlines reminiscent of the United States.

Another similarity to the United States was that the government lacked any precise figures about the number of overstayers. It settled for an estimate of between ten thousand and twelve thousand (Immigration Division, 1985). At a Pacific Island Church seminar on 10 April 1976, the minister, T. F. Gill, announced that while there would be no amnesty, there would be a "stay of proceedings" for all persons who had overstayed their temporary permits before that date and had remained unlawfully in New Zealand. The register for this respite from prosecution under the Immigration Amendment Act (1974) was open from 10 April to 30 June 1976. It produced a heated debate between the islanders' leaders and the Immigration Division. The leaders demanded to know the criteria of eligibility for permit extension and residence. The department wished to keep the criteria private to prevent overstayers from calculating their chances of eligibility and then deciding whether to register or not.

Race relations were again soured when the media reported the circumstances of random immigration status checks by the police in Auckland, Wellington, and Christchurch (Amnesty Aroha, 1987). Disappointed with the turnout and suspecting that island leaders had discouraged registering, the minister rejected local consultation and visited the governments in Western Samoa, Tonga, and Fiji. Determined that there would be no recurrence of overstaying, he reluctantly reopened the registers from 20 December 1976 to 30 January 1977. The total number of overstayers who registered was 5,381; of these 2,507 were from Tonga, 2,464 from Western Samoa, and 36 from Fiji. Almost 70 percent of those who registered (3,712) were accepted for permanent residence. Regarding the review to have been completed, and since no further stay of proceedings was intended, the minister released the criteria that had been used to determine acceptance for permanent residency. They were: marriage to a New Zealand citizen or permanent resident, or being the sole remaining member of a family unit permanently resident in New Zealand. Favorable consideration was also given to parents of New Zealand born children with a good employment record.

With supreme confidence the minister announced, "There will in the future be no need for a register. Our laws are now well understood" (Gill, 1977). Yet the first twelve months of a new computerized control system produced a list of 3,641 overstayers; 2,176 of these were from Western Samoa, Tonga, or Fiji. In view of the current situation it is noteworthy that 40 percent of the overstayers were not from the Pacific islands (Table 14.4). Claiming to be acting in the interest of job security for New Zealanders, the minister moved to amend the immigration bill. Temporary visitors were

TABLE 14.4
Overstayers in New Zealand as of July 1989

United States of America	708
United Kingdom	1,062
Fiji	1,111
Western Samoa	6,718
Tonga	4,614
Malaysia	253
Philippines	84
Others	3,069
Not Coded	1
Total	17,351

Source: New Zealand Immigration Service.

forbidden to work without authorization, and it was made an offense to employ those not authorized to work in New Zealand.[7]

The issue of illegal migration continued despite a markedly changed context from that of the 1970s. Throughout the 1980s, New Zealand had a big loss by emigration disturbing both in terms of numbers and caliber of emigrants (Figure 14.1). The early years of the decade saw constant denial from the government that there would be any future amnesty despite strong pleas, especially from the Tongan community, and after the Australian regularization of status program. However, those attempting to execute the immigration laws (the courts, lawyers and immigration division) agreed that the 1964 Act was no longer adequate for the migration conditions of New Zealand in the 1980's. Many of the Act's sections, in fact, dated from 1908, and one senior official claimed that thirty-seven of the fifty-seven sections were deficient or simply unworkable (Scrivener, 1984). Extravagant charges were made that it was minister Malcolm's frustration at court decisions, made on the technical deficiencies of entry documents that made "thousands upon thousands" of Pacific island overstayers de facto permanent residents, that stirred the government to action. In fact, there were two thousand of the so-called "limbo" cases.

FIGURE 14.1
New Zealand Net Migration

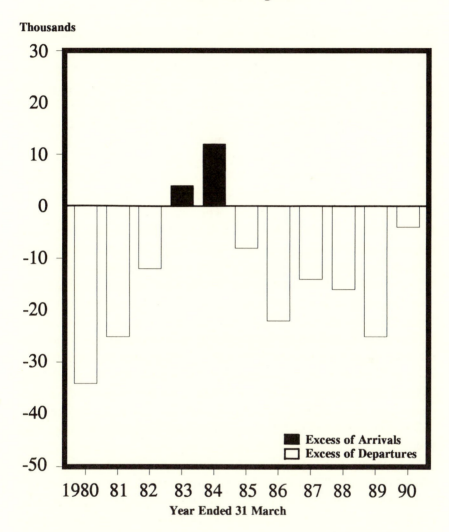

Inconsistencies in the New Zealand immigration law received the necessary wide public forum in the Lesa case (McManamy, 1982). This decision of the United Kingdom Privy Council was nullified by the citizenship (Western Samoa) Act (1983). While ensuring that a considerable proportion of the Western Samoan population would not be entitled to New Zealand citizenship, it was in effect a virtual amnesty for a cohort of Western Samoans in New Zealand on the day before the act came into force. The National government introduced a new immigration bill in December 1983, but it died following the government's defeat in the "snap" election of 1984.

The new Labour government was committed to review immigration law and policy. The two major changes in terminology and jurisdiction, in regard to status within New Zealand and the decriminalization of immigration offenses, were retained from the aborted 1984 act, but the previous government's intention to give immigration officers the power of arrest was abandoned. The immigration division followed the international debate on illegal migration; they knew that several countries had or were considering amnesty/regularization programs. The immigration division, while not accepting that the overstaying situation was out of control and not wishing to reward breaking of the law with amnesty, recommended another regularization program. The prime concern may have been the "limbo" cases, but it was also felt that other groups, who had been in a similar situation to Western Samoans before the 1982 act, might benefit from such a scheme.

The reports of the immigration division, discussions of the government caucus committees on Immigration and Justice, consultations with several departments including the Pacific Islands Affairs Advisory Council, and finally, consideration by cabinet culminated in a Review of Immigration Policy in August (Burke, 1986). An immigration bill was introduced concurrently that would eventually come into force on 1 November 1987.

Introducing the legislation, the minister declared a restricted but lenient legalization program. All who had arrived in New Zealand on or before 14 August 1983, and had no criminal record, would be granted permanent residence status. Persons who had arrived after 14 August could apply for permanent residence but this would only be granted if the new business, occupational, or family guidelines were met. Residence was granted to 2,567 persons under the program, including 805 from Tonga and 543 from Western Samoa.

The minister announced a "once only never to be repeated" opportunity for amnesty (Rodgers, 1987). Believing that a short period would encourage compliance, a three-month period was allowed during which a temporary permit would be issued automatically. The opportunity was then offered for an extension of that permit or even one for residence. The earlier the application after 1 November, the longer would be the currency of the initial permit. Thus, a permit obtained in November would expire on 30 June. A permit gained in December would end on 31 May. A last minute application between 1 January and 9 February would only run until 30 April. Acknowledging a lack of facilities and personnel, the immigration division retained a professional advertising consultant. Between 1 November and 9 February 3,115 people, including 1,523 from Tonga and 940 from Western Samoa, registered under the transitional provisions of the new act. Registration slightly less than 25 percent of the official estimate of overstayers as of 20 May 1987. To emphasize that this was not a general amnesty, the minister stressed "gift of time" and "clean the slate." However, all who applied for residence were approved if they had a job, adequate accommodation, all immediate members of their family in New Zealand, and no criminal convictions. Recognizing an anomaly, after the program had begun, the government decided to put all persons then legally in New Zealand on the "fast track" to residency if they so wished.

Yet, despite this seemingly lenient policy, the official number of overstayers in New Zealand at the end of April 1988 was 17,351 (Table 14.4). This number cannot be seen as evidence of successful elimination of illegal migrants. The total is higher than the pre-regularization estimate and considerably higher than in the decade before New Zealand embarked on a fifteen-year period of reform and regularization.

Sanctions and Discrimination

American states are currently reporting on whether or not sanctions reduced the attraction of the U.S. labor market. In Washington DC, Congress debates legislative proposals ranging from minor amendments to outright repeal of the sanctions provisions of IRCA. No such excitement and speculation exists in

New Zealand. Similar penalties have been in place for fourteen years, but no employer has been prosecuted for employing illegal workers. The New Zealand government cannot, and has no real desire to, enforce the sanctions law. Similarly, despite reminders from the opposition party and the media, the government's promise to follow the period of transition with the application of "the full force of the law" has proved empty. As in the United States, enforcement was curtailed for a period to allow the regularization provisions the maximum chance of success. However, in the twelve months following the resumption of enforcement in August 1988, only some 1,293 warrants were issued. Fifty-six persons were removed from New Zealand in that period, and a further 311 departed voluntarily.

Conclusion

After almost two decades of immigration reform debate, the United States and New Zealand governments remain concerned about the quantity and quality of their respective immigrants. New Zealand presents an apparent contradiction to the idea, still held by many American supporters of IRCA 1986, that the growth of an undocumented population is primarily the result of economic attraction. The precarious state of the economy, with high rates of unemployment resulting from massive restructuring, means that the pull in New Zealand is weak. Yet, the emigration push from the smaller neighboring islands remains, as indicated by the growth of the illegal population, despite the various schemes to eliminate it during the last seventeen years.

However, it may be that New Zealand should not be compared with the United States but rather with Mexico, an immigrant-sending country. In the year ending January 1989, 45,154 people moved from New Zealand to Australia as permanent or long-term residents. The figure for the previous year was 36,227 out of a total of 60,843 permanent and long-term departures. The New Zealand-born population of Australia probably now exceeds 250,000. Thus, thanks to the TTTA, New Zealanders treat the Tasman Sea as a "Porous Border" regarding themselves as participants in a common

Australasian labor market. Perhaps this also echoes a counterpart in North America's free trade zone.

Notes

1. Western Samoa was acquired under a League of Nations mandate in 1920. The United Kingdom ceded the Cook Islands and Niue to New Zealand in 1901 and the Tokelauan Islands in 1925. Western Samoa became self governing in 1962 and the Cook Islands attained complete internal self-government in 1965.
2. According to the 1986 Census 83.4 percent of the population was European; 8.2 percent of the population had been born in the United Kingdom and Ireland with a further 1.3 percent born elsewhere in Europe. In comparison, 12.5 percent were recorded as Maori and an additional 3.1 percent as non-Maori Polynesian.
3. Since employment is the basic requirement for migrants a higher percentage of them report an occupation on entry to New Zealand than of those entering the United States. The figures for 1987 and 1988 were 52 percent and 53 percent (New Zealand) compared with 40 percent and 44 percent (United States). The more dramatic, if simplistic, comparison should be with the United States third and sixth occupational preference categories, 3.9 percent and 2.0 percent in 1987 and 1988.
4. The maximum term for a New Zealand Government is three years. General elections were held in 1984 (when the long-standing National party was defeated by the Labour party), and in 1987 (when the Labour party returned).
5. Population pressure in the South Pacific islands has outstripped land and made the traditional economy untenable. Development of secondary and tertiary sectors is either nonexistent or very restricted.
6. Colloquial expression for New Zealand. Short for God's Own Country.
7. For further discussion of the "Overstayers" debate in the 1970's see De Bres and Campbell, 1975a, 1975b, 1976; Macdonald, 1978; New Zealand Coalition for Trade and Development, 1982.

References

Amnesty Aroha. 1987. "Proposals for Amnesty for Overstayers in New Zealand." Submission to the New Zealand Government. Auckland, New Zealand.

Bedford, Richard D., and Glynis Lloyd. 1982. "Migration between Polynesia and New Zealand, 1971-1981: Who are the Migrants?" *New Zealand*

Population Review 8, 1: 35-43.

Bedford, Richard D. 1986. *New Zealand, Country Report 11, SPC/ICO Series on Migration, Employment and Development in the South Pacific*, Noumea, New Caledonia: South Pacific Commission.

Burke, Hon. Kerry. 1986. *Review of Immigration Policy*, August 1986. Appendices to the Journal of the House of Representatives. Wellington, New Zealand: Government Printer.

De Bres, Joris, and Rob Campbell. 1975a. *Worth their Weight in Gold*. Auckland, New Zealand: Auckland Resource Center for World Development.

De Bres, Joris, and Rob Campbell. 1975b. "Temporary Labour Migration between Tonga and New Zealand." *International Labour Review*, 112, 6: 455-457.

De Bres, Joris, and Rob Campbell. 1976. *The Overstayers: Illegal Migration from the Pacific to New Zealand*. Auckland, New Zealand: Auckland Resource Centre for World Development.

Farmer, R. 1979. "International Migration." In *The Population of New Zealand: Interdisciplinary Perspectives*, edited by R. J. W. Neville and C. J. O'Neill. Auckland, New Zealand: Longman Paul.

Gill, Hon. Thomas Francis. 1977. "Statement on Immigration." *New Zealand Foreign Affairs Review* 10, 2: 67.

Hurrelle, Justin. 1988. "Immigration Policy." In *Report of the New Zealand Royal Commission of Social Policy* 4: 533-59.

Immigration Division. 1985. "Background Paper on Migration from the South Pacific." Wellington, New Zealand: Department of Labour.

Macdonald, Barrie K. 1986. "The Lesa Case and the Citizenship (Western Samoa) Act, 1982." In *New Zealand and International Migration: A Digest and Bibliography, No. 1*, edited by A. D. Trlin and P. Spoonley. Palmerston North, New Zealand: Department of Sociology, Massey University.

Macdonald, Barrie K. 1978. "Pacific Immigration and the Politicians." *New Zealand Quarterly Review*, New Series, 1: 11-16.

McManamy, John. 1982. "Lesa v Attorney General: The Story Behind the Judgement." *New Zealand Law Journal*, August: 273-78. Wellington, New Zealand.

Ministry of Foreign Affairs. 1983. *New Zealand Citizenship and Western Samoans*. Information Bulletin 4. Wellington, New Zealand: Ministry of Foreign Affairs.

New Zealand Coalition for Trade and Development. 1982. *The Ebbing Tide: The Impact of Migration of Pacific Societies*. Wellington, New Zealand.

Pool, D. Ian. 1977. *The Maori Population of New Zealand, 1769-1971*. Auckland, New Zealand: Auckland and Oxford University Presses.

Price, C. A. 1974. *The Great-White Walls are Built: Restrictive Immigration to North America and Australasia, 1836-1888.* Canberra, Australia: Canberra Australian Institute of International Affairs and Australian National University Press.

Rodgers, Hon. Stan, J. 1987. Press release, 7 October. Wellington, New Zealand: Ministry of Immigration.

Roy, W. Theo. 1970. "Immigration Policy and Legislation." In *Immigrants in New Zealand*, edited by K. W. Thomson and A. D. Trlin. Palmerston North, New Zealand: Massey University.

Scrivener, Mike. 1984. "The Immigration Bill, 1983-1984." *New Zealand Population Review* 10: 67-68.

15

Mexican Immigrants in California Today

Wayne A. Cornelius

When the *"bracero"* program of contract labor importation ended in 1964, and for up to a decade thereafter, Mexican migration to California consisted mainly of a circular flow of mostly undocumented, mostly young adult males who left their immediate relatives behind in a rural Mexican community to work in seasonal U.S. agriculture for several months (normally six months or less) and then returned to their community of origin. Most came from a small subset of communities, located in seven or eight Mexican states that for many years had sent the bulk of Mexican migrants to the United States. Thus, the typical undocumented Mexican worker of the late 1960s and early 1970s strongly resembled his legal contract-worker predecessor. In fact, in many cases the post-1964 illegal entrants had themselves worked in the United States as braceros up to 1984. This was the picture that emerged from data collected from apprehended "illegals" interviewed in the United States (North and Houstoun, 1976), returned migrants interviewed in traditional "sending" communities (Cornelius, 1976a), and a national sample of sixty-two-thousand Mexican households interviewed by CENIET, a Mexican government agency, in 1978 (Bustamante and Martínez, 1979; Zazueta and García y Griego, 1982; Ranney and Kossoudji, 1983).

Because of their research designs and data collection methods, these studies tended to understate the importance of permanent settlement in the United States by Mexican immigrant families. The 1980 U.S. Census, which some demographers believe counted a substantial portion of the illegal aliens in the United States at that time, found that most Mexicans were living with their immediate relatives (Warren and Passel, 1987; Borjas, 1990: 66-67). To the extent that living with their families in the United States can be treated as a proxy for permanent settlement, the 1980 U.S. Census depicted a much more settled stock of Mexican immigrants than the stereotypic illegal alien population dominated by transient, mostly male, farm workers living on their own or with unrelated persons. Of course, those enumerated in the U.S. Census were supposed to be settlers rather than sojourners; so short-stay Mexican migrants are virtually unrepresented in the census data. But recent studies done on both sides of the border have confirmed that Mexican migration to California has become much more heterogeneous, in terms of settlement patterns, gender, legal status, employment experience before and after migration to California, and in other ways -- so much so that it increasingly defies generalization.

I hypothesize that the erosion of the stereotype, which probably began in the late 1960s or early 1970s, has been intensified during the last ten years by four principal factors: (1) changes in the California economy that have affected the nature and magnitude of the demand for Mexican immigrant labor; (2) the long-running economic crisis in Mexico; (3) the 1986 U.S. immigration law (IRCA); and (4) the maturation of transnational migrant networks whose formation was initiated by earlier waves of migrants to California.[1]

Origins in Mexico

In the last ten to fifteen years, Mexican migration to California has become increasingly diversified in terms of its points of origin in Mexico. In 1973, 47.4 percent of the undocumented Mexicans apprehended in the San Diego area -- which accounts for more than 40 percent of all apprehensions along the U.S.-Mexico border -- originated in just two states: Jalisco and Michoacán which have towns and rural communities that have built up their own multigenerational traditions of migration to California. Other major sending states were Baja California Norte, Sinaloa, and Guerrero (Dagodag, 1975; Jones, 1984: 45-49).

More recent data on Mexican migrants in Southern California show greater diversity in states of origin within Mexico. In a random

TABLE 15.1
Points of Origin of Mexican Immigrants Employed in Southern California

State	Birthplace (N=315)	Last Place of Residence Before Most Recent Migration to U.S. (N=324)
Baja California Norte	8.6%	20.4%
Jalisco	24.8	18.8
Michoacán	13.0	11.1
Federal District (Mexico City)	6.7	9.9
Guerrero	9.8	7.1
Guanajuato	5.7	4.6
Oaxaca	4.1	3.4
Zacatecas	3.8	3.1
Nayarit	2.9	2.2
Chihuahua	1.6	1.9
Durango	2.5	1.9
Sinaloa	1.0	1.9
Puebla	1.6	1.5
Querétaro	1.3	1.5
Colima	1.6	1.2
Edo. de México (mostly Mexico City)	1.6	1.2
Sonora	1.9	1.2
Yucatán	1.0	1.2
Coahuila	1.0	0.9
Morelos	2.2	0.9
San Luis Potosí	1.6	0.9
Aguascalientes	0.6	0.3
Nuevo León	0.3	0.3
Tlaxcala	0.3	0.3
Veracruz	0.0	0.3
Hidalgo	0.3	0.0
Tamaulipas	0.3	0.0

Source: Personal interviews with Mexican-born workers employed in one hundred "immigrant-dependent" firms in San Diego, Orange, and Los Angeles counties, conducted in 1987-1988 by the Center for U.S.-Mexican Studies.

sample of 871 illegal Mexican entrants apprehended by the U.S. Border Patrol in the San Diego sector during calendar year 1987, only 28.7 percent had originated in Jalisco or Michoacán.[2] Among Mexicans (both legal immigrants and unauthorized migrants) employed in one hundred Southern California non-agricultural firms in 1987-1988, 37.8 percent had resided in Jalisco or Michoacán just before their most recent migration to California (see Table 15.1).

Twenty-seven out of Mexico's thirty-two states had sent migrants to these firms. An even more dispersed pattern is shown in our data collected from recently arrived, job-seeking, unauthorized migrants in Southern California in 1987-1988 (Table 15.2, column 2). Jalisco and Michoacán accounted for just 21.9 percent of these post-IRCA migrants, while six nontraditional sending states (the Federal District, Puebla, Hidalgo, Estado de Mexico, Morelos, and Oaxaca) accounted for 45.5 percent.[3] The state of Guerrero, while previously among the major sending states for Mexican migration to California, increased its relative contribution to the migrant flow in the 1980s.[4]

The increasing importance of the Mexico City metropolitan area (the Federal District and contiguous municipalities in the Estado de Mexico) as a source for unauthorized migration to California in recent years is particularly striking. Before the 1980s, the Federal District never ranked among the top seven sending states. Several sample surveys conducted among apprehended Mexican illegal entrants during the 1970s found that *capitalinos* constituted from 0.6 to 3.0 percent of those interviewed (Bustamante, 1979: 33-35). The Mexico City metropolitan area accounted for only 3 percent of the unauthorized Mexican migrants apprehended in the San Diego sector in 1973 (Jones, 1984: 45); in a 1987 sample of "illegals" apprehended in the same sector, it accounted for 8.2 percent.[5] Among 4,269 would-be illegal entrants interviewed from August 1987 through April 1989 as they prepared to cross the border in the Tijuana area, 11.7 percent came from the Mexico City metropolitan area.[6] The Federal District was the fourth most important sending state (after Michoacán, Jalisco, and Oaxaca) among migrants represented in this sample. Another study, based on interviews with 656 apprehended unauthorized immigrants interviewed in Laredo, Texas in the first half of 1986, found that the Federal District was the third most important state of origin -- accounting for 9.6 percent of the sample -- behind Nuevo Leon and Guerrero (Fatemi, 1987). As shown in Tables 15.1 and 15.2, among our 1987-1988 interviewees in Southern California, the Mexico City metropolitan area was the top-ranking sending area for recently arrived unauthorized migrants (23.1 percent of the sample, combining those whose last place of residence was either the Federal District or the Estado de Mexico),

TABLE 15.2
Points of Origin of Recently Arrived Unauthorized Mexican Migrants to Southern California

State	Birthplace (N=184)	Last Place of Residence Before Migrating to U.S. (N=187)
Federal District (Mexico City)	9.8%	17.7%
Guanajuato	11.4	11.2
Michoacán	12.5	10.7
Puebla	8.7	8.0
Guerrero	10.3	7.5
Hidalgo	7.1	7.0
Jalisco	5.4	5.9
Edo. de México (mostly Mexico City)	6.0	5.4
Baja California Norte	1.1	4.3
Morelos	3.8	3.7
Oaxaca	5.4	3.7
Chihuahua	2.2	2.7
Nayarit	2.2	2.1
Chiapas	1.6	1.6
Querétaro	1.6	1.6
Sinaloa	1.6	1.6
Sonora	2.7	1.6
Veracruz	1.6	1.1
Zacatecas	2.2	1.1
Aguascalientes	0.5	0.5
Colima	0.5	0.5
Nuevo León	0.5	0.5
Durango	1.1	0.0

Source: Personal interviews with job-seeking, unauthorized migrants who arrived in San Diego, Orange, and Los Angeles counties in 1987 or 1988, conducted by the Center for U.S.-Mexican Studies.

and the fourth most important sending area for more settled, employed immigrants (11.1 percent of the sample). In sum, the available evidence indicates that at least one out of ten Mexican migrants entering the United States clandestinely in recent years has come from their country's largest city.

Such evidence suggests that while traditional source areas have by no means dropped out of the U.S.-bound migration flow, important new ones have come "on stream" in recent years.[7] The economic crisis of the 1980s -- which reduced real wages for most Mexicans by 40-50 percent -- propelled into the migratory flow people from families, communities, and states *without* a long history of U.S.-bound migration. And the 1986 U.S. immigration law has not prevented the formation of new migrant networks originating in these nontraditional sending areas. To the contrary, the extensive publicity surrounding IRCA's legalization and "Replenishment Agricultural Worker" (RAW) programs seems to have attracted into the migratory flow persons from communities and states that heretofore had not participated significantly.[8]

Mexican migrants to California in the 1980s included skilled, urban-born workers from Mexico's principal cities, as well as destitute *campesinos* from some of Mexico's most underdeveloped states, such as Guerrero, Oaxaca, Hidalgo, and Puebla. These states all have large indigenous populations.[9] It is significant that several of the non-traditional areas now sending migrants to California are among the Mexican states most adversely impacted by the economic crisis of the 1980s (the Federal District, Morelos, Hidalgo, all of whose economies contracted by more than 2 percent during the 1980-1985 period; Guerrero and Puebla, whose economies contracted by 0.1-2.0 percent in the same years).

Another indication that the economic crisis of the 1980s pushed more residents of Mexico's principal cities into the U.S.-bound migration stream is provided by a comparison of migrants' birthplaces with their last place of residence in Mexico before migration. As shown in Table 15.3, one out of five migrants employed in our 1987-1988 sample of Southern California firms were "stepmigrants," who had moved initially to a major Mexican city and subsequently to California. Sixteen percent of our sample of

TABLE 15.3
Step-Wise Mexican Migration to Southern California via Large Cities in Mexico

| | Number of Step-Wise Migrants in | |
Migration Sequence	Sample of Employed Migrants (N=320)	Sample of Recently Arrived Migrants (N=184)
Birthplace---México City---S. Calif.	15 (4.7%)	18 (9.8%)
Birthplace---Guadalajara---S. Calif.	8 (2.5%)	3 (1.6%)
Birthplace---León, Gto.---S. Calif.	1 (0.3%)	3 (1.6%)
Birthplace---Baja Calif. N.**---S. Calif.	41 (12.8%)	6 (3.3%)
Total	65 (20.3%)	30 (16.3%)

**Includes cities of Tijuana, Mexicali, and Ensenada.
Source: Personal interviews with Mexican workers in San Diego, Orange, and Los Angeles counties, conducted by the Center for U.S-Mexican Studies, 1987- 1988.

recently-arrived, job-seeking, unauthorized migrants in Southern California also came via one of these Mexican cities.[10] Rather than simply absorbing internal migrants from the countryside and provincial cities as they have done for many years, Mexico's large urban centers today are serving increasingly as platforms for migration to the United States. In the 1980s, internal migrants encountered saturated labor markets, skyrocketing living costs, dangerously high levels of air pollution, and rising crime in Mexico City and other large cities. Having failed to solve their economic problems there, many of them headed for cities in California.

As our data suggest, the native-born populations of large Mexican cities have also become increasingly important sources of migration to California. Further support for this contention comes from several surveys conducted among the population of Guadalajara during the 1980s by Agustín Escobar-Latapí and Mercedes González de la Rocha. They found that in the 1982-1987 period, 23 percent of Guadalajara households were receiving regular cash remittances from household members living in the United States. Additional households had immediate kin in the United States who did not remit income to their Guadalajara relatives. In a separate 1982 sample of 1,223 Guadalajara workers in manufacturing, construction, and public-sector manual labor, 18.3 percent had worked in the United States. Another sample of Guadalajara manufacturing workers, interviewed in 1987, reported fewer sojourns in the United States. The researchers believe that this difference was not caused by fewer workers migrating to the United States, but occurred because more of them were staying there longer.[11]

This phenomenon is consistent with the widely held notion that, in relative terms, the economic crisis from which Mexico has suffered since 1982 has affected urban dwellers (especially residents of the largest cities) even more severely than the rural population. Prior to the economic crisis and the government austerity measures that it provoked, Mexico City and other large urban centers were heavily subsidized, as places to live and work. Moreover, they were major centers of government employment, and the wages of government workers filtered back into the general urban economy. Therefore, crisis-induced austerity has disproportionately impacted Mexico's large cities (Escobar-Latapí, Gonzalez, and Roberts, 1987).

Even with a sustained economic recovery in the 1990s, it can be anticipated that, by the end of this decade, the majority of new (first-time) Mexican migrants to California will come from urban Mexico. This trend reflects not only the emptying-out of traditional rural sending communities, as urbanization proceeds, but also the saturation of labor markets in Mexico's largest cities. Over half of the Mexican population now lives in large-scale urban areas (one out of every four in the Mexico City metropolitan area alone), and labor force growth rates in these cities remain quite high despite declining fertility.

California: The Preferred Destination

One of the constants in the profile of Mexican migration to the United States in recent decades is the leading role of California as a destination. A 1978 national survey of households in Mexico found that California was the destination of 47.3 percent of Mexican migrants to the United States (49.2 percent of "long-stayers").[12]

Although many parts of the United States attract Mexican labor -- including the Pacific Northwest, Chicago, and other midwestern cities, parts of the Southeast, and even New York City -- California now appears to be the preferred destination for the majority of Mexico's U.S.-bound workers and their dependents. This is reflected in national-level statistics on legal immigration and the unauthorized alien population, evidence gathered in Mexican sending communities, and applications for legalization under the two "amnesty" programs created by the 1986 Immigration Reform and Control Act (IRCA).

U.S. Immigration and Naturalization Service statistics show that since the 1970s California has absorbed about half of the total flow of legal immigrants from Mexico. In recent years, four of the top ten receiving metropolitan areas for legal Mexican immigrants have been located in California (Los Angeles-Long Beach, San Diego, Anaheim-Santa Ana, and Riverside-San Bernardino); these and seven other California urban areas accounted for 50 percent of all Mexican legal immigrants admitted to the United States in Fiscal Year 1988.[13] The Los Angeles-Long Beach metropolitan area received 6.6 times more legal Mexican immigrants than any other metropolitan statistical area in the country (INS, 1989b: Table 18, p. 38).

It is probable that the distribution of unauthorized Mexican migrants is roughly the same because most of them are now part of extended-family networks anchored by long-staying legal immigrants in California. Passel and Woodrow (1984: 651) have estimated that 67 percent of Mexican undocumented aliens counted in the 1980 U.S. Census lived in California. One-third of all censused, unauthorized immigrants in the United States (of all nationalities) were located in the Los Angeles metropolitan area alone.[14] Another study, based on a large, comprehensive sample of INS apprehension records covering the period from 1983 to 1986, found that among the thirty-five Mexican *municipios* having the highest density of unauthorized migrants to the United States per one thousand residents, more than half sent workers principally to a California destination (Jones, 1988: 16, Table 2).

Studies done at points of origin in Mexico have often found even higher proportions of California-bound migrants. In our study of three sending communities in the states of Jalisco, Michoacan, and Zacatecas, we found that among those residents who were considering a permanent or long-term move to the United States, more than 70 percent planned to go to California. California was even more dominant as a destination for short-term labor migrants from these communities. Among all residents aged 15-64 who had ever migrated to the United States, 81.7 percent had gone most recently to California, followed by Oklahoma (5.7 percent), Texas (5.0 percent), and Illinois (3.1 percent). Two of the three communities send virtually all of their migrants to California (95.5 percent and 99.0 percent, respectively); in the other community, 50.9 percent of those with U.S. migratory experience had chosen California as their most recent destination.

Another indicator of California's predominance in the Mexican migration stream is the distribution of applications for the regular and Special Agricultural Worker (SAW) legalization programs created by the 1986 immigration law. California accounted for more than 54 percent of total applicants for these two programs -- far more than any other state (INS, 1989a). The Los Angeles-Long Beach metropolitan area alone generated 36 percent of the national total of applications for the general "amnesty" program, and 24 percent of the SAW applicants. Together, the general amnesty program and the SAW program may have legalized up to 1.7 million Mexican immigrants in California's work force.[15]

A substantial portion of the recent growth of California's Mexican immigrant population is the inevitable product of the maturation of immigrant networks that began to form in the early 1950s (Rouse, 1989; Mines, 1981, 1984; Reichert and Massey, 1979; Massey et al., 1987; Fonseca, 1988; Fernández, 1988; López, 1986). Data from sending-community studies indicate that the social networks linking these communities to U.S. receiving areas have become the key factor affecting the choice of migration destinations. Among the interviewees in the three rural sending communities that we studied in 1988-1989 who were considering permanent emigration, 45.1 percent explained their choice of destination by citing the presence of relatives and friends in that place, and an additional 14.6 percent mentioned job opportunities (in many cases, to be arranged by relatives) as the principal attraction. New migrants generally tend to follow their predecessors, settling in the same U.S. communities and often working in the same firms, where they will be more likely to have social support as well as assistance in finding housing and jobs. Established migrant communities in the initial receiving areas have served as springboards for "settled-out" immigrants to move elsewhere in search of higher-paying, more stable (usually nonagricultural) employment and opportunities (Mines, 1984; Cornelius, 1990a).

California's attractiveness to the most recent wave of Mexican migrants also reflects the more robust, more diversified employment growth in that state, relative to other potential destinations. Following the 1980-82 recession, a boom occurred in most sectors of the highly diversified California economy. Since 1986, this boom has coincided with a sharp contraction in employment opportunities in oil-bust Texas, whose economy only recently has begun to revive. In the last two decades, employment growth in California has been far more robust than in the United States as a whole. During the 1970s, for example, blue-collar jobs increased in California at twice the national rate, and manufacturing employment expanded at nearly four times the national rate (Muller and Espenshade, 1985: 54-55). This pattern continued in the 1980s, and most economists expect it to persist into the next century. In Southern California alone, an estimated 7 million new jobs will be created during the next twenty years. While new technologies may eliminate many low-skilled jobs in manufacturing, data for the 1984-1989 period indicate that "low-tech" manufacturing continues to expand in California and other western states, thus more than offsetting job losses due to automation in "high-tech" industries (Birch, 1990).

In addition to its overall dynamism and diversity, these are certain structural features of the contemporary California economy that increase the demand for immigrant labor. For example, the system of contracting out labor-intensive tasks to small, largely non-union, immigrant-dominated firms in such industries as garment, electronics, and construction appears to be advancing more rapidly in California than in other parts of the nation (Bonacich, 1990: 4; Cornelius, 1990b; Fernández-Kelly and García, 1990). And while the demand for entry-level workers in manufacturing and construction is likely to remain strong, the largest numbers of new jobs to be created in California during the next twenty years will be relatively low-paying, low-skill, low-status jobs in restaurants, hotels, and other parts of the urban service sector -- precisely the kinds of jobs that are increasingly shunned by young, better-educated, native-born Californians.

As long as California's economy continues to out-perform the national economy, the state will be a strong magnet for future waves of Mexican migrants. Jobs in both California agriculture and nonagricultural industries are likely to remain plentiful, quick to obtain, and high-paying, at least in comparison with those in other southwestern states.[16] A strong feedback effect also operates, in which consumer spending by Mexican immigrants and their availability as a large, young, flexible labor pool stimulates the creation of new, locally owned small businesses (especially in the service sector), while helping to retain older labor-intensive industries like garment and shoe manufacturing (Birch, 1990; Cornelius, 1990b; Muller and Espenshade, 1985). This feedback effect is strongest in the largest metropolitan areas, where California's immigrant population is increasingly concentrated. Los Angeles, for example, became the principal manufacturing center in the United States during the 1980s because of its combination of "a first-world infrastructure and a third-world workforce . . . In the Los Angeles area, garment employment jumped even as it fell elsewhere" (Martin, 1990: 1). In addition to favorable labor-market conditions and mature immigrant networks, California offers to prospective migrants from Mexico a variety of other inducements, including a superior climate, less racial discrimination than in other potential destinations (such as Texas), and -- for those who enter clandestinely -- a relatively easy point of entry, the border city of Tijuana.

Gender, Family, and Duration of Stay

The shift from a migrant population consisting mainly of highly mobile, seasonally employed lone males (unmarried or without dependents in California) toward a more socially heterogeneous, year-round, de facto permanent Mexican immigrant population in California accelerated in the 1980s. To be sure, the absolute number of young, temporary Mexican male farm workers in the state did not decline during the 1970s and 1980s, but it grew slowly in absolute terms and, in relative terms, this fraction of the Mexican immigrant population was overtaken and overwhelmed by migrants who remained in the United States for long periods, accompanied by their dependents. Ethnographic and survey studies of both sending and receiving communities, interviews with would-be illegal migrants at the border, and INS apprehension statistics all show that there is now considerably more migration by whole family units (moving together), more family-reunification migration (women and children joining family heads already established in California), and more migration by single women than there was a decade ago (Bean et al., 1990; Bustamante, 1990; Cornelius, 1989, 1990a; Rouse, 1989).

Increased Female Migration

There are many indications that the female component of the Mexican migratory stock and flow has expanded in recent years. An analysis of data from the U.S. Census Bureau's Current Population Survey of June 1988 suggests that females may now constitute a majority of the settled undocumented immigrant population from Mexico (Woodrow and Passel, 1990). Our data from traditional sending communities in Mexico show that the probability of migration to the United States -- especially temporary migration -- is still much higher among males than among females. Nevertheless, we found substantial female participation in U.S.-bound migration in certain communities and age groups, especially women currently in their twenties (Cornelius, 1990a: 30-31). A study of Mexican immigrants residing in rural and urban areas of San Diego County conducted in 1981-1982 found that female immigrants are especially likely to originate in urban areas of Mexico; almost two-thirds declared their place of origin to be a city (Solórzano Torres, 1987: 45).

Increased female migration to the United States reflects, in part, generational changes in the attitudes and expectations of Mexican women. González de la Rocha (1989) has summarized her findings from a high-migration town in Jalisco as follows:

> During the last three years more women have left the town to be reunited with their husbands in the United States . . . Upon getting married, the woman no longer stays in the town . . . The young women do not want to repeat the loneliness that their mothers experienced nor the hardships that they had to endure [while their husbands worked in the United States].

The higher propensity of females to migrate to the United States in recent years is also a consequence of Mexico's economic crisis, which has driven more wives, single women, and children into the work force. Especially among Mexico's urban poor, the male family head's income is not nearly sufficient now to meet the family's needs.[17] Among our 1988-1989 Southern California sample of recently arrived undocumented migrants who still had no regular employment and were found looking for work in street-corner labor markets and other public areas, 8 percent were women; and among the male interviewees who were married, 17 percent had brought their spouses with them to Southern California.[18]

The 1986 U.S. immigration law also gave new impetus to female migration, by encouraging whole-family migration and family reunification in the United States. Frank Bean and his colleagues found that by the third year after IRCA's enactment, there was a statistically significant increase in the number and proportion of females and children being apprehended by the INS (Bean et al., 1990; cf. Bjerke and Hess, 1987:, 4-5). Another indicator of IRCA-related migration for family reunification is the 82 percent increase in non-immigrant visa seekers at the U.S. Consulate in Tijuana during the last quarter of 1989, as compared with the same period in 1988. Most of these visa applicants were dependents of persons who were granted amnesty under IRCA. In 1986, the Border Patrol apprehended and expelled an average of three to five unaccompanied children (aged five to seventeen) each day from California at Tijuana; in the first quarter of 1990, an average of fifteen such minors were returned to Mexico each day.[19]

In the immediate post-IRCA period, there was widespread fear in Mexican sending communities that the "door was closing" because of employer sanctions and the deadlines attached to the legalization programs created by the 1986 law.[20] Especially in the first half of 1988, thousands of undocumented women and children left Mexican sending communities with their husbands, many for the first time, in hopes of gaining legal-immigrant status.[21] Many others were summoned to the United States by family heads who had secured amnesty for themselves or made application for it; they used *coyotes* to guide them across the border. Many of these dependents were disappointed, since they could not possibly meet the five-year continuous U.S.-residence requirement for the general amnesty program. More of them were able to secure legalization under the SAW program since the eligibility criteria and documentation requirements for that program were much less stringent than for the general amnesty program.[22]

Female emigration to California has also been increasing because of the abundance of new employment opportunities for which women are the preferred labor source. There is a booming market in California's largest urban areas for undocumented female Mexican labor to provide child care, clean houses and offices, and iron clothes.[23] In the San Diego area, recently arrived female Mexican migrants now find housecleaning work by going door-to-door, as males have done (for gardening work) for many years. In San Diego and other U.S. border cities, such as El Paso, Texas, domestic work has become institutionalized as an occupation performed almost exclusively by unauthorized female immigrants (Solórzano Torres, 1987: 55-56; Ruiz, 1987). And Mexican immigrant women are still the preferred work force for low-level production jobs in California's garment firms, Silicon Valley semiconductor manufacturing firms, fruit and vegetable canneries, and packing houses (Hossfeld, 1989; Mummert, 1988: 290). Moreover, the recent relaxation of federal laws restricting "homework" for the apparel industry enables increased employment of recently arrived undocumented women in their own homes.[24]

Sojourners versus Settlers

The shift from a temporary to a long-staying or permanent Mexican immigrant population in California was well underway by the 1970s (Browning and Rodríguez, 1985; Cornelius et al., 1984), and it accelerated in the 1980s. Among Mexican workers employed in Southern California non-agricultural firms whom we interviewed in 1983-1984, 50 percent stated that they definitely intended to stay in the United States permanently; the proportion of permanent settlers among Mexicans working in the same firms in 1987-1988 was 69 percent. Traditional temporary migrants -- those working about six months in California during each sojourn, and returning regularly to their home community -- certainly have not disappeared, especially in the agricultural sector.[25] Even in urban areas, Mexican migrants still prefer to think of themselves as sojourners rather than permanent settlers (Chávez, 1988; Rouse, 1989). But the reality is that most of these urban-based immigrants are settled, more or less, permanently in California.

The shift toward more "settled-out" Mexican migrants in California is directly related to the maturation of transnational migrant networks during the last fifteen years. Kinship/friendship networks reduce the costs and risks of long-term stays in California and facilitate integration into U.S. society. They can offer extensive support systems for dependent family members. U.S.-born children and wives quickly become strong supporters of remaining permanently in California.[26] Teenagers are attracted to the life-style of California's young people, and housewives find that domestic chores are considerably easier in California, with all its modern conveniences, than in Mexico. Financial obligations -- debts owed to friends and relatives in California, home mortgages, and so forth -- accumulate. All these factors strongly increase the probability of permanent settlement. Indeed, many long-staying Mexican immigrants -- irrespective of their legal status -- feel trapped in California by these family and financial circumstances.

Greater "settling-out" is also very much related to changes in the California economy that have increased the demand for year-round low-skilled labor (Cornelius, 1990b). Even in agriculture, recent changes in crop mix and technology have made it possible for many growers to engage in year-round production and have increased the labor intensity of agricultural production (Palerm, 1987, 1989, 1990). Thus, year-round employment in California has become a realistic option for a growing segment of the Mexican migrant population. Many of the firms and industries in which Mexican migrants are now employed -- including construction, landscaping, light manufacturing, restaurants, and hotels -- are still subject to seasonal or cyclical fluctuations in demand for their product or service. Nevertheless, it is usually possible for migrants to ride out these slack periods. Thus, migrants have a strong incentive to remain in California, and their employers prefer to have them continuously available -- if not always on the payroll.

Accordingly, increasing numbers of Mexicans are being forced to choose, finally, between long-term residence in Mexico and long-term residence in California. With the option of more economically secure, year-round residence in California now open to them, more migrants from traditional sending communities view migration to California as a permanent change in their life situation, instead of just a short-term income-earning strategy. And high-emigration communities in central Mexico are being transformed increasingly into rest-and-recreation centers for families whose principal base is now in California (Cornelius, 1990a; Rouse, 1989).

Employment Patterns in Mexico and California

The Exodus from Agriculture

Since the late 1960s the share of Mexican migrants working in the agricultural sector of the U.S. economy has declined sharply. According to recent estimates, agriculture currently employs no more than 10 to 15 percent of the Mexican immigrants (legals and illegals) in California, Texas, and Arizona, and a much smaller proportion of the Mexicans working in Illinois (Wallace, 1988: 664-65).

Among the Mexico-born, non-U.S. citizen males included in the 1980 U.S. Census who had moved to the United States between

1975 and 1980, only 17.3 percent were employed in agriculture (or mining) at the time of the census; and an even smaller proportion -- 10.4 percent -- of post-1975 female Mexican immigrants were working in these sectors (Bean and Tienda, 1987: Table 4.12, p. 132). This occupational distribution is not surprising, since any census or household survey conducted in the United States will record very few temporary migrants, who are more likely to be agriculturally employed than permanent settlers from Mexico. This does not necessarily mean, however, that most temporary Mexican migrants are still employed in agriculture. In fact, only about one-third of the "short-stay" migrants to the United States detected in the 1978 CENIET survey of households in Mexico were employed in agriculture in the United States (Zazueta and García y Griego, 1982). And as noted below, there is more recent evidence from Mexico-based research indicating that the majority of unauthorized, mostly temporary migrants to the United States are now working in nonagricultural occupations.

Especially since the enactment of IRCA, there has been much speculation about the rate of attrition of Mexican labor from California agriculture. In our recent fieldwork, we found that Mexican migrants with extensive experience in the state's agricultural sector are not abandoning farm work in large numbers; but young workers migrating for the first time in the 1970s and 1980s were much more likely to choose less arduous, higher-paying jobs in nonagricultural enterprises as their point of entry into the U.S. labor market, and to remain in urban occupations for the duration of their U.S. migratory career. Those most committed to working in U.S. agriculture tend to be older men who began their migratory careers as agricultural workers and have remained in that sector, acquiring permanent legal immigrant status along the way.

Those who legalized themselves through the Special Agricultural Workers (SAW) program created by the 1986 U.S. immigration law are not required to keep working in the agricultural sector, and many of those who obtained SAW status actually had little or no previous agricultural employment experience. Among a statewide sample of applicants for SAW visas, only 28 percent gave farm work as their premigration occupation (CASAS, 1989: 5-7/5-8).[27] Moreover, only about one-third reported usually working in agriculture during the twelve months preceding the interview, and among those who had been agriculturally employed, 60 percent said that they planned to seek employment outside of agriculture. In this survey, urban-based SAW applicants are overrepresented (indeed, almost 50 percent of the SAW visa holders in this sample were drawn from Los Angeles County). Other surveys of SAW applicants in California have found higher levels of continued commitment to farmwork (see CASAS, 1989: 5-9). Similarly, a national survey of agricultural workers conducted by the U.S. Department of Labor to measure changes in the labor supply resulting from the movement of newly legalized farm workers from agriculture to other sectors found that in 1989 there was actually an increase in the number of SAW visa holders performing agricultural labor during the course of the year -- (i.e., the "exit rate" among SAW workers was negative) (*Rural California Report*, 1990: 9). Clearly, it is premature to reach any conclusions about the impact of IRCA's legalization programs on the sectoral distribution of Mexican migrants in the California economy.

The longer-term exodus from agriculture is reflected in the data from our recent field studies on both sides of the border. As shown in Table 15.4, more than three-quarters of the economically active population in the rural sending communities that we have studied who had U.S. migratory experience were employed primarily in agriculture in their home towns, immediately before their most recent trip to the United States.[28]

However, only 41 percent worked in agriculture once they got there (i.e., during their most recent U.S. sojourn). The proportion of migrants agriculturally employed in the United States varied considerably among the three communities (14.9 percent, 21.3 percent, and 88.6 percent, respectively). Seventy percent of the migrants in the three-community sample who were employed most recently in agricultural jobs in the United States were residents of a community in Michoacan that has long specialized in exporting labor to the strawberry fields of Watsonville, California. Even among migrants from this community, however, there is attrition out of the U.S. agricultural sector, especially among the youngest, better educated migrants, who prefer to work in urban services. The data reported in

TABLE 15.4

Sector of Employment of Migrants to the United States from Three Rural Mexican Communities, Before and During Their Most Recent Trip to the United States

Sector	Sector of employment before most recent migration (N=631)	Sector of employment during most recent stay in U.S. (N=891)
Agriculture	75.8%	41.0%
Services	5.4	15.2
Retail commerce (including restaurants)	5.9	12.5
Manufacturing	4.0	13.4
Construction	9.0	18.1

Source: Center for U.S.-Mexican Studies survey of three rural communities in Mexico, 1988-89. The sample consists of all members of 586 households in the three research communities who have ever migrated to the United States (N=1,126). Unemployed, retired, student, and other economically inactive persons are excluded from the tabulations.

TABLE 15.5

Sector of Employment of Migrants to the United States from Three Rural Mexican Communities, During Their Most Recent Trip to the United States, by Immigration Status

Sector	Legal Immigrants (N=257)	"Rodinos" (N=157)	Unauthorized Migrants (N=466)
Agriculture	51.8%	66.2%	26.4%
Services	15.2	7.0	17.6
Retail commerce	10.5	9.6	14.6
Manufacturing	12.5	7.0	16.1
Construction	10.1	10.2	25.3

Chi-square = 103.59; significance: p < .0000
Source: Same as for Table 15.4.

Table 15.5 show that, contrary to the popular stereotype, unauthorized migrants from our Mexican research communities were much less likely to be agriculturally employed in the United States than legal immigrants and those who were in process of legalizing themselves under the 1986 U.S. immigration law (popularly known as "Rodinos").

The migration profile of Tlacuitapa, Jalisco -- a community with about two thousand three hundred inhabitants located in the Los Altos region of Jalisco -- is particularly instructive. This community, which I initially studied in 1976 and restudied in 1988-89, sends some migrants to work in the orchards and flower fields of Oregon; but these agriculturally employed migrants are now outnumbered by those who go to Oklahoma City to work in highway and bridge construction, those who go to Las Vegas and Palm Springs to work in the hotel and restaurant industries, and those who migrate to the San Francisco Bay area to work in light industry and services. In 1976, 55.3 percent of Tlacuitapenos who had migrated to the United States had worked most recently in agriculture; in our 1988-89 survey of the same community, only 21.3 percent were employed in agriculture during their most recent trip to the United States. Between 1976 and 1988-89, the proportion of the community's U.S.-bound migrants employed in service activities more than tripled, and those in retail commerce and manufacturing nearly doubled (see Table 15.6). Similarly, in a 1982 sample of Guadalajara residents with U.S. migratory experience, 91 percent of those who had last migrated to the United States before 1962 had worked in agriculture, while 48 percent of those who had been in the United States between 1962 and 1972 and only 33 percent of those who had migrated after 1972 were agriculturally employed there (Escobar-Latapí et al., 1987: 50).

Most Mexican migrants to California today -- both legal and unauthorized -- are being absorbed into the urban service, construction, light manufacturing, and retail commerce sectors. In the service sector, Mexicans work primarily as janitors, dishwashers and busboys, gardeners, hotel workers, maintenance and laundry workers in hospitals and convalescent homes, car washers, house cleaners, and child-care providers (Cornelius, 1990b). The Mexicans filling these

TABLE 15.6
Sector of Employment in United States, among Migrants from a Rural Mexican Sending Community, During Most Recent Trip to the United States, 1976 and 1988-89

Sector	1976 Sample (N=76)	1988-89 Sample (N=300)
Agriculture	55.3%	21.3%
Services	6.6	21.0
Retail commerce (including restaurants)	10.5	20.7
Manufacturing	9.2	16.3
Construction	14.5	20.7

Source: Author's sample surveys in the community of Tlacuitapa, Jalisco. Unemployed, retired, student, other economically inactive persons, and missing cases are excluded from the tabulations.

types of jobs are increasingly likely to be persons whose previous work experience, if any, has been limited to nonagricultural employment (Bilateral Commission, 1988: 91-93). Among our sample of Mexican immigrants employed in Southern California nonagricultural firms in 1987-88, only 18.4 percent had been working in agriculture prior to their most recent trip to the United States (excluding those who had been economically inactive before migration). Nearly 14.6 percent had been factory workers in Mexico. Skilled craftsmen, small business owners, restaurant workers, white-collar workers, and other urban service workers were significantly represented. However, agricultural and horticultural enterprises in California that require only seasonal labor continue to attract mainly migrants with rural, agricultural backgrounds.

Wages and Impacts on California Wage Levels

Recent field studies have found that the majority of both legal and unauthorized Mexican immigrants in California are employed in jobs paying between $4.25 (the state's legal minimum wage, as of 1 July 1988) and $6.00 per hour. Among our sample of 146 regularly employed, unauthorized immigrant workers in Southern California in 1987-1988, most of whom were interviewed when the state's legal minimum wage was $3.35 per hour, the median hourly wage was $4.98. Among 154 "illegals" who had applied for amnesty, the median wage being earned was $5.16.[29] These wage levels may be upwardly biased because of our sample design, which excluded workers employed in very small, "underground economy" firms that are more likely to pay subminimum wages.

Wages in certain subsectors of California economy may have been depressed by the influx of Mexican labor in recent years. In the case of Los Angeles manufacturing industries, there is persuasive evidence that relative wage declines during the 1970s for low-skill jobs in these industries were related to the presence of large numbers of Mexican and Central American immigrants. In the apparel industry, for example, the wages of production workers grew considerably

TABLE 15.7
Median Hourly Wage Received by Workers in Southern California
Non-Agricultural Firms, 1983-1984 and 1987-1988, by Immigration Status

	Median Wage in:		Increase:
Immigration Status	1983-84 Sample	1987-88 Sample	1983-84 to 1987-88
Undocumented immigrants	$4.79 (N=235)	$4.98 (N=144)	$0.19
"Rodinos" (legalization applicant)	-- --	5.16 (N=154)	--
Legal immigrants	5.15 (N=102)	6.00 (N=98)	0.85
U.S. citizens	7.00 (N=110)	8.00 (N=93)	1.00

Source: Personal interviews with two different samples of production workers employed in "immigrant-dependent" firms in San Diego, Orange, and Los Angeles counties, conducted by the Center for U.S.-Mexican Studies in 1983-84 (N=447) and 1987-88 (N=489). Missing cases are excluded.

more slowly in Los Angeles than elsewhere in California between 1969 and 1977 (Muller and Espenshade, 1985: 110). In Southern California non-agricultural firms studied by the Center for U.S.-Mexican Studies in 1983-1984 and again in 1987-1988, the median hourly wage for unauthorized immigrants rose by only 19 cents per hour during the four-year interval between the surveys -- a real wage decline when inflation is factored in (see Table 15.7). Wages for legal immigrants in the two samples had risen by 85 cents per hour, and those of U.S.-citizen employees by $1.00 per hour.

Latino immigrant workers, especially unauthorized Mexicans, do tend to earn less than U.S.-born workers employed in similar job categories. But little evidence exists that immigration status is per se a crucial determinant of these wage differentials (Cornelius and Bustamante, 1990: 7-8; Tienda, 1990). Far more important are such factors as the particular region and sector of the economy in which the worker is employed, gender, the ethnicity of one's employer, and especially, labor union membership.[30]

Impacts of IRCA

The employer sanctions component of the 1986 U.S. immigration law was supposed to exert upward pressure on wage scales in immigrant-dominated industries by reducing the supply of unauthorized job-seekers and inducing firms to raise wages in order to retain their newly legalized immigrant employees. Thus far, however, there is little evidence of such an effect in California. Very few of the migrants who legalized themselves under IRCA have received pay increases as result of their new immigration status, and surveys of both agricultural and non agricultural employers in California show that only a small minority of them have any plans to wage raises, at least in response to any IRCA-related labor market changes (Cornelius, 1990b: 44; Martin and Taylor, 1990). In part, this is because IRCA thus far has failed to reduce the undocumented immigrant labor supply in most California industries that have come to rely on such labor. But econometric studies suggest that even if the labor supply were to be reduced by IRCA, real wage rates in agriculture would not rise significantly because many growers would introduce labor-saving technology or switch to less labor-intensive crops to avoid paying higher wages (Duffield, 1990).

There is no evidence that IRCA has reduced the total pool of Mexican migrants employed or seeking work in California's labor markets. In fact, the 1986 law seems to have augmented that pool by drawing into it thousands of first-time migrants who sought to take advantage of the SAW and general amnesty programs (Cornelius, 1989). IRCA has also increased the segmentation of the Mexican immigrant labor force, by opening up inter-firm and intersectoral mobility opportunities for the newly legalized segment (in theory, at least), and adding a new layer of highly vulnerable, economically desperate workers at the bottom of the labor force. This new under-class consists mostly of recently arrived, unauthorized migrants, especially those coming from nontraditional sending areas in Mexico, who are not attached to well-consolidated family support networks in California. Even though they are being enforced cautiously and selectively (Fix and Hill, 1990), employer sanctions have reduced the range of employment prospects available to these new arrivals, and have lengthened their job-search time. Unauthorized migrants without a prearranged job are still getting work in California, often using fraudulent or borrowed documents (Cornelius, 1989; Bach and Brill, 1990); but it takes them longer to find steady, full-time employment. Many of them must devote several weeks or even months to poorly paid, highly irregular day labor before finding steady employment.

One of IRCA's most conspicuous unintended consequences has been the proliferation of street corner labor markets in major urban areas (Bach and Brill, 1990; Kelley, 1990). In Los Angeles County, immigrant day-labor markets now operate at an estimated forty sites, and there are dozens of them in Orange and San Diego counties as well. These informal labor markets serve mostly nonagricultural employers -- small building contractors, painters, roofers, landscape maintenance businesses, individual homeowners who need help moving dirt, weeding yards, or moving furniture. The vast majority of workers who congregate in these markets are unauthorized, but some newly legalized SAW workers can also be found there, reflecting a general oversupply of low-skilled immigrant labor in some areas. Four Southern California cities (Los Angeles, Costa Mesa, Encinitas, and Carlsbad) have opened their own "hiring halls" to give migrant workers a regulated alternative to the chaotic, often highly exploitative street corner labor markets -- and, not incidentally, to get the migrants off the streets and away from retail businesses. Some of these hiring halls have failed to achieve their objectives, because city councils have restricted them to serving only legal immigrants, while unauthorized migrants continue to line the streets seeking work.[31]

IRCA has also contributed to the informalization of employment among California's Mexican immigrant population by encouraging the growth of sweatshops and other underground firms, homework (especially linked to garment subcontractors), and self-employment (street-vending, participation in swap meets, and so forth). Such enterprises were by no means absent in California in the pre-IRCA period (see, for example, Wolin, 1981), and it is difficult to estimate how much of their recent expansion is attributable only to IRCA. The proliferation of sweatshops, for example, is also associated with the intensification of competitive pressures within the garment industry resulting from the growth of imports and "offshore" production facilities (Bonacich, 1990: 35). It is clear, however, that such economic activities draw disproportionately on the pool of Mexican workers whose employment prospects have been most adversely affected by IRCA, (i.e., now "unattached" illegal arrivals and women who did not qualify for amnesty under the 1986 law).

Conclusion

Over the last one hundred years, Mexican migration to California has never been static. The changes or intensifications of preexisting trends that occurred during the 1980s, however, are particularly significant. The shift from short-term, shuttle migration to permanent settlement in California has accelerated considerably. Mexico's economic crisis has brought into the migration stream many rural communities as well as urban centers that had not been traditional labor exporters to California. The crisis has also discouraged many Mexican migrants already here from returning to their places of origin, as they might otherwise have done.[32] The 1980s brought major changes in the social composition of the flow; many more women and children, and more whole family units, are now participating in the migratory process. And the continuing dispersion of Mexican migrants outside of the agricultural sector is one of the most conspicuous features of the current wave of Mexican immigration to California.

Some of the patterns I have just noted are not really new, when viewed from a broader historical perspective. For example, there are important similarities between the profiles of Mexican migration to California in the 1920s and that which occurred in the 1980s. In both decades, points of origin within Mexico were relatively dispersed, and there was considerable employment of Mexican workers in nonagricultural sectors of the state's economy.[33] After the hiatus caused by the Great Depression, the *bracero* program of contract-labor importation greatly increased the proportion of short-stay, agriculturally employed migrants, and altered the migration flow in other enduring ways (García y Griego, 1983). Thus, in certain respects, the migratory profile of the 1980s represents a return to patterns established before the deformation of the migratory process caused by *bracerismo*.

In understanding the contemporary Mexican immigration phenomenon, we must also take care to distinguish analytically between absolute and relative changes. For example, while permanent emigrants may have grown considerably as a proportion of the total flow of Mexican migrants to California in the 1980s, this does not necessarily mean that short-term migration has diminished in absolute terms. The same caveat applies to the decline in the proportion of Mexican migrants who are agriculturally employed in California. This does not mean that agriculture has ceased to be an important employer of Mexican migrants in California; indeed, a 1983 survey of the state's farmworkers population found that 73 percent were Mexican-born, and 44 percent of these farmworkers admitted that they were unauthorized immigrants (Mines and Martin, 1986; Taylor and Espenshade, n.d.). In relative terms, however, Mexican migrants today are finding far more employment opportunities in the nonagricultural sectors of California's economy.

The profile of Mexican migration to California is changing in ways that raise new questions about the social and economic impacts of this population movement on the receiving areas. The shift from a Mexican immigrant population dominated by transient, "lone male" agricultural workers to a much more socially heterogeneous, year-round, urban-dwelling immigrant community is unlikely to be reversed, barring an economic calamity in California that would severely reduce the nonagricultural demand for Mexican labor. Already, this qualitative change has greatly increased the day-to-day visibility of the Mexican immigrant population, thereby intensifying the objection of the nonimmigrant population to their presence. Moreover, the legalization of a large part of the formerly unauthorized Mexican work force, combined with the steadily increasing proportion of women and children in the flow of migrants from Mexico, inevitably will increase the impacts of the Mexican immigrant population on housing, schools, and health care systems in localities that attract large numbers of migrants.

In the foreseeable future, Mexican immigrants in the United States -- both legals and unauthorized migrants -- are likely to remain concentrated in a few states and localities, with California alone receiving well over half of the total. Transnational migrant networks are now anchored in those places, and the networks will continue to expand. The character of the neighborhoods where Mexican immigrants cluster will change visibly. This high degree of spatial concentration will increase the perceived threat posed by Mexicans and other Spanish-speaking immigrants to the non-immigrant population.

It is important to underscore the *cultural* basis of that perceived threat. Polling data and anecdotal evidence show that most native-born Californians (not of Latino ancestry) and recent in-migrants from the East and Midwest do not see themselves as being in competition with Mexican immigrants for jobs or social services (Cornelius, 1983). They do see such people, however, as a very real threat to their high quality of life. As Los Angeles City Councilman Ernani Bernardi has put it, "The immigrants are resented strongly because of their impact on *livability*" (quoted in Kotkin, 1989: 8). They are blamed for rising local crime rates (Wolf, 1988), harassment of school children and other passersby, littering, and public health hazards. Local merchants complain that their regular customers are being driven away by migrants loitering or seeking work on nearby streets. For many members of the nonimmigrant population, racism and fears of a bilingual society are additional sources of hostility toward Latino immigrants.

The changing social composition and spatial concentration of the Mexican immigrant population will provide a stern test of California's capacity to develop as a multicultural society in the 1990s and beyond. The early signs are not particularly encouraging. Intolerance toward the Latino immigrant presence is rising in heavily impacted areas of the state. A case in point is the North County area of San Diego County -- home to more than 1.5 million largely middle and upper-income people, most of whom have migrated from other parts of the United States. For over three years, several of the principal North County cities have been in an almost continuous uproar over the presence of Mexican and Central American day laborers and the make-shift camps built of cardboard, used lumber, and plastic sheeting in which they live. IRCA has put more migrant day laborers -- the new underclass -- on the streets of these communities. Meanwhile, high-priced housing developments and shopping centers, sprouting up throughout the region during the 1980s, have encroached upon the vacant land where migrant farm workers in San Diego County have traditionally sought shelter. The cultural clash implied by upscale housing developments in immediate proximity to Third-World-style squatter settlements could hardly be more dramatic.

Statewide polling data[34] suggest that the majority of nonimmigrant Californians are unprepared to accept the notion of a settled, highly visible Latino immigrant presence in their immediate environments. If the futility of efforts to "stop them at the border" and other law enforcement approaches comes to be widely recognized, the focus of public debate in California will gradually shift to how to deal more effectively with Mexican immigrants as a settler population, and to the problems of "assimilating" the second and third generations. Such a shift in the terms of the public debate over immigration occurred during the 1980s in Western Europe, faced with the de facto permanent presence of millions of culturally distinct Algerian,

Moroccan, and Turkish immigrants (see Buechler, 1987; Layton-Henry, 1990). And as in Western Europe, the overall level of anti-immigrant hostility is likely to rise, as the majority population confronts this new and unwelcome kind of challenge.

Notes

1. This chapter draws upon field research conducted in California and Mexico between 1982 and 1989 on both sides of the border by the Center for U.S.-Mexican Studies at the University of California, San Diego. It was supported by grants from the Ford Foundation, the University of California's Pacific Rim Research Program, and the Commission for the Study of International Migration and Cooperative Economic Development. The research design, sampling methods, and data collection procedures are fully described in the final report submitted to the Commission for the Study of International Migration and Cooperative Economic Development, Washington, DC, in March 1990 (Cornelius, 1990a). This research included censuses, sample surveys, unstructured interviewing and ethnographic observation among U.S. employers, immigrant and U.S.-born workers employed in the same firms, recently arrived migrants who were seeking work as day laborers in Southern California's street corner labor markets, and returned migrants and prospective first-time migrants living in three traditionally labor-exporting rural communities in west-central Mexico. The comments of Manuel García y Griego and Jeffrey Weldon on an earlier draft are gratefully acknowledged.

2. Unpublished tabulation provided by the Statistics Division, U.S. Immigration and Naturalization Service (INS), Washington, DC, April 1990. The data were drawn from a border-wide sample of 1,575 "I-213" forms filled out by Border Patrol agents on apprehended Mexicans (Bjerke and Hess, 1987). The sampling interval was one out of every 500 Mexican I-213 forms. The sampling error for migrants originating in Jalisco was plus or minus 2.3 percentage points, and 2.4 percent for those originating in Michoacán (95 percent confidence level). It must be kept in mind that this sample was designed to be representative of those clandestine entrants who were apprehended by the Border Patrol (about 97 percent of whom, in recent years, have been Mexican nationals); it is not necessarily representative of the overall flow of unauthorized aliens into California. Information on state-of-origin within Mexico is collected continuously by the Border Patrol, as part of the I-213 forms completed on each apprehended alien. However, this information is not

keyed into the INS' computerized data base on apprehensions because of a shortage of data entry personnel, hence the need to draw special samples of I-213 forms.

3. For most of this century, about eight Mexican states have contributed the bulk of Mexican migrants to California (70 percent or more, according to most estimates). However, it has not always been the same eight states. For example, Sonora and Coahuila were important sending states in the 1920s, but are no longer important sources. The four entities that consistently have ranked among the top sending states are Jalisco, Michoacán, Guanajuato, and Zacatecas (see Jones, 1984). These, more than any others, merit the label" traditional sending states."

4. Reflected in data collected by El Colegio de la Frontera Norte, Tijuana, Baja California (Bustamante, 1990), and two surveys conducted in Southern California by the Center for U.S.-Mexican Studies, UCSD, in 1981-82 (Cornelius et al., 1984) and 1987-88 (Cornelius, 1990b).

5. Data from the Statistics Division, U.S. Immigration and Naturalization Service, from the above-referenced sample of "I-213" forms completed in the San Diego sector during calendar year 1987. The sampling error for migrants originating in the Federal District was plus or minus 1.5 percentages points; for those originating in the State of Mexico, it was 1.1 percentage points.

6. Unpublished data provided by the Canyon Zapata Project, El Colegio de la Frontera Norte (COLEF), Tijuana, Baja California, March, 1990, combining the shares of migrants from the Federal District (9.8 percent) and the State of Mexico (1.9 percent). Each weekend since August 1987, COLEF's research project has interviewed 75 persons in Tijuana, selected at random from those gathered at the two points of entry most frequented by migrants attempting clandestine entry into California (see Bustamante, 1990).

7. Nor does the available evidence indicate that, *within* principal sending states, U.S.-bound emigration has become less geographically concentrated than in previous decades. On the contrary, data from Border Patrol apprehension records for the 1983-1986 period (Jones, 1988) show that the bulk of unauthorized migration from Mexico to the United States continues to originate in a relatively small number of highly migration-prone *municipios*.

8. The same effect was observed in connection with the "bracero" program of contract labor importation, implemented beginning in 1942 (see Durand, 1988: 12). In 1989, the RAW program, which would provide short-term visas to foreign agricultural workers, attracted some 650,000 applicants, virtually all of them Mexican nationals. These applicants --

the majority of whom are already working in the United States, mostly in California -- are now in a registry maintained by the U.S. Immigration and Naturalization Service, awaiting the issuance of RAW visas. No such visas have been issued for 1990, and there is substantial doubt whether any will be issued in the remaining three years of the RAW program authorized by Congress as part of the 1986 immigration law because the U.S. Departments of Agriculture and Labor have determined through national sample surveys of farm workers and employers that there is an ample supply of legal resident farm workers to meet anticipated demands for labor in perishable crop agriculture. The government surveys and determinations of the farm labor demand and supply will be repeated annually through 1993, at which time Congress will reassess the RAW program.

9. On the "new" migration of Oaxacan Indians (especially from the Mixteca region) to California, Oregon, and Washington state, see Kearney, 1986; Kearney and Nagengast, 1988; and Zabin, 1991. For many Mixtecos, the agricultural areas of Baja California and the city of Tijuana have become important way stations (see Garduno et al., 1989).

10. This pattern of stepwise migration to California was not common in the 1960s or 1970s. For example, in Dagodag's (1984: 64) sample of apprehended unauthorized aliens, there was a very close (98 percent) correspondence between migrants' birthplace and their last premigration place of residence in Mexico.

11. Unpublished tabulations provided by Agustín Escobar-Latapí and Mercedes González de la Rocha (Centro de Investigaciones y Estudios Superiores en Antropología Social-Occidente, Guadalajara).

12. Long-stayers (designated as "Population V" in the CENIET survey) were defined as Mexicans fifteen years of age or older who were in the United States working or seeking work at the time of the December 1978 survey -- a time when most short-term or seasonal Mexican migrants traditionally have returned to their home communities (Zazueta and García y Griego, 1982).

13. The other seven principal receiving metropolitan statistical areas in California were San Jose, Oakland, Oxnard-Ventura, Fresno, San Francisco, Sacramento, and Stockton, in order of importance.

14. Unpublished data tabulations by Jeffrey S. Passel, U.S. Bureau of the Census, 1985.

15. The final number of legalized aliens will not be known for some time. Those who secured temporary legal status under the general amnesty program -- 70 percent of whom were citizens of Mexico -- have until sometime in 1989 or 1990 (depending on the date when their temporary *permiso* was issued) to apply for permanent legal residency. They must

also meet English proficiency and knowledge of U.S. history requirements during this period in order to retain their legal status. As of July
1989, only 4.2 percent of the applications for the general amnesty program had been disapproved, and 2.6 percent of the applications for the
SAW program had been denied, but two-thirds of the SAW applications
remained to be adjudicated (INS, 1989a). Only 250,000-350,000 SAW
applicants were originally expected; 1,301,970 applications -- 82 percent of them from Mexican nationals -- were actually filed by the 30
November 1988 deadline, leading some observers to argue that the
SAW program had been "too successful." Researchers at the University
of California, Davis, have estimated that as many as two-thirds of the
SAW applications from California could be fraudulent (Martin, 1990b;
Martin and Taylor, 1988).

16. Based on field interviews with illegal borders crossers conducted by El
    Colegio de la Frontera Norte in Tijuana and other Mexican border cities
    since 1986, Jorge Bustamante (1990: 98) concludes that "at any given
    time, close to 60 percent of the total of unauthorized immigrants from
    Mexico in the United States can be found in the state of California,
    where employer demand for Mexican unauthorized immigrants is higher
    and more diversified than in any other state, according to our survey
    data."

17. Field studies in Guadalajara by Agustín Escobar-Latapí and Mercedes
    González de la Rocha (CIESAS-Occidente, Guadalajara, Jalisco), 1982-
    1987.

18. Fieldwork in 1987-1988 by the Center for U.S.-Mexican Studies, Uni-
    versity of California, San Diego.

19. Data from the U.S. Consulate, Tijuana, Baja California; and Jorge
    Bustamante, El Colegio de la Frontera Norte, Tijuana, Baja California.

20. Interestingly, the abrupt shift toward restrictive immigration laws and
    policies in Germany and other West European countries in the last half
    of the 1970s had a similar effect -- increasing family reunification
    immigration and speeding up the process of permanent settlement in the
    host country. See Buechler (1987: 286) and Hollifield (1986).

21. Fieldwork by the Center for U.S.-Mexican Studies in three rural send-
    ing communities in Zacatecas, Jalisco, and Michoacan, 1988-1989; and
    a sample survey by German Vega (El Colegio de la Frontera Norte,
    Tijuana) in the municipio of Jalostotitlán, Jalisco, conducted January-
    March 1990. See also Cleeland (1989) and Escobar-Latapí and
    González de la Rocha (1989).

22. Experienced observers of the migratory flow from the state of Oaxaca to
    California have reported that IRCA's legalization programs stimulated a
    great deal of first-time migration by women and children in 1988 and

1989. They observed that male family heads already employed in California encouraged their dependents to join them there almost immediately after the family head applied for legalization. Since the vast majority of these family members could not qualify for amnesty themselves, and entered California illegally, they are now "stuck" in that country, unable to travel back and forth to their home community as easily as the family head. (Unpublished research reported at a workshop on "Oaxacan Migration to California's Agricultural Sector," Center for U.S.-Mexican Studies, University of California-San Diego, and California Institute of Rural Studies, 15 February 1990.)

23. Fieldwork by Rafael Alarcón and Macrina Cárdenas (El Colegio de Jalisco and Center for U.S.-Mexican Studies, University of California, San Diego), in the San Francisco Bay area, 1988.

24. In both the garment and electronics industries of California, large numbers of immigrant women are now employed as "homeworkers." See Fernández-Kelly and García (1990).

25. For example, Massey and his associates found that two-thirds to three-quarters of the household heads, and 55-65 percent of all U.S.-bound migrants from four Mexican sending communities surveyed in 1982 adopted a temporary migration strategy.

26. In a 1986 study of unauthorized Mexican and Central American immigrants in San Diego and Dallas, over 80 percent of the respondents believed that their children did not want to return to the parents' country of origin (Chávez and Flores, 1988).

27. The sample consists of 4,180 general-amnesty and 796 SAW applications, who were randomly selected from the statewide population of newly legalized persons who were enrolled in special educational programs operated by public and private agencies during the period of February- July 1989. The survey was conducted by the Comprehensive Adult Student Assessment System of San Diego, CA, under contract to California Health and Welfare Agency.

28. Among those agriculturally employed in Mexico, 44.1 percent were landless laborers; 25.2 percent were share-croppers; 21.9 percent were small private landowners or employed on the family's small private landholding; and 8 percent were ejidatarios or employed on the family's ejidal plot.

29. Personal, in-home interviews conducted by the Center for U.S.-Mexican Studies, University of California San Diego, in San Diego, Los Angeles, and Orange counties in 1987 and 1988. Legal immigrant workers interviewed for the same study (N=103) were receiving an average of $6.00 per hour.

30. Among our sample of unauthorized Mexican immigrants employed in

Southern California nonagricultural firms in 1987-1988, 17 percent were union members. This compares with 30 percent among legal immigrants, and 32 percent among U.S. citizen workers in the same sample. Our 1983-84 study of Mexicans employed in immigrant-dependent firms, which included firms located in Northern California where unionization levels traditionally have been much higher than in the South, found much higher proportions of union members, among both unauthorized and legal immigrants (see Cornelius, 1990b).

31. There are conflicting legal opinions about whether such city-run hiring halls can be "immigration status-blind" without violating the employer sanctions provision of the 1986 U.S. immigration law. The City of Los Angeles has chosen to run its hiring hall in this way, but the other three cities mentioned above have limited their halls to documented immigrants.

32. Roger Rouse (1989: 200-7), who has studied migration to Redwood City, CA from the town of Aguililla, Michoacán, found that the economic crisis of the 1980s had stimulated inflation in land and livestock prices in the community of origin, thereby preventing returning migrants from the United States from using their savings to good advantage.

33. For example, a survey of Los Angeles manufacturing industries in 1928 found that 17 percent of all workers were Mexicans. The single largest concentration of Mexican industrial workers was in textiles, but substantial numbers were also employed in construction and railroad yards (California Mexican Fact-Finding Committee, cited in Muller and Espenshade, 1985: 57).

34. For example, a *Los Angeles Times* Poll conducted in January 1989 found that 57 percent of the respondents agreed that there are "too many" immigrants in California.

References

Bach, Robert L., and Howard Brill. 1990. "Shifting the Burden: The Impacts of IRCA on U.S. Labor Markets." Interim Report to the Division of Immigration Policy and Research, U.S. Department of Labor: Washington, DC. February.

Bean, Frank D., and Marta Tienda. 1987. *The Hispanic Population of the United States*. New York: Russell Sage Foundation, Census Monograph Series.

Bean, Frank D., et al. 1990. "Post-IRCA Changes in the Volume and Composition of Unauthorized Migration to the United States: An Assessment Based on Apprehensions Data." In *Unauthorized Migration to*

California: IRCA and the Experience of the 1980s, edited by Frank D. Bean et al. Washington, DC: Urban Institute Press.

Bilateral Commission on the Future of U.S.-Mexican Relations. 1988. *The Challenge of Interdependence: Mexico and the United States*. Lanham, MD: University Press of America.

Birch, David. 1990. "The Contribution of New, Locally-Owned Firms to Growth in the U.S. Western Economy." Paper presented at the First Annual Broadmoor Symposium, "Beyond Decline: America's Resurgence in the New Century," sponsored by the Center for the New West, 22-23 January, Colorado Springs.

Bjerke, John A., and Karen K. Hess. 1987. "Selected Characteristics of Illegal Aliens Apprehended by the U.S. Border Patrol." Paper presented at the Annual Meeting of the Population Association of America: Washington, DC, May.

Bonacich, Edna. 1990. "Asian and Latino Immigrants in the Los Angeles Garment Industry: An Exploration of the Relationship between Capitalism and Racial Oppression." *Working Papers in the Social Sciences* 5, no. 13, Institute for Social Science Research, University of California, Los Angeles.

Borjas, George J. 1990. *Friends or Strangers: The Impact of Immigrants on the U.S. Economy*. New York: Basic Books.

Browning, Harley, and Nestor Rodríguez. 1985. "The Migration of Mexican *Indocumentados* as a Settlement Process: Implications for Work." In *Hispanics in the U.S. Economy*, edited by George Borjas and Marta Tienda. Orlando, FL: Academic Press.

Buechler, Judith-Maria. 1987. "A Review: Guest, Intruder, Settler, Ethnic Minority, or Citizen -- the Sense and Nonsense of Borders." In *Migrants in Europe: The Role of Family, Labor, and Politics*, edited by Hans Christian Buechler and Judith-Maria Buechler. Westport, CT: Greenwood Press.

Bustamante, Jorge A. 1979. "Emigración Indocumentada a los Estados Unidos." In *Indocumentados: Mitos y Realidades*, 23-67. Mexico, DF: El Colegio de México.

Bustamante, Jorge A. 1990. "Measuring the Flow of Unauthorized Immigrants: Research Findings from the Zapata Canyon Project." In *Mexican Migration to the United States*, edited by Wayne A. Cornelius and Jorge A. Bustamante. La Jolla, CA: Center for U.S.-Mexican Studies, Universtiy of California, San Diego.

Bustamante, Jorge A., and Gerónimo Martínez. 1979. "Unauthorized Immigration from Mexico: Beyond Borders but within Systems." *Journal of International Affairs*, 33, Fall-Winter: 265-84.

Calvo, Thomas, and Gustavo López, eds. 1988. *Movimientos de Población en el Occidente de México*. México, D.F. and Zamora, Mich.: Centre d'Etudes Mexicaines et Centramericaines and El Colegio de Michoacán.

Cárdenas, Macrina. n.d. "La Mujer y la Migración a los Estados Unidos en Chavinda, Michoacán." Unpublished paper, El Colegio de Jalisco, Guadalajara.

CASAS [Comprehensive Adult Student Assessment System]. 1989. *A Survey of Newly Legalized Persons in California: Prepared for the California Health and Welfare Agency*. San Diego: CASAS.

Chávez, Leo R. 1988. "Settlers and Sojourners: The Case of Mexicans in California." *Human Organization* 47, Summer: 95-108.

Chávez, Leo R., and Estevan T. Flores. 1988. "Unauthorized Mexicans and Central Americans and the Immigration Reform and Control Act of 1986." In Center for Migration Studies, Staten Island, NY, *In Defense of the Alien* 10: 137-56.

Cleeland, Nancy. 1989. "Many More Women Decide to Flee Mexico." *San Diego Union*, 27 August.

Cornelius, Wayne A. 1976a. "Outmigration from Rural Mexican Communities." In Interdisciplinary Communications Program, *The Dynamics of Migration: International Migration*. Washington, DC: Smithsonian Institution, ICP Occasional Monograph Series 2, no. 5.

Cornelius, Wayne A. 1976b. *Mexican Migration to the United States: The View from Rural Sending Communities*. Cambridge, MA: Center for International Studies, Massachusetts Institute of Technology, Monograph Series in Migration and Development.

Cornelius, Wayne A. 1982. "Interviewing Undocumented Immigrants: Methodological Reflections Based on Fieldwork in Mexico and the United States." *International Migration Review*, 16, no. 2, Summer: 378-411.

Cornelius, Wayne A. 1983. "America in the Era of Limits: Migrants, Nativists, and the Future of U.S.-Mexican Relations." In *Mexican-U.S. Relations: Conflict and Convergence*, edited by Carlos Vásquez and Manuel García y Griego. Los Angeles, CA: University of California, Los Angeles, Chicano Studies Research Center and Latin American Center, Anthology Series, no. 3.

Cornelius, Wayne A. 1989. "Impacts of the 1986 U.S. Immigration Law on Emigration from Rural Mexican Sending Communities." *Population and Development Review* 15, no. 4, December: 689-705.

Cornelius, Wayne A. 1990a. "Labor Migration to the United States: Development Outcomes and Alternatives in Mexican Sending Communities." Final report to the Commission for the Study of International Migration and Cooperative Economic Development, March, Washington, DC.

Cornelius, Wayne A. 1990b. "The United States Demand for Mexican

Labor." In *Mexican Migration to the United States*, edited by Wayne A. Cornelius and Jorge A. Bustamante. La Jolla, CA: Center for U.S.-Mexican Studies, University of California, San Diego.

Cornelius, Wayne A., and Jorge A. Bustamante, eds. 1990. *Mexican Migration to the United States: Process, Consequences, and Policy Options*. La Jolla, CA: Center for U.S.-Mexican Studies, University of California, San Diego, for the Bilateral Commission on the Future of U.S.-Mexican Relations.

Cornelius, Wayne A., et al. 1984. *Mexican Immigrants and Access to Health Care*. La Jolla, CA: Center for U.S.-Mexican Studies, University of California, San Diego.

Cornelius, Wayne A., and Manuel García y Griego. Forthcoming. *The Ties That Bind: Mexican Migration to the United States, Dependent Industries, and the Limits to Government Intervention*. Stanford, CA: Stanford University Press.

Dagodag, W. Tim. 1975. "Source Regions and Composition of Illegal Mexican Immigration to California." *International Migration Review* 9: 499-511.

Dagodag, W. Tim. 1984. "Illegal Mexican Immigration to California from Western Mexico." In *Patterns of Unauthorized Migration: Mexico and California*, edited by Robert C. James. Totowa, NJ: Rowman and Allanheld.

Duffield, James A. 1990. "Estimating Farm Labor Elasticities to Analyze the Effects of Immigration Reform." Agriculture and Rural Economy Division, Economic Research Service, U.S. Department of Agriculture, Staff Report No. AGES 9013, Washington, DC, February.

Durand, Jorge. 1988. "Los Migradolares," *Argumentos* (Universidad Autónoma Metropolitana, Mexico, D.F.), November: 7-21.

Escobar-Latapí, Agustín, and Mercedes González de la Rocha. 1989. "Efecto de IRCA en los Patrones Migratorios de una Comunidad en Los Altos de Jalisco." Report prepared for the Commission on the Study of International Migration and Cooperative Economic Development, November, Washington, DC.

Escobar-Latapí, Agustín, et al. 1987. "Migration, Labor Markets, and the International Economy: Jalisco, Mexico, and the United States." In *Migrants, Workers, and the Social Order*, edited by Jeremy Eades. Association for Social Anthropologists, Monograph no. 26. London and New York: Tavistock.

Fatemi, Khosrow. 1987. "The Unauthorized Immigrant: A Socioeconomic Profile." *Journal of Borderlands Studies*, 2(2), Fall 85-99.

Fernández, Celestino. 1988. "Migración Hacia los Estados Unidos: Caso Santa Inés, Michoacán." In *Migración en el Occidente de Mexico*, edited by Gustavo López Castro and Sergio Pardo Galván. Michoacán: El Colegio de Michoacán.

Fernández-Kelly, M. Patricia, and Anna M. García. 1989. "Hispanic Women and Homework: Women in the Informal Economy of Miami and Los Angeles." In *Homework: Historical and Contemporary Perspectives on Paid Labor at Home*, edited by Eileen Boris and Cynthia R. Daniels. Urbana: University of Illinois Press.

Fernández-Kelly, M. Patricia, and Anna M. García. 1990. "Economic Restructuring in California: The Case of Hispanic Women in the Garment and Electronics Industries of Southern California," In *The Changing Role of Mexican Labor in the U.S. Economy: Sectoral Perspectives*, edited by Wayne A. Cornelius. La Jolla, CA: Center for U.S.-Mexican Studies, University of California, San Diego.

Fix, Michael, and Paul T. Hill. 1990. "Enforcing Employer Sanctions: Challenges and Strategies." Program for Research on Immigration Policy, The Rand Corporation and The Urban Institute, Report JRI-04, Santa Monica, CA and Washington, DC, March.

Fonseca, Omar. 1988. "De Jaripo a Stockton, Calif.: Un Caso de Migración en Michoacán." In *Movimientos de Población en el Occidente de México*, edited by Thomás Calvo and Gustavo López. México, DF and Zamora, Michoacán: Centre d'Etudes Mexicaines et Centramericaines and El Colegio de Michoacán.

García y Griego, Manuel. 1983. "The Importation of Mexican Contract Laborers to the United States, 1942-1964: Antecedents, Operation, and Legacy." In *The Border that Joins: Mexican Migrants and U.S. Responsibility*, edited by Peter G. Brown and Henry Shue. Totowa, NJ: Rowman and Littlefield.

Garduño, Everardo, et al. 1989. *Mixtecos en Baja California: el caso de San Quintín*. Mexicali, Baja California: Universidad Autónoma de Baja California.

González de la Rocha, Mercedes. 1989. "El Poder de la Ausencia: Mujeres y Migración en una Comunidad de Los Altos de Jalisco." Paper presented at the XI Coloquio de Antropología e Historia Regionales, October 25-27, Zamora, Michoacán.

Hollifield, James F. 1986. "Immigration Policy in France and Germany: Outputs versus Outcomes." *The Annals of the American Academy of Political and Social Science* 485, May: 113-28.

Hossfeld, Karen J. 1989. "'Small, Foreign, and Female': Immigrant Women Workers and Racial Hiring Dynamics in Silicon Valley." Paper presented at the Annual Meeting of the American Sociological Association, September, San Francisco.

INS [U.S. Immigration and Naturalization Service]. 1989a. "Provisional

Legalization Application Statistics." Statistics Division, Office of Plans and Analysis, U.S. Immigration and Naturalization Service, Washington, DC, 20 July.

INS [U.S. Immigration and Naturalization Service]. 1989b. *1988 Statistical Yearbook of the Immigration and Naturalization Service*. Washington, DC: U.S. Government Printing Office.

Jones, Richard C. 1984. "Macro-Patterns of Unauthorized Migration between Mexico and the U.S." In *Patterns of Unauthorized Migration: Mexico and California*, edited by R. C. Jones. Totowa, NJ: Rowman and Allanheld.

Jones, Richard C. 1988. "Micro Source Regions of Mexican Undocumented Migration." *National Geographic Research* 4(1): 11-22.

Kearney, Michael. 1986. "Integration of the Mixteca and the Western U.S.-Mexican Border Region via Migratory Wage Labor." In *Regional Impacts of U.S.-Mexican Relations*, edited by Ina Rosenthal-Urey. La Jolla, CA: Center for U.S.-Mexican Studies, University of California, San Diego, Monograph no. 16.

Kearney, Michael, and Carole Nagengast. 1988. "Anthropological Perspectives on Transnational Communities in Rural California." Working paper, California Institute for Rural Studies, July, Berkeley, CA.

Kelley, Bruce. 1990. "El Mosco," *Los Angeles Times Magazine* 6, no. 11, 18 March: 11-20, 38, 42-43.

Kotkin, Joel. 1989. "Fear and Reality in the Los Angeles Melting Pot." *Los Angeles Times Magazine* 5, no. 45, 5 November: 6-19, 32-33.

Layton-Henry, Zig, ed. 1990. *The Political Rights of Migrant Workers in Europe*. London and Newbury Park, CA: Sage Publications.

López, Gustavo. 1986. *La Casa Dividida: un Estudio de Caso Sobre la Migración a Estados Unidos en un Pueblo Michoacano*. Zamora, Michoacán: El Colegio de Michoacán.

López, Gustavo, and Sergio Pardo Galván, eds. 1988. *Migración en el Occidente de México*. Zamora, Michoacán: El Colegio de Michoacán.

Martin, Philip L. 1990a. "Testimony Before the Immigration Task Force of the Committee on Education and Labor, and the Subcommittee on Immigration, Refugees, and International Law," 1 March, Washington, DC.

Martin, Philip L. 1990b. "Harvest of Confusion: Immigration Reform and California Agriculture." *International Migration Review* 24, no. 1, Spring: 69-95.

Martin, Philip L., and J. Edward Taylor. 1988. "California Farm Workers and the SAW Legalization Program." *California Agriculture*, November-December: 4-6.

Martin, Philip L., and J. Edward Taylor. 1990. "Immigration Reform and California Agriculture a Year Later." *California Agriculture* 44, no. 1,

January-February: 24-27.

Massey, Douglas S., et al. 1987. *Return to Aztlán: The Social Process of International Migration from Western Mexico*. Berkeley: University of California Press.

Massey, Douglas S., et al. 1990. "Effects of the Immigration Reform and Control Act of 1986: Preliminary Data from Mexico." In *Undocumented Migration to the United States*, edited by Frank D. Bean et al. Washington, DC: Urban Institute Press.

Mines, Richard. 1981. *Developing a Community Tradition of Migration: A Field Study in Rural Zacatecas, Mexico, and California Settlement Areas*. La Jolla, CA: Center for U.S.-Mexican Studies, University of California, San Diego, Monograph no. 3.

Mines, Richard. 1984. "Network Migration and Mexican Rural Development: A Case Study." In *Patterns of Unauthorized Migration: Mexico and the United States*, edited by Robert C. Jones. Totowa, NJ: Rowman and Allanheld.

Mines, Richard, and Philip Martin. 1986. "California Farmworkers: Results of the UC-EDD Survey of 1983." Unpublished report, Department of Agricultural Economics, University of California, Davis.

Morales, Rebecca, and Paul Ong. 1990. "Immigrant Women in Los Angeles." *Working Papers in the Social Sciences* 5, Institute for Social Science Research, University of California, Los Angeles.

Muller, Thomas, and Thomas J. Espenshade. 1985. *The Fourth Wave: California's Newest Immigrants*. Washington, DC: Urban Institute Press.

Mummert, Gail. 1988. "Mujeres de Migrantes y Mujeres Migrantes de Michoacán." In *Movimientos de Población*, edited by Thomás Calvo and Gustavo López.

North, David S., and Marion F. Houstoun. 1976. *The Characteristics and Role of Illegal Aliens in the U.S. Labor Market: An Exploratory Study*. Washington, DC: Linton and Co.

Palerm, Juan Vicente. 1987. "Transformation in California Agriculture." *UC MEXUS News* (University of California, Riverside), no. 21-22: 1-3.

Palerm, Juan Vicente. 1989. "Latino Settlements in California." In University of California Task Force on Senate Concurring Resolution no. 43, *The Challenge: Latinos in a Changing California*. Riverside, CA: University of California Consortium on Mexico and the United States.

Palerm, Juan Vicente. 1990. *The Formation and Extension of Chicano-Mexican Enclaves in Rural California*. Sacramento: Employment Development Department, State of California.

Passel, Jeffrey S., and Karen A. Woodrow. 1984. "Geographic Distribution of Unauthorized Immigrants: Estimates of Unauthorized Aliens Counted in the 1980 U.S. Census by State." *International Migration Review*

18(3), Fall: 642-75.

Ranney, Susan, and Sherrie Kossoudji. 1983. "Profiles of Temporary Mexican Labor Migration to the United States." *Population and Development Review* 9: 475-93.

Reichert, Joshua S., and Douglas S. Massey. 1979. "Patterns of U.S. Migration from a Mexican Sending Community: A Comparison of Legal and Illegal Migrants." *International Migration Review* 13: 599-623.

Rouse, Roger C. 1989. "Mexican Migration to the United States: Family Relations in the Development of a Transnational Migrant Circuit." Ph.D. diss. Stanford University, Stanford, CA.

Ruiz, Vicki L. 1987. "By the Day or the Week: Mexicana Domestic Workers in El Paso." In *Women on the U.S.-Mexico Border*, edited by Vicki L. Ruiz and Susan Tiano. Boston: Allen & Unwin.

Rural California Report. 1990. "Its Official: No RAW Visas Needed." *Rural California Report* 2, no 2, April: California Institute for Rural Studies, Davis, CA.

Solórzano Torres, Rosalía. 1987. "Female Mexican Immigrants in San Diego County." In *Women on the U.S.-Mexico Border*, edited by Vicki L. Ruiz and Susan Tiano. Boston: Allen and Unwin.

Tamayo, Jesús. 1990. "Las Areas Expulsoras de Mano de Obra del Estado de Zacatecas: su Desarrollo Económico y Social." Paper presented at the Annual Meeting of the Association of Borderlands Scholars, February, Tijuana, Baja CA.

Taylor, J. Edward, and Thomas J. Espenshade. n.d. "Foreign and Unauthorized Workers in California Agriculture," *Population Research and Policy Review*.

Tienda, Marta. 1990. "Mexican Immigration: A Sociological Perspective." In *Mexican Migration to the United States*, edited by Wayne A. Cornelius and Jorge A. Bustamante. La Jolla, CA: Center for U.S.-Mexican Studies, University of California, San Diego.

Wallace, Steven P. 1988. "Central American and Mexican Immigrant Characteristics and Economic Incorporation in California." *International Migration Review* 22(3): 657-71.

Warren, Robert, and Jeffrey S. Passel. 1987. "A Count of the Uncountable: Estimates of Undocumented Aliens Counted in the 1980 United States Census." *Demography* 24, August: 375-93.

Wolin, Merle L. 1981. "Sweatshop: Undercover in the Garment Industry." *Los Angeles Herald-Examiner*, 14 January-1 February (16-part series).

Wolf, Daniel. 1988. *Unauthorized Aliens and Crime: The Case of San Diego County*. La Jolla, CA: Center for U.S.-Mexican Studies, University of California, San Diego, Monograph no. 29.

Woodrow, Karen A., and Jeffrey S. Passel. 1990. "Post-IRCA

Unauthorized Immigration to the United States: An Assessment Based on the June 1988 CPS." In *Undocumented Migration to the United States*, edited by Frank D. Bean, Barry Edmonston, and Jeffrey S. Passel. Washington, DC: Urban Institute Press.

Zabin, Carol. 1991. *Migración Oaxaqueña a los Campos Agrícolas de California*. La Jolla, CA: Center for U.S.-Mexican Studies, University of California, San Diego, Current Issue Brief 2.

Zazueta, Carlos H., and Manuel García y Griego. 1982. *Los Trabajadores Mexicanos en Estados Unidos: Resultados de la Encuesta Nacional de Emigración a la Frontera Norte del País y a los Estados Unidos*. México, DF: Centro Nacional de Información y Estadísticas del Trabajo (CENIET).

Index

373